Japan's Industrialization
in the World Economy
1859–1899

To Helen

Japan's Industrialization in the World Economy 1859–1899

EXPORT TRADE AND OVERSEAS COMPETITION

Shinya Sugiyama

The Athlone Press
London and Atlantic Highlands, New Jersey

First published in 1988 by The Athlone Press
44 Bedford Row, London WC1R 4LY
and 171 First Avenue, Atlantic Highlands, NJ 07716

British Library Cataloguing in Publication Data

Sugiyama, S.
 Japan's industrialization in the world
 economy, 1859–1899; export trade and
 overseas competition.
 1. Japan—Commerce—History—19th
 century
 I. Title
 382'.0952   HF3824
 ISBN 0-485-11267-1

Library of Congress Cataloging in Publication Data
Sugiyama, S. (Shinya). 1949–
 Japan's industrialization in the world economy, 1859–1899: export
 trade and overseas competition / by S. Sugiyama.
  p.   cm.
 Bibliography: p.
 Includes index.
 ISBN 0-485-11267-1 : $70.00 (U.S. : est.)
 1. Japan—Commerce—History. 2. Exports—Japan—History.
 3. Japan—Industries—History. 4. Japan—Economic
 conditions—1868–1918. I. Title.
 HF3826.S77   1988
 382'.6'0952—dc 19

Typeset by BookEns, Saffron Walden, Essex
Printed and bound in Great Britain at
Billings Ltd, Worcester

Contents

List of Tables

Appendix

List of Figures

Notes on Usage

1. Japanese personal names are given in the order customary in Japan: family name followed by given name.
2. Unless otherwise stated, dollar means Mexican dollar.

Abbreviations

ADM	Admiralty Records, Public Record Office, London
BPP	*British Parliamentary Papers*
CAB	Cabinet Papers, Public Record Office, London
CI	Commercial Intelligence in the *North China Herald*
CR	British Consular Reports (Commercial Reports)
CS	Commercial Summary in the *Overland China Mail*
DCRTF	Diplomatic and Consular Report on Trade and Finance
FO	Foreign Office Papers, Public Record Office, London
IMC	China, Imperial Maritime Customs
JMA	Jardine Matheson Archive
LTES	Ohkawa Kazushi *et al.* (eds), *Chōki keizai tōkei* [Estimates of Japanese Long-Term Economic Statistics since 1868], 14 vols, 1966– .
MCC	Manchester Chamber of Commerce
NCH	*The North China Herald and Supreme Court and Consular Gazette*
PCMR	Prices Current and Market Reports in the Jardine Matheson Archive
PRO	Public Record Office, London

Measurement

1 picul = 16 kan = 100 kin = 133.33 lb = 60.48 kg
1 kan = 1,000 monme = 8.27 lb = 3.75 kg
1 koku = 10 kan (but in cocoon 1 koku = 3.25 kan)
1 bale of Japanese silk = about 100 lb
1 chō = 10 tan = 2.45 acres

Acknowledgements

This work is more or less based on my Ph.D dissertation, which was submitted to the University of London in 1981. I would especially like to express my thanks to my supervisor, Professor W.G. Beasley, who generally encouraged my research, expanded my interests, and has always been generous in his time and comments. I also wish to thank Professor Morishima Michio, Professor I.H. Nish, Professor B. Ranft and the late Professor G.C. Allen, for their various stimulating suggestions. I owe a debt to Mr A. Reid of Matheson & Co., who gave me permission to consult the Jardine Matheson Archive held at Cambridge University Library, and Miss Margaret E.A. Pamplin, the Archivist in the Library with special responsibility for the Jardine Matheson Archive. I also made use of the archives held in the Public Record Office, London.

Dr I.G. Brown and Professor Yamamoto Yūzō were kind and patient enough to read an initial draft of the whole book, while Professor Saitō Osamu read specific parts. Dr Brown, in particular, made valuable comments. I am very grateful for their help and advice, but any errors are mine. Miss Kusumoto Yukari has helped in various ways.

I must also thank the School of Oriental and African Studies, University of London, for financial assistance, in the form of first a bursary and then a Governing Body Postgraduate Exhibition. Without this, I would not have been able to complete my research. My three years as a research officer at the International Centre for Economics and Related Disciplines, London School of Economics, gave me the opportunity to develop my ideas further. The Fukuzawa Yukichi Memorial Fund of Keio University has provided publication assistance.

Finally, I would like to express my gratitude to my wife, Dr

Helen J. Ballhatchet, for her encouragement, patience and invaluable advice, and particularly for the ungrudging investment of her time. It is to her that I dedicate this book.

Foreword

The industrialization of Japan has become an important subject of study because of its relevance to Japan's place in the modern world and its implications for the development of Third World countries. Historically, the debate about how to explain it has focused on two principal topics. The first concerns economic and social change within Japan both before and after the commercial treaties of 1858, which ended two hundred years of near-isolation. One can ask, for example, how far domestic circumstance – the existence of a pre-modern commercial capitalism; an agrarian economy capable of generating significant capital accumulation without recourse to foreign borrowing; government initiatives in institutional and financial reform – is enough to account for Japan's ability to do what other non-Western countries proved unable to do until several generations later. Secondly, one can raise the issue of the international context in which industrialization was achieved: the relevance of the 'impact' of the world economy on Japan and the Japanese 'response' to foreign threat, which led in the end to both economic and territorial expansion.

There has long been disagreement about the relative weight to be attached to such domestic and international factors in Japan's industrial growth. In recent years, however, there has emerged a new generation of Japanese economic historians who have tended to set aside 'modernization theory' – the assumption that Japan has in some degree followed a Western 'model' – on the grounds that it attributes too little importance to the strictly economic continuities between pre-modern and modern Japan – hence to the possibility of alternative theories of development – and attaches too much significance to the change of political leadership in 1868: that is, the Meiji Restoration. One merit of Dr Sugiyama's book is that it provides an extended survey of this argument. Another is that it makes a start on filling what has hitherto been one of the lacunae in it: namely, how to relate developments in Japan to the world economy, if not through the concepts of 'impact' and 're-sponse'. By examining Japan's export trade in silk, tea and coal during the closing decades of the nineteenth century, he is able to demonstrate how an ability to meet the requirements of the international market with respect to price and quality accounts for success and failure in particular fields at particular times; in other words, to treat trade within the framework of commercial competition. This in turn provides an economic logic for the relationship between exports and industrial development.

He would be the first to admit that the argument is as yet incomplete. The present study needs to be complemented by others which consider in similar detail the growth of an export trade in industrial products, especially textiles, after 1880 as well as the import-substituting function of some Japanese industries. Nevertheless, by pointing the way towards a reassessment of the character and importance of foreign trade in the Meiji period, Dr Sugiyama has made a welcome start.

W.G. Beasley

East and Southeast Asia

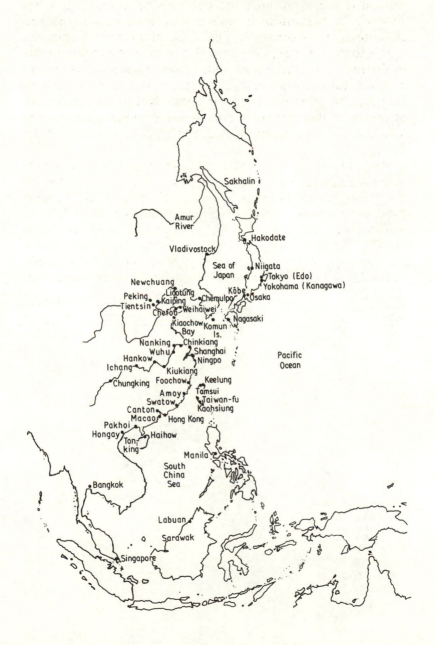

Japan: Prefectures (Provinces) and Major Place Names

1. Hokkaidō (Ezo)
2. Aomori (Mutsu)
3. Iwate (Rikuchū)
4. Miyagi (Rikuzen)
5. Akita (Ugo)
6. Yamagata (Uzen)
7. Fukushima (Iwashiro, Iwaki)
8. Ibaragi (Hitachi)
9. Tochigi (Shimotsuke)
10. Gunma (Kōzuke [Jōshū])
11. Saitama (Musashi)
12. Chiba (Shimousa, Kazusa, Awa)
13. Tokyo (Musashi)
14. Kanagawa (Sagami, Musashi)
15. Niigata (Echigo)
16. Toyama (Etchū)
17. Ishikawa (Kaga, Noto)
18. Fukui (Echizen, Wakasa)
19. Yamanashi (Kai [Kōshū])
20. Nagano (Shinano [Shinshū], Hida)
21. Gifu (Mino)
22. Shizuoka (Tōtōmi, Suruga, Izu)
23. Aichi (Owari, Mikawa)
24. Mie (Ise, Shima, Iga)
25. Shiga (Ōmi)
26. Kyōto (Yamashiro, Tanba, Tango)
27. Ōsaka (Kawachi, Izumi)
28. Hyōgo (Settsu, Harima, Tajima)
29. Nara (Yamato)
30. Wakayama (Kii [Kishū])
31. Tottori (Inaba, Hōki)
32. Shimane (Izumo, Iwami)
33. Okayama (Bizen, Bitchū, Mimasaka)
34. Hiroshima (Bingo, Aki)
35. Yamaguchi (Nagato [Chōshū], Suō)

36. Tokushima (Awa)
37. Kagawa (Sanuki)
38. Ehime (Iyo)
39. Kōchi (Tosa)
40. Fukuoka (Chikuzen, Chikugo, Buzen)
41. Saga (Hizen)
42. Nagasaki (Hizen)
43. Kumamoto (Higo)
44. Ōita (Bungo)
45. Miyazaki (Hyūga)
46. Kagoshima (Satsuma, Ōsumi)
   [Okinawa is not marked.]

1
Introduction

Approaches to Japan's Industrialization

This book is an attempt to analyse the industrialization of Japan in the second half of the nineteenth century from an international historical and economic perspective.[1] It is by now common knowledge that Japan was the only non-Western country to industrialize in the nineteenth century and that, moreover, she did so in an extremely short time. Attracted by this, and by the possible connection both with Japan's rapid post-1945 economic growth and with the problems of Third World industrialization, foreign scholars have for some time been paying special attention to her case. In addition to Japan specialists themselves, one can point to economic historians whose main interests lie in other areas[2] and also to many economists, from those concerned with economic development to dependency theorists.[3]

The starting point for all these scholars has been the search for the key to Japan's aptitude for rapid economic development. As a result, they have tended to adopt an inductive approach and focus on the reasons for Japan's 'success'. This approach is influenced by an assumption that the Western powers were the major force in nineteenth-century East Asian history, with China and Japan playing a role of passive response. The 'success' of Japan and 'failure' of China are therefore ascribed entirely to the different ways in which they responded to this foreign impact.[4] Certainly, in the Japanese case the power of the West gave intellectuals a sense of crisis which doubtless had a direct link with the speed at which Japan went about industrializing. However, the powerful impact which the threat from the West exerted on the Japanese must not be accepted unthinkingly, without a critical reassessment of the reality of that threat.[5]

The apparent rapidity of Japanese economic development has encouraged a tendency to stress the degree of discontinuity between modern and pre-modern Japan, with the Meiji Restoration uncritically accepted as the dividing line between the two. This, in turn, has led to an underestimation of the political and economic significance of the opening of Japan to foreign tıade in 1859 and an overestimation of the significance of the Meiji government and its policies. We are left with the impression that it was possible for Meiji Japan to achieve smooth industrialization simply as a result of intelligent government leadership. In addition, the speed at which this industrialization is thought to have been brought about gives us the picture of a Meiji government which had considerable power. However, these assumptions deserve careful examination. For a start, it should be clear from the difficulties at present being experienced by the countries of the Third World that industrialization cannot be achieved merely through government leadership and planning. Close scrutiny of Japan's modern history also makes it clear that industrialization did not proceed smoothly along the path first envisaged and that, particularly at first, it was very much a process of trial and error. Moreover, the fact that the process of industrialization also involved military expansion into Asia in order to secure existing economic and political interests suggests that we should not treat it as a 'success story' pure and simple.

It would be completely wrong to attribute the tendencies which I have been criticizing to non-Japanese scholars alone. We should first examine the approach to Japan's modernization of Japanese scholars themselves. Traditionally, Japanese economic historians have followed political historians in taking the Meiji Restoration as the dividing line between the pre-modern – that is, the Tokugawa period – and the modern – that is, the Meiji period onwards – and studied the two as completely distinct entities. Thus for specialists in the pre-modern era the Meiji Restoration was the ending point, while for specialists in the modern era it was the point of departure.

Since around the 1930s, specialists in modern Japanese history have been engaged in a debate about the meaning of the Meiji Restoration. On one side are ranged those who have concentrated on the agrarian structure. Pointing to the survival of feudal elements into the Meiji period, they deny that the Restoration was revolutionary and see it as representing either the establishment of absolutism or merely a rearrangement of feudalism. On the other side are those who have emphasized the post-Restoration development of capitalism. They interpret the Restoration more or less as a bourgeois revolution and see any remaining feudal elements as disappearing along with the development of capitalism.[6] Both sides in this debate have based their arguments on Marx's theory of the transition from feudalism to capitalism. Taking the European experience of history as a standard, they have tended to evaluate Japan's development according to its perceived distance from this. The debate continues to exert a great influence on some Japanese scholars, but recent changes in the understanding of modern Japanese history have led to a rapid loss of interest in such simplistic approaches to the problem.

The application of modernization theory represented a reaction on the part of foreign scholars against this tendency of Japanese historians to stress the warped and backward nature of Japanese development and its abnormality when compared with the West. In a reversal of this tendency, the modernization theorists drew attention to similarities rather than dissimilarities between Japan and the West, comparing Tokugawa Japan to feudal Europe and proclaiming that the key to her rapid industrialization was to be found in the advanced nature of pre-modern – that is, Tokugawa – Japan.[7] A paradoxical effect of this high evaluation of Japan's development has been the drawing of an even sharper barrier between the advanced countries of the West and the 'backward' countries elsewhere, encouraging a pessimistic attitude to the possibilities of modernization in the Third World. This is because, by interpreting 'modernization' in a narrowly Western sense and calculating the possibilities of success purely in terms of the number of 'Western' characteristics exhibited by a country, modernization theory effectively brings Japan over to the Western side of the divide and denies that it represents even a unique case of the successful industrialization of a non-Western country.

Other scholars, both Western and Japanese, have analysed Japan's industrialization from the viewpoint of theories of economic growth but on the basis of a variety of methodologies. For example, W.W. Rostow, clearly stimulated by modernization theory, described Japan's economic development as a process leading towards the goal of a mass-consumption society.[8] In general such approaches rely not so much on historical analysis as on the interpretation of the available quantitative material according to the national accounting framework. They neglect the role of international economic relations and tend to view development as a linear process within each country.[9]

However different, the approaches discussed above have two methodological characteristics in common. The first is the use of the historical development of the West as the sole criterion by which to analyse Japan. The danger of such a method is that factors which were important in the case of Japan, but not present in the West, may go unappreciated. The second is the narrow concentration on internal factors as the key to Japan's success. This has led to a virtual neglect of the role of the international economic situation.

Two important methodological developments are, however, causing great changes in these 'traditional' approaches to modern Japan. The first involves the invoking of a broader historical perspective, according to which the Meiji Restoration is seen as a turning point of political rather than economic significance; it therefore stresses the continuity between the socio-economic changes of the Tokugawa period and the subsequent Meiji process of industrialization. This approach is being pioneered in the field of quantitatively oriented economic history, challenging traditional interpretations that Tokugawa Japan was a stable and static feudal society.[10]

The second methodological development involves a broader regional perspective which rejects a Eurocentric standard of reference and encourages comparison between Japan and other non-Western, particularly Asian, societies. As particularly stimulating examples of this approach one can point to certain recent studies of early Tokugawa diplomacy and trade. Ronald Toby has analysed the 'seclusion' or 'isolation' policy of the Bakufu with regard to its internal and external political role, and interpreted it as part of an effort to establish Tokugawa legitimacy both in East Asia and within Japan itself. Tashiro Kazui has drawn attention to the scale and importance of foreign trade during the period of 'seclusion'.

Exports of silver from Japan continued in large quantities up until the mid-eighteenth century through trade with both Korea and the Ryūkyū Islands, and Japan formed part of an East Asian trade region centring on China.[11] Even though there is no direct connection between this trade and the trade which developed after the opening of Japan in the mid-nineteenth century, our understanding of the nature of the 'seclusion' policy has necessarily undergone considerable modification.

This broader regional perspective can be seen as a reaction against the previous neglect of international economic relationships. It also, however, reflects both the realization that the Western pattern of industrialization can have only limited relevance for Asian and African countries, with their very different non-economic and cultural characteristics, and the degree of industrialization which has in fact been successfully achieved in Asian countries such as South Korea, Hong Kong and Singapore. It should be noted that these two methodological developments are taking place side by side rather than in isolation.

Research on these lines is not entirely unprecedented. Over twenty years ago, Alexander Gerschenkron was pointing out the existence of fundamental differences in the industrialization patterns of backward and advanced countries, and stressing both the significance of native elements in the industrialization of backward countries and the effect of specific pre-industrial cultural developments upon their industrialization potential.[12] In *Asian Drama*, his famous work on South India, Gunnar Myrdal criticized the Eurocentric approach and emphasized the need for an ' "institutional" approach' which gave weight to non-economic factors.[13] As far as East Asia is concerned, William Lockwood stands alone in having discussed Japan's economic development in connection with the general issue of Asian industrialization, although he focused on Japan's development after World War I, and did not give much attention to the nineteenth century.[14]

Are we right to allow consideration of either external or internal conditons to lead us to abandon hopes of Third World industrialization? Has the Third World nothing to learn from Japan's experience? Surely there remain many points to be investigated before we reach such pessimistic conclusions. Failure to industrialize according to the Western model should be ascribed to the inappropriateness of the model rather than to the impossibility of industrialization itself. So long as it is interpreted as merely a modification of the Western pattern, therefore, Japan's historical experience can be of little significance to the rest of the world. On the other hand, in so far as no retrospective alterations can be made to the actual process of industrialization in Japan, its relevance now will in any case depend entirely on the extent to which conditions sufficient for a repetition exist in present-day underdeveloped countries. Macroeconomic analysis alone is clearly insufficient to ascertain this; detailed, concrete analysis is required of the similarities and dissimilarities in the external and internal factors affecting industrialization in Japan and underdeveloped countries. Unfortunately, few such studies have yet been carried out.

Japan's position as the only non-Western country to achieve industrialization in the nineteenth century means, on the one hand, that it is possible to compare her experience with that of the West. On the other hand, by virtue of being a late developer, Japan must also have many elements in common with other non-Western countries. Case studies of Japan therefore have a potentially very important role to play in providing a bridge between the two. For this reason Japan's industrialization should not be seen only in relation to Japan itself; it can properly be understood only through comparison with the contrasting historical experience of those Asian countries which were not able to industrialize in the nineteenth century. Moreover, through comparing the past and present situation of these Asian countries it should be possible to discover cultural elements foreign to the West in their past economic experience which they nevertheless have in common with Japan, and thus draw up an Asian model of industrialization. This should have more relevance than the Western model relied on until now, and it should even be possible to produce from it a further model which can be successfully applied to all non-Western countries. In this book I hope to adopt an approach to Japan's industrialization which will facilitate comparisons with non-Western as well as Western countries and thus help to show the unique bridging role which Japan can play between the two. It might even prepare the way for the formation of a new, less Eurocentric model of industrialization which will be of practical use to present-day developing or underdeveloped countries.

Internal and External Factors in Japan's Industrialization

The 'unequal' treaties of 1858 made Japan a reluctant member of the world economy and presented her with an utterly transformed external situation, which had inevitable internal repercussions. From being a virtually closed country with a closed economy, Japan became sharply exposed to the economic and political forces of the outside world. The economic and political development which followed the opening of the ports can therefore be understood only in relation to the changing international environment of the second half of the nineteenth century. It is impossible to understand Japan's industrialization without reference to this new dimension. Internally, the signing of the US–Japan friendship treaty of 1854 increased both distrust of Tokugawa rule and the general level of interest in politics, while the opening of foreign trade greatly disturbed the economy. Some sort of internal adjustment was inevitable and, in political terms, resulted in the Meiji Restoration in 1868. The assumption that these 'unequal' commercial treaties put Japan in a subordinate position is, however, misleading. While Japan's industrialization was in one sense a passive process during which the structure of domestic industry was reassembled under the impact of the world economy, it can also be seen as a dynamic process of interaction. For Japan herself had an undeniable effect on the international economic structure through coming to occupy a particular position in the overall international division of labour.

In general, when foreign trade with the West starts in a backward country, imports of manufactured goods, mainly consumer items, grow, destroying traditional domestic industry. At the same time, resource-intensive primary products come to form the main export items and exports often play a crucial role as a leading sector of economic development.[15] In Third World countries, however, the foreign currency obtained through exports of primary products does not lead to the development of modern industries which will allow import substitution. Furthermore, the introduction of foreign capital to aid industrialization does not link up with the domestic formation of capital, so that a dual industrial pattern develops of primary industries specializing in exporting and modern transplanted industries specializing in import substitution. According to the model based on the historical experience of the West, however, the export of primary products tends to be merely a means to industrialization, rather than an important part of the actual process. In other words, the basic criterion of industrialization is the establishment of modern industry, be it light or heavy manufacturing, and the traditional indigenous sector is something doomed to extinction and therefore without significance.

At the start of her industrialization, Japan faced an international environment similar to that encountered by developing countries today; she therefore had to begin trade on monoculture lines, exporting the products of her traditional industries and importing manufactured goods from economically advanced Western countries. In this sense, Japan was by no means exceptional. The 1880 report of the Competitive Exhibition for the Promotion of Cotton and Sugar describes the Japanese situation as follows:

Ever since the commencement of trade with foreign countries, there has been an excess of imports over exports for which we have compensated through the use of specie. . . . The outflow of specie grows more precipitate year by year. This is a source of lamentation for both government and people and some solution must be found. Our attempts to find a solution have not yet been successful, however, since any increase in exports in the morning has been followed by a similar increase in imports in the evening. Devastating loss of specie continues to this day. Could there be any worse crisis than this for Japan? If we investigate, products related to raw silk and tea manufacture take up just under 53 per cent of exports by value, and cotton and . . . sugar account for just under 49 per cent of imports by value. Foreign cotton manufactures and sugar are the greatest source of our trade problems and raw silk and tea make the biggest contribution to maintaining a balance. Therefore there is only one way in which to remove our disadvantage and improve our level of trade. We must expand our indigenous sources of national wealth and develop them where they are not yet developed; we must increase our production of key products and begin producing them where they are not yet produced. Raw silk and tea are the sources of wealth which should be most urgently expanded, cotton manufactures and sugar are the products which should be most urgently increased.[16]

Import substitution and the export of products of traditional industries were interdependent but separate aspects of Japan's industrialization. The experience of Japan as a latecomer country was that import substitution could not wait until exports of products of traditional industries had built up reserves of foreign currency, but had to take place at the same time. As I hope to demonstrate in some detail later, Japan's experience shows that it was traditional rural industry which provided the vital support for the early stages of industrialization; without this industrialization could never have been attained.[17] The expansion of exports of products of traditional industries had only an indirect link with the development of modern industry and was completely separate from industrialization through import substitution and the introduction of modern industry.

Japan's economic development in the Meiji period owed a great deal to exports of indigenous products such as raw silk and tea. The foreign currency obtained through these exports brought about conditions suitable to stable domestic economic development, through restraining the outflow of specie while at the same time limiting the potential entry of foreign capital, by keeping the imbalance of international payments to a minimum level. In addition, it produced the conditions essential to industrialization by increasing import capacity and in particular expanding the possible range of imports of production goods, which form the basis of import substitution. Since Japan had little indigenous raw cotton, any increase in exports of cotton cloth and cotton manufactures, production of which grew towards the end of the nineteenth century, meant a comparative increase in imports of raw cotton and therefore led to only limited gains in foreign currency. In contrast, raw silk and tea were indigenously produced and could therefore respond with great flexibility to changes in the structure of domestic production.

If one looks at the situation in China at the time, the contrast is striking. Table 1-1 shows movements in the exports of raw silk and tea from the two countries between 1871 and 1900. Up to 1899, when Japan recovered a degree of tariff autonomy, the two were placed in virtually the same international economic and political environment. In other words, both were subject to economic pressure from the Western powers and had no tariff autonomy; both were exporting raw silk and tea and importing manufactured goods. The production of raw silk and tea was dependent on natural conditions and both, as luxury goods, had to adapt to the requirements of the consumer. Increases in Japan's exports of these products were attained at the expense of Chinese exports, which had previously had an overwhelmingly dominant position in overseas markets. China had a negative balance of payments from 1865 onwards, with the sole exception of the years 1872 to 1876. This suggests that Japan's industrialization, made possible as it was through the export of the products of traditional rural industry, had a negative effect on China's balance of payments and increased China's financial dependence on the West, although imports of opium also contributed to the latter.

My intention in this study is therefore to examine the role of product exports of traditional industries in Japan's industrialization, in the international economic environment of the second half of the nineteenth century. This, however, is only the first half of the story. The industrialization made possible by exports of products of traditional industries was simply the stepping stone to fully fledged industrialization. The latter could not have taken place without the parallel process of import substitution. I hope later to write what amounts to the sequel to this book: a study of the later development of import substitution industries, centred on cotton spinning and sugar refining, and of the growth of heavy industry.

Throughout the present book I stress the complex interrelationship between Japan's industrialization, the international economic environment, and the East Asian policy of the Western powers. I cover the period from the opening of Japan to foreign trade in 1859 until the end of the treaty port system in 1899, when Japan attained partial tariff autonomy and obtained the abolition of extraterritoriality based on the 1894 Anglo–Japanese commercial treaty. This will allow me to con-

Table 1-1 Silk and Tea Exports from China and Japan, 1871–1900 (quinquennial annual average)

China				(in thousand Haikwan taels)	
	Total exports	Silk exports	(b)	Tea exports	(c)
	(a)	(b)	(a) %	(c)	(a) %
1871/75	69,444	24,920	(35.9)	39,589	(57.0)
1876/80	73,127	23,642	(32.3)	34,199	(46.8)
1881/85	68,228	18,747	(27.5)	31,544	(46.2)
1886/90	87,912	24,671	(28.1)	29,752	(33.8)
1891/95	118,312	32,376	(27.4)	30,375	(25.7)
1896/1900	161.680	49,572	(28.8)	29,033	(18.0)

Japan				(in thousand yen)	
	Total exports	Silk exports	(b)	Tea exports	(c)
	(a)	(b)	(a) %	(c)	(a) %
1871/75	18,912	8,418	(44.5)	5,534	(29.3)
1876/80	26,724	11,914	(44.6)	5,811	(21.7)
1881/85	35,213	15,802	(44.9)	6,566	(18.6)
1886/90	58,731	23,326	(39.7)	6,787	(11.6)
1891/95	101,940	39,501	(38.7)	7,814	(7.7)
1896/1900	173,218	50,131	(28.9)	7,997	(4.6)

Sources: Hsiao Liang-lin, *China's Foreign Trade Statistics, 1864–1949* (1974), pp. 22–23, 109, 117–18; Tōyō Keizai Shinpōsha, *Nihon bōeki seiran* (1935), pp. 3, 13–15, 52–55.

Notes: (1) Silk piece goods and products are excluded.

(2) The average exchange rate during the period 1874–96 was 1.53 yen per tael.

sider Japan's industrialization in the nineteenth century in comparison with China, which also attempted modernization in a similar international environment.

My analysis of Japan's industrialization process is founded on the following considerations. First, I stress both the domestic situation, with its roots in the Tokugawa period, and the international situation, with its roots in the changing world economy of the nineteenth century. Second, I regard not the Meiji Restoration but the opening of the treaty ports in 1859 as the turning point in Japan's industrialization. Third, I do not agree with the normal view that Japan's industrialization was created and engineered by the government working 'from above'. I consider the government to have been the organizer of the whole domestic economy, integrating the industrialization process, but stress that it relied very much on previous and continuing development 'from below'.

Chapters 2 and 3 of the book deal with the international institutional situation in the latter half of the nineteenth century and with the institutional framework for Japan's internal economic development. In Chapter 2, I discuss the structure of the world economy, focussing on Britain, the prime Western mover in East Asian affairs, briefly review the theory of the 'imperialism of free trade', and investigate the international political environment in East Asia through an examination of the operations of the British Royal Navy. In Chapter 3, I first review the commercial treaties which provided the external framework of Japan's industrialization and the way in which Western firms advanced into Japan. Then, through investigation of the actual nature of the treaty port trade brought into being by the 'unequal' treaties, both as regards the domestic Japanese distribution network and the activities of Western trading firms, I discuss the way in which this trade actually worked in Japan's favour as a non-tariff barrier.

Through Chapters 4 to 6, I focus on Japan's main export items, which were raw silk, tea and coal. I examine the domestic development of each industry in the context of movements in demand and international competition, and analyse the external and internal factors which made their development possible. The size of the overseas demand for any particular export article depended on the stage of economic development in the consuming country, and the only accurate way of judging the relative competitiveness of the same export article as produced in different countries is by comparing performance on the overseas market. I therefore pay great attention to the relative position of Japanese export articles overseas, in terms of price, quality, and quantities of supply.[18] Exports of raw silk and tea, both products of traditional industries, developed in connection with the European and American markets, where they competed with Chinese raw silk and tea; coal was developed as a modern industry by zaibatsu such as Mitsui and Mitsubishi for the Asian market, and sold in competition with exports from Britain and Australia. Chapter 4 examines the internal and external factors which enabled Japan to increase her silk exports in the changing world silk market, by considering the competition of Japanese silk with Chinese and European silk on the overseas market. Chapter 5 examines the competition between Japanese and Chinese, Indian and Ceylon tea on the overseas market, and shows why Japan failed to increase her tea exports. Chapter 6 examines the internal and external factors influencing Japan's coal exports and shows how Japan overcame competition from British and Australian coal in Asian markets such as Shanghai, Hong Kong and Singapore.

2
East Asia in the World Economy

The World Economy in the Nineteenth Century

The British Economy

For most of the nineteenth century Britain was the keystone of
the international economy, both in industrial production and
as a banking and monetary centre. In 1816 it had gone onto the
gold standard, and tariff rates had been cut to promote free
trading. The free trade movement reached its peak in the mid-
nineteenth century, with the abolition of the Corn Laws in 1846
and the repeal of the Navigation Acts in 1849. Through exporting industrial goods to non-industrialized countries in return
for imports of raw materials and foodstuffs, Britain in effect
transformed the world into a single interrelated international
trading and financial mechanism. One result of such international specialization between an industrialized Britain and
the non-industrialized – primarily agricultural – countries of
the world was that Britain was bound to have a decisive
influence on the infant industries in latecomer countries. A free
trade system would inevitably work against these countries as
rising British industrial production worked to bring down the
prices of industrial goods.[1]

In the mid-nineteenth century Britain was producing over
40 per cent of the total world trade in industrial goods, and
about a quarter of total international trade was passing
through British ports.[2] British production of textiles, coal,
ships and engineering products increased rapidly as the pattern of British international trade described above took shape.
Between 1845 and 1875 imports of foodstuffs and finished
goods grew while there was a decline in the proportion of imports of raw materials. Between 1854 and 1860, for example,
foodstuffs accounted for 32 per cent of total imports, raw
materials for 61 per cent and finished goods for 7 per cent.[3]
Textile goods, metals and coal were the major exports. Even as

late as 1914, over 65 per cent of Britain's total exports consisted of manufactured goods, two-thirds of which were textile goods such as cotton cloth and cotton yarn.[4]

Britain's position in the world economy was buttressed by her status as an international trade and financial centre. London became the centre of international trade, finance, insurance and shipping. The greater part of international trade was conducted in sterling, and bills drawn upon London were universally accepted for financial settlement. It was credit transactions of this type that made the expansion of world trade possible. British dominance in international trade was sustained by her remarkable development of a worldwide shipping network and long-distance telegraphic communications.[5]

In the mid-nineteenth century world trade was developing not only in the areas of transportation and technology but also in resources and markets. Its total estimated value increased rapidly, from £800 million in 1850 to £1,450 million in 1860, £2,890 million in 1872–73, and £3,900 million in 1895–99.[6] The annual average growth rate of world trade was 4.8 per cent between 1840 and 1860, and 5.5 per cent between 1860 and 1870. The corresponding growth rates for British trade were 5.5 per cent for 1840–60 and 4.3 per cent for 1860–70.[7]

As the above figures suggest, however, the industrialization of Europe and the United States increasingly came to threaten Britain's dominance over the international economic structure. Her share of world manufacturing production decreased from 31.8 per cent in 1870 to 26.6 per cent in 1881–85 and to 19.5 per cent in 1896–1900. In contrast, the share held by the United States increased from 23.3 per cent in 1870 to 28.6 per cent in 1881–85 and 30.1 per cent in 1896–1900, with a similar increase for Germany over the same periods: from 13.2 per cent to 13.9 per cent and then to 16.6 per cent.[8] The spread of industrialization led to a correspondingly rapid increase in demand for primary products. The newly industrialized countries themselves gradually became involved in developing close ties with non-European areas, both as export markets for their manufactured goods and as essential sources of primary products.[9] As a result, the international supply and demand relationship between the primary producing countries and the industrialized and industrializing countries became increasingly complicated.[10] The international trade in primary products rapidly increased in both volume and value. From the mid-1880s to World War I its quinquennial growth rate was 17 per cent. In quinquennial terms, the annual average world import of primary products increased in current value from 4.6 million US dollars in 1876–80 to 6.4 million US dollars in 1896–1900, while world exports of primary products increased from 3.7 to 5.5 million US dollars.[11] During this time, primary products maintained an average 61–65 per cent share of world trade. The proportion of primary products in the exports of underdeveloped countries was as high as 98 per cent for 1876–80 and 92 per cent for 1896–1900.[12]

As primary producing countries developed direct links with industrializing countries, there was a corresponding decrease in Britain's entrepôt trade. In quinquennial terms the annual average of re-exports decreased from 19.5 per cent of total imports for 1861–65 to 12.9 per cent for 1896–1900.[13] Between 1876 and 1880 Britain, the United States and France accounted for 53 per cent of the total world import of primary products, and for 1896–1900 the same three countries – together with Germany, Italy, the Netherlands and Switzerland – accounted for 75 per cent.[14] Since in this period prices moved in favour of primary products as opposed to manufactured goods, countries producing the former were able to increase their capacity to purchase the latter. In the 1880s and 1890s, however, increasing investment meant that new regions of primary production were becoming drawn into international trade, and the consequent rise in the availability of food and raw materials led to less favourable terms of trade for primary producers.[15]

The main cause of the decline in Britian's share of world trade was her failure to adjust domestically to the changes in the international economy.[16] As a consequence, British industrial goods lost competitiveness in their established export markets in terms of both production cost and selling price. Britain responded to intensified competition from the newly industrialized countries by adjusting her trade patterns and markets and reinforcing her position as the financial centre of the world. She shifted her major export markets from Europe and North America to still non-industrialized markets, particularly to India and East Asia, while increasing exports of capital to North and South America and her colonies.[17] In fact, British external trade of the traditional type – that is, the exchange of manufactured products against raw materials and foodstuffs – decreased from 65.9 per cent in 1854–63 to 34.5 per cent in 1893–1903. In contrast, for the same period, the exchange of manufactured products against other manufactured products increased from 8.8 per cent to 25.3 per cent, and the exchange of commodities against 'invisible items' increased from 14.2 per cent to 23.9 per cent.[18] Britain became even more dependent on the export of a small number of established goods such as textiles, iron and steel, and coal, thus restricting her trade opportunities in the more complicated network of multilateral trade.[19] Furthermore, the worsening terms of trade for the primary producing countries caused a decline in their purchasing power, adversely affecting exports of British manufactured goods.[20] The decline in exports of manufactured goods resulted in a continuous deficit for Britain's visible trade. This deficit reached an annual average of £125 million over the period 1876–80, but was more than compensated for by the invisible earnings from overseas investments and business services such as banking, insurance and shipping.[21]

Britain and East Asia

In the changing world economy of the second half of the nineteenth century, China and Japan appeared both as suppliers of raw materials and as markets for Western manufactured goods. British manufacturers and merchants had optimistic visions about the vast possibilities of the China market, while they were less sanguine about Japan.[22]

Table 2–1 shows Britain's trade with China and Japan in the second half of the nineteenth century. As a combined figure, imports from China and Japan took up a decreasing share of Britain's total imports towards the end of the century, until they formed less than 1 per cent. Together they accounted for a continuing share of 5–6 per cent of total exports of British products, Japan becoming the more important market.

The cotton industry was the leading exporter in the expanding British economy. By the mid-nineteenth century the overseas market for British cotton piece goods was shifting from Europe to Asia, with the Asian share of such imports increasing from 31.4 per cent in 1850 to 57.8 per cent in 1896. India was the single most important Asian market, taking 314 million yards (23.2 per cent of Britain's total exports in this field)

Table 2-1 Britain's Trade with China and Japan, 1850–1900
(in £ million)

Year	Imports			Exports[1]		
	Total	from China[2]	from Japan	Total	to China[2]	to Japan
		%	%		%	%
1850	100.5			175.4		
1860	210.5	9.3 (4.4)	0.2 (0.1)	135.9	5.3 (3.9)	–
1870	303.3	9.8 (3.2)	0.1 (0.0)	199.6	9.5 (4.8)	1.6(0.8)
1880	411.2	13.2 (3.2)	0.5 (0.1)	223.1	8.8 (3.9)	3.3(1.5)
1890	420.7	6.1 (1.4)	1.0 (0.2)	263.5	9.1 (3.5)	4.1(1.6)
1900	523.1	3.4 (0.6)	1.5 (0.3)	291.2	8.3 (2.9)	9.8(3.4)

Sources: Annual Statement of the Trade of the United Kingdom with Foreign Countries and British Possessions, corresponding years.
Notes: (1) British and Irish products. (2) Including Hong Kong but excluding Macao. For 1890 only Korea is included.

in 1850, and 2,038 million yards (39.1 per cent) in 1896. Exports to China, however, did not increase as much as had been expected. China took only 73 million yards (5.4 per cent of the total) in 1850 and 543 million yards (10.4 per cent) in 1896. In terms of value, the overall share of British cotton piece goods exports to the Asian market rose from 24.4 per cent in 1850 to 43.4 per cent in 1896, India accounting for 18.5 per cent in 1850 and 26.6 per cent in 1896 while China took up 3.6 per cent and 8.5 per cent respectively.[23] Since the overall share in yards rose faster than the overall share in value, it is clear that it was the cheaper, inferior goods which were finding an expanding market in Asia. In any case, by changing the market and the quality of manufactures Britain showed herself able to increase her exports of cotton piece goods in absolute terms.[24]

In cotton yarn, Britain faced strong competition both from the industrializing countries of Europe and America, and from the development of domestic cotton industries in her Asian export markets. According to the annual averages for 1880–84, Europe remained the most important market for British cotton yarn, taking 50 per cent of the total. India was taking about 20 per cent and China, Japan and other East Asian countries 16 per cent. From the 1880s onwards, however, Britain's cotton yarn exports decreased rapidly. On the European market, the development of the domestic cotton industry forced Britain to produce finer yarns; on the Asian market, Britain's cotton yarn exports gradually decreased in the face of competition from the rapidly developing cotton spinning industries of India, China and Japan. Increasing exports to China were produced first by Indian and later by Japanese mills.[25] As Asian countries produced mainly cheap, coarse yarns, Britain's production gradually became limited to yarns of medium and fine quality. In the 1890s in particular, British spinners attempted to solve the problem of declining cotton yarn exports by an increasing emphasis on yarn for hosiery and lace and on the production of finer count yarns.[26]

The significance of these exports must be relative. By comparison with India, Britain's cotton exports to both Japan and China seem small.[27] Although the factor of British rule makes it difficult to compare China and Japan with India, in the former two countries the rate of increase in imports of cotton manufactures was slower, and the traditional cotton weaving industry survived into a later period. Throughout the nineteenth century India was the single most important market for the British cotton industry and therefore the area at which the export effort was directed. Production of cheap fabrics of coarser yarn – that is, white and plain unbleached calicos which were dyed and printed into various types of designs and colours – increased to meet the vastly expanding Asian (mainly Indian) market, but not necessarily the needs of China and Japan. From the 1840s Blackburn became the main centre for producing these fabrics.[28] China and Japan were understandably regarded as of secondary importance despite the expectations that business groups held of the potentially enormous Chinese market.

China and Japan did not become attractive markets for British capital exports until the end of the nineteenth century. According to estimates by Feinstein, capital exports from Britain, including foreign holdings, amounted to £2,610 million by the turn of the century. Of this sum China absorbed only £50 million, 1.9 per cent of the total, 80 per cent of which was invested in the 1890s. Japan absorbed only £10 million, all of this again in the 1890s.[29] Even if one includes the two foreign loans raised in the early 1870s, capital investment in Japan was very low.

The significance of the Asian market in world trade grew until the first decade of the twentieth century. India and East Asia were becoming key elements in the British trading system and in the pattern of multilateral settlement.[30] At this point, some reference should be made to the relationship between the continuous depreciation in the gold price of silver from the early 1870s and the position of the East Asian countries in the international economy. Since they were on the silver standard, this depreciation, combined with a decline in ocean freight rates, was of great importance in both encouraging exports to the gold standard countries of the West, and discouraging imports from them.[31] Figure 1 shows the average price of bar silver per oz in London, the average rate of Japanese yen and the Chinese tael in sterling, and the average rate of the Japanese yen in American and Mexican dollars. This depreciation of silver occurred both because of the transition to the gold standard of Germany in 1871 and the United States in 1873, and because of an increase in world silver production. The decline of silver was extremely severe in the early 1890s. The average price per oz fell from 60.3d. in 1872 to 42.7d. in 1889, and 28.9d. in 1894. As we shall see later, this situation made it possible for Japan to increase her exports to European and American markets and to compete on easier terms with France and Italy in raw silk, for example, or with Britain and Australia in coal.[32]

The 'Imperialism of Free Trade' and Dependency Theory

The 'Imperialism of Free Trade' in East Asia

As this book is dealing with the international economic environment of the second half of the nineteenth century, some discussion of the theory of the 'imperialism of free trade' is inevitable. Since the theory was first put forward by John Gallagher and Ronald Robinson in 1953,[33] it has given great impetus to studies not only on mid- and late-Victorian Britain but also on European and non-European countries which have been influenced to varying degrees by British economic supremacy.

The inferences drawn by Gallagher and Robinson have, in addition, been the subject of lively debate. The workings of the

Figure 1 Depreciation in Silver Value and Fluctuations of the Yen, 1860-1900

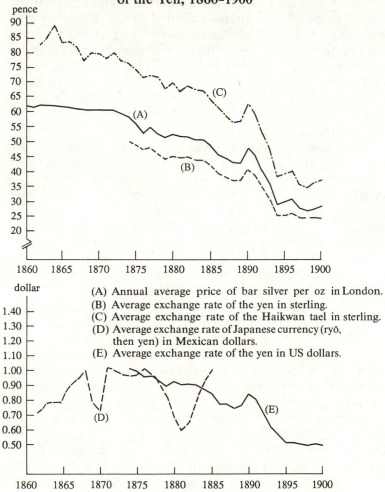

(A) Annual average price of bar silver per oz in London.
(B) Average exchange rate of the yen in sterling.
(C) Average exchange rate of the Haikwan tael in sterling.
(D) Average exchange rate of Japanese currency (ryō, then yen) in Mexican dollars.
(E) Average exchange rate of the yen in US dollars.

Sources: Ōkurashō, 'Kahei seido chōsakai hōkoku' (1895), pp. 29–31; Nihon Ginkō, *Honpō shuyō keizai tōkei* (1966), p. 318: Hsiao Liang-lin, *China's Foreign Trade Statistics, 1864–1949* (1974), pp. 190–1; Yamamoto Yūzō, 'Bakumatsu Meiji-ki no yōgin sōba', pp. 300, 307, in Shinbo and Yasuba, *Kindai ikō-ki no Nihon keizai* (1979).

Note: For figures in (D) before 1874 I have treated one Mexican dollar as equivalent to 45 silver monme.

theory have been tested against the historical experience of various countries in both the formal and the informal empires.[34] In their initial analysis, Gallagher and Robinson seem to have played down economic factors in favour of political ones in order to emphasize their departure from the Hobson-Lenin line. They therefore explained British overseas expansion largely in terms of the internal British political situation. In this sense one could say that their conceptual framework was not far from that of the British imperial historians whom they severely criticized.

Most scholars would seem to accept Gallagher and Robinson's first point, that British overseas expansion in the nineteenth century can no longer be understood without considering the informal as well as the formal empire, and without examination of political factors, whether positive or negative, as well as economic issues. The controversy, therefore, has centred on their second point, the question of continuity between mid- and late-Victorian British expansion; in other words, on the question as to whether after 1880 there was a different stage which one can call a 'New Imperialism'.[35]

One of the strongest critics of the theory of the 'imperialism of free trade' is D.C.M. Platt. Platt denies the existence of any consistent relationship between British policy and the interests of individual firms and traders abroad, and raises doubts about the readiness of the British government to establish and preserve British paramountcy.[36] These are issues which I will take up later.

Recent contributors to our understanding of British imperialism who have been stimulated, if only negatively, by Gallagher and Robinson, include C.C. Eldridge, and P.J. Cain and A.G. Hopkins. Eldridge put forward the view that the history of the British empire in the nineteenth century 'must be interpreted in the light of the economic situation, the international scene and the domestic politics of the period.'[37] P.J. Cain and A.G. Hopkins similarly stressed the subtly shifting links between British overseas expansion and domestic economic and political change.[38]

Robinson later revised his stand to emphasize the non-European foundations of imperialism,[39] but he did not change his view that non-European countries were purely passive partners in the 'imperialism of free trade' rather than fundamentally autonomous societies with their own socio-economic and cultural structures. Their development destined them for subordination to the European industrial powers. Even his later attempt to be 'non-eurocentric' is thus based on eurocentric assumptions, as can be seen in his continual use of only the two categories of European and non-European. In his eyes, there are no significant differences between the circumstances of Asia, Africa and Latin America in the nineteenth century. It is therefore inevitable that Gallagher and Robinson felt able to use the African encounter with the European powers to produce a general concept of the 'imperialism of free trade' which could then be applied without substantial amendment to the rest of the non-European world.

In their original article, 'The Imperialism of Free Trade', Gallagher and Robinson cited China to illustrate how 'British expansion sometimes failed, if it gained political supremacy without effecting a successful commercial penetration.' Their description of China is, however, too simplistic to be convincing: 'There were spectacular exertions of British policy in China, but they did little to produce new customers. Britain's political hold upon China failed to break down Chinese economic self-sufficiency.' The Opium War in 1840 and the Arrow War in 1856 put great strains on Chinese society, as the Taiping Rebellion showed. The British government was embarrassed and 'worked to prop up the tottering Pekin (*sic*) regime', but without using this 'as a lever for extracting further concessions':

> The value of this self-denial became clear in the following decades when the Pekin government, threatened with a scramble for China, leaned more and more on the diplomatic support of the honest British broker.[40]

Gallagher and Robinson thus recognized that Britain failed to penetrate the Chinese economy, which continued to be self-sufficient. To preserve their theory, they ascribe this failure to 'self-denial' on the part of the British government in order to avoid a total collapse of Chinese society. It is surely necessary, however, to prove that the British policy of support for the Chinese government was the result of true self-denial rather than the natural consequence of British inability to put further unilateral pressure on the Chinese government.

Platt criticizes Gallagher and Robinson on the grounds that for both silk and tea, which were significant British imports, 'the internal market in China was enormously larger than exports' and therefore 'In no real sense was China economically "dependent" on mid-Victorian Britain.'[41] He further stresses that trade, not political domination, was the fundamental motive behind Britain's expansion into East Asia and that fair and equal treatment for British trade and finance continued to be paramount in British foreign policy even after Britain had gone on to the economic and political defensive in the mid-1880s.[42]

In another critique of Gallagher and Robinson, B. Dean concludes that 'the non-economic criteria of informal empire seem to fit neatly the Anglo-Chinese relationship', but that 'the economic criteria are not satisfied' and '*on the whole* British merchants or British "free-trade imperialism" failed economically to effectively subordinate China to Great Britain or to British merchants.'[43] Dean thus points out that, since the 'imperialism of free trade' necessarily involves elements of both economic and political control, Britain's failure to manipulate the Chinese economy means that the theory cannot be applied to the Chinese case.[44]

In the article 'Non-European Foundations of European Imperialism', Robinson is clearly attempting to extend the approach taken in *Africa and the Victorians* to Asia and points to the lack of collaborators with the imperial powers both in China and Japan. In a later paragraph, however, Japan is discussed as a case where collaborators existed. He argues that

In Japan after 1869 (*sic*) the western samurai overthrew the Shogunate, perilously modernised its quasi-feudal institutions and exploited neotraditionalist nationalism and carefully calculated bargains with the West to protect their independence on the basis of 'rich country, strong army'. By 1914 these Japanese collaborators had achieved what otherwise only white colonists seemed able to achieve. They succeeded in translating the forces of western expansion into terms of indigenous politics. By adapting European style techniques and institutions, they managed to control them so that they strengthened, instead of destroying, Japanese government, and worked not for imperialism, but for Japan.[45]

However, he makes no attempt to prove that the Meiji government 'collaborated' with Western imperialism in the sense of trying to protect and promote British commercial and political interests. Indeed, the process of Japanese history provides no support for such a view.

Dependency Theory in East Asia

The contrast between Japan's industrial success in the nineteenth and twentieth centuries and the relative failure of the countries which are now thought of as belonging to the Third World has attracted the attention of dependency theorists. Dependency theory emphasizes the contribution of external as well as internal factors to underdevelopment. By giving underdevelopment an international dimension it has made a great contribution to the methodology of economic history. Since dependency theorists have analysed the causes of underdevelopment in Latin America in a variety of ways, it is not possible to provide one exact definition. The underlying hypothesis makes use of the categories of 'core' and 'periphery' to argue that the countries of Latin America were fated to suffer underdevelopment because of the external activities of the Western imperial powers.[46]

Dependency theory is thus based on the experience of Latin America, where internal factors were not strong enough to prevent Western economic encroachment. Some supporters of the theory have nevertheless tried to extend hypotheses drawn from Latin America and apply them to Africa and Asia. This approach seems similar to that of Gallagher and Robinson, who attempted to apply the experience of Africa to the rest of the world. It should be noted that, as with the 'imperialism of free trade', one of the crucial assumptions of dependency theory is that the imperialist countries of Britain and Europe were strong enough, both politically and economically, to subordinate non-European countries. In this respect, one can say that dependency theory is the 'imperialism of free trade' seen upside down: from the viewpoint of the subordinate countries rather than that of the Western imperial powers. Indeed, dependency theorists tend to accept the 'imperialism of free trade' without criticism.

Frances V. Moulder, for example, has attempted to apply Wallerstein's world system approach to an understanding of Japan's success at industrialization in the nineteenth century and China's failure.[47] Building on 'world economy theories', she tries to reinterpret Japan's development during the nineteenth century in an international context through comparison with China. Moulder argues that during the nineteenth century Japan remained relatively free from economic and political incorporation as a satellite in the world economy, while China was intensively and continuously incorporated. In the first phase until the 1880s, 'termed the "imperialism of free trade" ', China was of major trading interest to the West and Japan was not. In the second phase, of the 'new imperialism', China became a victim of the Western nations but by then Japan was militarily strong enough to deter European invasion. She concludes:

> The major way in which incorporation contributed to underdevelopment in China was the impact on the state. China's incorporation led to the dismantling of the already weak imperial state. Japan's greater autonomy, however, permitted transformation of the weak feudal state into a bureaucratic or national state. . . . Japan's success was due in part to the greater fiscal strength of the Meiji state but also, and importantly, to the absence of strong Western interests that in China blocked or undermined the success of such policies.[48]

In the second half of the nineteenth century, however, Britain's exports to Japan were actually increasing faster than her exports to China, and this seems inconsistent with Moulder's assumption that the former was less involved in the world economy than the latter.

Although Moulder does make use of information obtained from secondary works to develop her speculations in so far as it fits in with her framework, there are several occasions when her understanding of basic historical facts concerning China and Japan seems questionable. Moreover, her interpretation of Japan's industrialization is unbalanced. While she recognizes the role of exports of silk and tea, she does not realize their full significance. As I shall show in detail later, they were products of traditional rural industries, and cannot be discussed in isolation from other internal factors. However, she ignores all such factors, apart from the role of government, in favour of the external role of the Western powers. The view that traditional industries in a pre-modern economy might reach a high level of development is probably foreign to her conceptual framework, based as it is on the Latin American experience.

British East Asian Policy and the Limitations of British Power

There seem to me to be two decisive weaknesses in the theory of the 'imperialism of free trade'. One is the assumption that mid-Victorian Britain actually had the military strength to achieve the political and economic subordination of backward countries, through either formal or informal means. Second is the related assumption that it was possible for Britain to protect the overseas commercial interests of individual firms as and when required. The theory clearly assumes a strong and ubiquitous British military presence. But if such force really existed, why was Britain content to leave some countries merely as members of the 'informal' empire? Was it because these countries were in any case economically subordinate to Britain, as Gallagher and Robinson would have it? Or was it because Britain lacked the military power fully to subordinate them? In this section I shall discuss the nature of the British military presence in East Asia and thus examine the validity of the theory of the 'imperialism of free trade'.

The British Government and the Royal Navy

In the nineteenth century, the question of naval capability played a vital role in foreign policy. While there is general agreement that it was the British military presence which made her world supremacy possible, there has been little anlaysis of British naval performance. Even in the age of 'Pax Britannica' British sea power suffered from geographical limitations, of which statesmen in Britain were well aware, but the combination of British industrial supremacy and the naval weakness of rival countries enabled successive British governments to use the 'illusion' of British naval supremacy as a foreign policy weapon in order to stabilize the international balance of power.[49]

In 1834 the China Station was established as an outpost of the East Indies Station and as the base of the China Squadron. In 1844 it became an independent naval station with headquarters at Hong Kong.[50] The main activities of the China Station were the defence of Britain's commercial interests over a wide area – from Achin Head in Sumatra to the North Pacific and the Australian coast – through the suppression of piracy, and the general maintenance of maritime security in the China and Japan seas.[51] This required a considerable naval presence which it became increasingly difficult to ensure.

In the late 1850s the Crimean War (1853–56), the outbreak of the Arrow War in 1856, and the Indian Mutiny in 1857 forced increases in military expenditure.[52] For the period 1855 to 1859 the total excess of expenditure over revenue amounted to £36 million.[53] The financial strain caused by the ever-increasing costs of colonial defence and the growing burden this imposed on the British taxpayer made the government examine the possibility of reducing state expenditure in this area. The report of the Committee on Expense of Military Defences in the Colonies stated:

> We consider that this immunity [of the colonies themselves from almost any financial contribution], throwing as it does the defence of the Colonies almost entirely on the mother country, is open to two main objections. In the first place, it imposes an enormous burden and inconvenience on the people of England, not only by the addition which it makes to their taxes, but by calling off to remote stations a large proportion of their troops and ships, and thereby weakening their means of defence at home. But a still more important objection is, the tendency which this system must necessarily have to prevent the development of a proper spirit of self-reliance amongst our Colonists, and to enfeeble their national character.[54]

In the 1860s, under Gladstone and Disraeli as Chancellors of the Exchequer, successive British governments reviewed defence policy, both land and naval. The Admiralty was forced to reduce the level of naval expenditure through cutting the size of naval stations overseas and redistributing the fleet in order to achieve economies, as far as possible without adversely affecting efficiency and security.[55] Changes were made in British policy towards China in an attempt to avoid involvement in costly military intervention. In the early 1860s, despite pressure from mercantile communities, the British government became disillusioned about the potential of the Chinese market, and decided to support the tottering Ch'ing government, fearing increasing political instability in China. This change was officially announced by Lord Clarendon in December 1868, and force was now to be used only to protect British subjects and their property when there was immediate threat of danger.[56] In Japan too, as early as 1866, in anticipation of the outbreak of civil war, Britain had decided on a 'neutral' policy, seeking not 'political influence but merely the development of commerce in Japan', and this was unchanged at the time of the Meiji Restoration.[57] It was therefore possible to reduce the strength of the China Station greatly during the fleet redistribution of the late 1860s and early 1870s, the number of ships and men going down from 35 ships with 4,118 men in 1869 to 20 ships with 2,428 men in 1874.[58]

The Kagoshima Bombardment of 1863 is a nice illustration of the limitations of British naval power on the eve of this deliberate curtailment.[59] Britain needed to put pressure on Satsuma, one of the most powerful domains, and the Foreign Legation wanted Vice-Admiral Kuper to carry out a bombardment. However, Kuper was afraid that he could not both carry out a punitive expedition and continue to protect foreign residents at the open ports.[60] In a letter to the Admiralty he explained about:

> The very critical position in which the first act of hostility on my part would place the Foreign residents of Yokohama and the other open ports in Japan, which it would be entirely out of my power to defend, or to protect effectually against any sudden attack or outbreak on the part of the Japanese, partly from the want of sufficient disposable force and principally from their local position. Yokohama and Nagasaki are both surrounded and commanded by heights, without being in the possession of which, the settlements would be untenable, and this would require a large Military force.[61]

Nevertheless, in August a British squadron of seven ships left Yokohama and entered Kagoshima Bay. It seized ships and destroyed the town of Kagoshima, the capital of Satsuma, but suffered heavy damage in a gunnery engagement with the Satsuma batteries and was forced to withdraw and return to Yokohama. Facing a reduction both in its fleet size and in the man power at its disposal due to the government's underlying policy of economy, and strained by the need to protect the treaty ports in China in the unstable political situation caused by the Taiping Rebellion, the Royal Navy was unable to undertake any long term involvement in the Kagoshima affair. Far from being able to exert direct military pressure at will, it was barely managing to perform its minimum task: the protection of British interests and British nationals at the treaty ports and the maintenance of maritime security on the China and Japan seas.

British Colonial Defence and Coaling Stations

A major factor limiting British military and naval strength in East Asia was the question of coaling the Royal Navy in eastern seas. Distant coaling stations had to be supplied with coal, and contingency plans had to be made for supplying these stations, and defending them, in times of war.[62] In the late 1870s the issue of coaling was therefore prominent among the logistical problems with which the British Empire had to contend as it contemplated the defence of its colonies. In 1879, an eight-man commission was formed under the Earl of Carnarvon, Henry Howard Molyneux:

> to inquire into the condition and sufficiency of the means both naval and military, provided for the defence of the more important sea-ports . . . and of the stations established or required [within British colonial possessions and dependencies] . . . for coaling, refitting, or repairing the ships of Our Navy, and for the protection of the commerce

of the British colonies with Britain and other countries. They were to take into account questions of strategic and commercial importance; the scale of defence needed, including the stationing of garrisons of imperial or local troops and the provision of local naval organizations and armaments; and the proportions of the cost of such measures to be borne by the British government and the colonies. They were also to suggest the best means of meeting the coaling requirements of the British fleet and mercantile marine in time of war.[63] The average coal-carrying capacity of naval ships was only 14 per cent of their displacement, in comparison with the 40 per cent of merchant vessels when equipped for war purposes.[64] Having this relatively small coal capacity, naval ships therefore needed regular coal supplies at suitable coaling stations.[65] The commission drew the following conclusion:

> No addition to the number and fighting power of your Majesty's ships will make up for the want of coaling-stations, which to be of use must be able to defend themselves. We desire to impress upon your Majesty's Government the paramount importance to the British Empire of secure coaling-stations . . . In a man-of-war, the limited capacity for carrying coal, taken in connection with the high rate of consumption, necessarily limits the range of effective action. Without secure and well-placed coaling-stations your Majesty's ships, however numerous and powerful, will be unable to protect trade, or perhaps even to reach distant parts of the Empire.[66]

Coal supplies were therefore vital to the maintenance of the China Squadron, upon which British security in East and Southeast Asia depended. In 1870 the squadron consisted of thirty-six ships with an aggregate tonnage of 22,034. By 1900 this had risen to thirty-nine ships with a considerably greater aggregate tonnage of 111,334.[67] More coal was therefore required. As time went on, the development of new naval technologies and the growing naval power of other imperial countries increased the vulnerability of British seaborne trade, and forced changes in British naval strategy.[68]

Most of the coal used by the China Squadron was needed for journeys north of Hong Kong. Purchases of coal varied from year to year, depending on the degree of political tension in the region. For the three years from 1857 to 1859 it was supplied with a total of 66,299 tons at Hong Kong, 8,008 at Shanghai and 13,900 at Singapore, through public tender, casual officers, or commission agents.[69] On an annual average for

these three years the British government purchased 203,310
tons of Welsh and North Country coal for the use of the Royal
Navy.[70]

The Admiralty officially classified 'the various coaling depots and places and stations at home and abroad' into three
categories in accordance with the way in which they were
supplied with coal. First, there were twenty-three Admiralty
depots which were kept supplied with coal sent from England
or other places by the Admiralty; second were seven places in
different parts of the world to which coal was not sent by the
Admiralty but where it was obtained by local agreements or
contracts, the contractors being bound to keep a certain fixed
quantity of coal in store; and third, other places where coal
was purchased in the open market, whenever required. In the
area covered by the China Station, there were the following
Admiralty sites classified under the first and second categories:
Hong Kong (storage room under cover 7,000 tons), Nagasaki
(3,200 tons), Hyōgo (3,800 tons) and Yokohama (all first category), and Singapore, Amoy, Shanghai and Labuan (second
category). With the exception of Hong Kong, Singapore and
Labuan, these were located in foreign territories and might be
closed to British naval ships during time of war. This would
mean that along the steam route from Ceylon to Japan, Britain
would 'lose all stations to the north of Hong Kong, Japan being
closed during war, and . . . have no position on the coast of
Corea (*sic*), unless the H. [Hamilton, Komun] Islands could be
obtained.'[71]

As the ability to defend British colonies and protect British
commercial interests became an urgent matter of concern, so
also did the ability to ensure regular supplies of coal in sufficient quantities at remote stations such as China. Although
on average no naval ship at the China Station spent more than
47 days a year 'under steam making good the distance
logged',[72] for 280 days a year ships were 'kept in readiness for
unforeseen employment' at anchor, but consumed coal for
various firing and other practices.[73]

In 1881, in reply to a proposal concerning coal supplies for
the China Station by G.O. Willes, Vice-Admiral and Commander-in-Chief of the Station, the Admiralty issued an in-
struction for the trial use of Takashima coal (from Japan) in
some ships, admitting that 'from the proximity of the source of
the former [Takashima coal], greater dependence could be

placed upon timely supplies in case of emergency.'[74] It directed that Takashima coal be used in the usual proportion of one-third to two-thirds Welsh coal, but also instructed that a trial should be made in some ships of equal quantities in view of the cost of freighting Welsh coal to China and Japan.[75]

The situation became more urgent with the issue the following year of regulations relative to 'Coals, Coaling, and Economy of Fuel', in which the Admiralty noted the extremely high prices of coal in some places.[76] After the trial mixing of Takashima coal with Welsh coal or patent fuel in fourteen naval ships from October 1882 to August 1883, the Admiralty drew the conclusion that 'it does not appear desirable, at present, to depart from the usual practice of issuing two thirds Welsh, to one third Takashima, to the Ships on the China Station.'[77]

Around 1880 the total amount of naval coal consumption at Nagasaki and Yokohama was less than 4,000 tons per year. Coal was brought from Cardiff or purchased as required from local consignors.[78] There were annual limits on the amount of coal which the China Station was allowed to purchase locally at Nagasaki (1,000 tons) and Hyōgo and Yokohama (both 800 tons), although there was no such limit for Hong Kong.[79] Rises in political tension in the area in both the early 1880s and the late 1890s brought increases in imports of Cardiff coal for naval use. In 1900 total consumption of coal by the British at the China Station amounted to 102,064 tons, a third of this being used for cruising.[80] Early in the first decade of the twentieth century, it was estimated that the China Squadron would require on average 16,000 tons of coal per month, 12,000 tons of which was to be sent from Britain with the balance of 4,000 tons being supplied from local contractors during times of 'peace'.[81] We shall look at the overall role of British coal in the East Asian coal market in Chapter 6.

The non-intervention policy of the British government in East Asia remained unchanged until the mid-1890s. This was in parallel with the decrease in British military force due to the reduction in military expenditure in this area. This decrease, coupled with the difficulties in coal supply, restricted the activities of the Royal Navy to the protection of British interests at the treaty ports. Even if Britain had intended to expand territorial and political control, therefore, it would have been impossible for her to do so.[82]

3

Japan's Incorporation into the World Economy

Western Firms in Japan

Commercial Treaties with the West

The United States took the initiative in opening Japan because of her immediate and practical need for coaling stations on the long-distance Pacific steamer line to China, and for ports of refuge for whaling vessels in the Northern Pacific.[1] In 1858 Japan reluctantly signed commercial treaties with the United States, the Netherlands, Russia, Britain and France, so committing the country to open to foreign trade the ports of Kanagawa (Yokohama), Nagasaki and Hakodate in 1859, Niigata in 1860, Hyōgo (Kōbe) in 1863, and the two cities of Edo (later Tokyo) and Ōsaka in 1862 and 1863 respectively.[2] This marked the beginning of Japan's incorporation into the world economy.

The commercial treaties were based on the principle of free trade and were fundamentally 'unequal' in their main provisions concerning extraterritoriality, tariff rates, and the 'most-favoured nation' clause. The Japan trade therefore developed within an institutional framework, known as the treaty port system, which had initially been established to provide security and commercial advantage to Western merchants on the China coast. Its extension to Japan ensured close links between the foreign merchants and firms engaged in trade with the two countries, as well as many similarities in trading methods. The epithet 'unequal' tends to obscure the fact that the system was not without its attractiveness to the Bakufu. It helped to isolate the Japanese from both Western people and Western influence and also gave the Bakufu the opportunity to control and restrict trade with the West, thereby offsetting to some extent the lack of tariff autonomy. We shall examine this other, neglected, aspect of the treaty port system in more detail later in this chapter.

For Western firms, the existence of low tariff rates was very important. Tariff rates for all articles were stipulated in the commercial treaties and additional trade regulations. All export duties were set at 5 per cent *ad valorem*, gold and silver coins and copper in bars being duty free. Import duties were in general set at 20 per cent *ad valorem* with 5 per cent *ad valorem* for cotton and woollen manufactures, steam machinery, rice, coals, minerals such as zinc, lead and tin, and 35 per cent for liquor.[3] There were no duties on the import or export of gold and silver, coined or uncoined, but the import of opium was prohibited. The commercial treaties further set exchange rates between currencies of the same metallic base. Both Japanese and foreign currencies were to circulate freely for trade purposes. Three hundred and eleven *ichibus*, Japanese silver coins, were to be equivalent to 100 Mexican dollars, which had been circulating widely in Southeast and East Asia as a standard trading currency since 1535.[4]

In 1866, in response to renewed foreign pressure – chiefly concerning imperial ratification of the 1858 treaties and the promised opening of Hyōgo – Japan consented to tariff revision, which came into effect in July 1866.[5] Both export and import duties were then fixed on a basis of 5 per cent *ad valorem*, tariff rates equivalent to those stipulated in the 1858 Tientsin Treaty with China. Imports of metals and of cotton and woollen manufactures were subject to specific duties. General import duties were reduced from 20 per cent to 5 per cent. The standard for all tariffs was based on the average export price of each article in the exporting country calculated over several preceding years. Import duties were therefore independent of price fluctuations in Japan. These new tariff rates for imported goods were already less than 5 per cent at the time of the revision, and were in effect reduced to 2–2.5 per cent by increasing inflation in the early Meiji period.[6]

Thirty-seven articles, including raw silk, tea and coal, were subject to specific export duties, the duty on raw silk being 75 *ichibus* per picul, tea 3.50 *ichibus* and coal 0.04 *ichibus*. Saltpetre, and grains such as rice, paddy and barley, were among the goods which were not to be exported. Many other goods were subject to a fixed *ad valorem* duty of 5 per cent, which was set as a rate calculated from the average home-market value over the five years.

The attainment of tariff autonomy and the abolition of extraterritoriality were the main targets of treaty revision. The tariff rates stipulated in 1866 lasted until 1899, when Japan obtained partial tariff autonomy through the enactment of the Fixed Tariff Law as a result of the 1894 treaty revision carried out successfully with Britain. This still left conventional tariff rates from 5 to 15 per cent on many items. It was not until 1911 that Japan finally recovered complete tariff autonomy.[7]

The Advance of Western Firms into East Asia

The opening of China and Japan, in 1842 and 1859 respectively, signified a new phase in East Asian trade. The development of ocean shipping routes for steamers and the extension of telegraphic communication were bringing the area closer to the European and American markets. The opening of the Suez Canal in 1869 had particularly dramatic results: the distance from London to Bombay was reduced by 41 per cent, from 10,667 nautical miles via the Cape of Good Hope to 6,274 nautical miles; the distance to Singapore was reduced by 29 per cent, from 11,740 nautical miles via the Cape to 8,362 nautical miles; the distance to Hong Kong by 26 per cent, from 13,180 nautical miles via the Cape to 9,799 nautical miles, and to Shanghai by 24 per cent, from 14,050 nautical miles via the Cape to 10,669 nautical miles. The number of merchant steamers passing through the Canal increased rapidly, from 1,042 in 1876 to 1,534 in 1880, and 2,514 in 1885.[8] Since conditions in the Red Sea were not favourable to sailing ships, the opening of the Canal encouraged the shift to steamers and stimulated the development of new, faster types.[9] More important, it also led to a rapid growth in Indian and East Asian trade. In the late 1870s, seven-eighths of China trade was carried by steamers and almost all China trade was through the Canal.[10]

The Peninsular and Oriental Steam Navigation Co. started a fortnightly service to China in 1853, and in 1859 commenced a regular service between Shanghai and Nagasaki which was extended to Yokohama in 1864. Messageries Impériales opened a regular monthly service between Shanghai and Yokohama as an extension of the Marseilles-Shanghai line in 1865. The Pacific Mail Steamship Co. began a regular service between San Francisco and Hong Kong in 1867. Other shipping companies such as the Blue Funnel, Castle, and Glen lines entered the East Asian trade in the 1860s and 1870s. Later, in 1887, Canadian Pacific started a regular monthly service between Vancouver and Hong Kong via Yokohama and Shanghai.[11] In the 1860s and 1870s freight rates fell rapidly, largely as a result of the increasing competition among shipping companies. Shipping conferences were formed as a way of curtailing damaging competition by fixing freight rates, and making possible concerted measures against shipowners who were not members.[12]

Direct telegraphic links betwen East Asia and the European and American markets did not exist until 1871, when the Eastern Extension Australasia and China Telegraph Co. (a British firm) constructed a cable between Singapore and Hong Kong and the Great Northern Telegraph Co. (a Danish firm) extended a line across Siberia to Nagasaki and thence to Shanghai and Hong Kong.[13] This extension of the telegraphic network revolutionized established commercial patterns and the nature of financial procedures, through making possible both telegraphic transfers and the reception of immediate information about current prices on the European and American markets.[14]

Western firms which had been engaged in the 'country trade' between India and China moved into Hong Kong in 1842 when it was ceded to Britain by the Treaty of Nanking which followed the Opium War (1840–2).[15] The number of Western firms increased to over a hundred in the 1860s. They included the British firms of Jardine, Matheson & Co., Dent & Co., Gibb, Livingston & Co., Gilman & Co., Holliday, Wise & Co., Lane, Crawford & Co., and Butterfield and Swire, although they did not open their China branch until 1867; the American firms of Russell & Co., Augustine Heard & Co., and Olyphant & Co.; the German firms of Siemssen & Co., and Pustau & Co., and Indian firms such as Sassoon Sons & Co. These firms were all commission, or agency houses and engaged in the buying and selling of commodities either on their own account or on commission for the European and American markets, while providing other facilities for trade such as shipping insurance, banking and warehousing.[16]

Table 3–1 shows the number of Western trading firms, including branches, at the open ports in East Asia for the years 1869, 1880 and 1893.[17] Their aggregate number increased from 440 in 1869 to 466 in 1880, and 692 in 1893. Fifty per cent of the firms were located in mainland China, 25 per cent in Japan, and 20 per cent in Hong Kong. The numbers listed in the directories seem fairly accurate, but it should be noted that there were a number of small Chinese and Indian merchants in competition with them. Western firms faced severe competition from Chinese as well as other Western firms, and in the second half of the 1860s in particular, the mortality rate of firms was as high as 51 per cent in Hong Kong, 47 per cent in Shanghai and 62 per cent in Yokohama.[18]

Western firms engaged in the East Asian trade were able to obtain finance from Western banks. The main role here was played by British colonial banks such as the Agra Bank, which was founded in London in 1833; the Oriental Bank Corporation, founded in London in 1842; the Chartered Mercantile Bank of India, London and China, which was founded in London in 1854; and the Chartered Bank of India, Australia, and China, which was founded in London in 1858. The Hongkong and Shanghai Banking Corporation, which was founded in Hong Kong in 1865 to serve British business interests, opened its Yokohama branch in 1866. The Comptoir d'Escompte de Paris, founded in Paris in 1848, was also engaged in the East Asian trade. Such banks generally had branches at Hong Kong, Shanghai, Foochow, Hankow, and Yokohama. They played a crucial role in providing the finance for foreign trade, either by buying and selling bills of exchange drawn on London, Hong Kong and Shanghai, or by providing Mexican dollars and issuing their own bank notes.[19]

In various senses the 1860s proved to be a crucial decade for East Asian trade. The development of the Suez route, the opening of regular services by ocean shipping, and the advance of commercial banks into the area, made it possible for merchants with small capital to join in the trade and compete with the larger Western firms which were already established in the area.[20] To add to the severe competition which

Table 3-1 Western Firms in East Asia, 1869, 1880 and 1893

Place	1869	1880	1893	Place	1869	1880	1893
Hong Kong	87	92	120	*Formosa*			
				Tamsui	2	5	8
China				Keelung	2	3	–
Shanghai	94	94	131	Kaohsiung	2	6	8
Canton	28	27	43	Taiwan-fu	1	–	–
Hankow	24	20	36				
Foochow	22	35	32	*Japan*			
Amoy	15	18	19	Yokohama	61	60	106
Ningpo	13	9	6	Nagasaki	26	12	9
Tientsin	11	16	31	Kōbe	14	22	70
Macao	9	7	–	Ōsaka	4	1	1
Chinkiang	7	7	9	Hakodate	6	3	2
Chefoo	5	7	5	Niigata	–	3	–
Swatow	4	7	5	Tokyo	–	–	1
Newchuang	3	4	3				
Kiukiang	–	3	6	*Korea*			
Wuhu	–	2	3	Chemulpo	–	–	3
Haihow	–	2	2				
Peking	–	1	2	Vladivostock	–	–	18
Chungking	–	–	6				
Ichang	–	–	5	Totals	440	466	692
Pakhoi	–	–	2				

Sources: The Chronicle and Directory for China, Japan and the Philippines, 1869, 1880, 1893.
Note: Figures represent totals of firms listed under 'merchants' and 'commission agents'.

inevitably resulted among Western merchants, a trend also developed by which Chinese compradores, who had acted as managers in Western firms, started business independently on their own account. The competition from small merchants of both kinds threatened the agency house system, as we shall see in detail later on. For the two decades of the 1860s and 1870s, Western merchants suffered severely from decreasing profits, particularly in product transactions. While reducing their dealings in commodities and increasingly carrying out produce trade on joint accounts with other firms in order to decrease the risk, they also became more concerned with shipping, insurance, banking and the provision of treaty port utilities.[21]

Western Firms in Japan

With the opening of Nagasaki, Kanagawa and Hakodate in 1859, Western firms already engaged in the China trade advanced to Japan. Western banks which had been established in India and China also advanced to Japan in the 1860s. The Chartered Mercantile Bank of India, London and China opened its Yokohama branch in 1863; the Oriental Bank Corporation in 1864; the Hongkong and Shanghai Banking Corporation in 1866; and the Comptoir d'Escompte de Paris in 1867. The Chartered Bank of India, Australia, and China also wanted to open a branch in Japan, but could not do so until 1880.[22] Of these banks, the Hongkong and Shanghai Banking Corporation was particularly influential and financed most foreign trade with Japan until the mid-1880s.[23] All the banks faced business difficulties and some of them were forced to withdraw from Japan around 1880,[24] when the Japanese monetary system was in the process of formation.

Table 3–2 shows the number of firms and foreign residents in the treaty ports and open cities by nationality from 1870 to 1895. The number of Western firms remained more or less constant up to 1890, but increased rapidly between 1890 and 1895. British firms accounted for over 40 per cent of the total number of Western firms, and British residents formed just under 50 per cent of the total number of Western residents. American firms gradually increased in number, German firms remained constant, and the importance of French firms gradually decreased towards the end of the century. It is clear from details of the number and location of Western firms that they tended to congregate in Yokohama and Hyōgo. Nagasaki, where Chinese merchants were dominant, rapidly declined in importance to Western firms in the late 1860s. Of the 256 Western firms in Japan in 1870, 119 (46 per cent) were located in Yokohama, 75 (29 per cent) in Hyōgo and Ōsaka, and 24 (9 per cent) in Nagasaki. In 1880, out of the total of 258 Western firms, 159 (62 per cent) were located in Yokohama, 79 (31 per cent) in Hyōgo and Ōsaka, and 12 (5 per cent) in Nagasaki. In

Table 3-2 Number of Foreign Firms and Residents at Japanese Treaty Ports by Nationality, 1870–95

Firms

Year	American	British	French	German	Others	European (total)	Chinese	Grand total
1870	33	101	39	45	38	256	n.a.	–
1875	30	109	42	43	33	257	n.a.	–
1880	40	108	37	41	32	258	102	360
1885	46	91	18	33	22	210	139	349
1890	53	113	30	36	27	259	305	564
1895	73	148	38	57	39	355	33†	388

Residents

Year	American	British	French	German	Others	European (total)	Chinese	Grand total
1870*	229	782	158	164	253	1,586	n.a.	–
1875	353	1,282	254	279	415	2,583	n.a.	–
1880	407	1,057	184	309	402	2,359	3,584	5,943
1885	447	1,065	201	269	316	2,298	3,876	6,174
1890	495	1,236	236	333	507	2,807	4,373	7,180
1895	584	1,424	252	347	603	3,227	3,373	6,598

Sources: (1) CR, Japan for 1870, Returns of Foreign Residents, etc., at Treaty Ports. (2) For 1875, CR, Parkes to Derby, Yedo, 18 July 1876, (H). (3) CR, General Report on the Foreign Trade of Japan for 1880, (H). (4) DCRTF, No. 47, Foreign Trade of Japan for 1885. (5) DCRTF, No. 961, Foreign Trade of Japan for 1890. (6) DCRTF, No. 1727. Hakodate for 1895; No. 1758, Nagasaki for 1895; No. 1779, Yokohama for 1895; No. 1786, Hyōgo and Ōsaka for 1895 (Niigata and Tokyo are excluded).

Notes: (1) The term 'firm' is liable to a different interpretation at different ports (Summary of Commercial Reports for 1876, p.10) and includes not only mercantile establishments but also storekeepers and other concerns of every description (DCRTF, No. 47, p. 5). (2) Foreigners employed by the Japanese government in the interior are probably excluded (Summary of Commercial Reports for 1876, p. 10). (3)* Females other than British are excluded. (4)† Females other than British are excluded. (4)† Nagasaki and Hakodate only.

1895, out of 355 Western firms, 212 (60 per cent) were located in Yokohama, 119 (34 per cent) in Hyōgo, and 21 (6 per cent) in Nagasaki. Figures for the number of Chinese firms seem unreliable but in 1884, out of a total of 346, 209 were located in Yokohama, 56 in Hyōgo and Ōsaka, 70 in Nagasaki, 7 in Hakodate and 4 in Tokyo.[25]

Table 3–3 shows shares in exports and imports of foreign and Japanese merchants. In the year 1865/6 British merchants handled 73 per cent of the total imports of 10,592,341 dollars and 56 per cent of the total exports of 16,186,110 dollars; American merchants handled 9 per cent of imports and 19 per cent of exports.[26] Japanese merchants began to increase their share of both exports and imports from the second half of the 1890s. However, even in 1900 foreign merchants were handling 63 per cent of exports and 60 per cent of imports, and not until 1912 did Japanese merchants gain control of more than half of trade.[27]

If we consider the percentages of export and import articles handled by Western and Japanese firms in Yokohama in 1889 in relation to the nationality of the partners, and ignore Chinese firms, for which no figures exist, it is clear that British firms had a 90–95 per cent share of imports of cotton manufactures and 75–99 per cent of imports of sugar. German firms competed with the British in mousselines, and iron and steel; the French had half of the business in wines, and the Americans half of that in kerosene oil. Japanese firms took the lead in handkerchiefs (47 per cent) and raw cotton (33 per cent). Swiss firms handled 42 per cent of all silk exports, while British firms controlled only 21 per cent; British firms took up two-thirds of tea exports and American firms a third.[28]

Chinese merchants played a great role in the Japan trade in the period under consideration. Along with the Dutch, they had been allowed to trade at Nagasaki under Bakufu jurisdiction even before the general opening of the port to foreign trade in 1859. They continued to trade in tea and marine products despite having the status of non-treaty residents until the Sino–Japanese commercial treaty of 1871. Since Chinese merchants already had an established network of business at Nagasaki, Western merchants found it particularly difficult to compete with them there. The Chinese presence was accordingly given as one of the reasons for the failure of direct trade

Table 3-3 Exports and Imports by Japanese and Foreign Merchants, 1877–1900 (in thousand yen)

Year	Exports						Imports			
	by Japanese	%	by foreigners	%	by government	%	by Japanese	%	by foreigners	%
1877	842	(4)	21,689	(96)	410	(1)	426	(2)	26,995	(97)
1880	4,486	(16)	23,020	(84)	665	(2)	1,939	(5)	35,031	(93)
1885	3,394	(10)	31,390	(90)	1,258	(4)	2,345	(8)	25,725	(88)
1890	6,124	(11)	48,768	(89)	1,174	(1)	19,522	(24)	61,033	(75)
1895	26,329	(20)	107,188	(80)	2,000	(2)	38,829	(30)	88,432	(68)
1900	73,382	(37)	124,682	(63)	1,091	(0)	112,737	(39)	173,434	(60)

Sources: Naikaku Tōkeikyoku, *Nihon teikoku tōkei nenkan*, for 1880, 1888, 1901; Ōkurashō, *Dainihon gaikoku bōeki nenpyō*, for 1885, 1890, 1895.

Notes: (1) Re-exports and re-imports are excluded. (2) Exports 'for ships' use' are excluded.

with the West at Nagasaki to increase.[29] According to the *Nagasaki Express*, in 1869 Chinese merchants handled 52 per cent of the total exports of 1,537,000 dollars and 52 per cent of the total imports of 3,052,580 dollars.[30] Once Western firms were established in Ōsaka after the opening of the city in 1868, they employed an increasing number of Chinese. There were also twenty wholly Chinese trading firms in Ōsaka by 1882. They were mainly from Canton and Foochow and were engaged in exporting marine products to China and importing sugar, rice, grains and medicine from there.[31] In this district too the Chinese continued 'to remain formidable competitors with the foreign import trade'. They purchased goods, although usually of inferior quality – generally at auction in Shanghai –, sent them over in return for products purchased in Japan, and sold them to purchasers at a rate too low for Western merchants to compete. All trade in shirtings, for instance, was in the hands of Chinese merchants.[32]

The Development of Japan's Foreign Trade

A Review of Japanese Trade Statistics

As anyone who has looked at Japan's pre-war trade statistics will know, there are various irregularities in the way they have been compiled. Attempts are in progress to reconstruct complete and compatible records including those for invisible trade after 1868,[33] but no substantial effort has been made to link the pre–1868 trade statistics with those after 1868. It is necessary, therefore, to start this section with a review of the statistics available at present.

Trade statistics exist for the period 1859–72 as compiled by the customs authorities at each open port, but these are not entirely reliable due to changes in the definitions used in their compilation and to the inexperience of the custom house officials.[34] In 1872, when the administration of custom houses at the open ports was transferred from local government to the Ministry of Finance, trade statistics began to be prepared on an improved system. Statistics after this date are fairly reliable in terms of quantities of commodities, but the same cannot be said of valuations.

There are two time series of basic trade statistics available, although the standards according to which they were compiled vary from period to period. One is the time series of trade statistics available in British consular reports after 1859. These are given in Mexican dollars. The other is the series of official Japanese statistics which became available after 1868 and are given in yen. The yen did not come into existence until the New Currency Act of 1871, and trade figures prior to 1871 seem to have been converted from old Japanese currency into yen. Since there are no official Japanese statistics for the period 1859–67, one must rely on the figures in the British consular reports. These figures seem to have been compiled on the basis either of Japanese customs returns or of reports by the Chambers of Commerce organized by Western merchants at the open ports; but the method of compilation is not clear.

There are various problems concerning the trade statistics for the period under consideration.[35] For the period before 1868, not only are the figures incomplete but it was usual for both export and import goods to be greatly undervalued at the time of declaration to the customs house. Imported goods were probably even more undervalued than exports in order to reduce the liability for those taxes which were levied on an *ad valorem* basis. Another reason for undervaluation was the decline in the value of Mexican dollars to Japanese currency in the first half of the 1860s.[36] The customs returns do not include figures for imports of ships, for smuggling (of course), or for the outflow of gold and silver, either as coins or bullion. One hundred and eleven ships were purchased by the Bakufu and feudal domains, mainly from Britain and the United States, at a cost of 7,815,000 dollars.[37] Smuggling seems to have been very active in Nagasaki and Hakodate.[38] In particular there seems to have been a considerable business in arms and ammunition, only a small portion of which was reported to the customs house.[39]

The system of valuation given in the official trade statistics varies from period to period. In the period 1868–1903, the valuation of exports was based on market prices at the port of clearance. After 1904 packing charges were added to the above value, and after 1912 the f.o.b. (free on board) system was adopted. In the period 1868–98, the valuation of imports was based on prices at the port of origin. After 1898 the c.i.f. (cost,

Table 3-4 Japan's Foreign Trade in Commodities, 1860–1900
(current prices) (in thousand yen)

Year	Exports	Imports	Total	Balance
1860	7,547	3,116	10.663	4,431
1861	4,911	3,318	8,229	1,593
1862	10,662	6,891	17,554	3,771
1863	13,283	7,278	20,561	6,005
1864	12,545	10,129	22,673	2,416
1865	20,800	17,922	38,722	2,878
1866	18,692	18,664	37,356	28
1867	13,638	23,649	37,287	(−) 10,011
1868	22,988	19,350	42,338	3,637
1869	12,909	21,659	34,567	(−) 8,750
1870	14,543	35,004	49.547	(−) 20,461
1871	17,969	22,076	40,044	(−) 4,107
1872	17,027	26,175	43,201	(−) 9,148
1873	21,635	28,107	49,743	(−) 6,472
1874	19,317	24,487	43,804	(−) 5,170
1875	18,611	31,899	50,511	(−) 13,288
1876	27,712	26,544	54,256	1,167
1877	23,349	29,979	53,327	(−) 6,630
1878	25,988	37,722	63,711	(−) 11,734
1879	28,176	38,015	66,191	(−) 9,839
1880	28,395	42,246	70,641	(−) 13,850
1881	31,059	35,767	66,825	(−) 4,708
1882	37,722	33,354	71,076	4,367
1883	36,268	32,449	68,717	3,819
1884	33,871	33,617	67,488	254
1885	37,147	33,499	70,646	3,648
1886	48,876	37,364	86,240	11,512
1887	52,408	53,153	105,561	(−) 745
1888	65,706	65,455	131,161	250
1889	70,061	66,104	136,164	3,957
1890	56,604	81,729	138,332	(−) 25,125
1891	79,527	62,927	142,455	16,600
1892	91,103	71,326	162,429	19,777
1893	89,713	88,257	177,970	1,456
1894	113,246	117,482	230,728	(−) 4,236
1895	136,112	129,261	265,373	6,852

1896	117,843	171,674	289,517	(−) 53,832
1897	163,135	219,301	382,436	(−) 56,166
1898	165,754	277,502	443,256	(−)111,748
1899	214,930	220,402	435,332	(−) 5,472
1900	204,430	287,262	491,692	(−) 82,832

Sources: CR, Summary of Foreign Trade in Japan for the Year 1878, p.25; CR, 1865–1868; M. Paske-Smith, *Western Barbarians in Japan and Formosa in Tokugawa Days* (1930), p. 303; *Nihon bōeki seiran*, p. 2; Baba and Tatemoto, 'Foreign Trade and Economic Growth in Japan: 1858–1937', p. 185.

insurance, and freight) system was adopted.

Attention should also be paid to the valuation of imports in the official statistics for the period 1871–87. Trade statistics for the period from 1871 to 1887 were calculated on a basis of both gold and silver yen. The silver yen was the basis used in the period 1888–97 but after 1897, when Japan went on to the gold standard, the basis shifted to the gold yen. During the period 1871–87, imports from gold-standard countries were converted in terms of Japanese gold yen, while those from silver-standard countries were calculated in terms of Japanese silver yen. Despite the changing difference in value between gold and silver, however, a simple total was made from these figures. It is therefore necessary to correct the figures so that they stand wholly on the basis of silver yen.[40] No revision is required for the period 1871–73 as the difference between the prices of gold and silver in Japan was negligible. Revised import figures for 1874–87 are shown in Table 3–4.

I have attempted to compile a complete set of trade statistics from 1860 to 1900 by revising the available figures. For the period 1859–67 Ishii Takashi has given his own estimates, but his figures seem to have been put together in a random fashion from different sources which he considers appropriate, rather than according to a coherent system.[41] For the period 1860–68 I have therefore used the time series given in the British consular reports.[42] However, the figures seem undervalued and have been upwardly revised, taking 1869 as the standard year, since the figures for 1869 given in both the British and Japanese time series are relatively close. Since there are no figures for Kanagawa in 1866, owing to the destruction of the records by fire, I have used the estimates of Paske-Smith[43] and added these to the surviving original figures for Nagasaki and Hakodate. Since the figures given in the British commercial reports are probably based at least partly on Japanese customs house returns, it would seem a good idea to turn to the official Japanese trade statistics once these become available from 1868. However, there are great differences between the figures given in the British commercial reports and the official Japanese trade statistics for the year 1868. If one considers the political and administrative turmoil which occurred with the advent of the new government, it seems reasonable to assume that the former, which also drew on the records of foreign Chambers of Commerce in the treaty ports, are the more likely to be reliable. After 1873 there is a fair degree of consistency between the two series of figures; I have been unable to find a reasonable explanation for the continuing discrepancy in the period 1869–72.[44] For the period until 1874, the prices of any ships imported during the corresponding year have been added, since ship imports only appear in the official Japanese statistics from 1875. For the period 1874–87 I have used statistics revised to account for the use of both the gold and silver yen. It did not seem necessary, however, to calculate the trade figures according to the f.o.b. and c.i.f. systems, since I only had to use the c.i.f. basis for the years 1899 and 1900, and a complete revision of all the earlier figures to the two systems would have further increased the inaccuracy of the pre-1869 figures. Finally, as Figure 2 shows, the terms of trade in general improved from the late 1870s to the first decade of the twentieth century, a situation which worked in favour of Japanese exports.

Trade and Politics

The opening of Japan to foreign trade in 1859 had a decisive effect both on the country's economy, and on the internal political situation. Structural changes occurred in the traditional economy, most rapidly in major export and import sectors such as the silk and cotton industries. Domestic prices in general were influenced by the prices of export and import

Figure 2 Indices of Export and Import Prices and Terms of Trade, 1874–1900

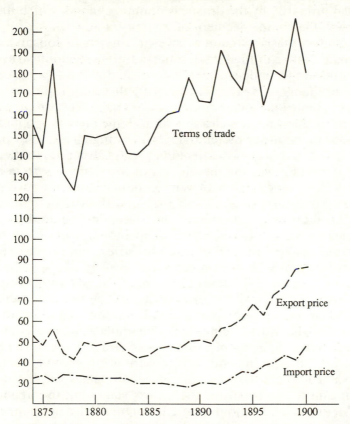

articles until they became equal with international levels, an upheaval which could be called 'the Japanese price revolution'.[45] The Tokugawa Bakufu planned to stabilize its political and financial position by monopolizing the benefits from foreign trade, but its efforts ended in failure. Meanwhile, a powerful anti-Bakufu group formed on the initiative of the south-western domains of Satsuma and Chōshū. The radical economic changes, combined with the emergence of this powerful opposition group, hastened the collapse of the Bakufu and in 1868 the Meiji government was established.[46] There is no doubt that the Meiji Restoration marked a turning point in Japanese political history, but the Meiji Restoration was itself caused primarily by the drastic economic changes which had followed the commencement of foreign trade.

The urgent task of the new government was to consolidate the nation into a unified state, while maintaining political and economic independence in the face of the Western threat. This inevitably led to the adoption of policies for rapid political, economic and social modernization on a Western model. The new leaders made a clean break with the previous political and economic order by removing remaining elements of the feudal system, such as the hereditary class structure. Particularly important was the dissolution of the domain system in 1871, which unified the country. In economic terms, the government tried to carry out on a national level the self-strengthening policies which had emerged on a domain level in the late Tokugawa period. Initial attempts to modernize simply by introducing Western institutions, industries, and science and technology met with little success, however.

In the long term, the financial base of the government was too weak to allow it to carry out any systematic industrialization on its own. While it did play an important role in forming the infrastructure for industrialization, in organizing the domestic economy, and in encouraging the development of domestic industries, its contribution should not be overvalued. Local industrialists and manufacturers played a significant role, not only in these early stages but throughout the Meiji period. Without their entrepreneurial and financial resources Japan's industrialization would not have been possible. In addition, the Tokugawa period had seen considerable investment in well-developed transport networks, and in water supplies and irrigation for agricultural purposes. This legacy doubtless enabled the new government to economise on its investment in social capital during the difficult early years.

The major elements of Meiji economic policy were land tax reform, the abolition of the stipend system, and the promotion of industry. Land tax reform stabilized government revenues, and the dissolution of the samurai class through the abolition of the stipend system lightened the burden of annual expenditure. This gave the government a firm financial base. After the return of the Iwakura Mission from its tour of America and

Europe in 1873, concrete steps were taken to draw up coherent plans for promoting industry, under the leadership of Ōkubo Toshimichi (1830–78) and with Ōkuma Shigenobu (1838–1922) as Finance Minister. This policy began to take shape in the mid-1870s amidst a growing anxiety that the outflow of specie which had been occurring as a result of the increase in imports since the late 1860s might completely destabilize the economy, and in time threaten Japan's independence from the West. Since the commercial treaties deprived Japan of tariff autonomy, it was not possible to nurture infant industries through protective tariff barriers. The only way of overcoming the crisis caused by the continued outflow of specie therefore lay in promoting exports and in finding indirect ways of restricting imports. Accordingly the government concentrated both on promoting traditional export-related industries, and on hastening the development of import substitution through introducing and nurturing modern industries.

Having decided the general direction of its industrialization policy, the government limited itself to fostering private industry through offering institutional, legal, and financial assistance, while taking upon itself the initial risks in sectors such as munitions, which served vital national interests, or in those where private initiatives could not be expected. Unfortunately, the outbreak of the Satsuma Rebellion in 1877 increased inflation. The worsening financial situation which followed forced a change in the policy of promoting industry before it had had a chance to get started. In addition, the assassination of Ōkubo in the following year destroyed the political balance within the government. Ōkuma Shigenobu and Itō Hirobumi (1841–1909) clashed with increasing ferocity over both economic problems, such as the inflation which had followed the Satsuma Rebellion and the continued outflow of specie, and constitutional policy, such as how to deal with the People's Rights Movement, and in particular over the timing of any introduction of parliamentary government. Their clashes ended with Ōkuma's expulsion from the government in 1881; soon afterwards Matsukata Masayoshi (1835–1924) became Finance Minister.[47]

Matsukata took stringent deflationary measures to balance the state budget and thus permit the redemption of devalued paper money. His chief objective was to reform the monetary system and so accumulate a specie reserve in order to redeem all inconvertible paper money. He combined this redemption with the establishment of a stable modern currency and credit system, and in 1882 established the Bank of Japan as a central bank. The Yokohama Specie Bank had an important role to play in Matsukata's policy of accumulating specie and providing finance for foreign trade. At the same time, growing tension with Ch'ing China over Korea led to increases in military expenditure. The fiscal 'success' of Matsukata's policies, and the recovery of economic stability, led to a boom in private industry during the second half of the 1880s. Railway construction and cotton-spinning were the prime instigators of this boom, but the economy over-heated as a result of the excessive expansion of the credit system, and consequently entered a depression in 1890.

The expansion of military expenditure in anticipation of a confrontation with China bore fruit in the Sino–Japanese War of 1894–5. The Treaty of Shimonoseki which ended that war, and the Triple Intervention which deprived Japan of some of the territorial fruits of her victory, had a decisive effect on Japan's subsequent fiscal and economic development, and led to a policy of military expansion which saw Russia as the potential enemy. The adoption of the gold standard in 1897 stabilized the yen's position as an international currency, making it easier for Japan to increase imports of armaments and machinery, and to raise foreign loans in gold standard countries. On the other hand, it had unfavourable repercussions on export industries.

Treaty Port Trade: The Paradox of the 'Unequal' Treaties

The Treaty Port System

In this section I should like to look at the actual workings of the system behind the statistics; this has not been done before. As is widely known, both in China and Japan trade with the West was conducted under the system stipulated in the commercial treaties and known as the treaty port trade.[48] This system had initially been developed to give Western merchants both security and commercial advantage. There is no doubt that in backing the system Britain was guided by its confidence in Ricardian comparative advantage theory, which gave support to the idea of Britain's supremacy in the world economy. The idea was to make trade with backward countries work in favour of the industrially advanced Western countries, with the former importing industrial goods from the latter and specializing in exporting primary products. Western merchants would therefore be able to engage in trade and commerce on advantageous terms under the protection of low tariff rates as well as of extraterritoriality.

Both contemporary participants (including the Bakufu) and most later scholars have tended to assume that the treaty port system could only work in favour of the West. Much effort has therefore been expended in trying to explain why China and Japan were able to escape economic colonization in the late nineteenth century. According to the 'imperialism of free trade' theorists, Japan and China were able to escape the network of the formal empire because elites formed there to promote collaboration with Britain, while other countries which opposed British supremacy had membership of the network forced upon them. The quite natural assumption is that it was easy for individual Western merchants to function profitably under the privileged institutional and legal protection afforded by the 'unequal' treaties. However, a brief look at the average mortality rate of the independent British firms which operated in East Asia in the mid-nineteenth century seriously undermines this view.

Here I should like to pursue the activities of Western trading firms in more detail through case studies drawn mainly from the Jardine Matheson Archive.[49] The materials in the Jardine Matheson Archive allow one to build up a picture of the activities of Western firms engaged in the China and Japan trade. The regular weekly correspondence between the partners in Hong Kong and Shanghai and the branches and agents in East and Southeast Asia contain advices and reports which give one much information on the market in each district. The only stricture necessary is that since the reports are concerned with the short term, one must be cautious in using the information to extrapolate long-term trends.

The commercial activities of Western firms were strictly confined to a limited area of 10 *ri* (24.4 miles) around each treaty port, and foreign merchants were not allowed to go into the interior of Japan for commercial purposes. They could therefore only hope to penetrate the inland market by sending their Japanese employees or by offering advances to Japanese merchants to obtain export articles in the interior. There are several known cases of Western firms in Japan engaging in this type of activity in order to purchase raw silk and tea.[50] For example, as I shall show later, in the 1860s Jardine, Matheson & Co. made advances of 870,000 Mexican dollars to Takasuya Seibei, a silk merchant, for 'country purchase'. Similarly the American firm of Smith, Baker 4 Co. sent Ōtani Kahei to Ōsaka to purchase 700,000 kin of tea valued at 268,000 *ryō* for export.[52] Alternatively, Western firms could provide funds for Japanese merchants who were suffering from a shortage of capital. Thus Iwasaki Yatarō seems to have borrowed from the American firm of Walsh, Hall & Co. for funds to help in the development of Mitsubishi. Similarly, the house of Mitsui had a close financial relationship with the Oriental Bank in the early Meiji period.[52]

Western firms also attempted to invest in export-related industries such as tea, coal and raw silk, shipbuilding, and shipyards.[53] For example, they founded tea-refiring places in the treaty port areas employing Japanese workers. In 1867 there were six tea-refiring places in Nagasaki operated by Western merchants, and in 1873 there were fifteen in Yokohama and eleven in Kōbe. At the busiest season, it was reported, one tea-refiring place might employ 1,500–2,000 workers.[54] Glover & Co. provided funds to the Saga domain for the development of the Takashima coal mine and constructed a slip dock in Nagasaki.[55] In the 1870s Jardine, Matheson & Co. provided loans to Gotō Shōjirō for running the Takashima coal mine, and Gotō's failure to repay them eventually led to a court case.[56] The French firm of Ludwig & Co. provided a Japanese merchant with funds for the establishment of a steam-powered filature in Yamanashi in return for the raw silk which would be produced there.[57]

In 1869 Jardine, Matheson & Co. were planning to found a filature in Japan if the Japanese government would support the undertaking. After visiting some silk districts, Mr Adams, a Secretary at the British Legation, had written that the reason why silk production did not increase in Japan was that producers 'had not the facilities to reel off the silk quickly' as 'they were too poor to get them out', 'consequently every year a great many cocoons are wasted.' Therefore, 'it is not at all unlikely that a Filature would answer here very well & if we could have the support of the Government its success could almost be guaranteed.' In addition, 'It would be a good means for the Government raising a revenue & by their having a share in the concern it would in a measure give us a sort of monopoly.'[58] The Maebashi domain was keen to purchase machinery from Jardines' filature in Shanghai, which had suspended operations. Jardines wanted to operate the new filature as a joint-concern with the Maebashi domain, but the latter desired complete control.[59] Jardines gave up the idea of a joint operation and concentrated on the sale of the machinery, but Maebashi arranged the establishment of a filature with the Swiss firm of Siber and Brennwald.[60] However, this, and other similar projects, all came to an end in the mid-1870s, when the Meiji government adopted a policy hostile to foreign investment in Japan.

Exports of Raw Silk: The Takasuya and Nanbu Affairs

The branches and agents of Jardine, Matheson & Co. situated at treaty ports both in China and Japan engaged in export and import activities in accordance with instructions from the partners in Hong Kong and Shanghai. In Japan, Jardine, Matheson & Co. had a branch in Yokohama from 1859, agents in Nagasaki and Hakodate from the same year, and in Hyōgo (Kōbe) and Ōsaka from 1868. Branches and agents were generally given instructions about the type and quantity of goods in which to deal, and were also supplied with minimum and maximum price limits based on prices of commodities in London or other prime markets. These price limits were of overriding importance and could not be disregarded. If a branch did wish to disregard the guide lines with which they had been issued, either by purchasing goods at higher prices, or by selling imported goods at lower prices, they had to seek special permission from a partner. However, as these instructions or replies from partners took time to come, they frequently missed the chance to enter the market for raw silk and tea on advantageous or reasonable terms, since both markets changed very rapidly.

As we will see in Chapter 4, silk was Japan's most important export article. At first, Western merchants tried to work through Japanese intermediaries, but these attempts ended in failure. In the case of Jardine, Matheson & Co. loans to such intermediaries, for the purchase of raw silk, only took place in the first half of the 1860s. One of them, a Japanese silk merchant called Takasuya Seibei, defrauded Jardines of substantial funds. His story reveals the difficulties which Western traders faced, and must in many respects present features typical of Western dealings with Japanese merchants in the 1860s.[61]

William Keswick, Jardines' representative in Yokohama, seems to have started his dealings with Takasuya for upcountry purchases of silk in the 1860/1 season.[62] At first Takasuya 'always proved himself honest & upright in his dealings',[63] and 'Keswick put the greatest confidence' in him.[64] Takasuya's first transactions with Keswick amounted to 484,784 dollars[65] and in May 1862, when Keswick left Japan for Shanghai and Samuel J. Gower took over the Yokohama end of the business, the balance of his account was about 36,000 dollars.[66] In the new silk season of 1862, Bakufu restrictions on the silk trade made it difficult to obtain raw silk for export purposes. Prices rose and, as a result, Japanese silk merchants started to sell raw silk for cash only. This made it difficult for Jardines' Yokohama branch to enter the silk market, because of their 'great scarcity of funds'.[67] At the same time, increasing prices also meant that they were unable to purchase silk within the limits instructed by their partners. They were therefore forced to stop all purchases on the Yokohama market and attempt to secure silk at cheaper than market prices through 'country purchases'.[68]

As Bakufu policy towards the silk trade became more restrictive Jardines became more and more dependent on country purchases, particularly through Takasuya, who was the 'purchaser of nearly all the silk obtained from the country': 'if his business was lost, we should never be able to get anything like the same quantity or advantage in silk.'[69] To increase purchases of silk in the interior Gower continued to make advances to him in accordance with instructions from James Whittall, Jardines' senior partner in Hong Kong, but confessed: 'I am rather afraid of encreasing (*sic*) too much the already large amount sent into the country.'[70] In March 1863 the unsettled political situation and the exhaustion of Jardines' funds prompted Gower 'to recover the money sent into the country'.[71] The silk purchased through Takasuya was not delivered satisfactorily, while the overdraft of his account gradually increased. Gower's anxiety grew rapidly and, his confidence in Takasuya severely shaken, he referred the matter formally to the British Consul at Kanagawa, Charles A. Winchester.[72] By June Takasuya's debt against Jardine, Matheson & Co. amounted to 120,882 dollars at an interest rate of 1 per cent a month.[73] Keswick expressed his regret that his own 'confidence in Takasia [Takasuya] induced Mr Gower to believe in his [Takasuya's] statements & to trust him too far', but he was sanguine about the chances of settling the account, 'as I believe Takasia to be a man of wealth & of position.'[74] Keswick visited Yokohama and was satisfied with Takasuya's assurances that he was in perfect solvency and that the full balance of the silk would be delivered as soon as prices declined. He therefore thought that it would be better 'to give him the time requested than to precipitate matters', 'staying proceedings against him through the Consul'.[75]

At the end of June 1863 Takasuya agreed to deliver 120 bales of silk per month at market prices, 10 per cent of this being used to settle his debts on the mortgage of his properties.[76] However, as the control exerted by the Bakufu on the silk trade through the silk guild in Edo grew and the terrorizing of Japanese merchants by anti-foreign extremists increased, Takasuya closed his business and only a few bales of silk were delivered.[77] In view of the fact that as long as 'the restrictions on silk are not removed it is almost impossible that Takasia can deliver the article', Keswick informed Gower that he should take the steps 'necessary to establish the responsibility of the Japanese Government for the loss we shall inevitably sustain', through the intermediacy of the Consul, Winchester.[78] Winchester, however, replied that he had 'no power to make the Japanese Government responsible for Japanese debts.'[79] Gower urged Takasuya to deliver the promised raw silk in order to liquidate his debts, but Takasuya always put him off with excuses about difficulties in the interior and the Bakufu restrictions.[80] Gower appealed to the Consul again, requesting the arrest of Takasuya and the seizure of his property,[81] but all Jardines' efforts – whether private or official – to recover Takasuya's debts failed.[82]

In December 1863, the Governor of Kanagawa sent an 'unsatisfactory & obscure' reply to Winchester, recommending that Takasuya should be spared bankruptcy. Since it was impossible for Takasuya to repay all his debts immediately, Gower would gain nothing from his bankruptcy.[83] Gower was 'at a loss what is the best course to pursue'. Even 'if his property is seized & the claim pushed to the utmost', since Japanese claims would have priority,

> I see no hope of the claim being paid that way. On the other hand, there appears no great probability of the present unsettled & unsatisfactory state of affairs coming to a speedy termination, so there appears so little to be gained by giving further time, & I fear the only thing to be done is to let matter (*sic*) take their course through the British Consul.[84]

Keswick, however, instructed Gower 'not [to] let the matter rest' and suggested that it be brought as far as negotiations at a ministerial level.[85]

In April 1864 Gower brought the case to the British Minister, Rutherford Alcock.[86] On receiving Gower's report on Takasuya, Keswick had reached

> the conclusion that no forbearance should be shown him, under whatever circumstances he may have been prevented from carrying out his engagements . . . It is very probable that nothing will be gained by severe measures, but it is only just that an example should be made when dishonesty of either the merchant or the government is so apparent, as it is in this case.[87]

Although Alcock was very pessimistic about the outcome, he requested the Bakufu authorities to repay the debts by liquidating Takasuya's property.[88] The Governor of Kanagawa was urged by the Bakufu authorities to examine the case, and summoned Takasuya that same April.[89] By June 1864 Takasuya had received loans totalling 763,243 dollars from Jardine, Matheson & Co. and had sold them produce, mainly raw silk, valued at 669,742 dollars, leaving a balance against him of 93,501 dollars.[90] In late June the Governor proposed a settlement: of the total debt of 93,500 dollars, 3,500 dollars was to be paid immediately, 4,000 by the end of 1864 according to the Japanese calendar, 2,240 every year for 25 years from 1865 (56,000 dollars) and the remaining 30,000 in portions of 5,000 every year from 1867.[91] C.S. Hope, then acting agent for Jardines' Yokohama branch, discussed the matter with Winchester and asked for instructions from Keswick with the comment:

> It is a melancholy business altogether and the proposals of the Japanese Government are far from being satisfactory. I do not, however, see that any advantage is to be gained by refusing the pittance offered.[92]

Jardine, Matheson & Co. accepted this proposal once it had been arranged on a diplomatic level between the British Consul at Kanagawa and the Governor of Kanagawa, and the case seemed to be over by June 1864.[93] Takasuya's debt had been transferred to Jardines' Shanghai branch by August 1865 and was probably written off as irrecoverable.[94]

For the season 1864/5, Keswick instructed Gower to purchase Japanese silk to 'as large an extent as possible' because the export of silk from China for the season was going to be very limited and prices would be so high that 'a little or no good will be done.'[95] When the silk trade in Japan was suspended in mid-1864 as a result of increasing intervention by the Bakufu, the Yokohama branch was therefore in a dilemma. It was at this time that Takasuya suggested that he would be able to secure 4,000–5,000 bales of silk at Hakodate without difficulty, since there were no restrictions in force there. Gower considered that if this were true, it might be worth sending a ship to Hakodate.[96] Takasuya spoke several times about the cheapness of silk in the interior and asked for advances in order to secure Ōshū silk. Gower promptly refused this proposal, but feeling that Takasuya 'certainly appears to be most anxious to do what is right & if possible to retrieve his lost character', he gradually became inclined to give him the chance to pay off a large portion of his debt 'should he be able to secure a good amount of silk in the way he proposes'.[97]

For a while after the allied Western bombardment of Shimonoseki in September 1864, little raw silk was brought to the Yokohama market. Some was smuggled, but in Gower's opinion there was

> considerable risk in bringing down in this manner, for in the event of discovery the whole would be confiscated, and it is certain the Native dealers would not incur the risk themselves and consequently the greater portion of any loss would be sustained by the Foreigners who had advanced for the Silk.[98]

Some Western firms sent ships to Hakodate to secure silk there, and Gower was also ready to send Hope with funds to buy all the silk available.[99] Keswick insisted that 'no advances are to be made to Takasia until value has been received' and that 'in the event of no silk being forthcoming at Hakodadi (*sic*) the expenses incurred by sending a steamer to that Port should be defrayed by him.'[100] Unable to obtain advances, Takasuya at one point had to abandon his idea of obtaining silk at Hakodate. Sympathizing with him, Gower relented and gave an advance of 3,200 dollars, not directly to Takasuya but through another Japanese merchant, Hanbei, who would be responsible for the funds which Takasuya needed to bring down silk from Edo.[101] The silk Takasuya brought was good and cheap and Gower advanced him a further 10,000 dollars through Hanbei.[102] Gower wrote to Keswick that Takasuya

> appears so prompt now in bringing silk & so very anxious to retrieve his former good name, that with your permission I would almost be again inclined to give him a fair trial & a little more help, in order that he may secure larger quantities.[103]

Keswick was still cautious about advances to Takasuya, but for the time being answered: 'I leave you a little more free to act with him as you think best, only remarking that we are not disposed again to put ourselves in his power to any considerable extent.'[104]

By the end of September 1864 restrictions on the silk trade had been removed, but prices on the Yokohama market were increasing rapidly. Takasuya brought silk regularly. In early 1865 Gower was very optimistic that Takasuya's debts would be cleared up in March or April.[105] In March Gower left Japan, and Hope became responsible for Jardines' Yokohama branch. He found that 84,566 dollars of Takasuya's old debt still remained and that his new debt amounted to 55,737 dollars.[106] Hope became 'very uneasy about Takasia for he delivers his silk with most aggravating tardiness, & has the assurance to demand further assistance.'[107] Takasuya was obviously unable to repay either the old or the new debt, and his case was again brought to the consideration of the British and Japanese authorities. After the agreement over his old debts, Takasuya had been advanced 116,200 dollars and had sold 87,153 dollars' worth of silk to Jardine, Matheson & Co.; the balance of his new account was therefore 29,047 dollars.

The Governor of Kanagawa ordered Takasuya to pay up immediately, while warning Jardine, Matheson & Co. that they had known of his poor financial situation. Takasuya was, however, insolvent and proposed to repay his new debt in annual instalments. When this offer was refused, he suggested liquidating his properties in Yokohama and then gradually repaying the remaining balance. After making their own investigations Jardines demanded that he secure the money by selling all his properties not only in Yokohama but also in the provinces.[108] The Governor, however, replied that Takasuya did not possess any properties other than those in Yokohama.[109] The main point at issue concerned the treatment of these Yokohama properties. Hope considered that if the Governor took up the case, it would be possible for Jardines to recover the whole of Takasuya's new debt. But the Governor evaded this issue, fearing that Hope or other foreigners would probably settle in the Japanese residential area outside the foreign settlement. He therefore refused to let Jardines take over the houses, and would agree only to sell them and then transfer the money.[110] In August 1866 Hope, realizing that such was the Governor's decision, brought the matter to negotiation between the British Minister, Harry S. Parkes, and the Bakufu authorities.[111] The case was, in fact, 'in a most deplorable state'.[112] In October 1867 the Governor made the same proposal for settlement as before: through the sale of Takasuya's Yokohama properties.[113] Meanwhile, his new debt had been transferred to the Hong Kong office of Jardine, Matheson & Co.[114]

Complicated negotiations with the Japanese authorities over Takasuya's debt are mentioned in subsequent letters from the Yokohama branch. A letter dated 28 September 1870 mentions that the matter 'has received the constant attention of the [British] Consul and The Saibansho'. According to the same letter, one of the problems seems to have been that 'The Authorities I think want the property realised for the benefit of *all* his creditors, which of course cannot be permitted.'[115] Jardines were resigned to the fact that they could not hope to see all their money returned and concentrated on the relatively small sum of 12,000 dollars.[116] On 31 December 1870 E. Whittall reported that Takasuya had paid 2,000 dollars and the remaining 10,000 dollars was to be paid in various instalments.[117] The last 4,000 dollars was paid over a year later, in 1872, by the buyers of Takasuya's properties.[118]

The other big Jardines loan to a Japanese contact was to the Nanbu (Morioka) domain of Northern Japan. In January 1865 Gower made an advance of 60,000 dollars on an exclusive contract basis to the commercial agents of the domain in order to purchase all their silk for the subsequent three years at market prices.[119] After the trouble he had had with Takasuya – and against the background of rapid increases in silk prices which prevented him from purchasing it within the instructed price limits – Gower probably thought it was a good idea to secure a quantity of silk in this way and at the same time to build up close ties with the financially reliable Nanbu domain.[120] In the circumstances Keswick could not but accept Gower's action, but expressed strong disapproval that he had advanced a sum as large as 60,000 dollars without prior consultation.[121] On succeeding Gower, Hope determined not to give any further advances until the previous ones had been cleared as Nanbu was slow in delivery. Accordingly he had no intention of giving any advances in the following year.[122] In the first half of 1865 alone the Nanbu domain had been given three advances, amounting to 150,000 dollars. Of this, 23,653 dollars was not settled. Hope had to bring this affair also the consideration of the British Minister.[123]

The Takasuya affair was probably atypical, 'a bad case',[124] but it shows clearly that the method of giving advance payments to Japanese merchants, however unsatisfactory, was the only prompt commercial response – excluding diplomatic channels – which Western firms were able to make in the face of official restrictions on the silk trade and the confinement of their activities to the treaty ports. As Gower himself wrote, when restrictions were tight it was not possible to obtain a single bale without advances.[125] Even so, it is difficult to understand why Jardines or their agents continued to make such large advances to Takasuya without proper security. Jardine, Matheson & Co. should have realized that he depended on funds from them for his business activities. Cut off as they were from accurate information on the state of the interior market, Jardines presumably had no alternative but to do business with him. Whatever his financial situation, Jardines seem to have had confidence in him as long as he kept up his deliveries of raw silk.

Keswick's confidence in Takasuya greatly influenced Gower's judgement because Gower was only Jardines' Yokohama agent, while Keswick was a partner in the firm. After mid-1863, when loans to Takasuya had caused Jardines great pecuniary inconvenience, Gower seemed more cautious and suggested: 'With reference to advances, it is my decided opinion that great risk is increased by advancing to Japanese Merchants and that it is much better to adhere strictly to cash transactions.'[126] There was doubtless a communication gap between the partners and their agents. In dealing with markets elsewhere partners had to depend on reports from their agents, while the agents had to find a swift response to rapid changes in the business situation. Gower therefore had a difficult path to chart between the partners' sometimes 'unrealistic' instructions and the rapid changes in the 'real' Yokohama market. There was not enough time to wait for instructions from the partners, which in any case would be out of date by the time they arrived. It was not only the inflexibility of the agency house system of Western firms which lay behind cases like the Takasuya affair, however, but also the treaty port system itself and the restrictions which it placed on travel into the interior by foreign nationals. The other big Western firms seem to have had similar problems.

By mid-1865 worsening pecuniary troubles with both Takasuya and the Nanbu domain had made Jardines reluctant to give further advances to Japanese. Even if they might profit from such transactions, neither now nor in the future could they be sure of avoiding similar difficulties. All accounts with those to whom Jardines made advances showed losses against the firm: as of May 1865, the adverse balance of Takasuya's new account was 29,047 dollars; Hanbei's balance was 8,451 dollars; Taguchiya's balance 100 dollars; and the Prince of Nanbu's 16,580 dollars. All these cases eventually had to be laid before diplomatic channels.[127]

What effect did the uncertainties of the Takasuya affair have on the attitude of Jardines' Yokohama branch towards the use of advances to secure Japanese raw silk? Luckily, the branch's cash books are available for the period from July 1864 to June 1865, with the exception of January 1865.[128] In this season Jardines' Yokohama branch advanced a total of 268,533 dollars to Japanese merchants: Takasuya received 75,200 dollars, including a loan transferred into Hanbei's account; Hanbei 24,000 dollars, Taguchiya 19,333 and Nanbu 150,000. During the same period, cash transactions with Japanese export merchants amounted to 452,208 dollars. Advances therefore accounted for only 37 per cent of total silk purchases. Cash had become the main method of transaction, and advances had lost their former importance. Seventy per cent of Jardines' cash business was with five Japanese export merchants who were already established in the Yokohama market. In fact, from the mid-1860s it is clear that a transaction system was gradually being formed between Western firms and respectable Japanese export merchants in the treaty ports.[129] However attractive the financial rewards of direct country purchasing might have seemed, Western firms had become aware of the risks of making cash advances and presumably decided, if reluctantly, that it was more prudent to do business on a commercially stable basis with Japanese firms of a similar status.

Imports of Cotton Manufactures

Jardine, Matheson & Co. imported cotton and woollen manufactures, sugar, rice, metals and peas, while exporting silk, tea and marine products. In the case of imports to Japan, their branches and agents were given minimum price limits within which to sell, and the Hong Kong or Shanghai branches of Jardine, Matheson & Co. sent goods for sale to other branches and agents, either at their own discretion or on the receipt of advices from branches and agents in the various open ports. However, with the former method, goods sent sometimes had to be returned unsold as there was no demand, and with the latter method it sometimes happened that the advantageous market conditions had already been lost by the time the goods could be delivered.

Cotton manufactures were the major import into Japan in the decades following the opening of the ports despite the fact that cotton growing and weaving was the most developed industry in Tokugawa Japan. Like many other latecomer countries, Japan faced rapid increases in imports of manufactured goods from the already industrialized West. Cotton and woollen manufactured goods, mainly from Britain, accounted for 82 per cent of total imports in 1865 and 67 per cent in 1872.[130] Table 3–5 shows imports of raw cotton, cotton yarns, and cotton manufactures into Japan. Imports into Japan of cotton yarn gradually increased to 63.3 million lb valued at 13.6 million yen in 1888, but rapidly decreased after this date as the Japanese cotton industry developed. Those of cotton goods, including grey, bleached and dyed shirtings, decreased after reaching a peak of 87.6 million yards valued at 4.7 million yen in 1879, and then increased again from the mid-1890s to retain an important position up until World War I.[131] Imports of cotton yarn increased much more rapidly than imports of cotton piece goods in the period up to the late 1880s, as a result of the increasing demand from the domestic weaving industry. This cotton yarn market had not even existed before the opening to foreign trade. On the other hand, piece goods imports fluctuated, and also exhibited a high degree of product differentiation, since they were affected by consumer preference with regard to factors such as the quality of texture or design. For yarns, however, product differentiation was lower and substitutability correspondingly higher.

Since comparative advantage theory would lead one to expect a steady increase in all imports from industrialized Britain, what is the significance of the fact that British cotton piece goods were able to penetrate into the Japanese market only to

Table 3-5 Imports of Raw Cotton, Cotton Yarn and Cotton Piece Goods into Japan, 1870–1910

Year	Cotton, ginned		Cotton yarn		Cotton piece goods	
	mil. lb	mil. yen	mil. lb	mil. yen	mil. sq. yard	mil. yen
1870	3.1	0.6	11.8	4.5	37.1	3.0
1875	3.8	0.4	18.0	4.1	64.7	5.0
1880	1.9	0.2	38.1	7.7	78.5	5.5
1885	5.9	0.6	28.5	5.2	50.2	2.9
1890	34.8	4.1	42.5	9.9	58.5	4.1
1895	191.3	24.3	19.5	7.1	75.8	6.9
1900	328.5	58.5	12.1	7.0	133.8	18.4
1905	557.7	109.3	3.0	1.7	132.0	17.9
1910	637.9	157.8	0.4	0.3	97.8	13.7

Source: Tōyō Keizai Shinpōsha (ed.), *Nihon bōeki seiran* (1935), pp. 229, 230, 240, 241.

Note: It was not possible to calculate all cotton piece goods in terms of square yards.

a limited extent? It may seem plausible to argue that the main reason lay with the preference of the Japanese consumer for domestic goods.[132] This would imply that from the first there was no chance that British cotton manufactures might penetrate the Japanese domestic market. However, there was an overall increase in imports of manufactures into Japan in which Britain had a comparative advantage, such as machinery, metals, electrical goods and chemicals. With cotton manufactures, the general trend was for Japanese consumers to become interested in an increasing variety of imported cotton fabrics. Their quality deteriorated, however, and in the late 1870s and early 1880s they faced fierce competition from domestically produced goods of improved quality, which used imported cotton yarn. British consular reports frequently noted the decline in quality and the failure to vary patterns as two elements which made British cotton piece goods less competitive and therefore limited their penetration into the Japanese market.[133] While it is true that the development of the Japanese cotton spinning industry from the mid-1880s led to a rapid decrease in imports of cotton yarn, expanding demand for various types of fabric which were not yet competitively produced in Japan meant a general increase in fabric imports from the mid-1890s. These facts suggest that the difficulty lay not with a a Japanese preference for domestic goods, but rather with institutional and structural elements linked to the treaty port system itself which worked to obstruct a natural increase in imports. In this section I shall review various factors relating to production, distribution and consumption in an attempt to find the answer to this question.

The following contemporary descriptions of the import trade and the way in which British merchants conducted their business indicate the existence of other, more deep-seated, restraints on penetration in addition to problems connected with the actual goods on offer.

Foreign merchants have been forced to reside and carry on all their business within the narrow limits of small settlements situated at the few open ports in the country, where it has been quite impossible for them to cultivate direct friendly relations with the principal Japanese merchants, or themselves to study or inquire into the wants and tastes of the Japanese people at large. They have been obliged to conduct all business transactions with a class of brokers ... on whom a monopoly of foreign business has been conferred. It is on these men that foreign importers have been forced to rely for information as to the class of goods which will find a market here, and it is to them alone that all sales have had in the first instance to be made. Every imported article passes, therefore, through their hands before it reaches the Japanese wholesale dealer in Tokyo or elsewhere, and the price at which it can then be sold is, of course, enhanced by the heavy commission levied by them.[134]

Or again:

few foreign firms at this port can afford to import large quantities of goods, and store the same for an indefinite period until there is a demand for them, and, therefore they do not import to any large extent, and keep only samples; it follows that when a Japanese wishes to make a purchase, say, of a quantity of piece-goods, he is informed on application to the foreign merchants that they have not in store the goods he requires, but can contract to deliver them within a certain time by importing them either from Europe or China. *As the Japanese merchants generally only buy when there is a demand, they are averse to contracting, and naturally prefer purchasing on the spot, if the goods they require are obtainable in the place.* They, therefore, apply to the Chinese merchants, who, being well supplied, are often in a position to accommodate them with the merchandize they are in want of, and at a cheaper rate than foreigners would be willing to contract for. Many of the Chinese hongs at Nagasaki are agents for wealthy Chinese merchants in China, who keep them well furnished with a large stock of goods suitable for the Japan market, and which are purchased in China when prices are low, and they can afford to allow these goods to remain in store for a long time, and often in order to effect sales either barter them against produce suitable for the China market, or sell them to the Japanese on credit.[135] (emphasis added)

It is clear from this account that there was severe competition between Western firms and Chinese merchants. There was also competition between the Western firms themselves, to such an extent that in 1869 Edward Whittall of Jardine, Matheson & Co. wrote that 'there are too many firms engaged in the Import trade for any good to be done in it just at present.'[136] The descriptions above also suggest the existence of two related and vitally important factors: the differences between the commercial system adopted by British and other Western trading firms as opposed to that of Chinese firms, and the network by which imported goods were distributed inland from the open ports.

Jardine, Matheson & Co. supplied British cotton and woollen manufactured goods to Japan by two routes: they either purchased goods which had already arrived in Hong Kong or Shanghai and sent them to Japan; or sold on a commission basis goods which had been sent directly from Britain. The latter practice began in the late 1860s. According to correspondence in the Jardine Matheson Archive they received fabrics directly from Sam Mendel in Manchester and from Kraentler & Mieville, Murdoch's Nephews, and Schuster, Son & Co. in London, but the volume of these transactions was small.[137] Since Japanese importers tended to purchase at only 'the quotations ruling for the small requirements of immediate wants', demand fluctuated in the short term and Jardines had to keep stocks of a variety of fabrics to meet this fluctuating demand.[138] A British commercial report pointed out that

> Japanese taste is so fluctuating that the market has to be watched very closely, and where before shipments could be ordered without exceptional care as to detail, it is now necessary to accompany almost every order with an indent, minutely particularizing every article, and so timing the arrival as to meet the immediate wants of the consumer.[139]

1870 is a relatively well documented year in the Jardine Matheson Archive.[140] If one takes that year as an example and compares the market situation of grey shirting using the prices of 8¼ or 8⅙ lb grey shirting – this being the main type of cotton piece goods imported into Japan – the fluctuations in price would seem to reflect changes in both delivery and stock rather than demand. From January to March the market was active and the total stock of all grey shirtings at the end of each month was less than 35,000 pieces. This was reported to be 'not large'.[141] Prices increased from 3 dollars per piece in early January to 3.05–3.075 in early March. However, the market became inactive after April and stocks increased from 35,000 to 58,000 pieces in late May, prices conversely reaching at their lowest 2.77–2.81 dollars. The market returned to activity from mid-July and the total stock, which had reached 90,000 pieces in late July, decreased to 55,000 in early August. It increased once again, to 100,000 pieces, in early September, but suddenly decreased to about 40,000 towards the end of the month. The price recovered slightly to 2.78 dollars towards late December. Although prices of grey shirtings were obviously moving in inverse proportion to stock volumes from January to May, during the summer season prices increased with increases in stock, probably as a result of strong demand. From October prices once again moved in inverse proportion to stock. Although nothing is known of the nature of the demand from Japanese dealers, both deliveries of goods and fluctuations in the volume of stocks seem to have occurred irregularly and without any apparent relationship between them.

Stocks of cotton piece goods at Jardines' Yokohama branch sometimes underwent a sudden increase due to the simultaneous arrival of goods supplied directly from Britain and goods sent by Jardines' branches in Hong Kong and Shanghai, both without reference to the Japanese market situation.[142] Herbert Smith, Jardines' Yokohama agent, wrote to Jardine, Matheson & Co. in Hong Kong: 'As regards direct shipments of Cotton Yarns & Cotton manufactures, moderate supplies will I think meet with a more satisfactory sale, than re-shipments from the China Ports.'[143] In the case of sugar, regular panics were caused by similar simultaneous arrivals.[144] When imported goods were unsaleable, they were reshipped back to China.[145] However, Western merchants hesitated to do this because of the absence of a drawback system in Japan.[146]

This market situation probably discouraged Western firms from importing in large quantities. They were unwilling to risk increasing their stock of unsaleable goods, since holding of such goods caused heavy losses.[147] Conversely, when imported goods which they wished to buy were not available, Japanese merchants would purchase domestically produced goods instead. Japanese goods were therefore able to maintain a high substitutability for imported cotton piece goods. The Japanese bought imported cotton piece goods because of their cheapness and fine quality. When these advantages disappeared, domestic products using imported yarn easily provided strong competition. Given the combined factors of price and durability, it was economically reasonable for Japanese consumers to turn from imported cotton piece goods of low price and bad quality to domestically produced goods of high durability and a reasonable price.

In their import activities, as we have already seen, Western firms were separated not only from the Japanese consumer but also from the wholesale dealers in the large cities. They were able to develop only indirect links with them, through Japanese merchants living or working in the treaty ports who specialized in the import business on a commission basis. Western firms, at this time mainly British, usually waited at their offices in the treaty ports for inquiries from Japanese import merchants. They scarcely made any efforts to do research in order to develop the market for imported goods, nor did they embark on positive sales activities. This was partly because the treaties did not allow them to travel outside the treaty ports for commercial purposes and partly because they knew little of either the Japanese language or the economic and political situation. Even if they had attempted to do market research, however, they would have been dependent on Japanese merchants for information. There is an increasing contrast between the British approach and the commercial activities of German firms in the 1880s. Instead of waiting in their Yokohama offices for customers to turn up, German merchants diligently sought out customers, aided by Japanese partners established in Tokyo.[148] As we saw above, Chinese merchants active in Japan also had a different commercial system, which tended to be more effective than the systems adopted by Western firms.

Distribution by Japanese Import Merchants

Few substantial studies have been made of the activities of Japanese import merchants.[149] They visited Western firms in the treaty ports in order to purchase goods. Although sometimes purchasing goods on their own account, they usually provided their customers with accommodation in the treaty port while finding the goods they required, and then took their customers to purchase them. Business was usually transacted in cash, not only because Western firms did not trust Japanese merchants but also because, as we have already seen, Japanese importers fully reciprocated this feeling. Because of the Western merchants' rights of extraterritoriality, their Japanese counterparts knew they would be at a disadvantage if they wanted to take them to court. They therefore naturally tried to avoid, where possible, forward transactions without goods available on the spot. Any Japanese merchant who wished to purchase import goods therefore required a certain amount of capital[150] and the market was inevitably closed to those un-

able to raise sufficient money for purchasing. The number of
buyers was therefore limited, and the business in imports had
to be conducted on a limited scale. Money exchange dealers
lent funds, presumably gained from foreign trade, to import
merchants who required cash.[151]

There seem to have been two different routes for the distribution of imported goods. In some cases export merchants
purchased such goods with the money they had received in
exchange for exports. Imported goods obtained in this way
were probably distributed directly to the places where these
export merchants were located. In most cases, however, goods
were – quite naturally – distributed by Japanese import merchants. As the goods were transacted in cash, Japanese import
merchants generally maintained links with wholesale dealers
in the large cities. Imported goods were then distributed to the
local market through the traditional Tokugawa networks of
recognized merchants in the cities, and through local merchants in the agricultural areas. Thus imported grey shirtings
and yarns probably found their way to agricultural areas
through the markets in large cities such as Edo, Ōsaka and
Kyōto.[152] Two distribution networks for cotton yarn and cotton piece goods had been established by the late 1870s. At first
Yokohama was the main distribution centre and goods were
sent from there to wholesale dealers in Tokyo or Ōsaka. From
Tokyo they went on to the eastern part of Japan, and from
Ōsaka to the western part. During this period, 'considerable
quantities' of yarn and one-third of all piece goods were
transferred from Yokohama to the Hyōgo-Ōsaka district. By
the late 1880s, however, Kōbe had become the main distribution centre for western Japan.[153]

The distribution network for imported cotton manufactures
has not yet been studied in enough detail for a clear picture to
be obtained. There are, however, some studies of sugar, another
main import.[154] During the Tokugawa period sugar was usually
designated an important local product, so that both production and sales were under the control of the feudal domain.
There was a sugar market managed by recognized Ōsaka
merchants. Sugar was brought from the producing districts of
Satsuma (Kagoshima) and Sanuki (Kagawa) to Ōsaka and
thence distributed to consuming cities such as Edo through
brokers and wholesale dealers. These privileged wholesale

dealers with monopolies in domestically produced sugar gradually lost their importance in sugar transactions, their position being usurped by dealers in imported sugar who developed close connections with traditional city merchants. In the early years only a limited number of Japanese sugar import merchants were buying foreign sugar from Western and Chinese firms in Yokohama and Kōbe. These merchants in turn sold to sugar dealers in Tokyo and Ōsaka who had been wholesale dealers or brokers in the Tokugawa period. They proceeded to distribute the imported sugar all over Japan through the traditional distribution network. Sugar import merchants worked between the foreign firms and large whole-sale dealers in Tokyo and Ōsaka on a commission basis, usually at 1 per cent of the original Yokohama and Kōbe purchasing price, although around the turn of the century they came to dominate the wholesale dealers.

In 1868 the Meiji government formally abolished the traditional guild system of privileged city merchants by issuing the 'Guidelines for Commerce', which permitted freedom of activity in commerce, industry and trade. However, members of the same trade did not therefore cease to associate and organize themselves, and the traditional market system and commercial customs continued. The old distribution network remained substantially unchanged, although the difference between wholesale dealers and brokers disappeared. From 1877 various associations of dealers in each trade were formed. Although these were not exclusive and privileged organizations like the old guilds, as the example of the Tokyo Association of Wholesale Dealers in Cotton Piece Goods shows, almost all the executives belonged to families which had been traditional cotton cloth dealers in the Tokugawa period.[155] These trade associations were formed voluntarily and their success contrasts with the failure of commercial corporations which had been set up under government control in the early Meiji years.

Government trade policy was, however, successful in promoting the development of export-related industries. In the late 1870s, an overseas documentary bill system was started as a way of protecting Japanese merchants and recovering Japan's commercial rights through the encouragement of direct exporting. In the early 1880s, with the establishment of the modern monetary and credit system and the consolidation of the domestic market system around Japanese export merchants, the focus of government policy changed. Now the emphasis was on the expansion of trade within the already established treaty port system through extending the business of drawing foreign exchange bills to Western merchants, in order to facilitate the accumulation of specie.

The experience of Western firms in China was similar, even though their activities were less restricted. In addition to reducing basic tariff rates to 5 per cent *ad valorem*, the Treaty of Tientsin of 1858 gave foreigners the right of participation in the coastal and river carrying trade and of travelling in the interior for commercial purposes.[156] Despite this, Western firms were entirely dependent on Chinese compradores, merchants and shroffs with their detailed knowledge and understanding of Chinese business methods. The trade and distribution of goods for both selling and buying were in the hands of Chinese guild merchants.[157] There were already flourishing self-sufficient local markets in the interior, but these did not develop into an interrelated nationwide network.[158] In various respects, therefore, treaty port trade developed as an extension of the established traditional Chinese economic system rather than as a newly created Western-style commercial system. Despite the right of travelling into the interior which was denied foreigners in Japan, the business activities of Western firms were effectively confined to the treaty ports, and treaty port trade developed in isolation from the overall Chinese economy.[159]

The above analysis of the actual working of the treaty port system clearly implies that far from promoting and protecting the activities of the Western merchants in Japan and China, it in fact worked to obstruct them. In Japan in particular, by several ironic twists of fate, the system worked in favour of the Japanese merchant, whether he was exporting or importing. On the export side, the opening of the ports was followed by a rapid increase in the outflow of primary products such as raw silk and tea as a result of the very strong Western demand for these goods. Both Western firms and Japanese merchants were actively involved in this business and, true to the supply–demand relationship, prices for silk rapidly increased. Competition among Western merchants for business with the small number of Japanese merchants in a position to obtain silk for export put the former in a disadvantageous position. It was a sellers' market which ultimately worked in favour of the Japanese merchants.

If in exports the demand 'pull' factor from the West was strong, in imports comparative advantage theory would lead one to expect the supply 'push' also to be comparatively strong, with the industrial supremacy of the West working in its favour. Both external and internal factors, however, meant that this was not so. India was Britain's most important market for cotton goods, and production was therefore regulated to suit India rather than Japan. In marketing British firms were hampered first by the inflexibility of the agency house system and by the excessive competition with other foreign merchants, both Western and Chinese, and second by the well-organized Japanese commercial and distribution system which dated back to the Tokugawa regime. Under the control of Japanese import merchants, the treaty port system acted as a non-tariff barrier to economic penetration by the industrialized West and protected the domestic market from Western manipulation. Unable to participate in distribution or to develop their own separate distribution networks, Western merchants suffered increasingly heavy losses in the import trade.[160] It was a buyers' market which once again ultimately worked in favour of the Japanese merchants.

The economic depression in the early 1880s led to a decline in imports of Western goods due to a decline in purchasing power of the middle and lower classes.[161] Imports of Western goods were further hit by the decline in the gold price of silver from the mid-1870s.[162] This discouraged Western firms from importing goods into Japan, while at the same time encouraging exports. It was more obviously in the interests of Western firms to concentrate on exports, favoured as these were by the international economic situation, than to try to improve the unprofitable and unpromising import business. This situation facilitated the development of stable business relationships with established Japanese merchants within the treaty port system rather than encouraging Western merchants to form their own independent networks using Japanese employees or non-established Japanese merchants.

In practical terms, however paradoxical it must seem, the 'unequal' treaties, and the treaty port system they created, had ceased to function as they were expected long before they formally came to an end in 1899. This state of affairs, completely unforeseen by either the Western or the Japanese signatories of the treaties, set the general framework for Japan's industrialization in the second half of the nineteenth century. In fact, the methods of business described in this section had become so well-entrenched that they continued into the twentieth century.[163]

4

The Development of Silk Exports

Japanese Silk in the World Silk Market

The combination of international and domestic factors described in the previous chapters formed the political and economic background to the development of export industries such as silk, tea and coal, which I will now analyse. During the period under consideration, raw silk was Japan's single most important export article. Success in this area depended on the competitiveness of Japanese raw silk in the world market. Table 4–1 gives the figures for world raw silk production in the second half of the nineteenth century, when Japan had become involved in the world market. It indicates that Italy, China and Japan became the main suppliers of raw silk to the world market. France was a major silk manufacturing country throughout the nineteenth century, but during the middle years her output was affected by the silkworm disease *pebrine*. This made it easier for imports of raw silk from China and Japan to make headway in Europe. As we shall see later, the United States was to emerge as a major silk manufacturing country after 1870. France and the United States did not need to compete against each other as far as the finished product was concerned, however, since the former was primarily producing high-quality silk fabrics for Europe, while the latter concentrated on producing ordinary silk fabrics for its ample domestic market behind a protective tariff barrier.[1]

The raw silk-producing countries of Italy, China and Japan became caught up in the growing demand for raw silk from France and the United States, the two major silk-manufacturing countries, and competed over quality and price in the world market. Silk fabric was becoming popular, but was not yet an item of ordinary wear, as cotton was. The demand for

Japan's Industrialization

Table 4-1 World Raw Silk Production, 1871–5 and 1896–1900 (annual average in thousand kg)

Country	1871–75		1896–1900	
		%		%
Europe				
France	658	(3.9)	650	(2.6)
Italy	2,880	(17.1)	4,215	(16.6)
Others	138	(0.8)	355	(1.4)
Europe Total	3,676	(21.8)	5,220	(20.6)
Levant and Central Asia	676	(4.0)	1,552	(6.1)
Asia				
China	10,560	(62.5)	9,737 †	(38.4)
Japan	1,414*	(8.4)	8,524	(33.7)
India (export only)	562	(3.3)	293	(1.2)
Asia Total	12,536	(74.2)	18,554	(73.3)
Total	16,888	(100)	25,326	(100)

Sources: (1) For Europe, Levant and Central Asia, and India, J. Schober, *Silk and Silk Industry* (1930), p. 102.

(2) For China, IMC, *Silk* (Special Series No. 3 (1881), pp. 7–8; L. Clugnet, *Géographie de la Soie* (1877), pp. 26–28; Tōa Kenkyūjo, *Shina sanshigyō kenkyū* (1943), pp. 2–4. Figures for 1898 are calculated from cocoon production on the basis that 1 picul of raw silk was produced from 17.5 piculs of fresh cocoons, according to the information in Tōa Dōbunkai, *Shina keizai zensho*, vol. 12 (1908), pp. 54–55.

(3) For Japan, *Fuken bussan-hyō* for 1874; Nōshōmushō, *Nōshōmu tōkei-hyō* for 1896–1900.

Notes: *for 1874 only. † for 1898 only.

silk was elastic, since it was affected by fluctuations in both price and the income of customers; moreover, raw silk production was very sensitive to changes in natural conditions such as weather, temperature and humidity. Since silk fabrics were also associated with affluence, the demand for raw silk was greatly influenced by economic fluctuations in the con-

sumer countries and the silk industry itself was highly
unstable and sometimes speculative.

As I have already mentioned, silk constituted a major
export for Japan. The ratio of silk exports to total exports
shows a relative decline from 46 per cent in the 1870s to 43 per
cent in the 1880s and 35 per cent in the 1890s, but their absolute
value increased, from 9.8 million yen in the 1870s to 19.0
million in the 1880s and 41.6 million in the 1890s.[2] Raw silk
was the main silk export item, although until 1873 silkworm
eggs were also important. From 1868 to that date they comprised 28 per cent of total silk exports.[3]

Table 4–2 shows the geographical distribution of raw silk
exports from Japan. In the early 1860s Japanese raw silk was
mainly exported to Shanghai and thence re-exported to Britain.[4]
The decrease in exports to Shanghai and the increase in direct
exports to Britain was a result of the extension of the regular
P & O service, which rendered reshipment from Shanghai un-
necessary. By the mid-1860s exports to Shanghai had decreased,
but from then on exports to Marseilles increased rapidly. This
reflected the positive turn taken by French foreign policy towards Japan under Léon Roches, in part motivated by interest
in the possibility that imports of Japanese silkworm eggs
might help the French silk industry to recover from the rav-
ages of silkworm disease.[5]

The rapid expansion in the value of raw silk exports was
due to sharp price rises, influenced by the depreciation in
silver value, rather than to any increase in actual quantities. In
fact, silk-reeling productivity had reached its limits, given the
existing level of expertise, and this was actually hindering an
increase in exports.[6] There was a clear correlation between
raw silk exports and overall Japanese exports to France before
the mid-1880s and those to the United States from the mid-
1880s onwards, with 1884 as the watershed year. The sharp
contrasts between the three destination countries can easily be
seen: the rapid increase of exports to the United States, the
gradual decline of those to France, and the sharp decrease of
those to Britain.

Japanese raw silk was divided into six categories in the
overseas market, according to the method of production and
the type of dressing. These were filatures, re-reels, hanks (or
Maebashi), Kakeda, Ōshū, and Hamatsuki. Re-reels

Table 4-2 Annual Average of Raw Silk Exports from Japan, 1861–1900 (in piculs)

Year	USA	France	Britain	Others	Total
	%	%	%	%	%
1861/65	40(0.3)	1,403(10.7)	5,724(43.7)	5,928(45.3)	13,095(100)
1866/70	349(3.4)	3,798(37.2)	6,019(59.0)	34(0.3)	10,200(100)
1871/75	209(1.8)	4,725(41.5)	5,216(45.9)	1,225(10.8)	11,375(100)
1876/80	2,914(17.4)	7,787(46.5)	5,295(31.6)	738(4.4)	16,734(100)
1881/85	9.714(39.3)	12,027(48.6)	2,845(11.5)	139(0.6)	24,725(100)
1886/90	18,365(55.1)	12,776(38.4)	1,389(4.2)	777(2.3)	33,307(100)
1891/95	28,843(56.0)	19,426(37.7)	835(1.6)	2,372(4.6)	51,476(100)
1896/1900	30,363(57.8)	17,722(33.8)	342(0.7)	4,081(7.8)	52,508(100)

Sources: For 1861–72, Yokohama Prices Current and Market Report, in JMA, PCMR, 46, 74, 75, 76; for 1873–1900, *Yokohamashi-shi*, Shiryō-hen, vol. 2, p. 165.

Notes: For 1861–72 figures are calculated from numbers of bales, at 0.80 picul per bale. Up to 1872, years refer to the period from 1 July to 30 June of the next year.

described silk produced by sedentary reeling machines which had then been re-reeled for export purposes to divide the silk according to size and quality. Hanks referred to the silk produced in the Gunma district by sedentary reeling machines, while Kakeda was the same type of silk, but produced in the Fukushima district. Ōshū was the silk produced in the northern part of Japan proper by hand or sedentary reeling machines, and Hamatsuki was the silk produced in the Hokuriku district by the same method.[7]

The characteristics of the three main production methods are shown in Table 4–3. In the 1870s and 1880s filatures had only twice or three times the productivity of sedentary reeling machines. The basic difference between sedentary reeling and filature methods lay in the provision of a special twisting apparatus in the latter, and in whether the small spool which wound the silk thread from the cocoons was revolved separately by each operator or whether several small spools fixed to a rod were revolved at the same time by manual, water or steam power. In both cases the reeling itself was performed by

Table 4-3 Types of Silk Reeling Machines in Japan

Reeling method	Quality of silk produced	Name of finished product	No. of pans (boiling & reeling)	No. of threads reeled	Revolving	No. of reels per machine	Joining method	Twisting method	Main producing districts
Hand	coarse	Hanks etc.	1	1	manual	1	manual	manual	Fukushima
Sedentary	coarse/ medium	Hanks/ Re-reels	1	1	manual/ foot/water	1 (mainly)	manual	manual/ apparatus	Fukushima Gunma
Filature	medium/ fine	Filature	2	2, 3 or more	water/ steam	many	manual	apparatus	Nagano

Source: Compiled from various sources.

manual labour. In this sense, there were no great differences between the production methods of filature, re-reels and other silk. The crucial distinctions in this period were regularity in size and efficiency in sorting and packing large quantities. Consequently, as hanks and other silk were usually produced as a small-scale household industry, it was not difficult to compete with filatures through reductions in production costs and the unification of the re-reeling and packing processes. Demand could therefore be met without adopting the machine-reeling system, through expanding production by the sedentary reeling system under strict quality control.[8]

Raw silk produced by sedentary reeling machines initially played a great role in the development of silk exports. In the 1860s and 1870s hanks and Ōshū formed the major silk exports from Japan. In the seasons 1873/4–1876/7 hanks took 74 per cent of the total quantity of raw silk exports, with Ōshū, Kakeda and Hamatsuki all together at 20 per cent, while filatures took only 4 per cent.[9] The ratio of both filatures and re-reels to the total volume of raw silk deliveries into Yokohama for export increased steadily from 15 per cent in 1878 to 61 per cent in 1885 and 82 per cent in 1890, replacing hanks and Ōshū and Kakeda silks.[10] Sedentary reeling products continued to develop in absolute terms, however, partly because – as we have seen – there was little difference between the reeling methods of sedentary machines and filatures, and partly because of the continuous expansion of the overseas and domestic markets.[11]

The quality of filatures was mostly below average. The Annual Report on Commerce and Industry for the fiscal year 1879 stated:

> The best filatures are appreciated as similar to Italian and French silk of good quality in the European and American markets. However . . . the producers of the best filatures are still few and it is therefore regrettable that the quality of filatures delivered to Yokohama is to a great extent below medium.[12]

The quality of raw silk is related to its price. As we review the price of Japanese raw silk on the overseas market later, we shall see the change in quality of exported Japanese raw silk.

The relative merits of Japanese raw silk as compared with European and Chinese lay, first, in its very white colour, which made it suitable for light-coloured fabrics; second, in the fact that it was less boiled-off in weight in the process of manufacturing; and third, in its price, which lay between the more expensive European silk and the cheaper Chinese variety. Its demerits arose from inferior reeling and finishing techniques and from low cocoon quality.[13]

Table 4–4 shows the quality indices of the Japanese raw silk exported to both the United States and France.[14] It is clear that the silk exported to the United States was the more expensive, but the difference in export prices to the two countries gradually lessened. The quality indices of the raw silk (mainly filatures) exported to the United States steadily decreased towards the early 1890s and slightly recovered in the second half of the decade while those to France – in which sedentary produced raw silk took a large share – remained fairly steady. The fact that exports to the United States rose, even though there was an overall decrease in quality, was accounted for by the increasing exports of inferior silk.

Since Chinese silk was a major competitor of Japanese silk in the international market, a brief review of Chinese raw silk exports is necessary. Table 4–5 shows the distribution of raw silk exports from Shanghai from 1861 to 1900 by country and description in quinquennial terms. Shanghai was a major raw-silk-exporting port because it was near the silk-producing districts of Kiangsu and Chekiang. Raw silk from the inland areas of central and northern China such as Hankow and Tientsin was also transmitted to Shanghai for export. Until the first half of the 1870s over half the raw silk exports from Shanghai were destined for Britain. Exports to France increased in the 1870s and 1880s, but slightly decreased in the period 1896 to 1900; exports to the United States show little change from 1876–80 to 1891–5. If one compares these figures with the information about the type of silk being exported, a clear picture emerges. Until 1890 almost all the silk was of the sedentary-produced white and yellow type, and went mainly to Europe. The increase in the United States' share after 1895 is clearly related to the increase in re-reels and filatures, but the latter accounted for only 16 per cent of the total in 1896–1900. Canton silk was mainly filature and exported to Europe

Table 4-4 Quality Indices of Japanese Raw Silk Exports,
1875–1900

To	United States		France	
Year	Quality indices	Average export price per picul	Quality indices	Average export price per picul
1875	100	596 yen	100	473 yen
1880	85	660	91	559
1885	81	552	93	506
1890	78	667	94	637
1895	84	831	103	809
1900	85	1011	96	904

Sources: Dainihon gaikoku bōeki nenpyō, corresponding years; Yamazawa and
Yamamoto, *Bōeki to kokusai shūshi* (1979), p. 192.
Note: The price indices of exported raw silk have been deflated in accordance
with the export price indices of textiles.

via Hong Kong, to be used as a substitute for Italian silk,
rather than to the United States.[15]

Chinese raw silk for export can be divided into four
categories: 'raw white', produced from white cocoons, 'raw
yellow', produced from yellow cocoons, 're-reeled', and 'steam
filature'. The first two were apparently exported to Europe,
while re-reels and filatures were destined for the United States.
The first three types of raw silk were produced by sedentary
reeling machines, but re-reels were reprocessed to meet the
overseas demand. These were inferior to Japanese re-reels:
more uneven with many breaks (caused during reprocessing)
and a lower tensible strength. 'Raw white' and 'raw yellow'
produced in the district of Chekiang and Kiangsu were called
'Tsatlee' (20–40 deniers); when produced in other areas they
were called 'Taysaam'.[16] As the annual total silk production in
China in the early 1870s was estimated at 10,560,000 kg and
the annual average exports of raw silk from Shanghai and
Canton for 1871 to 1875 amounted to 3,877,000 kg, 37 per cent
of total production was therefore destined for export.

Table 4–6 shows the annual average export prices of Japanese and Chinese raw silk. Since one tael was equivalent to one

Table 4-5 Annual Average of Raw Silk Exports from China, 1861–1900
(in thousand piculs)

Year	From Shanghai							Total (with others)	From Canton
	By destination			By category					
	Britain	France	USA	White	Yellow	Re-reel	Filature		
	%	%	%	%	%	%	%	%	
1861/65	41.5(83)	6.1(12)	0.5(1)	–	–	–	–	50.0(100)	5.8*
1866/70	26.0(76)	7.3(21)	0.3(1)	–	–	–	–	34.2(100)	12.3†
1871/75	26.8(56)	14.9(31)	3.5(7)	45.8(95)	2.0(4)	–	–	48.1(100)	16.0
1876/80	18.4(33)	26.8(48)	5.7(10)	50.7(91)	4.8(9)	–	–	55.6(100)	15.7
1881/85	9.5(22)	24.2(56)	6.0(14)	37.5(86)	6.0(14)	0(0)	–	43.5(100)	14.7
1886/90	4.0(9)	30.2(67)	5.4(12)	36.6(81)	8.6(19)	0(0)	–	45.2(100)	18.8
1891/95	3.3(6)	35.0(58)	8.2(14)	43.7(72)	10.6(18)	3.9(6)	2.1(4)	60.3(100)	21.2
1896/1900	2.7(5)	28.3(48)	10.6(18)	28.0(48)	9.2(16)	12.2(21)	9.1(16)	58.5(100)	30.6

Sources: Holdsworth Silk Circular, Shanghai, 4 July 1866, and 4 July 1867, both in JMA, PCMR 46; Jardine, Matheson & Co.'s (General Circular), Shanghai, 5 June 1868, in JMA, PCMR 72; Shanghai Price Current and Market Report, No.138, Shanghai, 2 June 1871, in JMA, PCMR 74; IMC, *Returns of Trade at the Treaty Ports*, Pt II, Shanghai, 1870–81; IMC, *Returns of Trade at the Treaty Ports, and Trade Reports*, Pt II, Shanghai, 1882–86; IMC, *Returns of Trade and Trade Reports*, Pt II, Shanghai, 1887–1900.

Notes: (1) Figures for 1861–7 are from 1 July in the previous year to 30 June, and those for 1868–70 from 1 June in the previous year to 31 May. (2) * 1864–5. (3) † 1867–70.

Table 4-6 Annual Average Export Price of Japanese and Chinese Raw Silk, 1866–1900

| Period | Japanese silk | Shanghai silk | | | Canton silk[3] |
		Tsatlee Taysaam	Re-reels	Filature	
	yen	tael	tael	tael	tael
1866/70	657[1]	478	–	–	514
1871/75	557	416	–	–	370
1876/80	599	347	–	–	267
1881/85	545	304	–	–	253
1886/90	627	316	–	–	305
1891/95	705	307	410[2]	558[2]	343
1896/1900	885	392	489	665	396

Sources: Nihon bōeki seiran, p. 55; IMC, *Returns of Trade*, Shanghai and Canton, corresponding years.
Notes: (1) 1868–70. (2) 1894–5. (3) Export price for Hong Kong.

and a half yen until Japan's establishment of the gold standard in 1897, it is clear that Japanese raw silk fetched lower prices than Chinese raw silk in the period 1866 to 1870 and drew level between 1871 and 1875. After 1875 the export price of Chinese raw silk fell below that of Japanese silk.

Silk Exports and the European Markets

Japanese Silk in the London Market

London reigned supreme as the distribution centre of the world silk trade until the mid-1880s, when it was replaced by Lyons in Europe and New York became very important for the United States. Raw silk exported from China and Japan was first transported to London and distributed from there to the silk-manufacturing districts of Europe.[17] British predominance in shipping and banking networks throughout the world was obviously the reason for London's importance. For the period 1861–5 to 1876–80, 40 to 48 per cent of the raw silk imported into Britain was re-exported. Up to 1880 an annual average of over 70 per cent of total re-exports went to France and 12 per cent to other European countries. Since Britain's position in the world silk trade clearly depended on the volume of raw silk transactions in London, as imports decreased towards 1880 her importance gradually declined with them.[18]

Table 4–7 gives details of the imports of raw silk into Britain during the period 1831 to 1873. Most raw silk imported into the London market came from China, Bengal, Italy and, from 1859, Japan. Raw silk imports increased steadily, and those of Chinese silk particularly rapidly after the mid-1840s. Before imports of Japanese silk began Chinese silk held the dominant position in the London silk market, with a 63–75 per cent share of Britain's total raw silk imports, while Bengali silk took 19–23 per cent. For the period 1861 to 1870, 64 per cent of Chinese silk was Tsatlee type, 25 per cent Taysaam and 11 per cent Canton. From 1876 to 1890 Chinese silk continued to dominate, taking 67 to 80 per cent of Britain's total raw silk imports, while the Japanese share remained at only 7–8 per cent.[19]

The period during which Japanese raw silk was brought to Britain coincided with an expansion in Britain's raw silk imports. Japanese silk was welcomed with enthusiasm, partly because the European cocoon crop was still suffering the effects of silkworm disease and partly because it was better in quality and cheaper than Chinese and Bengali silk. J.M. Jaquemot, a French silk merchant in Yokohama, wrote to the British Consul Howard Vyse:

> When the first importation of Japanese raw silk arrived in England it caused a general curiosity, owing to its intrinsic excellent quality, being far superior to anything that had been before received, either from Bengal or China. The experiments which were made by practical men soon confirmed the first favourable impression, and a general demand ensued, which has been growing every day larger, and extends now to most of the consumers of raw silk in Europe and America.[20]

A Durant & Co. circular made the following comment on the silk trade in 1860:

Table 4-7 Annual Average Imports of Raw Silk into Britain, 1831–1873
(in thousand lb)

Year	China	%	Japan	%	Bengal	%	Persia	%	Brutia	%	Italy	%	Total	%
1831/35	755	(24)			971	(31)	109	(3)	301	(10)	1,020	(32)	3,156	(100)
1836/40	923	(24)			1,221	(32)	145	(4)	405	(11)	1,129	(30)	3,823	(100)
1841/45	483	(13)			1,444	(37)	142	(4)	548	(14)	1,243	(32)	3,860	(100)
1846/50	2,035	(45)			1,243	(27)	147	(3)	307	(7)	798	(18)	4,530	(100)
1851/55	3,820	(63)			1,413	(23)	226	(4)	146	(2)	495	(8)	6,100	(100)
1856/60	6,582	(75)	429*		1,691	(19)	141	(2)	45	(1)	355	(4)	8,814	(100)
1861/65	4,806	(61)	1,398	(18)	1,090	(14)	210	(3)	20	(0)	340	(4)	7,864	(100)
1866/70	3,663	(65)	812	(14)	1,016	(18)	27	(0)	28	(0)	118	(2)	5,664	(100)
1871/73	4,806	(72)	912	(14)	770	(11)	7	(0)	72	(1)	154	(2)	6,721	(100)

Source: Durant & Co.'s Circular, 1 January 1874, in JMA, PCMR 42.
Notes: (1) Calculated from figures in bales in the original table. Average net weights per bale were as follows: Chinese and Japanese 103 lb, Bengali 150 lb, Persian 75 lb, Brutia 170 lb (200 lb after 1842) and Italian 250 lb (280 lb after 1839). (2) Thrown silk is excluded. (3) *for 1859 and 1860 only.

The chief feature of the year and almost the only feature, was the importation from Japan – a most welcome and seasonable addition to our sources of supply. The only drawback to its advantage is the very small 'breaks' in which it comes forward, but this is comparatively unimportant, and will no doubt be remedied in time. The grand point [is], that it promises to be an increasing supply, and that the nature of the Silk is intrinsically good and much of it of a size to render it especially available.[21]

At first imports of Japanese silk increased rapidly, from 0.6 million lb in 1860 to 2.3 million lb in 1863, by which time it represented 27 per cent of Britain's total raw silk imports. As imports increased, however, it was remarked that 'the quality has not been found equal to the expectations at its early introduction.'[22] Japanese silk became less popular, and it was consequently reported that 'the prices of this class [Japanese silk] show a very large reduction' due to 'less care in the reeling – a greater mixture and greater variation in size of thread in the same skein than formerly'.[23] In fact the maximum price fetched by Japanese silk fell from 31s. in 1860 to 24s. in 1862. Since raw silk prices are generally related closely to quality, it is clear that Japanese silk had lost its golden reputation less than two years from its first importation. A Durant & Co. circular commented, with reference to 1863, that:

In Japan Silk we had happily most opportunely a largely increased supply. The general size and character of this Silk is very available, so that notwithstanding manifest evidence of diminished care in the reeling it continues in great favor, too much confidence must not however be placed on this, as most assuredly it will be displaced by European Silk whenever the supply becomes more abundant unless the Japanese Reelers return to their previous standard of quality.[24]

Despite the continuous suggestions that there was 'ample room for improvement in the sorting and packing' of Japanese silk,[25] there were no signs that this might in fact occur.

Chinese silk imports, Japan's main competitor, consisted chiefly of Tsatlee. This was generally sedentary reeled silk

produced in Chekiang and Kiangsu. In the 1860s Tsatlee was
joined by Taysaam, sedentary-reeled silk produced in other
areas, and in the 1870s by Canton silk. In the same period
Tsatlee accounted for 66 per cent of the total imports of
Chinese silk, which continued to be in demand chiefly for
goods manufactured in France for export to the United
States.[26] When the Taiping Rebellion caused a dramatic decline
in both quality and production, imports to Britain decreased
from 6.8 million lb in 1862 to 2.6 million lb in 1864, and the
Chinese share of total raw silk imports fell to below 50 per
cent.[27] This led to a reciprocal rapid increase in imports of
Japanese silk. It was said that 'the deficiency has to a great extent been supplied from Japan', and therefore that 'Japan silk
continues to be the leading article.'[28] Despite the decline in
quality, Japanese silk was still better than Chinese.

The possibilities for further market expansion of Japanese
silk were to depend on its ability to compete not only with
Chinese and Bengali silk, which were generally of inferior
quality, but also with European silk, which was generally
superior. The overall demand for Asiatic silk was sensitive to
the movements of European silk. Just as the circulars quoted
above had predicted, consumption of the former was reduced
in 1863 owing to 'the abundance and relative cheapness of
European Silk'.[29]

In the second half of the 1860s, annual imports of raw silk
into Britain decreased from an average of 8.1 million lb in the
first half of the 1860s to an average of 5.6 million lb. The market for Japanese silk became restricted, partly because of the
recovery of Chinese and European silk and partly because of
the increased competition between the various types of Asiatic
silk caused by the opening of the Suez Canal in 1869. As a
consequence it was stated that 'Japans and Bengals ... are in
more direct competition with European silk'[30] and neither was
able to expand.

In the 1860s Japanese raw silk was imported into Britain
primarily in the form of hanks. Fine Maebashi was most in
demand, and 'freely bought by manufacturers in place of Italian
silks at a much lower cost.'[31] In the late 1860s, however, complaints about the deteriorating quality of Japanese silk were
still being made. The deterioration was blamed on 'the bad
reeling and the immense export of silkworms' eggs of the best

quality.' If such complaints were loud in 1868 they were deafening in 1869, and in 1870 it was said that 'the effect of the export of 700,000 to 800,000 annual cards [of silkworm eggs] in 1869 was more than ever visible in the deteriorated quality of the silk.'[32] While hanks went out of favour in the late 1860s demand for Ōshū silk grew, owing to its cleanness of thread and regularity of size. Ōshū silk remained in demand on the European market until the late 1870s.[33] This preference for a particular type of raw silk resulted from the fact that fewer silkworm eggs had been exported from Ōshū than from Shinshū (Nagano) and Jōshū (Gunma). Ōshū silk was therefore of comparatively higher quality.[34] In most Japanese silk, however, there was obvious irregularity in the size of thread, leading European buyers to complain bitterly that it could be sold only as waste silk.[35] During the period 1867 to 1869 the average price of Japanese silk on the London market was from 21s. 3d. to 22s. 6d. This was nearly the same as the price fetched by Chinese Taysaam and Bengali silk, and shows that Japanese silk was considered as an alternative to these. Although the best and finest Japanese varieties continued to be in demand, Japanese silk was largely replaced by Chinese silk, which was used for the same purposes, and had been 'almost always neglected'. The medium and lower sorts of Japanese silk were particularly difficult to sell, and stocks became large in the late 1860s.[36]

Figure 3 shows the average price of imported raw silk in the London market from 1860 to 1899. A conspicuous characteristic of Japanese – as opposed to Chinese and Bengali – silk is that there was a wider spread between the highest and lowest price. This implies that the quality of Japanese silk ranged from the very superior to the very inferior. The difference between the highest and lowest prices of Japanese silk became increasingly obvious in the late 1860s. Between 1867 and 1869, while the lowest price of Japanese silk remained stable at 7s., the highest prices fluctuated from 35s. 6d. to 39s. Such disparities in price undoubtedly reflected an underlying deterioration in quality. Even in the early 1870s, when the price of Japanese silk recovered temporarily, it was stated:

[Japanese silk] has been fluctuating heavily from time to time; business has generally had to be forced, and the only

Figure 3 Price Fluctuations of Imported Raw Silk in the London Market, 1860–1899

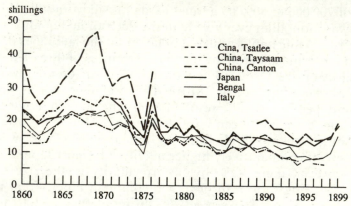

Sources: (1) 1860, 1861: Eaton's Circular. London. 3 Jan. 1862. in JMA. PCMR 41. (2) 1863–5: ibid., 6 Jan. 1865. in JMA. PCMR 41. (3) 1866: *Economist*. Nos 1167–1218. (4) 1867–9: H.W. Eaton & Son's Circular. London. 4 Jan. 1869. in JMA. PCMR 40. (5) 1870: *Economist*. Nos 1376–1427. (6) 1871. 1872: ibid., 4 Jan. 1873. in JMA. PCMR 41. (7) 1873: ibid., 5 Jan. 1874. in JMA. PCMR 41. (8) 1874–99: *Economist*. Nos 1635. 1687. 1740. 1792. 1844. 1896. 1948. 2001. 2053. 2105. 2157. 2209. 2261. 2314. 2366. 2418. 2470. 2522. 2575. 2627. 22679. 2731. 2783. 2835. 2888 and 2940.
Notes: (1) Quotations for 1862. 1865 and 1869 are those on 1 Jan.
(2) After 1874 quotations are for the last whole week of each year. and Japan is represented by Maebashi silk. Bengal by Cossimbuzar silk. and Italy by Milan silk.

moments of activity have been speculative . . . unfortunately, no real consuming demand has stepped in to help this silk, and importers have for months been helpless in a stagnant market.[37]

Japanese Silk in the French Silk Market

The French manufactured silk primarily for export, and by the mid-nineteenth century France had become the world's largest silk-manufacturing country. Lyons was the centre for French silk manufacture. The production of cocoons in Europe was severely hit by the silkworm disease *pebrine*, which first appeared in France in 1840 and spread to Italy in the early 1850s, reaching a peak in the 1860s. French production of cocoons in the areas of Gard, Ardèche, Drôme and Vaucluse decreased dramatically, from 26 million kg in 1853 to only 4 million kg in 1865,[38] and Italy was also severely affected. To cope with this catastrophic fall in cocoon production, both countries introduced high-quality silkworm eggs from Japan. In France, cocoon production recovered to reach 16 million kg in 1866, but after that never again reached even 12 million kg. French production of raw silk accordingly remained stagnant at an annual average of 664,500 kg for 1866–75, 597,200 kg for 1876–85, and 706,800 kg for 1886–95.[39] In Italy, production based on indigenous eggs quickly recovered, increasing from 27 per cent of total Italian cocoon production in 1880 to 50 per cent in 1885 and 84 per cent in 1890. Annual average cocoon production had recovered by the end of the 1860s, but decreased from 48 million kg in the period 1871 to 1875 to 28 million kg in 1875–80, and then remained stagnant at 39 million kg for 1881–90 and 41 million kg for 1891–1900.[40]

After the 1860s France was never able to supply sufficient raw silk to meet growing domestic demand and came to depend significantly on imported raw and thrown silk, particularly raw silk from China and Japan. The rapid rise in raw silk prices caused by *pebrine* and the subsequent increased demand for imported Asian raw silk encouraged manufacturers to move to new, lower-quality fabrics which used cheaper Asian raw silk.[41] Until the mid-nineteenth century France had obtained its foreign raw silk by re-importing through London. The extension of the regular service of Messageries Impériales to Shanghai and Yokohama in 1865 and the opening of the Suez Canal in 1869 had the effect of encouraging some direct imports from East Asia to Marseilles. The raw silk which arrived at Marseilles was mostly from Persia, Bengal, China and Japan. For the period 1862 to 1870, the annual average quantity of Japanese silk inspected at the Lyons Conditioning House amounted to 310,642 kg. This represented 26 per cent of the total of 1,198,753 kg of silk inspected, as opposed to 213,671 kg of French raw silk and 260,379 kg from China.[42]

Up to the late 1870s, however, Chinese and Japanese raw silk was not normally landed at Marseilles. Many shipments for France from Japan were on an arrangement labelled 'Marseilles optional', under which they were ordered on to London or Lyons from Marseilles.[43] The situation regarding Chinese silk was probably the same. Although it is difficult to estimate the volume of re-exports from Marseilles to London, it is thought that large amounts of raw silk were reshipped, exclusively by British vessels, until around 1880.[44] The dependence of French silk merchants on British firms for supplies of East Asian raw silk was by then decreasing, as Lyons began to replace London as the central distribution point and direct imports started from Shanghai. This shift from London to

France was due to the increased facilities granted by French banks for drawing upon goods shipped to France.[45] The new credit system gave fresh direction to silk merchants and Lyons developed from a market for European silk to a market for East Asian silk.[46] Silk merchants in Lyons centralized orders from manufacturers and acted together in purchasing raw silk from Shanghai, Canton and Yokohama. In the mid-1870s more than half of the total silk exports from China was earmarked for direct shipping to France.[47]

Table 4–8 gives details of French imports of raw silk and thrown silk for 1866 to 1895. Total imports increased by 87 per cent while imports of thrown silk, mainly Italian in origin, gradually decreased after the 1870s. Imports of Italian silk gradually decreased after 1880 along with a decrease in thrown silk, so that the significance of Italian raw silk in the French market gradually declined. This was the result of a rapid increase in Italian exports to the United States in the 1880s and of French restrictions on imports of Italian silk imposed in 1888 after the annulment of the French–Italian Treaty.[48] As we have already seen, the decrease in re-exports of raw silk from Britain reflected the central silk market's shift from London to Lyons in the late 1870s. Imports of Chinese silk to France showed a steady increase, taking a market share of nearly 50 per cent, but imports of Japanese silk remained unchanged throughout the 1870s and 1880s, with a market share of around 15 per cent.

Imports of Japanese silk were relatively stagnant in the London market, both in quantity and in the extent of their share, after the sudden increase of 1863. As we have already seen, the deterioration in quality had not been stopped, and Japanese silk was consequently in demand only when Chinese silk was in insufficient supply and poor quality, or there was a poor crop of cocoons in Europe. In 1872 it was noted that Japanese silk temporarily 'occupied a more satisfactory position' due to 'a marked improvement both as regards fineness of size and firmness of thread', so that 'the trade is willing again to employ the finer qualities of this [Japanese] Silk as a substitute for European.' Chinese silk, moreover, deteriorated seriously both in quality and size in 1873: 'in consequence some consumers have been compelled to abandon the use of Chinas in favor of European and best Japan.'[49]

Table 4-8 Annual Averages of Raw Silk and Thrown Silk Imports to France, 1866-95
(in thousand kg)

Year	Raw Silk												Thrown Silk
	China	%	Japan	%	Turkey	%	Italy	%	Britain	%	Total	%	
1866/70	782	(23)	409*	(12)	333	(10)	244	(7)	1,272	(37)	3,451	(100)	1,007
1871/75	1,196	(28)	668	(16)	307	(7)	471	(11)	1,118	(27)	4,205	(100)	1,398
1876/80	2,108	(43)	680	(14)	269	(5)	571	(12)	693	(14)	4,912	(100)	1,332
1881/85	2,091	(42)	638	(13)	363	(7)	1,018	(20)	226	(5)	4,958	(100)	1,077
1886/90	2,700	(49)	786	(14)	473	(9)	961	(17)	167	(3)	5,529	(100)	689
1891/95	2,984	(46)	1,258	(20)	735	(11)	938	(15)	65	(1)	6,444	(100)	431

Sources: France, Direction Générale des Douanes. Tableau Décennal du Commerce de la France, 1857–66 (1869); ibid.. 1867–76 (1878); ibid. 1877–86 (1888); ibid.. 1887–96 (1898).
Note: * for 1867–70.

By the mid-1870s, however, the deterioration in the quality of Japanese silk was widely acknowledged, with a consequent decline in European demand and consumption. In particular, as the production of fine silk recovered both in France and Italy, Japanese silk was driven 'in a great measure out of the European markets' by French and Italian competition, and raw silk exports from Japan fell off accordingly.[50] Although the better classes of Shinshū and Maebashi were most in favour even in the early 1870s, fine-reeled Japanese silk was 'assimilated in a greater degree to French and Italian silk, and consequently . . . suffers proportionately from the disfavour and decline of prices which have attacked the European products.'[51] Japanese silk faced continuous direct competition in the European market from Chinese and Bengali silk up to the mid-1870s, chiefly because of its steady deterioration in quality and the consequent decline in price. In the 1870s its price rose slightly and came between Chinese Tsatlee and Taysaam. In the late 1870s and early 1880s Japanese silk was also affected by the abundant supply of European silk at a cheaper price.

Figure 4 shows the average price of each description of imported raw silk in the Lyons market, using figures for the end of December in each year from 1860 to 1899. Prices as a whole tended to rise up to 1865 after the trough in 1861 and were generally steady up to 1872; but they subsequently declined sharply until 1875. 1876 prices were double those of 1875 due to the poor crop of cocoons in Europe,[52] but declined again towards the end of the century. The price of Japanese hank silk (Maebashi) ranged from 73 to 77 francs in 1862, making it one of the highest-priced raw silks, along with Italian silk. In fact from 1863 to 1867, with the exception of 1864, Maebashi was the highest-priced of all raw silks. Reflecting a deterioration in quality, however, it fell sharply from 100–106 francs in 1868 to 72–75 francs in 1870 and 44–45 francs in 1875. Even so, from 1868 to 1879, Maebashi was second in price only to Italian silk. Ōshū silk was priced at 65–67 francs in 1863, which was slightly higher than Chinese Tsatlee. In 1865, however, it rose to third place behind Maebashi and Italian silk, at 93–94 francs. In 1866 it overtook Italian silk, and rose to 98–101 francs in 1868. In both 1869 and 1870, Ōshū silk was fetching the highest prices in the Lyons silk market. It remained higher than Maebashi even after 1869, when Maebashi prices began to fall.

Figure 4 Price Fluctuations of Imported Raw Silk in the Lyons Market, 1860–99

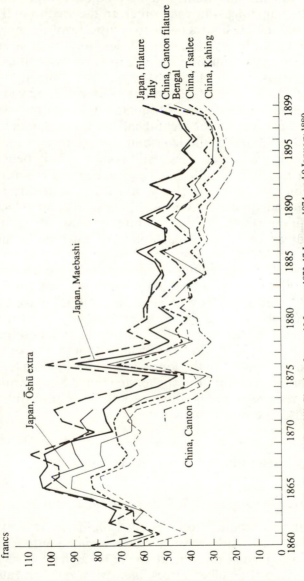

Sources: Arlès-Dufour & Co. (Silk Circular), Lyons, 10 January 1873, 17 January 1874, and 9 January 1880,
in JMA, PCMR 41, 43; Japan, Nōshōmushō, *Yushutsu jūyōhin yōran*, Sanshi (1901), pp. 407–8.
Note: Prices are for 31 December of each year.

In the first half of the 1860s the price difference between types of raw silk was small, and it is possible to argue that they were all competing with each other. In the second half of the 1860s only Italian silk was able to compete with Japanese silk at similar price levels. However, the deterioration in Maebashi quality caused a reduction in price in Lyons as well as in the London market, and Maebashi had to face competition from Chinese and Bengali silk. From the 1870s prices moved generally in parallel, so that the silk market was relatively stable.

As we have seen, as the second half of the nineteenth century proceeded, Japanese silk deteriorated in quality on the European market, although it was still comparatively better than Chinese and Bengali silk. At first it fetched continuously high prices, but these fell towards the mid-1870s, as quality deteriorated. In both quality and price, Japanese silk had to face keen competition from Italian, Chinese and Bengali silk. Possibilities for market expansion were restricted by the stagnation of domestic raw silk production, technological deficiencies in silk reeling, and the consequent decline in quality. Since the use of Japanese hank silk was confined to the weft[53] and supplies were limited, it did not have to be of outstandingly good quality to meet the demands of the market. However, since any real expansion in Japanese raw silk exports to Europe would be difficult without a marked qualitative improvement, in the long run Japan would have to shift its export market from Europe to the United States, which did not yet require a fine quality raw silk. This shift did in fact occur after the mid-1870s.

Silk Exports and the United States Market

The Development of the Silk Industry in the United States

Raw silk was produced on a small scale in the United States from the eighteenth century in Georgia, South Carolina, Pennsylvania and Connecticut. In the 1830s there was a mania for speculation in mulberry trees, *morus multicaulis*, and attempts were made in Pennsylvania and Connecticut to begin sericulture on a large scale. Most of these early undertakings resulted in failure, however, owing to the absence of the necessary sericulture experience, the lack of skilled labour, and the unprofitability of silkworm rearing.[54] Growth in demand for – and consumption of – silk fabrics gradually created a serious shortage of material for silk manufacturers.

Asiatic silk was first brought to the States in 1828, and from 1840 the number of silk manufacturers who used imported raw silk began to increase. Imports of raw silk were estimated at 120,010 lb and 401,385 US dollars in 1850, increasing to 297,877 lb and 1,340,676 US dollars in 1860.[55] Chinese silk was transported to New York via London, but the small quantities of raw silk involved meant that this rather roundabout route did not cause serious difficulties. Imports were promoted by the abolition in 1857 of import duties on directly imported raw silk; and the import duty on Asiatic silk brought via Europe, which had been levied at 10 per cent *ad valorem*, was removed in 1865.[56]

The development of the silk-manufacturing industry in the United States during the period 1850 to 1910 is shown in Table 4–9. Steady development began after the American Civil War (1861–5), and silk manufacturing made relatively greater progress than any other textile sector between 1870 and 1890.[57] Imports of silk manufactures, mainly from France, which were confined to high-quality novelties, hand-made velvets and laces, remained at around 30 million US dollars annually. In contrast, the domestic production of silk goods increased steadily, supplying 56 per cent of the total consumption in 1880 and 78 per cent in 1900.

Table 4–10 shows the distribution by value of silk products between 1875 and 1910. In 1860, 89 per cent of all raw silk was used for sewing silk and twist.[58] The principal products in the 1870s were machine-twist and sewing silk and narrow manufactures like ribbons, laces, upholstery goods and trimmings. In the 1880s and 1890s, however, silk products diversified and the production of broad silk manufactures, especially of plain dress silks, increased rapidly. In 1900, broad silk goods accounted for 62 per cent of total production and 67 per cent of total consumption.[59]

The development of the silk industry in the United States after 1870 was characterized by the introduction and diffusion of the power loom. This spread swiftly and widely, replacing the hand loom in the 1880s and 1890s. The number of power

Table 4-9 Development of the Silk Industry in the United States, 1850–1910
(in thousand US dollars)

Year	Total value of products[1] (A) thousand dollars	Number of establishments	Capital thousand dollars	Capital per establishment thousand dollars	Number of wage-earners[2]	Wage-earners per establishment	Imports of silk piece goods (B) thousand dollars	$\frac{(A)}{(A)+(B)}$ %
1850	1,809	67	678	10	1,723	26	17,640	9
1860	6,608	139	2,927	21	5,435	39	32,726	17
1870	12,211	86	6,231	72	6,649	77	23,904	34
1880	41,033	382	19,125	50	31,337	82	32,189	56
1890	87,293	472	51,008	108	49,382	105	38,686	69
1900	107,256	483	81,082	168	65,416	135	31,129	78
1910	196,912	852	152,158	179	99,037	116	32,888	86

Sources: 1o.1th Census (1880); Eleventh Census (1890); Twelfth Census (1900); Thirteenth Census (1910); USA, Department of Commerce, Statistical Abstract of the United States, for 1910, p. 712.
Notes: (1) Figures include organzine, tram and spun silk yarn, but silk used in other industries is excluded. According to the Thirteenth Census, 'Production in other industries' amounted to 5.8 million US dollars in 1910.
(2) Proprietors, firm members and salaried employees are excluded.

Table 4-10 Distribution of the Value of Products in the United States Silk Industry, 1875–1910 (in thousand US dollars)

Year	Machine-twist & sewing silk[1]	Broad silks		Upholstery goods & trimmings	Ribbons & laces[3]	Braids & bindings[4]	All other products	Total value of products[5]
		Dress goods, figured & plain	Velvets, plushes, etc.[2]					
	%	%	%	%	%	%	%	%
1875	6,463(30)	1,413(7)	2,679(13)	3,991(19)	4,979(23)	383(2)	1,361(6)	21,269(100)
1880	7,009(20)	4,115(12)	3,228(9)	8,307(24)	6,460(19)	1,000(3)	4,401(13)	34,520(100)
1890	8,918(13)	15,183(22)	9,000(13)	12,267(18)	17,343(25)	2,771(4)	3,672(5)	69,155(100)
1900	9,972(10)	52,153(56)	4,960(5)	4,002(4)	19,270(21)	1,523(2)	1,269(1)	92,451(100)
1905	10,146(9)	66,918(56)	4,502(4)	5,797(5)	22,636(19)	3,494(3)	5,228(4)	118,534(100)
1910	10,521(6)	107,881(63)	6,873(4)	5,543(3)	34,096(20)	4,483(3)	4,496(3)	172,256(100)

Sources: US Department of the Interior, *Tenth Census* (1880), 'Report on the Silk Manufacturing Industry of the United States', by W.C. Wyckoff (p.21); *Eleventh Census* (1890), Pt III, 'Silk Manufacturing', by B. Rose (pp. 213, 227); *Twelfth Census* (1900). vol.IX, 'Manufactures', Pt III, 'Silk Manufactures', by F. Allen (pp. 209, 228); *Thirteenth Census* (1909), vol. X, 'Silk Manufactures', pp. 152, 163.

Notes: (1) includes fringes, knitting, embroideries, wash and floss silks. (2) includes tie silks, scarves, tailor's linings, and satin (until 1900). (3) includes nets, veils, and veilings. (4) handkerchiefs and mixed goods. Figures for 1890 include 1,156,172 US dollars for hosiery and knitted goods. (5) Total figures for 1900, 1905, and 1910 are not consistent because of duplication in calculations.

looms increased from 1,251 in 1870 to 5,321 in 1880, 20,822 in 1890 and 44,257 in 1900; hand looms, on the other hand, increased to 3,153 in 1880 but rapidly decreased thereafter: to 1,747 in 1890 and 173 in 1900. In 1880, 63 per cent of all looms were power looms; by 1890 this had risen to 92 per cent. This increase was linked to the rapid development in the production of broad silk goods.[60]

The production of silk manufactures was diversified by location and geographical specialization. The main silk-manufacturing districts were New Jersey, Pennsylvania, New York, Connecticut and Massachusetts. Paterson in New Jersey remained the leading ribbon-manufacturing town throughout the late 1860s and early 1870s. In the 1870s broad silk goods and laces were introduced, and many ribbon manufacturers added the production of the former to the output of their mills. Paterson took advantage of its proximity to the consuming areas on the east coast and the major silk market of New York.[61]

The rapid growth of the silk industry in the United States was facilitated by three main factors. First, there was a high tariff on silk manufactures to protect the infant industry from imported goods. Duties on general silk goods were imposed *ad valorem* until the Dingley Act of 1897. Duties on silk dress piece goods, ribbons and velvets were generally maintained at 60 per cent *ad valorem*. These were reduced to 50 per cent by a tariff revision in 1884, but remained in force until 1897. Duties on some items such as handkerchiefs and laces were increased by the Mackinlay Tariff in 1891. The Dingley Act introduced specific rates, but average duties remained at around 64 per cent.[62] The second favourable factor was the general expansion of the domestic market. This was due to population growth and also to increasing incomes, which led to a rise in living standards. The population was rising at a rate of 26 per cent every ten years between 1860 and 1890: from 31.4 million in 1860 to 62.9 million in 1890.[63] American manufacturers concentrated on producing the medium-grade goods which were most in demand in the domestic market. The last factor was rapid technological improvement in throwing and weaving machinery.

One of the most important improvements in the early stages of the industry was the friction roller for winding, doubling and spinning devised by Nathan Rixford, which was introduced in Paterson around 1838. Among developments in throwing were the double-decking winding frame and doubling frame, which led to economies in space and time. Around 1880 came the introduction of newly-invented automated throwing machinery, which could operate at speed. In the 1890s it was stated that such improvements in throwing machinery had led to savings of about 40 per cent in floor space and of about 20 per cent in production costs, compared with older systems. As early as 1890 spindles were being operated at a speed of 7,500–10,000 revolutions per minute: by 1900 this had risen to 11,000–12,000 revolutions.[64] Developments in weaving included the highly efficient power loom, which was 'equipped with mechanical devices designed for the saving of both time, labor, and material, such as the numerous multipliers, two-weave, leno, swivel, embroidery motions, and many other devices, all arranged to operate automatically'.[65] In silk ribbon production, the high-speed ribbon loom invented in 1889 replaced the Swiss and German power looms. These automatic devices raised productivity two to four times.[66]

Raw Silk Imports into the United States in the 1870s

Asiatic silk was greatly in demand on the American market. Table 4–11 gives the annual average figures for imports of raw silk from 1866 to 1900; prices of each type of imported raw silk are shown in Figure 5. Raw silk imports from Britain, transmitted from London to New York, presumably included both Chinese and Japanese silk. The imperfect reeling of Chinese silk made it unsuitable for ribbon production, which required clean and uniform threads.[67] Since most of the silk industry in the United States was not in a position to use the finer raw silks until the 1880s, Chinese silk was actively in demand. However, as demand increased, shortages and the great distance involved in shipping via London gradually became more of a problem.[68] Moreover, as the power loom became more widely used in the production of broad silk goods in the 1870s, the pattern of raw silk imports began to alter. It was at this stage that Japanese silk began to be imported and to provide serious competition for Chinese silk, which had hitherto been predominant in the American market.

Imports of Chinese silk decreased drastically between 1874

Table 4-11 Annual Average of Raw Silk Imports into the United States, 1866–1900
(in thousand lb)

Year	China	%	Japan	%	Italy	%	France	%	Britain	%	Total	%
1866/70	154	(22.6)	49	(7.2)	–		34	(5.0)	315	(46.2)	682	(100)
1871/75	424	(38.7)	228	(20.8)	1	(0.1)	73	(6.7)	194	(17.7)	1,095	(100)
1876/80	1,007	(53.7)	548	(29.2)	1	(0.1)	157	(8.4)	143	(7.6)	1,874	(100)
1881/85	1,172	(33.4)	1,443	(41.1)	402	(11.5)	408	(11.6)	45	(1.3)	3,507	(100)
1886/90	1,126	(21.7)	2,744	(52.8)	956	(18.4)	264	(5.1)	37	(0.7)	5,193	(100)
1891/95	1,932	(26.9)	3,629	(50.6)	1,223	(17.0)	317	(4.4)	15	(0.2)	7,175	(100)
1896/1900	2,696	(28.7)	4,542	(48.4)	1,782	(19.0)	316	(3.4)	2	(0.0)	9,384	(100)

Source: US Treasury Department, *Commerce and Navigation of the United States,* corresponding years.
Note: Years run from 1 July to 30 June of the next year.

Figure 5 Annual Average Price of Raw Silk Imports into the United States, 1864–1900

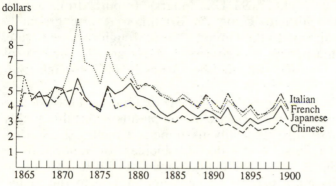

Source: US Treasury Department. *Commerce and Navigation of the United States.* for 1864–1900.

and 1876, but this decrease was compensated by a parallel increase in Japanese silk, which came to hold an important position in the American raw silk market after 1875, if only for a short time. The rapid decrease in imports of Chinese silk into the United States in 1874–6 reflected American silk manufacturers' reluctance to purchase because of the deterioration in quality. Even so, imports of Chinese silk continued in large quantities after 1877, despite continuing complaints about quality. This is firstly because, as Figure 5 shows, Chinese silk remained cheaper than Japanese; secondly because, despite the deterioration in quality, Chinese silk was needed to satisfy the increasing demand from the American industry; and finally because Japanese silk did not maintain a high quality either.[69] In other words, imports of Chinese silk continued because of the failure of Japanese silk to meet the rise in demand created by the rapid growth of the American silk-manufacturing industry.

In the second half of the 1870s, silk from China and Japan accounted for 80 per cent of raw silk imports into the United States. This rapid increase in imports of Asiatic silk into the American market after 1875 was closely related to the completion of the Trans-Continental Railway in 1869. San Francisco had not previously been an important port for raw silk imports, but after this date it was possible for Asiatic silk to be transmitted by rail from the west coast to the silk-manufacturing districts in the eastern states.[70] In 1871 imports of raw silk into San Francisco reached 449,295 lb (2,013,081 US dollars), surpassing imports into New York, which amounted to 343,670 lb (1,827,893 US dollars). Imports from Japan, which had hitherto come via Britain, were also gradually diverted directly to the United States through this new route. During the period 1875 to 1885, on average, 77 per cent of imports of raw silk to the States came through San Francisco.[71]

As with the European market, the first half of the 1870s saw a constant stream of American complaints about the quality of Japanese silk, especially its imperfect reeling.[72] Even so, 1875 and 1876 showed a decisive increase of imports to the United States. This meant that Japanese silk had begun to change its main export market from Europe to the States, which did not require such a fine-quality raw silk.[73] This increase in imports was simply the result of the fact that, however imperfect the reeling, Japanese silk was still of more suitable quality for American silk manufacturers than was Chinese silk. This shift made it likely that raw silk production in Japan would gradually adapt to meet the increasing demand of the American market for quantity, and later for quality as well. In a later section we shall see this happening, after technological developments in filatures in the late 1870s onwards.

The quality indices of Japanese and Chinese raw silk imported into the United States between 1876 and 1900 are shown in Table 4–12. Despite annual variations, the quality of Japanese silk did not reach its 1876–80 level again during the following two decades, while the quality of Chinese silk was consistently below that of Japanese. The high quality index for 1876–80 can probably be attributed to the relatively high quality for the time of the first filatures exported to the States. Imports of Japanese silk rapidly grew in quantity after 1876–80, but it is obvious from the quality indices that the less expensive types of raw silk were increasing. This does not, however, necessarily mean a deterioration in overall quality. Rather, it implies that quality could not improve fast enough to meet the increasingly high standards required by the American silk industry after 1880 as the use of power looms spread.

The types of raw silk most in demand on the American market were filatures and Kakeda. While the European market wanted fine thread of from 11 to 13 deniers, the United States

Table 4-12 Quality Indices of Imported Raw Silk to the United
States, 1876-1900
(Quinquennial average taking 1875 as the basic year)

Periods	Japanese silk	Chinese silk
1876/80	154	134
1881/85	129	115
1886/90	138	128
1891/95	134	116
1896/1900	149	127

Sources: US Treasury Department, *Commerce and Navigation of the United States*, corresponding years; US Department of Commerce, Bureau of the Census, *Historical Statistics of the United States*, Pt I (1975), pp. 200–201.
Note: I have adjusted the price indices of imported raw silk in accordance with the Warren and Pearson wholesale price indices of textile products for 1875–90 and BLS for 1890–1900, as cited in the latter.

was satisfied with coarser thread of from 14 to 18 deniers.[74] It is not possible to know the exact purposes for which Chinese and Japanese raw silk were used. Considering both the respective quantity and quality of imports and the distribution by fabric of silk products, Japanese raw silk was probably used mainly for the warp of narrow silk fabrics, while Chinese was probably used both for the weft of narrow silk fabrics and for sewing silk and machine-twist.[75]

Raw Silk Imports in the 1880s

Japanese silk competed with Chinese silk on the American market throughout the 1870s, but towards the end of the decade competition between European and Japanese silk also became very keen. In 1878, so much European silk was being imported that it became a great influence on the American market. One of the causes of this increase in European silk imports was a decline in prices in the late 1870s and early 1880s which sometimes made it cheaper than Japanese silk. The competition between European and Japanese silk concerned price rather than quality, but the expansion of outlets for the latter was also being undermined by its increasing inferiority.[76]

A modest 'swing back' from Asiatic silk to European silk of superior quality occurred in the early 1880s, when the pattern of raw silk imports began to change both quantitatively and qualitatively. The two principal causes of this 'swing back' were the introduction of new technology for the manufacture of plain silk goods and a change from the hand to the power loom, which required thread of superior quality, uniformity and strength.[77] Imports of raw silk from France increased in the early 1880s, and Italian silk imports increased rapidly after 1883. Japanese silk moved closely with the changing pattern of the American market,[78] imports increasing in line with the rapid increase in European silk and a relative decline in Chinese silk. In 1882, imports of Japanese silk surpassed those of China and thereafter took a position of relative predominance in the American market. In 1887 the Japanese share rose to over 50 per cent. In the 1880s, as a whole, Chinese silk took on average 31 per cent of total American raw silk imports, while Japanese silk took 44 per cent, Italian 13 per cent, and French 9 per cent.

Filatures (13–16 deniers) and re-reels (14–20 deniers) were in most demand on the New York silk market. Low-quality Japanese silk such as Kakeda and other Ōshū types competed with – and were strongly influenced by – Chinese re-reeled Tsatlee from Shanghai.[79] A general feature of Japanese silk was that it ranked between European and Chinese, not only in quality but also in price. The relationship between quality and quantity, which can be found in the figures for the distribution of raw silk imports and the state of the American silk industry, suggests that in the 1880s Italian and French silk was used exclusively for the warp, while Japanese silk was used in almost equal quantities (taking the decade as a whole) for both the warp and the weft;[80] Chinese silk was used mainly for the weft. It would seem that increasing European silk imports, stimulated by the development of the United States silk industry, had reduced Japan's dominance of the warp market and were gradually pushing it over into the weft. Japanese silk came to compete with Chinese silk, and partially ousted it from the weft market.

Raw Silk Imports in the 1890s

Production of broad silk goods had developed considerably in the 1880s. In 1900 such goods had come to occupy 62 per cent of total production by value. As Table 4–11 shows, raw silk imports into the United States continued to increase in both quantity and value throughout the 1890s, maintaining a pattern of imports by country which was on the whole similar to that of the 1880s. The Japanese share was 49 per cent on average in the 1890s, in comparison with Chinese at 28 per cent, Italian at 18 per cent and French at 4 per cent. One new feature in the mid-1890s was that a small amount of Shanghai steam filatures began to be imported for use as the warp.

Imports of Japanese raw silk did not grow in volume, but their value increased because of a sharp rise in export prices. This stagnation should be seen in the context of the rapid increase in imports of Japanese silk piece goods, particularly *habutae*. Imports of Japanese silk fabrics into the United States increased from 1,695,866 US dollars in 1890/1 to 2,804,906 in 1895/6, and 3,421,144 in 1899/1900.[81] The decline in the quality of Japanese hank silk had already been observed in 1880, and as a result its price declined sharply in the mid-1890s.[82] Although American silk manufacturers were demanding superior-quality Japanese silk, it was hardly ever good enough for fine fabrics and was used instead in the coarser grades of silk manufactures.[83]

The decline in the quality of Japanese silk became even more obvious after 1890. A British consular report for 1891 states:

> Japan silk possesses the virtue of strength and of good white colour, but at present is said to be open to the re-proach of 'nibbiness' and irregularity of colour and size, faults which the exercise of greater care in the process of preparation would correct.[84]

Complaints were mainly directed at the re-reels of Gunma and Ōshū, although the filatures of Nagano and Yamanashi were also deteriorating. This deterioration swiftly caused Japanese silk to lose its reputation among American manu-facturers.[85] Its roots lay in the rapid expansion in demand, which meant that reeling and packing had to be performed at speeds faster than the existing equipment allowed, even though techniques in reeling had improved following the development of filatures. In other words, technological development in Japan was unable to keep up with the much faster pace of technological development in the United States. The reason for the decline in quality in the 1890s was therefore completely different from the reason behind the earlier decline of the 1870s, which was the poor quality of the cocoons themselves.

Warnings about the poor quality of Japanese silk and the need for improvement were made repeatedly, and stemmed from a recognition of the constant threat from Italian and Chinese silk.[86] Despite this there were no indications of improvement, and Japan was unable to supply superior silk suitable for the American market. Japanese silk of medium and coarse thread was therefore largely ousted from the warp market to the weft market, from which it in turn expelled Chinese silk. Japanese silk was also used for sewing silk and machine-twist, according to its quality. In the late 1890s it was estimated that only 10 to 20 per cent of Japanese silk was for the warp, European silk and Chinese filatures providing the rest.[87] The reason why Japanese silk was able to remain dominant in the 1890s, despite the keen competition and the decline in quality, was its flexibility in use – since both in quality and price it came in between European and Chinese silk – and the comparatively large quantities available.

The Development of the Silk Industry in Japan

Increase in Production

The emergence of foreign markets and a continuing increase in demand for Japanese silk overseas stimulated the development of the silk industry in Japan, both in production methods and in the adoption of technologies of sericulture and silk reeling. After the opening of the ports, there was a rapid spread in the use of improved reeling machines in the main silk-producing districts such as Fukushima, Gunma and Nagano. Traditional hand reeling machines were gradually replaced by improved sedentary reeling machines, which doubled productivity. Overseas demand for Japanese raw silk was high because of the continuing poor cocoon harvests in the main European silk-producing countries. The consequent rise in raw silk prices naturally encouraged Japanese silk producers to concentrate on the quantitative expansion of production rather than on the maintenance of quality. In the late 1860s, silkworm eggs of the best quality were exported to France and Italy in large quantities. Exports increased to 2,106,171 cards valued at 4,199,138 dollars in 1868.[88] However, this meant that only eggs of inferior quality were left for domestic use; as an inevitable consequence, the quality of Japanese raw silk for export declined. On the European market, this silk which had been produced from inferior-quality cocoons had to face keen competition from European silk which had been produced as a result of the introduction of superior-quality silkworm eggs from Japan. As cocoon production in Europe recovered, the demand for Japanese silkworm eggs rapidly decreased and there was a rapid fall in price. In 1874, 400,000 cards of silkworm eggs originally destined for export had to be destroyed in Yokohama.[89] Apart from the problem of egg quality in the late 1860s, the fundamental reason for the stagnation in demand was that, given the existing technological levels, it was impossible to increase production of raw silk without harming quality.

By the mid-nineteenth century, sericulture was already well developed in the mountainous areas of Japan as a subsidiary industry for farmers. Predictably, cocoon production increased rapidly in line with the increase in raw silk exports. According to the estimates of the silk guild in Edo, after the opening of the ports the annual production of raw silk in Japan doubled to 40,000 bales (1,360,000 kg), three-quarters of which were for export, the remainder being for domestic use. Since total raw silk production in 1874 was recorded at 377,000 kan (1,414,000 kg), however, it would seem that production was stagnant throughout the 1860s and early 1870s.[90]

In 1868, European and American silk merchants asked the Yokohama General Chamber of Commerce to communicate with Japanese silk merchants and producers about the deterioration in the quality of Japanese raw silk. They complained about various defects including false trade labels, bad winding, irregularity of size and thread, dirtiness, a lack of strength, and the weight and irregularity of the paper ties. They went on:

> the disease of the silkworms has diminished the silk crops of some countries of Europe. For this reason foreigners have paid for the Japan silks high prices as long as they were good; but now they are neglected by the manufacturers on account of their inferiority. The disease of the silkworms cannot last for ever; when it is cured, can foreigners be expected to buy bad silk in Japan whilst they produce good silk in their own countries?[91]

Introduction of Western-style Filatures

Both the private and public sectors saw the improvement of raw silk quality as an urgent task; they therefore embarked on attempts to establish modern Western-style filatures. Thus in 1870 the Maebashi domain, aided by C. Müller, a Swiss engineer, established an Italian-style filature in the hope of solving its financial difficulties through exports of the famous Maebashi hank silk.[92] In 1871 Ono-gumi, a wealthy city merchant house, employed Müller to set up the Tsukiji Filature in Tokyo. Unfortunately both these trials had to be abandoned after a couple of years, due to various managerial failures. However, all was not lost. The reeling machines of the Tsukiji Filature were transferred to the Miyamada Filature in Nagano, and many female reelers went to the Nihonmatsu Filature in Fukushima.

The Meiji government was also seriously concerned about the declining reputation of Japanese silk on the European market. In 1872 the Tomioka Filature was founded in Gunma by the Ministries of Home Affairs and Finance as a pilot firm, to improve the quality of Japanese silk. Total expenditure for its establishment reached 200,000 yen. The Tomioka Filature, operated under the supervision of Paul Brünat and other French instructors,[93] was equipped with French reeling machines and had 300 basins with steam power for killing chrysalises and boiling cocoons. In 1873 the Italian-style Kankōryō Filature, with twenty-four basins, was founded by the Ministry of Industry for the purpose of diffusing silk-reeling technologies. However, this had to be transferred to private ownership in the following year due to managerial inadequacies. The establishment of both these filatures was clearly a government-level response to the deterioration in the quality of Japanese raw silk.

These Western-style filatures were initially introduced without regard to conditions in the Japanese industry. It was therefore natural that they should fail in the face of managerial inefficiency and difficulties in supplying suitable cocoons and in finding skilful reelers.[94] With the exception of the Tomioka Filature, they were all either closed or transferred to other owners before completing three years of operation. Even the Tomioka Filature was not profitable; its operational losses up to mid-1876 amounted to 187,000 yen.[95] However, it cannot be denied that these trials encouraged silk producers through the diffusion of improved methods and technologies in machine reeling. Local silk manufacturers either visited the filatures themselves or sent their reelers, and were anxious to employ female reelers who had been trained in the filatures.

In the following years the silk industry developed, aided by institutional and financial support from the government. The government held competitive exhibitions and fairs, which played an important role in improving the quality of raw silk and in encouraging production. It also dispatched government officials to Italy to study sericulture and silk-reeling technology, and established experimental institutions and schools to teach new techniques. Regulations to form a Silk Inspection House were issued in 1873, partly to establish a new system for delivering raw silk from the producing districts to Yokohama under the control of Yokohama export merchants. The preface to these regulations emphasized the declining reputation of Japanese silk in overseas markets brought about by the deterioration in quality, and the urgent need to cope with this matter as soon as possible:

> silk culture is an industrial pursuit of the highest importance to this Empire [Japan], and it is not only profitable to the persons engaged in it, but also contributes largely to the increase of national wealth.

However, the regulations met with fierce opposition from local silk producers and had to be abolished in 1877. Throughout the 1870s the government circulated and issued notifications and regulations concerning the sericulture and silk reeling industries.[96] This suggests that it was in fact unable to gain effective control of the development of the silk industry at a private level. Indeed, its failure to improve quality eventually led to a further decline in the competitiveness of Japanese silk on the European market.

Response to the Increasing Demand in the American Market

The emergence after 1870 of the United States in addition to France as a major silk-manufacturing country provided a favourable opportunity for Japanese silk to find a temporary solution to increasing competition in Europe by shifting its export market to that country. The increase in demand for raw silk in the States thus made it possible for Japanese silk of a medium and coarse type of thread, which faced keen competition on the European market due to the deterioration in quality, to find a ready market. This change in the overseas market stimulated domestic raw silk production for export to the United States without requiring drastic changes in production methods. On average 64 per cent of annual domestic raw silk production between 1878 and 1899 was directed to exports.

Table 4-13 shows the production of all types of cocoons and raw silk in the main producing prefectures such as Fukushima, Gunma and Nagano from 1876 to 1900. The increase in cocoon production was facilitated by the spread of double cropping, and the quality of cocoons was raised through improving the mulberry trees and the introduction of more scientific breeding methods. The average annual growth rate of cocoon production was 14.4 per cent for 1876–80, −0.9 per cent for 1881–90, and 6.4 per cent for 1891–1900; that of raw silk production was 15.1 per cent, 9.5 per cent, and 5.4 per cent respectively.[97] The production of both cocoons and raw silk rapidly increased until 1880; in the 1880s raw silk production continued to rise, but cocoons experienced a negative growth rate. The cocoon/raw silk ratio rapidly decreased until 1885–90, but remained constant after that time. This data suggests that the increase in raw silk production up to 1880 was probably sustained by the expansion in cocoon production and that the increase in raw silk production in the 1880s was due to a rise in productivity through improvements either in silk-reeling technology or in cocoon quality. In the 1890s, as in the period until 1880, the increase in raw silk production was due to the increase in cocoon production.

The silk reeling industry developed rapidly, but there were regional differences. Two major patterns can be discerned in the response to expanding overseas demand: in the old silk-producing districts, such as Gunma and Fukushima, raw silk production was increased without any fundamental change in either sedentary or hand reeling methods, simply through unifying the re-reeling and/or finishing processes; in relatively new silk-producing districts such as Nagano, however, production methods were changed from traditional sedentary reeling to filature.

The silk reeling industry in the Fukushima district had originally developed as a putting-out system controlled by local city merchants, and the traditional hand and sedentary reeling methods were used.[98] The produce of this district, generally known as Kakeda silk, continued to remain in fair demand on the European market until the late 1870s despite thickness problems, owing to its cleanness of thread and regularity of size. Production methods did not change even after the opening of the ports, and sedentary reeling remained until as late as around 1910. It is said that in about 1890 95 per cent of Fukushima raw silk was produced by this reeling method, mainly using manual power. From the late 1880s, joint packing factories were founded to control the quality of silk on its collection, prior to being taken to Yokohama by local silk merchants. Joint factories for the finishing process were operated either by silk merchants or by producers, the process varying from unification of re-reeling and packing to the packing process only. However, Fukushima silk could not adjust its production methods to meet the overseas demand for better quality. It eventually lost competitiveness on overseas markets and became of significance for domestic use rather than as an export.

In Gunma, the silk reeling industry had developed since the early nineteenth century as a small-scale household industry under a putting-out system. In the town of Maebashi and its vicinity (formerly the Maebashi domain) the system

Table 4-13 Cocoon and Raw Silk Production in Japan,
1876–1900 (in thousand kg)

Cocoon

Year	Fukushima	Gunma	Nagano	Saitama	Gifu	Yamanashi	Total (with others)	Area of mulberry plantation mil. acres
1876	1,176	891	1,169	479	756	427	7,291	n.a.
1880	1,268	2,237	2,638	n.a.	1,093	743	14,418	n.a.
1885	3,697	3,278	4,522	1,577	2,286	1,601	32,984	17.2*
1890	4,614	4,639	6,956	2,948	2,580	1,913	44,292	24.4
1895	6,804	7,919	18,429	6,486	5,143	3,860	85,321	26.6
1900	7,618	10,309	16,009	7,652	4,469	3,950	104,051	30.1

Table 4-13 continued

Raw Silk

Year	Fukushima	Gunma	Nagano	Saitama	Gifu	Yamanashi	Total (with others) (A)	Exports (B)	(B)/(A)
1876	144	205	147	42	67	85	1,238	1,127	91
1880	232	446	245	n.a.	107	127	2,014	884	44
1885	256	609	273	114	70	136	2,441	1,486	61
1890	392	656	941	231	187	240	4,396	1,276	29
1895	642	1,549	1,892	403	330	411	8,689	3,514	40
1900	623	1,580	1,786	457	403	408	9,426	2,801	30

Sources: Calculated from Nōshōmushō, *Nōsan-hyō*, for 1876, 1880, and *Nōshōmu tōkei-hyō*, for 1885, 1890, 1895 and 1900; *Nihon bōeki seiran*, p. 55.
Note: * Estimate.

was under the control of privileged silk merchants; in other areas it was controlled by wealthy farmers who were themselves cocoon raisers.[99] With the commencement of foreign trade demand for silk from this district rapidly increased, helped by its proximity to Yokohama. Prices rose sharply, and silk merchants and local silk producers began to expand their production and transactions. Raw silk from Gunma was known as Maebashi or as hanks, and featured prominently among the various raw silks for export. With the sudden increase in overseas demand silk reeling techniques in Gunma improved and the sedentary reeling method replaced low-productivity hand reeling.

From the late 1870s silk manufacturers, worried by the stagnation in exports caused by the deterioration in quality, began to form their own associations and set up joint factories for re-reeling, to produce large quantities of silk with size regularity. In other words, the silk industry in this area developed not through the establishment of Western-style filatures but by improving traditional production methods. In the Maebashi area the silk merchants were by this time operating small-scale factories as well as the putting-out system. They formed associations such as the Kōshin-sha, the Tengen-sha and the Shōryū-sha. In other areas, farmers who were producing silk on a small family basis founded joint factories such as the Usui-sha, the Shimonida-sha and the Kanraku-sha for the same purpose. These associations consisted generally of several small divisions. Re-reeling was performed by each division, and only the packing was done by the association as a whole. In both cases, re-reeling and finishing were conducted under strict examination in order to sort and maintain quality.

Despite such improvements, there were complaints from the American market around 1890 about the poor quality of re-reels. This was reflected in demands for silk manufacturers in re-reel producing districts such as Gunma to improve their methods of production immediately. In the event, rather than respond to such demands, the Maebashi silk market gradually became domestic- rather than export-orientated.[100]

The Development of Filatures in Nagano

In the Nagano district, the silk reeling industry had developed as a household industry under a putting-out system. The opening of the ports had a great impact and in the early 1860s the improved sedentary reeling method was introduced from Gunma, spreading rapidly and widely into the small-scale factories. The centre of production shifted from the north of the district – from areas such as Ueda, which produced mainly sedentary raw silk – to the central and southern parts such as the Suwa area, which produced filatures. In this area, for example, several middle-sized independent farmers expanded their silk production, employing seasonal labourers in their own small factories. Central and southern Nagano were in fact to play a crucial role in Japanese silk exports in the late nineteenth and early twentieth centuries.[101]

As we saw earlier, from the late 1860s better-quality silk-worm eggs began to be exported to France and Italy. Sericulture was carried out by peasant families in addition to rice culti-vation. Mulberry trees were planted on surplus land unsuitable for other agricultural purposes and double cropping spread widely and rapidly. As the mulberry leaves were more suitable for the silkworms which emerged from spring cocoons than for those from summer and autumn cocoons, however, the raw silk produced from summer and autumn cocoons was inferior. Summer–autumn cocoons were reared at a time when no labour was needed for rice planting, and enabled sericulture peasants to increase their cocoon pro-duction. Since the better-quality silkworm eggs obtained from spring cocoons were destined for export, however, only the inferior quality eggs from the summer–autumn cocoons remained for use in domestic silk production.[102] In the late 1870s, when exports of silkworm eggs rapidly decreased, spring cocoons also came to be reeled for export.

The first filature in Nagano was the Italian-style Miyamada Filature established in Suwa in 1872 by Ono-gumi, the merchant house which had set up the Tsukiji Filature the year before. Under the influence of the Miyamada Filature, local silk manufacturers started to found filatures on a small scale. Unfortunately almost all the filatures established in Nagano in the first half of the 1870s failed, mainly due to difficulties in raising sufficient capital, the inexperience of the reelers, and problems in obtaining and preserving cocoons. The establish-ment of Nakayama-sha in 1875, however, marked a turning point. Nakayama-sha operated under a factory system, adapt-ing Western techniques to indigenous economic conditions.

The reeling machine was a mixture of the Italian and French styles, called 'Suwa-type', which utilized cheaper, domestically-made wooden or wood-and-metal machines, and ceramic basins instead of iron ones. In addition, it operated on water power rather than on steam. These modifications made it possible for manufacturers to start operating with only a small capital outlay.

From the late 1870s, the increase in demand from the United States, which required quantity rather than quality, encouraged the growth of the Japanese silk industry. The poor cocoon crop in Europe, and a rise in raw silk prices in 1876, promoted the establishment of a large number of small-scale filatures each equipped with under 30 basins, many operating only from mid-June to late October or early November each year. They were, however, considerably affected by a subsequent rapid fall in raw silk prices. From 1877 small silk manufacturers began to form associations, such as the Tōkō-sha and the Kaimei-sha, for joint delivery to Yokohama in order to mitigate the effects of price fluctuations. The number of filatures employing over ten reelers increased, from 60 in 1876 to 361 in 1879, 340 of which were equipped with less than 50 basins. The number of producers' associations increased from 45 in 1885 to 116 in 1890. These associations also functioned as units for obtaining loans from export merchants in Yokohama.[103]

From the early 1880s, silk export merchants in Yokohama started financing not individual producers but associations of producers, by making forward charges of documentary bills and sometimes giving loans for silk even without such documentary bills. From the 1880s, merchants also began to make advances to producers to help provide the large amounts of capital needed around June to purchase the new cocoons which were appearing on the market. Local banks started financing the silk producers in their districts as well. Export merchants had difficulty in providing sufficient funds from their own financial resources. In order to loan to producers at a favourable interest rate, they usually borrowed from their banks in Yokohama by discounting promissory notes which they had received from producers. Banks in Yokohama, such as the Yokohama Specie Bank, obtained funds for this in turn from the Bank of Japan, by rediscounting bills of exchange which they had discounted for export merchants. Until around 1905, local producers were financed for around 80 per cent of the estimated sales value of raw silk. The loans supplied by local banks were financed directly by the Bank of Japan through the head office, or its local branches, by rediscounting these same bills. In 1889, when government financial support for the foreign exchange business of the Yokohama Specie Bank was withdrawn, the Bank of Japan started to supply capital to the Yokohama Specie Bank by rediscounting foreign bills of exchange. This organized credit system under guarantee from the Bank of Japan not only solved the problem of insufficient capital accumulation but also prevented the further encroachment of foreign capital into the domestic market.[104]

The rapid development of filatures from the late 1870s onwards was helped by several favourable domestic factors: the advance in commercialization, the large Tenryū River, which provided a convenient source of water power, an abundant female labour force from neighbouring agricultural areas in the deflationary period of the early 1880s, the appearance of many innovative silk manufacturers, and the increase in cocoon production through the introduction of double cropping. A major additional factor was probably the availability of finance from export merchants in Yokohama. Silk manufacturers were able to devote their own capital to the expansion of production, as they could use loans from export merchants to purchase cocoons.

Filatures were exported to the United States, albeit in small quantities, 'to supplement the shortage of European silk'.[105] Silk manufacturers were anxious to introduce simple reeling machines in order to increase production and meet the rapidly increasing demand. They paid little attention to quality, such as regularity in size and strength of thread.[106] However, as power looms were widely used in the States, both regularity in size and strength of thread became necessary, if exports to that market were to be increased.

Nagano responded quickly to the increasing demand from the States. From the mid-1880s joint re-reeling factories, such as the Hirano-sha and the Ryūjō-kan, were established to produce large quantities of standardized silk at a reduced cost and under strict quality control. Steps were also taken to improve cocoon quality. In the mid-1880s courses on silk-worm-rearing and on methods of inspecting eggs and elimi-nating diseases were frequently held in various places throughout Nagano. The local authorities energetically pro-moted improvements in quality through microscopic exami-nation of silkworm eggs and the plantation of special mulberry trees for summer and autumn cocoons. Nagano stood out from the other main cocoon-producing districts because of its high ratio of summer and autumn cocoons to total cocoon production. For the period 1886 to 1890 spring cocoons took 61 per cent of the total cocoon production in Nagano, while summer cocoons took 27 per cent and autumn cocoons 7 per cent. In contrast, over the same period, the corresponding figure for spring cocoons was 81 per cent in Gunma and 88 per cent in Fukushima. The figure for spring cocoons in Nagano decreased further, to 52 per cent for 1891–5 and 50 per cent for 1896–1900.[107]

Since summer and autumn cocoons were inferior in quality to spring cocoons, increases in total raw silk production did not necessarily mean that quality had been improved. In fact, the general quality of Japanese silk remained below the 1876–80 level throughout the last two decades of the nineteenth century (Tables 4–4 and 4–12). This situation led Nagano silk manu-facturers to start purchasing better-quality cocoons from out-side Nagano – after 1890, sometimes even from China – and to establish silk-reeling factories in districts which were closer to good-quality cocoons.

Table 4–14 shows the development of the silk-reeling industry in the Suwa district, which continued to be a major centre of filatures, accounting for 30 per cent of total raw silk production in Nagano. In the decade after 1885 raw silk production in Suwa grew by a factor of as much as 8.5. This was linked to an increase in the number of basins and in the production per basin. There was a 6.1 increase in the former and a 1.4 increase in the latter during that decade. Since the general quality of summer and autumn cocoons in particular improved only after 1900, the increase in raw silk production was probably due to the rise in productivity in the reeling pro-cess. Methods of drying and storing cocoons improved, and cocoons were carefully selected for either export or domestic use. Various improvements were also introduced in reeling

Table 4-14 Development of the Silk Reeling Industry in the Suwa District, Nagano, 1876–1900

Year	No. of basins (in 100 basins)	No. of workers (in 100 workers)	Raw silk production (in 1000kg)	Production per basin (in kg)	Average annual working days (in days)	Average daily wage of a female reeler (in sen)	Average daily production per female reeler (in g)	Average production costs per picul (in yen)	Average filature silk price per picul (in yen)	Ratio of Suwa out of the total production in Nagano (in %)
1876	n.a.	n.a.	n.a.	n.a.	115	n.a.	103[1]	151[2]	n.a.	n.a.
1880	14[3]	16[3]	25[3]	18[3]	143	10.5	139[3]	172	n.a.	7.0[3]
1885	22	26	67	30	198	11.0	146[4]	124[5]	645	24.9
1890	73	86	263	36	211[6]	12.0	203	n.a.	650	28.2
1895	135	151	576	43	n.a.	10.0	263	117[7]	830	30.7
1900	110	120	553	50	225	20.0	n.a.	144	1,068	31.2

Sources: Hiranomura Yakuba (ed.), *Hirano sonshi*, vol. 2, pp. 480–1, 483–6; Eguchi and Hidaka (eds), *Shinano sanshigyō-shi*, vol. 3, pp. 1138–9, 1340–1.

Notes: (1) for 1874 (2) for 1877 (3) for 1881 (4) for 1884 (5) for 1883 (6) for 1889 (7) for 1896.

instruments such as boiling basins. Steam power was used for boiling cocoons, and water power for revolving reels.[108] However, since the reeling process itself was not mechanized and therefore depended on the manual skill of female reelers, the increase in production would not have been possible without an intensification of their labour. The average number of working days per year increased to about 200 in the early 1880s and the number of working hours in each day, including meals and intervals, grew from twelve to thirteen in the mid-1880s.[109] The average daily production of the individual reeler steadily increased. If we take the average daily production of 1884 as 100, this had risen to 139 in 1890 and to 180 in 1895, but the average real wage over the same period remained roughly the same.[110]

The export price of silk was decided in accordance with prices in the international market, and export prices in turn determined the price of both cocoons and raw silk for domestic use. The decrease in production costs – excluding purchasing cocoons – in the 1880s was probably attained by both establishing joint re-reeling factories and maintaining labourers' wages. The cost of purchasing cocoons accounted for 70-80 per cent of the total production costs. The fact that cocoon prices were fairly stable in the late 1880s and early 1890s therefore worked greatly in favour of Suwa silk manufacturers. This is further demonstrated by the fact that as exports of raw silk increased, producers became more and more interested in trying to purchase cocoons at lower prices to make production profitable. It can therefore be said that it was low cocoon prices, as well as technological developments in sericulture and silk reeling, which made it possible for Japanese silk to increase its competitiveness on the international market. Since wages for female workers constituted only 4–5 per cent of total costs, the importance of low wage labour should not be allowed to overshadow the role of low cocoon prices.[111]

I do not want to deny the significance of low-wage female labour entirely. The reeling processes for finding the beginning of filaments and joining them were performed by female reelers until the mid-1920s, when reeling machines with joining apparatus became widely used; the quality of raw silk therefore depended upon their skill. Female workers were drawn from poor neighbouring agricultural districts and were aged mainly from sixteen to twenty-two. They usually spent one to three years in unhealthy working and living conditions under strict supervision, staying at company dormitories. They worked for over thirteen hours a day in the summer season, with only a thirty-minute break, and were paid on a differential wage scale with reward and penalty points, their wages being decided by the amount and fineness of the raw silk they reeled.[112]

The increase in productivity was therefore clearly linked to the intensification of the female reelers' labour, which seemed to have reached its maximum by the mid-1890s. The need for even further labour intensification resulted in a deterioration in the quality of raw silk for export and in fierce competition among silk manufacturers to employ more skilled reelers. As a consequence, female reelers from outside Nagano began to be employed. Linked to the shortage of skilled labour in the 1890s there was a halt in the rapid development of filatures which had been taking place since the mid-1870s. In sericulture, however, alongside further improvements in cocoon quality through strict selection of eggs, mulberry trees suitable for summer and autumn silkworms were introduced.

In the late 1890s, several large-scale silk manufacturers such as the Katakura-gumi, the Oguchi-gumi, the Yamajū-gumi, the Yamaichi Hayashi-gumi and the Ozawa-gumi began to operate their filatures independently of the silk manufacturers' associations. Their activities were made possible by the availability of production funds, mainly for purchasing cocoons, supplied by export merchants who did not require bills of exchange. Several producers were therefore able to invest all their own profits into the expansion of their factories and the adoption of further improved reeling machines which operated on steam power.[113] In 1894, for the first time filatures were responsible for producing more silk than sedentary machines.[114]

Table 4–15 shows the results of a survey into the silk-reeling factories of Japan carried out at the turn of the century, and Table 4–16 puts the Japanese situation into an international comparative perspective. From around 1905 a different type of silk manufacturer – who wanted to produce export silk of a superior, fine quality of thread – emerged alongside the established type of silk manufacturer, who produced silk of ordinary quality and concentrated on expansion of output or

Table 4-15 Japan's Silk Reeling Industry in 1900

	Nagano			Gunma			Fukushima			Total (with others)		
	F	S	Total	F	S	Total	F	S	Total	F	S	Total
No. of factories by scale:												
10–49 reelers	195	23	218	38	58	96	13	27	40	1,269	404	1,673
50–99	66	0	66	14	33	47	11	1	12	523	43	566
100–499	59	0	59	5	107	112	5	25	30	262	136	398
over 500	11	1	12	1	5	6	0	3	3	18	14	32
Total	331	24	355	58	203	261	29	56	85	2,072	597	2,669
No. of basins	32,336	2,370	34,706	2,813	29,925	32,738	1,713	12,613	14,328	122,166	55,022	177,188
No. of female reelers	32,813	2,410	35,225*	3,019	32,271	35,290	1,637	12,972	14,609	117,861	58,045	175,906
Cocoon consumption (in thousand koku)	380	3	383	20	90	110	11	28	39	1,086	75	1,261
Raw silk produced (in thousand kin)	2,202	20	2,222	177	545	722	64	156	220	6,222	1,031	7,253
Waste silk produced (in thousand kin)	469	9	477	56	157	212	19	47	66	1,408	285	1,693
Raw silk produced per basin (in kin)	68	9	–	63	19	–	37	12	–	48	27	–

Table 4-15 *continued*

Production costs per 100 kin (in yen)	144	108	-	136	130	-	142	124	-	156	129	-
Power for reeling:												
Steam			40			7			8			965
Water			270			7			21			786
Manual			45			216			56			918
Total			355			230*			85			2,669
Method for boiling cocoons:												
Steam			301			30			25			1,612
Charcoal			54			231			60			1,057
Total			355			261			85			2,669

Source: Nōshōmushō, Nōmukyoku, *Zenkoku seishi kōjō chōsa-hyō*, for 1900 (1902).
Notes: (1) F: Filature, S: Sedentary reeling. (2) * Totals are inconsistent, but this stems from inconsistencies in the original figures.

Table 4-16 Comparison of Silk Reeling in Italy, China, and Japan (filatures only)

	Italy	China	Japan
1) Daily production per operative	400–500 g (14.1–17.6 oz.)	310–400 g (11–14 oz.)	225–375 g (8.0–13.4 oz.)
2) Wages	19.3–21.2 cents	13–18 cents	7.5 cents
3) Working hours	11–12	10–	12–15
4) Annual working days	250–280	60	250
5) Cocoons needed to produce 1 kg of raw silk	10–12 kg	16–17 kg	14 kg

Source: 'Sericulture in Italy, China, and Japan', in US Department of Commerce and Labor, Bureau of Statistics, No. 296, *Monthly Consular Reports* (May 1905).
Notes: (1) Figures for Italy are for Lombardy. (2) Figures for China are for Chekiang.

on the improvement of existing silk reeling technologies. The new type aimed to compete with Italian fine-thread silk by using improved silk reeling machines, by going over to electric power to reduce production costs, and by making exclusive contracts with producers to be sure of obtaining good-quality cocoons. Such manufacturers, however, were rare.[115] According to the statistics available for 1905, 67 per cent of all filatures in Japan had fewer than ten reelers; furthermore, nearly all the 355,000 factories operating for the domestic market according to the traditional sedentary reeling method also had fewer than ten reelers.[116] The fact that only 10–20 per cent of the raw silk delivered to the Yokohama market was transferred back to the domestic sector seems to imply that raw silk for export had a market system largely separate from that for domestic use.[117]

The Silk Trade and the Transportation of Silk

So far I have concentrated on factors affecting Japanese silk exports and their overseas markets. To complete this account of the silk trade, I shall now examine external marketing and transportation.

Table 4–17 shows the amounts of raw silk shipped by Western and Japanese merchants respectively. Western merchants had a position of overwhelming predominance, and even in 1900 handled two-thirds of the silk trade. Exports by Japanese merchants increased after the late 1890s, with the aid of institutional changes such as the abolition of the treaty port system in 1899. Mitsui Bussan Kaisha and Kiito Gōmei Kaisha were the two largest Japanese shippers, but not until 1912 did Japanese merchants come to handle over half of all silk for export. Western merchants gradually lost their power in the silk business, but the export and transaction system remained unchanged. In other words, powerful Japanese merchants – Mitsui Bussan in particular – took over where Western merchants had left off.[118]

Silk was purchased by Western merchants either directly from producers or indirectly from Japanese export merchants, most silk for export coming via the latter route. The general pattern of silk marketing in Yokohama was as follows. Raw silk was delivered from the producing district by the producers themselves or through local consignors to export merchants in Yokohama. These were Japanese commission agents who undertook to sell to Western merchants. This was the only way local producers without knowledge of the international market could export their product. Raw silk for export was entrusted either to Japanese export merchants at Yokohama, who then went to Western firms, or directly to export merchants specializing in silk. Among these were both Japanese and Westerners. The former, indirect, route was, however, the more frequent. Local producers drew documentary bills through local banks on their export merchants in Yokohama and were financed for about 70 per cent – sometimes over 80 per cent – of the estimated selling value. Export merchants received the silk dispatched by local producers and were able to take the parcels of raw silk to their godowns on settling bills of exchange with interest. Local producers could either give export merchants complete discretion over the time of selling and the price, or could attach conditions. In practice, however, the former method was most common.

Prices of silk were first negotiated between Western mer-

Table 4-17 Raw Silk Exports by Western and Japanese Merchants,
1875-1920 (in thousand lb)

Year	Western	%	Japanese	%	Total	%
1875	1,522	(100)	–		1,522	(100)
1880	2,310	(86)	368	(14)	2,678	(100)
1885	2,886	(88)	390	(12)	3,276	(100)
1890	2,516	(89)	298	(11)	2,814	(100)
1895	6,499	(84)	1,248	(16)	7,747	(100)
1900	3,738	(67)	1,836	(33)	5,574	(100)
1905	6,125	(64)	3,423	(36)	9,548	(100)
1910	10,555	(54)	8,990	(46)	19,545	(100)
1915	9,051	(38)	14,924	(62)	23,975	(100)
1920	4,408	(20)	17,319	(80)	21,727	(100)

Sources: Ōkurashō, *Shōkyō nenpō*, for 1875 and 1880; Ōkurashō, *Dainihon gaikoku bōeki nenpyō*, for 1885, 1890, 1895; Fujimoto Jitsuya, *Kaikō to kiito bōeki* (1939), vol. 2, pp. 380–2.

chants and Japanese export merchants on the basis of samples. Once a price had been agreed, Western merchants took all the raw silk which they intended to purchase to their godowns, without remitting any payment or issuing any documents. This was only a preliminary to the actual transaction. Japanese merchants could not obtain a sale until quality inspection, weight measurement, and other procedures had been completed. After the export merchants had received their remittances – either in cash or in bills of exchange – they would pay the local producers after first making deductions from the bills for interest, commissions and for other expenses.[119]

The number of raw silk export merchants in Yokohama ranged from twenty to forty, the speculative nature of the trade making bankruptcies frequent. Hara Zenzaburō, Mogi Sōbei, Shibusawa Sakutarō and Ono Mitsukage were the four biggest merchants, handling between them 60–70 per cent of the raw silk sold after the late 1880s. After the mid-1890s they began to own large-scale silk filatures, but since the amount of raw silk produced in their own filatures remained small in comparison to the total silk they handled, they were still dependent on their commission.[120]

Western sources frequently complain about the 'immorality' of Japanese silk merchants, mentioning various illicit methods of bringing bales of silk up to the required weight.[121] On the other hand, Japanese sources emphasize the way in which Western merchants took advantage of the protection offered by extraterritoriality to trick and defraud Japanese merchants.[122] For example, Western merchants frequently held silk in their godowns for several days – sometimes more than ten – before inspecting it, while they waited for favourable market quotations. If they received good news of the overseas market they would complete the remaining procedures and purchase the silk. If market prospects were dull, however, they would cancel the purchase on the pretext of finding faults in the silk. Again, when a Western merchant wanted to purchase 500 bales of raw silk, he might promise at first to buy 800 bales. After taking the 800 into his godown, he would use them as security to gain finance from foreign banks, and then cancel the 300 which he did not really want. Since it was the Japanese export merchants who had to bear all the expense involved in transportation to and from godowns, they suffered heavy losses from any cancellation. When Japanese merchants made accusations of dishonesty in such cases, they were often threatened with violence. Western merchants also used various means to defraud Japanese merchants in the measuring of silk.

In addition, it was reported to be customary for Western merchants exporting silk to the United States to employ the following complicated tactics in order to make large profits through price manipulation. They would first send a circular to their American customers, advising them to abstain from purchasing Japanese silk as there was a sign that prices would fall in the near future. Manufacturers in the States would follow their suggestion and suspend purchases. When Yokohama was informed of the inactivity of the American market, Japanese merchants would start to sell their silk at even lower prices. Western merchants would gradually buy up silk, and then produce artificially high prices on the Yokohama market by getting their American agents to send telegrams to Japan stating that demand in the United States was rising again. Western merchants would then purchase some silk at a relatively high price to raise quotations for Japanese silk, and send tele-

grams to the States saying that prices were rising. Thinking
that prices would soon shoot up, American manufacturers
would hastily order from Western merchants at current high
Japanese prices. Finally, Western merchants would sell the
silk which they had bought cheaply to American manufacturers, charging the latter a relatively high price.[123]

Such practices must have been common, although it would
be misleading to give the idea that they were typical of the silk
trade as a whole. In any case, they inevitably provoked a reaction. In the early 1880s the government began to develop a
policy of encouraging direct exporting, to accumulate specie
reserves. This coincided with an upsurge of economic nationalism in the form of a movement for the recovery of commercial
rights. This movement reached a climax in the campaign of
the Yokohama Allied Silk Warehousing Association in 1881.
Silk export merchants in Yokohama, supported by local
producers, suspended transactions for two months in an
attempt to gain equal business terms with Western merchants.
They did not secure any substantial concessions, but they did
force Western merchants to accept the existence of the export
merchants' system in the treaty ports in order to continue
business.[124]

Hoshino Chōtarō attempted direct exporting of raw silk in
1875. His efforts were well received by American brokers and
manufacturers, and he organized an association for direct
exporting with forty producers in his village in Gunma. The
Nihonmatsu Filature, established in 1873 in Fukushima
Prefecture, also exported its products direct to the United
States. Mitsui Bussan attempted direct exporting of raw silk to
France and the United States in 1880, but discontinued their
efforts from 1885 until 1896. Further direct-exporting firms
were established in the early 1880s. Dōshin Kaisha was
founded in Gunma in 1880, and was engaged in the direct
silk-exporting business until 1909. Bōeki Shōkai was also
established in 1880, with support from Mitsubishi. Other
firms, such as Iroha Shōkai and Fusō Shōkai, also commenced direct exporting in the early 1880s. However, these
attempts resulted largely in failure, due to a variety of
unfavourable factors: insufficient information about – and
knowledge of – overseas markets, insufficient capital, wide
fluctuations in silver value and silk prices, and a change in the

direct-exporting policy of the government in the mid-1880s.[125]

There were two methods of direct export. The direct-export merchant was either consigned with silk by local producers or consigned with orders for silk from manufacturers or merchants in New York and Lyons. In both cases the direct-export merchant would match his raw silk with the appropriate market, and arrange the issue of documentary bills to local producers at the Yokohama Specie Bank for 80–85 per cent of the estimated value of the order. This included an allowance for various expenditures. When the raw silk reached its final destination and was sold to manufacturers or silk import merchants in New York or Lyons, their branches or agents there would settle these documentary bills in foreign currency with overseas branches of the Yokohama Specie Bank. Transactions were usually performed on a deferred-remittance basis of from ten days to six months in the United States, and of 100 days in France.[126]

In the mid-nineteenth century raw silk was transported to Europe by the two main shipping companies: the British P & O and the French Messageries Impériales. Steamers of both companies were used for transportation to both Britain and France, showing that foreign merchants used steamers as they became available, regardless of nationality.[127] In the late nineteenth century raw silk was transported to Europe by P & O, Messageries Maritimes and North German Lloyd, and to New York by Pacific Mail, Canadian Pacific and Northern Pacific, by a combination of steamer and train through San Francisco or Tacoma.

The cost of raw silk transportation – including freight, insurance and all other expenses – came to an estimated 10 to 15 per cent of the original production cost. Other costs amounted to less than 4 or 5 per cent, including the commission for sale (2.5 per cent), the commission for middlemen, and the charge for warehousing. In contrast with coal, freight charges did not form an important part of the selling price on the overseas market. Silk freights to Europe cost 7–7.60 dollars per cwt in 1880 and 5.60–8 dollars (5–7 cents per lb) in the 1890s. Silk freights to New York by Pacific Mail cost 8 cents per lb in 1880 and 4–8 cents per lb in the 1890s. In the 1890s Canadian Pacific and Northern Pacific were charging 3–6 cents per lb.[128]

Since, as we have seen, Japanese and Chinese silk were in competition on the European market and put to primarily the same use in weaving, exporting firms which handled both found that any increase in exports of Japanese silk meant a reciprocal decrease in Chinese. Furthermore, with the wide fluctuations in both the exchange rate and in silk prices, the silk business did not always give Western merchants a profit margin.[129]

Tablet 4–18 shows the profit/loss balance up to the mid-1880s in the main silk accounts of Jardine, Matheson & Co., including figures for Chinese and Japanese silk, while Table 4–19 shows the distribution of raw silk exports handled by the firm for the season 1884/5. The firm was a major exporter, dispatching 2,144 bales of Japanese raw silk in the season July 1877 to June 1878. This put it in third place behind Siber & Brennwald (2,916 bales) and Hecht, Lilienthal & Co. (2,419 bales). In 1884/5 Jardines exported 2,511 bales of silk, valued at 1,106,807 dollars, 84 per cent of which went to consignors in France: Arlès-Dufour & Co. and Hecht, Lilienthal & Co.[130] Fifty-two per cent of the total was exported on a joint account with Hecht, Lilienthal & Co., probably to reduce the risks involved. Although the silk trade was temporarily profitable in the early 1860s, it is obvious from Table 4-18 that the main trend after 1870 was unprofitable. John Swire & Sons, too, made losses of approximately £78,000 between 1868 and 1880 on silk imported into England.[131]

The more vulnerable Western merchants with small capital had to specialize in both the market to which they exported and the type of silk in which they dealt, in order to obtain high profits. The smaller the firm, the clearer the tendency to such specialization became. This situation made them act in a speculative manner, which disrupted the silk market, and their mortality rate was generally high.[132] A large number of such small, specialist firms had therefore disappeared by the late 1870s. This meant that the raw silk trade lost its speculative aspect and became a stable business.

Table 4-20 shows raw silk exports by firm for the season 1890/1. By this time Japanese firms were dealing with about 8 per cent of all exports. The surviving Western silk exporting firms may be classified into three categories. The first consists of the firms which shipped raw silk exclusively to Europe. The

Table 4-18 Profit/Loss Balance in the Main Silk Accounts of Jardine, Matheson & Co., 1859/60-1885/6 (* = loss) (in Mexican dollars)

Account Year	Silk to England	Silk to France	Silk to New York	Japanese silk	Total (with others)
1859/60	306,626	64,659		13,171	384,456
1860/61	* 7,185	8,337		20,958	30,408
1861/62	180,980	10,475		20,004	211,458
1862/63	11,478	–		21,500	46,599
1863/64	* 29,463	* 101		8,041	* 21,523
1864/65	n.a.	n.a.		n.a.	
1865/66	178,473	* 1,479		* 434	214,719
1866/67	88,855	12,169	6,608	* 588	113,695
1867/68	64,767	9,491	1,738		75,733
1868/69	* 90,813	* 9,177	3,536		* 95,796
1869/70	6,447	24,911			31,612
1870/71	* 40,919	* 12,884			* 53,803
1871/72	* 20,175	* 6,905			* 27,080
1872/73	* 55,549	* 28,985			* 82,618
1873/74	* 68,861	* 31,702			*104,738
1874/75	* 34,747	* 2,878			* 36,034
1875/76	41,417	* 3,519			37,897
1876/77	181,899	*101,355			121,727
1877/78	56,561	* 13,217			43,344
1878/79	* 15,700	* 46,622	* 4,550		* 66,074
1879/80	* 10,513	* 86,806			* 99,415
1880/81	* 5,590	* 1,903	* 325		* 18,310
1881/82	–	* 15,747	* 1,141		* 16,713
1882/83	–	* 46,560	2,779		* 51,665
1883/84	* 5,000	*137,859	* 2,484		*144,406
1884/85	* 725	* 31,671	* 2,210		* 51,728
1885/86	* 2,331	* 15,342	11,201		11,298

Sources: JMA, Ledgers, A1/52, 54, 55, 57–74; Miscellaneous Accounts, A7/292, 298–301, 384. There are no figures either for 1864/5 or for the years after 1885/6.

Notes: (1) This table is constructed using the figures available for each year. According to the summary accounts, for instance, the total for 1875/6 was (−)2,591 dollars. (2) Years refer to the period from July to the next June up to 1868/9, June to April for 1869/70, and May to April after 1870/1. Figures for final accounts are slightly different from the figures for each year. (3) Joint accounts and waste silk are included.

Table 4-19 Silk Export Accounts by Jardine, Matheson & Co. for the Year 1884/5
(in bales and Mexican dollars)

From / To	Canton		Shanghai		Yokohama		Total			
	bales	$	bales	$	bales	$	bales	%	$	%
Silk to France										
Arlès-Dufour & Co.	191	76,579	207	65,051	211	94,607	609		236,237	
Hecht, Lilienthal & Co.	100	34,348	–	–	99	44,660	199		79,008	
Joint Account with Hecht, Lilienthal & Co.	–	–	264	90,127	1,044	511,588	1,308		601,715	
Sub-total							2,116 (84)		916,960 (83)	

Table 4-19 continued

	bales	$	bales	$	bales	$	bales %	$ %
Silk to New York								
C.A. Auffm Ordt & Co.	–	–	–	–	25	12,493	25	12,493
G.L. Montgomery	25	8,934	78	38,404	241	124,197	344	171,535
Sub-total							369 (15)	184,028 (17)
Silk to England								
H.T. Gaddum	–	–	20	3,323	6	2,496	26 (1)	5,819 (1)
Total	316	119,861	569	196,906	1,626	790,041	2,511	1,106,807
(%)	(13)	(11)	(23)	(18)	(65)	(71)	(100)	(100)

Source: Jardine, Matheson & Co., Account 1884–5 (JMA A7/301).

Table 4-20 Silk Exports by Major Firms for the Season from July 1890 to June 1891 (in bales)

Shippers		To Europe	To USA	Total	Order
Bavier & Co.	(S)	1,002	1,866	2,868	3
China & Japan Trading Co.	(A)	0	1,511	1,511	10
Dourille, P.	(F)	471	19	490	17
Fraser, Farley & Co.	(A)	0	1,563	1,563	8
Frazer & Co.	(A)	0	237	237	22
Girand & Co.	(F?)	972	0	972	12
Griffin & Co.	(B)	169	742	911	13
Gouilloud, L.	(F)	328	0	328	21
Jardine, Matheson & Co.	(B)	858	892	1,750	7
Kingdon, Schwabe & Co.	(B)	215	0	215	23
Middleton & Co.	(A)	0	406	416	18
Nabholz & Osenbruggen	(S)	1,936	290	2,226	5
Otto Reimers & Co.	(G)	0	4,218	4,218	2
Robison & Co.	(B)	1,506	33	1,539	9
Schoene & Mottu	(F)	491	11	502	16
Siber & Brennwald	(S)	2,855	3,648	6,503	1
Sieber & Co.	(S)	356	479	835	14
Smith, Baker & Co.	(A)	0	351	351	19
Strachan & Co.	(B)	997	20	1,017	11
Ulysse, Pila & Co.	(F)	1,666	105	1,771	6
Ziegler & Marian	(S)	680	0	680	15
Others (Foreign)		89	0	89	
Dōshin Kaisha	(J)	380	1,952	2,332	4
Bōeki Shōkai	(J)	336	0	336	20
Others (Japanese)		12	0	12	
Total		15,349	18,343	33,692	

Source: Jardine, Matheson & Co., 'Silk Shippers from Yokohama for Season 1890/1891', in JMA, PCMR 82.

Note: A: American; B: British; F: French; G: German; J: Japanese; S: Swiss.

second is the type of firm which shipped raw silk exclusively to the United States, and comprised mainly American firms like the China & Japan Trading Co., Fraser, Farley & Co., and Smith, Baker & Co. The third includes firms which shipped raw silk almost equally to Europe and to the United States: these were relatively large general trading firms such as Siber & Brennwald and Jardine, Matheson & Co.[133] For this season, sixteen firms out of a total of twenty-eight sent over 80 per cent of their shipments to Europe; seven specialized to the same extent in shipments to the United States; four sent almost equal shipments to Europe and to the United States.

5
The Development of Tea Exports

Japanese Tea in the World Market

As an export, tea came second in value only to raw silk during the period immediately after the opening of the ports to foreign trade in 1859. At the time when Japanese tea exports were beginning, China dominated world tea production and controlled the world market.[1] By the late nineteenth century, however, India, Ceylon, Japan and the Dutch East Indies had also become major producers of marketable tea. Table 5–1 gives details of the total area under plantation, the volume of production, and the quantities of exports for the main tea-producing countries in the late nineteenth century.

Britain, Russia, the United States, Canada and Australia were the main tea-importing countries. Britain was the biggest, purchasing an annual average of 121 million lb during the period 1866 to 1875. Of this, 108 million lb, 89 per cent of the total, came from China. Between 1876 and 1885 British imports steadily grew to an annual average of 163 million lb, of which 118 million (72 per cent) came from China and 45 million (28 per cent) from British India.[2] Annual average tea imports for 1896 to 1900 were: Britain 279 million lb, Russia 107 million lb, the United States 80 million lb, and Canada and Australia around 23 million lb each.[3]

Tea can be roughly divided into three basic classes according to the different methods of manufacture: black or fully fermented, green or unfermented, and Oolong or semi-fermented. Japan produced mostly green tea. The preparation of green tea requires only three principal operations: steaming or panfiring, rolling, and firing. There is no need for fermentation, as with black or Oolong tea. Leaves intended for manufacture into green tea are steamed when fresh instead of being sub-

Table 5-1 Production and Exports in the Main Tea-Producing
Countries (annual averages for 1896-1900)

Countries	Area under plantation (acres)	Production (thousand lb)	Exports (thousand lb)
British India	488,645	169,388	154,116
Ceylon	361,200	124,458	125,177
China	n.a.	n.a.	207,966
Japan*	139,298	67,580	43,646
Dutch East Indies	n.a.	11,111	11,130

Source: Nōshōmushō Nōmukyoku, *Chagyō gairan* (1914), pp. 52, 54.
Note: *Formosa is excluded. For 1896-1900 the annual average of exports from
   Formosa was 19,876,000 lb.

jected to the slow process of natural withering which is essential
to black tea preparation.[4]

Table 5-2 gives figures for Japanese tea production and export
for 1868 to 1900. In the early 1860s tea was exported almost
equally from both Yokohama and Nagasaki, but by 1865
Yokohama had established its position as the main tea-
exporting port.[5] It remained dominant into the Meiji period,
accounting for 54-68 per cent of all tea exports in quantity and
59-71 per cent in value annually between 1871 and 1888.[6]
Eighty-five per cent of all Japanese tea exports between 1868
and 1900 were of green tea. Product differentiation in tea was
naturally very strong. This meant that the demand for Japanese
tea – and consequently the prices it fetched – depended more
on economic conditions and preferences in the consumer
markets than on the state of production in Japan or on fluctuations in exchange rates.[7] The amount of tea exports remained
stable at between 200,000 and 310,000 piculs for 1875 to 1885
and at between 300,000 and 400,000 piculs for 1886 to 1900.
The overall value of tea exports did not rise as much due to a
decline in export prices, which were at a relatively lower level
after 1876 and remained low until the end of the century.

The country distribution of tea exports from Japan during

Table 5-2 Annual Averages of Japan's Tea Exports and Production, 1868–1900
(in thousand piculs)

Period	Exports				Total (with others)		Price per picul	Price per picul (Green)	Total Production (B)	(A)/(B)
	Green	Green (coarse)	Black	Dust	Quantity (A)	Value (thousand yen)				
1868/70	82	17	–	4	103	3,399	32.2	38.8	–	–
1871/75	149	11	–	5	165	5,534	33.4	36.3	176*	94
1876/80	214	7	–	22	243	5,811	23.7	26.4	179†	136
1881/85	245	9	–	30	286	6,566	23.0	26.2	363	79
1886/90	297	10	1	36	348	6,787	19.5	22.1	437	80
1891/95	313	11	1	50	381	7,814	20.6	24.0	480	79
1896/1900	267	6	5	43	327	7,997	24.5	27.8	508	64

Sources: Tōyō Keizai Shinpōsha, *Nihon bōeki seiran* (1935), pp. 13–15; Nōshōmushō, Nōmukyoku, *Chagyō gairan* (1914), pp. 21–5; Chagyō Kumiai Chūō Kaigisho, *Nihon cha bōeki gaikan* (1935), pp. 116–8; for production in 1874. *Fuken bussan-hyō*, quoted by Yamaguchi Kazuo, *Meiji zenki keizai no bunseki* (1963), p. 19.

Notes: (1) Figures for production during the years 1878–1880 are undervalued because of incomplete statistics (see *Nihon cha bōeki gaikan*, p. 96). (2) Prices per picul are 5-year annual average. (3) * 1874 only. † 1878–80.

**Table 5-3 Green Tea Exports from Japan by Country, 1862–1900
(in thousand lb)**

Period	Britain	USA	China	Canada	Total (with others)
	%	%	%	%	%
1862/65	1,993(33.7)	3,073(51.9)	852(14.4)	–	5,918(100)
1866/70	507(4.5)	10,754(95.4)	15(0.1)	–	11,277(100)
1871/75	307(1.6)	18,330(93.4)	667(3.4)	–	19,625(100)
1876/80	533(1.7)	30,043(94.9)	717(2.3)	–	31,659(100)
1881/85	149(0.5)	32,213(98.6)	214(0.7)	–	32,672(100)
1886/90	91(0.2)	35,507(86.6)	272(0.7)	3,865(9.4)	41,022(100)
1891/95	197(0.5)	33,956(81.4)	57(0.1)	7,066(16.9)	41,730(100)
1896/1900	63(0.2)	28,933(81.3)	85(0.2)	6,217(17.5)	35,603(100)

Sources: (1) 1862–8: Yokohama Prices Current and Market Report, No. 36 (10 July 1868), JMA, PCMR 46, and No. 62 (10 July 1869), JMA, PCMR 74.
(2) 1869–72: H. Gribble, 'The Production of Japan Tea', *Transactions of the Asiatic Society of Japan*, vol. 12 (1885), p. 21.
(3) 1873–1900: *Nihon bōeki tōkei* (1980), p. 139.
Notes: (1) Figures prior to 1873 include all types of tea. (2) Figures for 1862–8 are exports from Yokohama only, and those for 1869–70 are the total of exports both from Yokohama and Kōbe. (3) Figures for the USA before 1886 include Canada.

the period from 1862 to 1900 is shown in Table 5–3. Although a British consular report for 1862 had already pointed to a demand for Japanese tea on the American market, exports to Britain accounted for from 35 to 48 per cent of all tea exports until 1865, after which they rapidly decreased. Most Japanese tea originally sent to Britain, however, was re-exported to the United States.[8] A British consular report for 1867 stated that British ships 'generally return via New York with tea for the American market.'[9] Meanwhile exports from China for reshipment to England or the States sharply decreased, and by 1865 the transshipment ports of Shanghai and Hong Kong had lost their tea transit trade to San Francisco.[10] Direct exports to the States increased from 1,978 piculs (263,727 lb) – 42 per cent of Japan's total tea exports – in 1863/4, to 6,534 piculs (871,178 lb) – 87 per cent – in 1865/6. From 1866 over 90 per cent of Japanese green tea was exported to the States, and

Table 5-4 Annual Averages of Tea Exports from China by Description, 1866-1900
(in thousand piculs)

Period	Black	Green	Brick	Total (with others)
	%	%	%	%
1866/70	1,099(79.6)	218(15.8)	55(4.0)	1,381(100)
1871/75	1,388(80.5)	230(13.3)	106(6.1)	1,725(100)
1876/80	1,534(79.4)	186(9.6)	201(10.4)	1,931(100)
1881/85	1,601(77.8)	205(10.0)	242(11.8)	2,057(100)
1886/90	1,419(72.2)	194(9.9)	343(17.5)	1,965(100)
1891/95	1,073(63.6)	220(13.0)	382(22.6)	1,688(100)
1896/1900	779(53.0)	199(13.5)	483(32.9)	1,470(100)

Sources: IMC, *Returns of Trade at the Treaty Ports*, 1871–81; IMC, *Returns of Trade at the Treaty Ports, and Trade Reports*, 1882–6; IMC, *Returns of Trade and Trade Reports*, 1887–1900.

Note: Totals do not include the figures for tea exported to Hong Kong and Macao in junks.

Table 5-5 Annual Averages of Main Distribution of Green Tea Exports from China by Country, 1868-1900
(in piculs)

Period	Britain	USA	Total (with others)
	%	%	%
1868/70	74,932 (32.8)	140,984 (61.7)	228,505 (100)
1871/75	75,435 (32.9)	127,158 (55.4)	229,522 (100)
1876/80	55,571 (29.8)	119,320 (64.0)	186,362 (100)
1881/85	66,958 (32.7)	121,656 (59.3)	205,054 (100)
1886/90	54,354 (28.0)	107,903 (55.5)	194,285 (100)
1891/95	46,672 (21.2)	127,289 (57.7)	220,457 (100)
1896/1900	33,496 (16.8)	104,101 (52.2)	199,435 (100)

Sources: IMC, *Returns of Trade at the Treaty Ports*, 1868–81; IMC, *Returns of Trade at the Treaty Ports, and Trade Reports*, 1882–6; IMC, *Returns of Trade and Trade Reports*, 1887–1900.

this situation continued until Canada emerged as a separate destination for Japanese tea in 1887.[11] Figures in Table 5–3 do not necessarily show the full picture, however, since a consular report remarked that 'All tea destined for Canada passes through the United States.'[12] More will be said about this later.

China, India and Ceylon

Chinese tea was produced by native farmers on small plots of land using the family as a labour force. These farmers usually had other crops and therefore paid little attention to plucking. Chinese brokers went around from farm to farm buying tea, which they brought to the market nearest the tea district and marketed through Chinese tea hongs.[13]

Table 5–4 shows the annual average of tea exports from China from 1866 to 1900. Black, not green, tea formed the main export, accounting for 70 per cent of all Chinese tea exports until 1886–90. Exports of green tea were small, remaining at an annual average of about 200,000 piculs (27 million lb) throughout the period 1886 to 1899, with an average share of total tea exports of from 10 per cent to 16 per cent. Table 5-5 shows the annual average distribution of green tea exported from China in terms of quantity. Shanghai was the main port for green tea exports during the period under consideration. In 1877 nearly two-thirds of all green tea exported was brought to Shanghai from Kiukiang and Ningpo for shipping. In the mid-1880s this proportion grew to nearly 100 per cent.[14] On average, 58 per cent of all Chinese green tea went to the United States and 27 per cent to Britain. Most green tea shipped to London was subsequently re-exported to the States, making the latter easily the world's major importer. After 1890, however, the demand for Chinese green tea in India increased.[15]

In India and Ceylon tea production was carried out on large estates owned by big producing companies and managed by Europeans. Machines were used, producing tea which was cheap and regular in quality. Ninety-nine per cent of the tea was black. Tea production began in India in the 1830s and took place in Assam, Cachar, Sylhet, and Darjeeling. The area under plantation increased from 124,836 acres in 1875/6 to 344,827 in 1890 and 522,487 in 1900. Production increased rapidly too, from 1.4 million lb in 1860 to 13.2 million in 1870, 36.4 million in 1877, 112.0 million in 1890 and 197.5 million in 1900.[16] Tea production in Ceylon began only after 1880. The area under plantation increased rapidly from 9,300 acres in 1880 to 236,000 in 1890 and 405,000 in 1900. Tea production increased accordingly, from 1 million lb in 1882 to 46 million in 1890 and 149 million in 1900.[17] Exports also increased, from 0.2 million lb in 1880 to 45.8 million in 1890 and 149.3 million in 1900, and tea became a crucial export for Ceylon.[18] Almost all Indian and Ceylon tea was exported to Britain.

Competititon in the United States Market

In order to secure export markets Japanese tea had first to overcome the dominance of Chinese green tea. It had been recognized by 1865 that 'the quality [of Japanese tea] is more suited to the American than the English market.'[19] British and American tastes in tea were completely different: while the prevailing taste in England was for black tea, the United States preferred green or uncoloured tea.[20]

The official statistics, as given in the *Commerce and Navigation of the United States*, do not provide us with figures suitable for reviewing the market structure of tea in the United States, since both black and green tea are subsumed under the single heading 'tea'. Moreover, in reviewing the American tea market it is necessary to consider not only black and green tea but also coffee and cocoa, as Japanese green tea faced keen competition from coffee as well as from black tea. Both economic factors, such as income, and non-economic factors such as preference in taste and life-style, should also be included in our analysis if we are to be able to draw any general conclusions. It is not sufficient to explain market conditions on the basis of the competition between tea and coffee alone.[21]

Table 5–6 shows imports of tea, coffee, and cocoa and chocolate into the United States between 1851 and 1900. Imports of tea increased from 24 million lb in 1851–5 to 60 million in 1871–5 and 91 million in 1891–5. Imports of coffee also increased, however, to 303 million in 1871–5 and 762 million in 1896–1900. For 1881 to 1897 coffee took 83–89 per cent of total coffee and tea imports, tea taking only 11–17 per cent.[22] Imports

Table 5-6 Imports of Tea, Coffee, and Cocoa and Chocolate into the United States, 1851–1900 (quantity in thousand lb)

Period	Tea			Coffee			Cocoa & Chocolate	
	Quantity	Average import price per lb	Imports per capita	Quantity	Average import price per lb	Imports per capita	Quantity	Average import price per lb
		cent	lb		cent	lb		cent
1851/55	23,874	28.7	0.76	179,914	8.3	6.6		
1856/60	27,444	26.8	0.76	226,467	9.7	7.1		
1861/65	27,509	26.6	0.74	125,169	11.7	3.5		
1866/70	42,378	29.4	1.08	221,410	10.5	5.8		
1871/75	60,132	33.9	1.37	302,647	14.5	7.2		
1876/80	63,792	26.9	1.30	361,202	15.1	7.3	} 5,132	13.8
1881/85	74,773	22.7	1.32	507,675	9.6	8.9		
1886/90	83,962	16.9	1.38	518,404	12.2	8.3	} 13,504	14.0
1891/95	90,673	15.4	1.35	585,270	16.8*	8.7		
1896/1900	87,648	13.2	1.18	761,715	9.3	10.1	} 29,408	14.0

Sources: US Department of Commerce, *The World's Production and Consumption of Coffee, Tea and Cocoa* (1905), and *Commerce and Navigation of the United States*, corresponding years, quoted from Nōshōmushō, Nōmukyoku, *Chagyō ni kansuru chōsa*, pp. 253–6, 281–4.

Notes: Year means fiscal year from 1 July of the previous year to 30 June. *Figures are overvalued due to the depreciation of Brazilian milreis.

Table 5-7 Annual Averages of Tea Imports into the United States by Country, 1861–1900 (in thousand lb)

Period	Britain	China	Japan	India	Total (with others)
	%	%	%	%	%
1861/65	2,792(10.1)	23,956(87.1)	280(1.0)	–	27,509(100)
1866/70	2,339(5.5)	30,746(72.6)	8,196(19.3)	–	42,378(100)
1871/75	3,518(5.9)	36,381(60.5)	16,195(26.9)	–	60,132(100)
1876/80	2,953(4.6)	31,603(49.5)	28,351(44.4)	–	63,792(100)
1881/85	1,384(1.9)	38,868(52.0)	33,773(45.2)	–	74,773(100)
1886/90	3,839(4.6)	42,616(50.8)	36,462(43.4)	–	83,962(100)
1891/95	3,258(3.6)	47,582(52.5)	38,450(42.4)	–	90,673(100)
1896/1900	3,268(3.7)	45,826(52.3)	34,439(39.3)	2,410(2.7)	87,648(100)

Sources: US Department of Commerce, *The World's Production and Consumption of Coffee, Tea and Cocoa* (1905), and *Commerce and Navigation of the United States,* corresponding years, quoted from Nōshōmushō, Nōmukyoku, *Chagyō ni kansuru chōsa,* pp. 260–2.
Notes: China excludes Hong Kong.

of coffee were therefore five times greater than those of tea. More coffee than tea was drunk, and the average import price was lower. The market for green tea therefore occupied only a small part of the total market for hot, non-alcoholic drinks. Tea prices were probably influenced by coffee prices. While coffee prices remained relatively stable, however, tea prices decreased considerably. In the absence of official statistics, estimates by a tea dealer suggest that over the period from 1886 to 1895 green tea accounted for 68 per cent of all tea imports, black tea for 8 per cent and Oolong tea for 24 per cent.[23]

Tea consumption in the United States increased after the Civil War. It was encouraged by the abolition in 1872 of the duty of 25 cents per lb on directly imported tea, although a duty of 10 per cent continued on tea imported indirectly.[24] This 'gave an over-impetus to the trade in green [tea] with the United States'. As a result, 'over-competition created serious loss' and led to 'the depressed and unsatisfactory condition of the tea market' in the mid-1870s.[25]

Table 5–7 shows tea imports to the United States by country for 1861 to 1900. China and Japan were clearly the main exporters. Japanese green tea was mainly consumed in the agricultural districts around Chicago, on the western Pacific coast and in the vicinity of New York, while Chinese green tea was mainly consumed in the central part of the States.[26]

Since the market for Japanese green tea was confined to the United States after 1865, Japan's tea exports were influenced to a great extent by changes in American market conditions, and her tea trade business was vulnerable even to rumours concerning the American market.[27] Japanese tea faced continuous competition from Chinese tea, particularly green tea. Since the annual American consumption of green tea was estimated to be about 20 million lb in the second half of the 1870s,[28] we can gain some idea of the intensity of the competition when we consider that total green tea imports stood at 32 million lb in 1875 and rose to 50 million in 1880.[29] Both quality and price were therefore vital factors in increasing sales of Japanese tea.

Chinese tea soon felt the effects of Japanese competition. A report for 1869 by the Chinese Imperial Maritime Customs warned that before long competition from the other tea producing countries, Japan and India, might be felt; by the mid-1870s it was being noted that green tea exports to the United States had seriously decreased as a result of successful Japanese competition.[30] The decrease was rapid: from 21.7 million lb in 1872 to 15.0 million in 1874 and 8.0 million in 1875.[31] Japanese tea overtook Chinese green tea in 1874 and, although China soon recovered some of its lost ground, exports to the United States remained at less than half the amount exported by Japan. Just as Chinese green tea was being threatened by Japanese tea on the American market, in the mid-1870s Chinese black tea was facing a similar threat on the British market from the rapid increase in imports of Indian black tea. China was losing ground in the world's tea markets as a whole to the challenge from Japan and India.[32] A Chinese Imperial Maritime Customs report for 1876 suggested the need for a considerable reduction in the price of Chinese tea, pointing to minor defects in Chinese green tea and the relative cheapness of Japanese green tea.

The competitive weakness of Chinese tea was attributed to high prices caused by likin and heavy export taxation, and also to deteriorating quality.[33]

Japanese green tea continued to threaten Chinese on the United States market, causing stagnation in exports of green tea from China. However, the prospects for Japanese tea on the American market were not totally bright. The rapid increase in tea exports from Japan after 1871 inevitably meant hurried and careless preparation, and a consequent deterioration in quality.[34] Complaints about the dusty and broken character of Japanese tea were reported in the late 1860s. A British consular report for 1868 warned that 'unless a decided stand is made to discountenance this adulteration, Japan tea will fall into disfavour in the United States, where it chiefly has to seek a market.'[35]

After mid-1875 the price of Japanese tea began to decline as a result of new competition from Formosan tea, which was similar to Japanese in quality.[36] In 1876 Japanese teas were 'losing their former great popularity with consumers in the United States', as quality deteriorated due to hasty overproduction.[37] A British consular report considered that the continuous decline in the value of Japanese tea exports from 1874 to 1876 showed that 'there is a limit to the demand for Japan teas' in the United States market, 'partly attributable to faulty preparation' and stated that 'it is evident that the Japanese must pay more regard to the quality . . . if they are to compete successfully with Chinese growers.'[38] As we have already seen, since the annual consumption of green tea in the States was estimated at about 20 million lb it seemed that 'unless some fresh outlet is speedily discovered, prices must continue to decline.'[39] A British consular report for 1881 commented:

> The popularity of Japan teas seems now seriously on trial in America . . . it must be admitted that the quality of Japan tea is steadily deteriorating, thus seriously endangering this country's [Japan's] trade in one of its staple articles of produce.[40]

In New York, Japanese tea was disposed of 'by auction at ruinously low prices'.[41] This deterioration continued throughout the 1880s and 1890s.

An Act of 1883 which prohibited the importation of low-quality tea into the United States led to a considerable reduction in the amount of ordinary tea from China and Japan.[42] In fact, imports from China and Japan decreased from 37.6 million lb for Japan and 34.4 million lb for China in 1882/3, to 33.2 and 31.0 respectively in 1883/4.[43] Japanese tea imported at San Francisco decreased by more than a quarter in 1883 compared with the previous year.[44] In such circumstances it was clearly vital for Japanese teas 'to maintain the reputation they have enjoyed for many years' in order to overcome competition and ensure a market.[45]

The 1890s saw the beginning of a radical shift in consumption from green to black tea in many areas of the United States. At the same time Japanese tea was suffering from continued competition, from a steady deterioration in quality, and also from price rises. India and Ceylon started an active marketing campaign after the International Exhibition at Chicago in 1893. Indian tea began to invade the Japanese tea market, albeit in only small amounts.[46] As had been already pointed out in the late 1870s, the question was 'whether these [Japanese] teas can be produced at prices low enough to enable them to compete favourably in foreign markets with China and Assam tea.'[47]

The severe competition in the United States led Japanese tea gradually to shift its export market to Canada. Before 1890 it was mainly the coarse type of tea, which had by then lost popularity in the States, that was sent to Canada, but in the 1890s the demand for better-quality tea increased around the Quebec and Ontario districts.[48] As Table 5–3 shows, Canada took 17 per cent of Japan's total tea exports in 1891–1900.

Table 5–8 shows the distribution of tea imports into Canada by country. In the second half of the 1880s Japanese tea was already accounting for over 40 per cent of the total imports. Tea from Britain – in other words, re-exports of Indian and Ceylon tea – was taking 35–40 per cent of the market. The market share of Japanese tea remained at over 40 per cent until the turn of the century, but was then replaced by the rapidly increasing Indian and Ceylon tea. The ratio of green to black tea stood at 55 per cent for 1886–90, 54 per cent for 1891–95, and 47 per cent for 1896–1900, but rapidly decreased to 28 per cent for 1906–10. Japanese green tea took about 85 per cent of

Table 5-8 Annual Averages of Tea Imports into Canada by Country,
1886-1905 (in thousand lb)

Period	India	China	Japan	Britain	US	Total (with others)
	%	%	%	%	%	%
1886/90	42(0.2)	2,576(13.6)	7,664(40.6)	7,716(40.9)	876(4.6)	18,875(100)
1891/95	219(1.1)	3,305(16.6)	8,838(44.3)	6,903(34.6)	674(3.4)	19,948(100)
1896/1900	3,864(16.5)	4,182(17.9)	9,791(41.9)	5,153(22.0)	399(1.7)	23,393(100)
1901/05	10,812(43.5)	2,135(8.6)	6,172(24.8)	5,390(21.7)	334(1.3)	24,844(100)

Source: Nōshōmushō, Nōmukyoku, *Chagyō gairan* (1914), pp. 72–4.
Note: Year means fiscal year from 1 July of the previous year to 30 June.

total green tea imports up until 1902, and then decreased to
50–60 per cent.[49] In the late nineteenth century tea accounted
for 85 per cent of combined consumption of tea and coffee in
Canada, and remained at over 75 per cent for the 1900s. Coffee
consumption increased as prices came down below tea prices.
The annual average import price per lb of tea for 1893–5 was
15.5 US cents, while coffee was 18.7 US cents. For 1901–5,
however, tea was 14.5 US cents and coffee 9.0 US cents.[50] An
official Japanese report attributed the decline in Japanese tea
imports into Canada to a combination of positive marketing
by Indian and Ceylon tea and the close relationship between
India, Ceylon and Canada through the British Empire.[51] Thus
in Canada, even more than on the American market, Japanese
tea faced severe competition from Indian and Ceylon tea,
which it was unable to withstand.

The Development of the Tea Industry in Japan

The first tea exported from Japan after the opening of the
ports in 1859 came from existing producer districts such as
Yamashiro (Kyōto), Ōmi (Shiga), Ise and Iga (Mie), Yamato
(Nara), Suruga and Tōtōmi (Shizuoka), Shimousa (Chiba)
and Musashi (Saitama).[52] Tea was sent directly from producing
districts by local consignors on a contract basis to tea merchants
in Yokohama, who sold it to Western merchants for export.
These tea merchants had originally come to Yokohama from

the main tea-producing districts, in particular Suruga and Ise, and kept a close relationship with their home district. This direct connection between producing districts and the treaty ports implied the destruction of the traditional distribution system controlled by privileged guild merchants in large cities such as Edo and Ōsaka. Tea from districts in the Kinki region such as Yamashiro and Yamato was sent to Yokohama for export until the opening of Kōbe in 1868. Thereafter Yokohama was sent tea from the eastern parts of Japan such as Mie and Shizuoka, while Kōbe exported tea from areas to the west, such as the Kinki region, which was mixed with other, inferior tea from the Chūgoku and Shikoku regions.[53]

The increase in demand for Japanese tea from overseas markets stimulated domestic tea production and gave rise to changes or improvements in methods.[54] The quality of Japanese tea was from the first appreciated by Western merchants. However, it had been refired only once and needed to be refired again to extract almost all its moisture in preparation for long-distance transportation: 'China leaf finds its way to the hands of the foreign purchaser fully cured and packed and ready for exportation', but

> Japan leaf . . . comes to the market in a comparatively raw state, though partially sun-dried, or fired, and is then submitted to a thorough process of firing at the hands of the foreign exporter, either in his own or in another's establishment at a fixed rate of charge.[55]

In 1860 two Western firms had private tea-refiring establishments in Yokohama, but apparently most Japanese tea was sent to Shanghai for refiring and then shipped to England or the United States.[56]

Nagasaki was another important port for tea exports: 'In Nagasaki an imitation of Chinese green tea is prepared and exported under the [brand] names of Gunpowder, Hyson, Young Hyson, and Twankay.'[57] As the Custom House passed all tea in raw leaf as 'bancha' (coarse green tea) and charged only a low scale of duty, a large proportion, usually of inferior quality, was exported 'in an unprepared state, principally to Shanghae (*sic*) by Chinese shippers'. From Shanghai it found its way to the European markets, 'either separately prepared or mixed with the China leaf, or was marketed locally.[58] Better quality tea was shipped from Nagasaki to Yokohama or Kōbe 'for the purpose of being mixed with the tea of those districts which have commanded higher prices than usual for the American market'.[59] Although tea started off as Nagasaki's largest export item after coal, exports decreased sharply in 1873 and by 1887 tea had 'virtually ceased to be an article of export, except to the north of China'.[60]

The opening of Kōbe in 1868, following the revision of the tariff treaty in 1866, gave Western merchants the chance of access to the most important tea-producing districts in the Kinki region. This led to changes in both the prospects for tea exports and the system by which tea was exported. At first, considerable quantities continued to be sent to Yokohama for refiring, 'some by the native merchants themselves, and some by the foreign agents of Yokohama houses, from whom the native merchants received advances on the shipments.'[61] This left a satisfactory profit margin for the Western merchants.[62] In late 1868, however, some of the Western merchants began to erect tea-firing establishments at Kōbe in order to prepare tea for export on the spot, without the need to send it to Yokohama. The number of these establishments increased year by year. In 1872 there were eleven, with a total of about 1,500 pans.[63] The returns of the Kōbe (Foreign) Chamber of Commerce show a rapid increase in the proportion of Kōbe tea exports which were shipped directly to the outside world: from only 6,266 lb out of a total of 2.5 million lb (0.2 per cent) in 1868; to 780,350 out of a total of 2.2 million (36 per cent) in 1869; 2.2 million out of a total of 3.2 million (68 per cent) in 1870; and 4.2 million out of a total of 4.8 million (89 per cent) in 1871.[64] As tea exports from Kōbe increased, however, the small number of tea-firing establishments meant that the Kōbe market often suffered from over-supply, so that some tea still had to be transported to Yokohama. In 1887 over 6.7 million lb, or 36 per cent of the total tea actually shipped from Kōbe, was sent to Yokohama for this reason.[65]

Tea production in Japan expanded in response to the firm foreign demand. Producers were particularly attracted by the rising price of tea for export. In the 1872/3 season, production was reported to be at 121,000 piculs, or 16 million lb.[66] According to the 1874 Survey of Prefectural Products it was 17.6

million kin (23.5 million lb), of which Kyōto produced 8.3 million kin, Shiga 1.6 million and Shizuoka 1.1 million. These three prefectures were therefore responsible for 62 per cent of Japan's tea production.[67] The land under plantation throughout Japan doubled during the decade from 1872 and then continued to increase, from 42,024 chō in 1881 to 63,648 chō in 1892.[68] As Table 5-2 shows, the annual average production of tea increased from 363,411 piculs (48.5 million lb) for 1881 to 1885 to 437,492 (58.3 million lb) for 1886 to 1890; 480,384 (64.0 million lb) for 1891–95 and 507,581 (67.7 million lb) for 1896–1900. An average 76 per cent of total annual tea production was exported between 1881 and 1899.

We have already seen that Japanese tea was exposed to keen competition in the United States and was constantly on the verge of losing its market there because of deteriorating quality, even though it was able to maintain a predominance over Chinese tea, which was deteriorating at a faster rate. This situation threatened the economic policies of the Meiji government, which relied on exports of tea (as well as raw silk) to obtain the foreign currencies needed for industrialization. The government therefore took positive steps to improve quality and expand exports. It attempted by various means to control and facilitate green tea production and to start black tea production. It also encouraged direct exporting by Japanese merchants.

One measure taken by the government was the creation in 1874 of an office in the Home Ministry for the organization and control of tea production. The government held competitive exhibitions and fairs which played a crucial role in improving the quality of tea and encouraging its production. It also advertised Japanese tea abroad by participating in international exhibitions at Philadelphia in 1875 and at Sydney in 1879, and promoted sales in Europe. Government officials were sent to investigate the demand for tea in overseas markets.[69] A slight improvement in quality had occurred by the late 1870s, but this created a rise in prices which in turn caused over-production and a renewed deterioration.[70]

The government also encouraged the development of tea plantations in Shizuoka, as a way of helping the former samurai class. This was done with such success that in 1877 tea production in Shizuoka exceeded that in Yamashiro.

From the early 1880s Shizuoka became the central tea-producing area, accounting for 43 per cent of total deliveries into Yokohama in 1885, 60 per cent in 1890 and 77 per cent in 1896. In 1889 Shizuoka found itself literally at the centre of Japan's tea-exporting industry when the Tōkaidō Railway Line and the special port of Shimizu were opened.[71]

Attempts to stimulate production of black tea began in 1874, with the dispatch of government officials to India to learn the methods of production. In the second half of the 1870s, as prices of Japanese tea declined on overseas markets, the government tried to engineer a shift in production from green to black tea.[72] In 1878 the Bureau for Encouraging Agriculture of the Home Ministry issued regulations for training people in black tea production. However, all attempts resulted in failure, due to lack of care and because technology was not sufficiently developed to overcome the unsuitable nature of the Japanese climate. This was clearly illustrated by the failure in 1881 of an attempt to export black tea to Melbourne by the Yokohama Black Tea Co., which had been formed under government sponsorship.[73] As British consular reports for 1881 and 1882 commented, Japan's 'climate and soil . . . appear unfitted to the growth of plants producing a leaf of the quality necessary to make good black', with the result that the manufacture of black tea 'has been almost given up'.[74]

Both Western merchants and Japanese producers and dealers must bear the responsibility for complaints about the quality of Japanese tea. It was pointed out at the time that Western merchants added colouring during the refiring process and failed to pack tea properly, while Japanese producers would try to make a quick profit by picking a third, fourth and even a fifth crop when prices were high.[75] The desire for direct shipments by Japanese merchants grew, and in 1872 the Tea Improving Co. was established for this purpose by Ōtani Kahei, one of the main tea merchants in Yokohama, whose aim was also to ensure that only high-quality Japanese teas were exported. 1876 saw the first – unsuccessful – attempts by Japanese trading firms such as Mitsui Bussan and Ōkura-gumi to export tea directly to New York, with government support.[76] Government-sponsored attempts at direct exporting continued, however, as a British consular report indicated the following year:

Native shippers still continue to consign tea on own account to America, but the results, as far as can be ascertained, are not very satisfactory. They seem deficient in the knowledge of the right preparation of the raw staple as required on the American market. . .[77]

In the second half of the 1870s attempts at direct exporting began in producing areas with the establishment of tea companies by wealthy farmers. In Saitama Prefecture, for example, the Sayama Tea Co. was formed in 1876. In Shizuoka Prefecture the Sekishin-sha was formed in 1876, the Yūshin-sha and the Shizuoka Tea Co. in 1878, and the Shizuoka Direct Tea-Exporting Co. in 1885. In Mie Prefecture, the Mie Tea Exporting Co. was established in 1881. This was succeeded by the Mie Tea Co. in 1882 and by the Mie Prefectural Tea Co. in 1883. Further tea exporting companies were established in Ōsaka, Kyōto and Kōbe in 1887. However, almost all these attempts at direct exporting failed after a few years due to management difficulties, the fall in tea prices, and inadequacies in technology. The percentage of direct tea exports by Japanese merchants reached 4.5 per cent of total Japanese tea exports in 1887 and 1888, but decreased after this date. This reflects the failure of direct shipments as a whole, despite positive government support.[78]

The government was compelled to reconsider its policy on tea production in the early 1880s. This followed the failure of the various attempts to produce black tea and the strict implementation of the 1883 United States Act prohibiting the importation of inferior teas, at a time when the deterioration in Japanese green tea was again obvious. A conference of domestic tea producers and dealers held in 1883 made two proposals to the government: first, that a law should be issued prohibiting the production and sale of inferior teas; second, that an association of tea producers should be organized in order to improve the general quality.[79] At a meeting of producers and merchants held in 1883, the following four subjects were discussed: (1) the history and present situation of the industry; (2) the history and present situation of transactions; (3) measures to rectify poor methods of production and improve quality; and (4) the removal of bad trade practices and the expansion of overseas markets. Ōtani Kahei urged the establishment of

Japanese-owned refiring factories in tea-producing districts, and the need for more information on overseas markets. The latter would help to prepare for the possible closure of the American market to Japanese tea, following the continuous deterioration in its quality.[80]

In 1884, on the basis of these proposals, the government issued the Working Rules of the Tea Association. This brought about the formal organization of tea producers and dealers in order to improve the quality of tea both for export and for domestic use. These rules lacked provisions for enforcement, however, and were replaced in 1887 by the stronger Regulations of the Tea Association.[81] In 1888 the Tea Association was re-organized into the Japan Central Tea Association, its principal objects being 'to correct any abuses existing between the producers and the purchasers, to enforce close attention to the preparation and packing of teas, and to ensure the fulfilment of contracts in a creditable manner.'[82] In accordance with the Regulations of the Tea Association, local associations were formed at a prefectural level. A conference of producers and dealers held in 1889 described the market conditions for Japanese tea:

> the tea industry in Japan has not recently been prosperous, because of the fall in prices, and the prospects for tea production are bad, because the market for Japanese tea is narrow and confined only to the United States. Particularly in the United States, Japanese tea has faced keen competition from India, Ceylon and China, so that stocks of Japanese tea have increased and prices have in consequence fallen sharply.[83]

In 1890 the Japan Tea Co. was organized with the help of financial support from the government, to strengthen Japan's commercial rights through expanding the black tea market in Russia and meeting the demand for tea in the United States, but unfortunately it proved unsuccessful and was dissolved the next year.[84] In 1894, in the midst of the commercial rights recovery movement, the Japan Tea Society was formed with the encouragement of Maeda Masana, former government official.[85] In 1895 the Japan Tea Co. and the Kōbe Tea Exporting Co. were established to extend Japan's commercial rights through fostering direct shipments.[86] At a meeting of the

Central Tea Association in 1897, Ōkuma Shigenobu, then Minister of Agriculture and Commerce, made a stirring speech:

> tea has been recently imported [into the United States] from India and Ceylon, and their market is developing. They are our most formidable rivals in the tea trade. The government has approved a proposal for a subsidy to help competition with these teas. . . With only a little financial help [70,000 yen annually for seven years], it will be difficult to compete with Indian and Ceylon teas . . . production in India is far cheaper than in Japan. This is why Japanese tea should be improved. . . If tea producers do not brace themselves, it will be difficult even to maintain the current market position of Japanese tea in the United States.
>
> Your urgent task is surely not only to compete with Indian and Ceylon teas in the Unites States, but also to expand your markets into northern China, Siberia, Russia, Canada, Central America, South America and elsewhere.[87]

Despite such strenuous encouragement and support from the government tea exports from Japan did not develop successfully, although the process of preparation was simplified by the invention by Japanese of several machines for tea manufacturing and refiring.[88]

The main reason for the failure of Japanese tea in the United States lay in the low profit margin, which was a great disadvantage in Japan's fierce competition not only with tea from China, India and Ceylon but also with coffee and cocoa. While the import price of Japanese tea was higher than any other, its retail price had to be kept the same. The high import price was caused by the rise in production costs and by the complicated marketing routes between producers and consumers in which margins and commissions were added by merchants and brokers.[89]

Table 5–9 shows the average import prices of Japanese tea in the United States, the average export prices from Japan, and the average domestic prices of tea destined for export. While import prices in the States decreased, export prices were pushed up further by a rise in domestic tea prices so that the difference between the American import price and the Japanese

Table 5-9 Annual Average Prices of Japanese Tea, 1871–1900
(per lb)

Period	Import prices in the United States		Export prices of green tea from Japan	Domestic prices of Shizuoka green tea*
	US$	yen	yen	yen
1871/75	0.36	(0.36)	0.27	–
1876/80	0.27	(0.29)	0.20	0.22†
1881/85	0.21	(0.24)	0.20	0.23
1886/90	0.14	(0.18)	0.16	0.15
1891/95	0.14	(0.22)	0.18	0.14
1896/1900	0.13	(0.26)	0.21	0.18

Sources: US, *Commerce and Navigation of the United States,* 1871–1900;
Nōshōmushō, *Chagyō ni kansuru chōsa* (1912), pp. 45–7; Nōshōmushō,
Nōshōmu tōkei-hyō, for 1878–1900.
Notes: * Yokohama prices for 1878–88, and Shizuoka for 1889–1900.
† 1878–80 only.

export price gradually narrowed, reducing profitability. The amount of profit to be gained from producing and exporting tea depended on the price at which it could be sold, but this was determined by the structure of the importing market. The cost of tea manufacturing increased steadily, mainly because of rises in wages and in the price of charcoal.[90] This restricted the scope for reducing production costs. Although these had to be reduced to promote exports, a combination of the domestic factors mentioned above and severe competition in overseas markets made the industry unprofitable. Indian and Ceylon tea was regular in quality due to machine manufacturing and was superior to Japanese tea in both production methods and marketing. A crucial factor in production was the size of plantations and the consequent economy of scale.[91]

The Tea Trade and the Transportation of Tea

As with silk, the tea trade remained almost completely in the hands of Western merchants despite various attempts by the government to promote direct exporting. In the period immediately following the opening of the ports, almost all Japanese export merchants and Western merchants were involved in tea. However, as the trade developed specialist tea firms gradually emerged, and the overall number engaged in the tea business decreased. This was partly because many Western merchants lacked sufficient capital. Apparently only a few large firms such as Jardine, Matheson & Co. and Walsh, Hall & Co. were able to deal in cash; other merchants often had financial problems in their business with Japanese merchants.[92] Since Japanese merchants also lacked sufficient capital, both sides were under pressure to concentrate on specific lines of business. Thus in Yokohama, the number of Western firms and Japanese export merchants engaged in the tea business decreased from 20 and 109 respectively in 1885 to 15 and 43 in 1895. The main Western firms dealing in tea were Mourilyan, Heimann & Co., Smith, Baker & Co., Jardine, Matheson & Co., Middleton, Smith & Co., Hellyer & Co., and Hunt & Co. Mourilyan, Heimann & Co. and Jardine, Matheson & Co. had their own branches in the United States and exported tea on their own account. The other firms were commission merchants. The main Japanese export merchants were Ōtani Kahei, Nakajō Junnosuke, Okano Rihei and Yoshinaga Nizō in Yokohama, and Yamamoto Kametarō, Nishiguchi Seisuke and Kawaguchi Seiji in Kōbe.[93]

Tea transactions were similar to silk transactions.[94] Usually tea was purchased by local tea brokers or wholesale dealers and then sent to Japanese export merchants, who sold it to Western merchants in the treaty ports. The export merchants purchased on their own account or were entrusted by local consignors on a 5 per cent commission basis. They took samples of tea to Western merchants for negotiating purposes, and made verbal agreements with them. Starting in October every year the Western merchants would make provisional purchases on the basis of these samples, either on their own account or on a commission basis. When they received orders from tea importers or wholesalers in the United States and elsewhere, they would also receive letters of credit from them, generally for 75 per cent of the value at which they were instructed to buy. These they would use to obtain bank loans from foreign banks, or from the Yokohama Specie Bank, so that they could complete their provisional tea purchases. At this point, the Japanese vendors would bring the tea to the

Western merchants' godowns. The size of the parcels differed according to the time of year:

> Early in the season there are usually ten or twelve piculs in a parcel; but later on, parcels are sold of 100 or 200 piculs, or even more. The ordinary teas come down in rough-made chests, prepared inside, each chest containing on an average 60 lbs; but the finest descriptions come down in jars, holding from 35 to 36 lbs.[95]

After the tea had been inspected for quality and weighed the Japanese merchants would be given 70–80 per cent of the value, the balance being paid after refiring. The drying, mixing, colouring, refiring, sorting and packing operations were all performed in the Western merchants' refiring establishments.[96]

Direct exporting continued on a small scale after the mid-1880s, but direct tea export companies had to entrust both the export and sale to already established Japanese trading firms such as Mitsui Bussan and Ōkura-gumi or to Western merchants, owing to a lack of sufficient knowledge of the international market. Not until 1910 did Japanese merchants come to handle larger quantities of tea than Western merchants.[97]

As in the case of the silk trade, there are claims that Western merchants engaged in speculative activities, imposed high charges, and employed various tactics to manipulate both quality and price in order to make profits.[98] Japanese merchants, lamenting the failure of their overseas tea market to expand, also assigned part of the blame to the 'malpractices' of Western firms which had their sights fixed only on a good profit. However, there is little evidence that Western merchants did in fact make large profits. Moreover, it seems unlikely that a Western merchant would consciously have damaged the long-term reputation of his firm among Japanese merchants or the reputation of the tea which it was his business to sell.

In the early years profits for Western merchants in the tea business were as high as 40 per cent, but this did not last. As increasing demand led to higher prices on the domestic Japanese market, profit margins shrank.[99] Table 5–10 shows the profit/loss balance up to the mid-1880s for both Chinese and Japanese tea, on the main tea accounts of Jardine,

Matheson & Co. Table 5-11 shows the distribution of the tea exports handled by that firm for the season 1884/5. Jardine, Matheson & Co. exported tea to London, New York, Melbourne, and Rotterdam. As Table 5-10 shows, the tea trade remained basically profitable until the early 1870s, but from then on exports to both London and New York became unprofitable. This tendency remained fundamentally unchanged until the mid-1880s. In 1884/5, for example, Jardine, Matheson & Co. handled mainly Chinese tea. Japanese tea accounted for only 5 per cent of all their tea exports and for 11 per cent of total invoice value. Sixty per cent of all the tea handled by Jardine, Matheson & Co. went to England and 23 per cent to New York. The invoice prices for New York were, however, disproportionately high, probably because much of the green tea exported by Jardines was dealt with on a joint basis to reduce the risks involved.

By the mid-1870s the old tea clippers had been almost driven out of business by the advent of the steamer which was quicker, albeit more expensive. In 1874 tea freight from Shanghai to London per ton (40 cubic ft) cost £3 to £3.10s. From Shanghai to New York freight rates stood at £5 to £5.10s. per ton (40 cubic ft) for steamers and £2.10s. to £3.10s. for sailing vessels.[100] In June 1882 the freight rates levied by the Pacific Mail for steamer and rail transport to New York and Canada were reduced from 5 to 2 cents per lb gross. This facilitated shipments of tea.[101] Table 5-12 shows the distribution of Japanese tea exported from Yokohama by destination and by route for 1881-3 and 1890-1. Japanese tea was exported to the United States mainly by British firms in British vessels.[102] In the early 1880s 53 per cent of the total tea exports from Yokohama were destined for New York and Boston, and much of the tea sent to New York was probably sent on to Chicago and other cities. In 1881-3 23 per cent of the tea exported from Yokohama was carried by American vessels, the remaining 77 per cent by British ships.[103] According to Table 5-12, in 1881-3 steamers carried 90 per cent of the tea exported from Yokohama; 49 per cent was transported to the States via Suez and 42 per cent was sent directly across the Pacific Ocean. However, the greater speed of steamers became less important after the opening of the Canadian Pacific Railway in 1881 and its extension to Tacoma in 1885. In 1886 seven fast

Table 5-10 Profit/Loss Balance of the Main Tea Accounts of
Jardine, Matheson & Co., 1859/60–1885/6 (*=loss)
(in Mexican dollars)

Year	To England	To Melbourne	To Sydney	To New York	To Rotterdam	Japanese tea a/c	Tea a/c
1859/60	31,494	8,738	23,750	25,687		38,131	44,685
1860/61	* 2,205	4,277	8,781	95,941		20,539	45,948
1861/62	245,485	12,792	1,040	582		8,679	65,521
1862/63	–	5,628	2,645	2,345		14,571	67,775
1863/64	* 43,192	7,585	3,787	–		–	50,730
1864/65	n.a.	n.a.	n.a.	n.a.		n.a.	n.a.
1865/66	238,349	32,193	8,063	18,489		* 6,820	70,952
1866/67	* 28,351	22,656	9,501	* 35,086		–	55,861
1867/68	* 14,988	–	10,324	* 11,194		–	89,455
1868/69	* 53,391	5,003	600	6,701	321		33,176
1869/70	23,440	6,638	–	7,715	96		38,045
1870/71	133,934	5,269	–	15,962	40,235		23,114
1871/72	51,667	8,337	419	* 44,783	9,674		38,710
1872/73	* 23,770	15,380	900	* 57,371	* 3,160		35,492
1873/74	n.a.	n.a.	n.a.	n.a.	n.a.		n.a.
1874/75	* 20,979	27,994	–	* 53,810	2,615		21,086
1875/76	* 57,516	16,629	1,672	* 13,987	9,945		16,575
1876/77	* 73,216	1,200	810	*107,952	577		13,332

Table 5-10 continued

Year	To England	To Melbourne	To Sydney	To New York	To Rotterdam	Japanese tea a/c	Tea a/c
1877/78	n.a.	n.a.	n.a.	n.a.	n.a.		17.300
1878/79	* 72,449	3,337	* 446	* 1,877	*10,633		16,203
1879/80	138,450	–	–	499	*10,633		26,665
1880/81	* 35,730	3,902	* 2,572	* 511	* 9,051		20,370
1881/82	* 6,958	182		564	* 2,553		18,171
1882/83	* 19,483	1,754	–	* 5,642	3,571		n.a.
1883/84	* 45,594	* 1,874	–	700	* 563		27,012
1884/85	* 43,847	869	–	12,268	6,577		26,098
1885/86	13,944	7,064	–	* 31,576	8,718		25,763

Sources: JMA, Ledgers. A1/52, 54, 55, 57–74: Miscellaneous Accounts, A7/292, 294–301, 389. Figures for 1864/5 and years after 1885/6 are not available.
Notes: (1) Figures for each account are generally on a July-to-June basis. (2) Figures in joint accounts are included.

Table 5-11 Tea Exports by Jardine, Matheson & Co. for the Year 1884/5 (in packages and in Mexican dollars)

To	Canton	Hankow	Foochow	Shanghai	Amoy	Yokohama	Total	Profit/Loss (*=loss)
England								
Own a/c		24,884 ($209.375)					18,358[3] ($187,148)	*$25,909
Joint a/c[1]	4,905 ($11.091)		56,074 ($316,462)				85,863 ($536,928)	*$17,937
Sub-total							104.221 ($724,076)	60.3% (53.7%)
New York								
Own a/c				7,447 ($106,432)		4,561 ($82,043)	12,008 ($188,475)	$ 3,873
Joint a/c[2]					23,391 ($247,425)	3,601 ($48,267)	26,992 ($295,692)	$ 8,395
Sub-total							39,000 ($484.167)	22.5% (35.9%)

Table 5-11 continued

Melbourne			15.965 ($ 55,384)				15.965 ($ 55,384)	9.2% (4.1%)	$ 869
Rotterdam			10,321 ($ 78,417)				10,321 ($ 78,417)	6.0% (5.8%)	$ 6,577
New Zealand			3,450 ($ 6,183)				3,450 ($ 6,183)	2.0% (0.4%)	$ 506
Total	4,905 ($11,091)	24,884 ($209,375)	85,810 ($456,446)	7,447 ($106,432)	23,391 ($247,425)	8,162 ($130,310)	172,957 ($1,348,227)	100% (100%)	$10,976 (with others)

Source: JMA, A7/301. In the case of joint accounts, only J.M. & Co.'s share of the invoice prices is given.
Notes: (1) with Koenigsberg Commercial Association (2) with Mosle Bros and Fearon Low & Co. (3) ports unknown.

Table 5-12 Annual Averages of Tea Exports from Yokohama by
Destination and Route, 1881–3 and 1890–1
(in thousand lb)

Destination and Route	1881–83		1890–91	
To		%		%
USA				
New York & Boston	11,322	(53.4)	6,588	(23.0)
San Francisco	3,852	(18.2)	4,253	(14.8)
Chicago & other cities	2,955	(13.9)	8,029	(28.0)
Canada	2,823	(13.3)	9,445	(32.9)
England & Europe	267	(1.3)	377	(1.3)
Total	21,220	(100)	28,692[3]	(100)
By				
Suez Steamers[1]	10,518	(49.6)	6,437	(22.4)
P & O or Occidental & Oriental				
steamers	5,830	(27.5)	9,945[4]	(33.6)
Pacific Mail steamers	3,067	(14.5)		
Canadian Pacific steamers or				
steamers in connection with				
Union Pacific Railway	–		5,301[5]	(18.5)
Sail to San Francisco	1,805[2]	(8.5)	339	(1.2)
Sail & rail via Tacoma	–		6,655	(23.2)
Sail via the Cape to Canada	–		30	(0.1)
Total	21,220	(100)	28,707[3]	(100)

Sources: CR, Kanagawa, 1881–3; DCRTF, No. 922, Kanagawa for 1890, and
No. 1084, Kanagawa for 1891.

Notes: (1) 'Suez steamers to London' from 1881 to 1883 are included. (2) Figures
for 1881 include tea carried by sailing vessels to New York. (3) The discrepancy in the figures is due to a difference in the original figures.
(4) 'Steamers to San Francisco' for 1891 are included. (5) Figures for 1890 are
calculated by deducting total quantities by route from those by destination.

sailing vessels chartered by Canadian Pacific carried silk and tea from China and Japan to Canada for the first time. Thereafter tea was carried to the western ports of Canada and sent on from there to the eastern cities of Canada and the United States. In the early 1890s slightly less than 50 per cent of tea from Yokohama was exported via Canada. Canadian Pacific carried an average of 42 per cent of all tea exported from China and Japan during the period 1887 to 1892.[104] Its freight rates were generally lower than those charged by Pacific Mail and the Occidental and Oriental lines.[105]

Exports from Kōbe, the other main tea port, reached slightly over half the amount shipped from Yokohama. In 1896 28 million lb was exported from Yokohama and 15 million from Kōbe; in 1900, 25 million from Yokohama and 13 million from Kōbe. In 1889, 18 million lb was shipped from Kōbe: 7 million for New York and other cities in the eastern United States, 5 million for California, 1 million for Chicago and 5 million for Canada.[106]

In the early 1890s, steamers faced increasing competition in tea transportation from fast sailing vessels as a result of the opening of the Canadian route. During this time, tea coming from Yokohama was transported by sailing vessels via either Tacoma or Vancouver. Exporting to the United States and Canada via Suez by steamer decreased to 21 per cent of the total in 1891, while Canadian Pacific came to play an important role in exporting across the Pacific by steamer and then railway. In the first half of the 1890s freight rates to the States and Canada ranged from 1.25–1.50 cents to 3 cents per lb gross.[107] Since freight costs constituted about 10 per cent of the export price, the decline in rates helped exports of Japanese tea to the States and Canada. Had freight rates not been low, Japanese tea would have been driven out of these markets.

6
The Development of Coal Exports

Coal and East Asia

Together with raw silk and tea, coal was one of Japan's main exports in the second half of the nineteenth century. During the period 1868 to 1899 coal exports formed on average 5.8 per cent of total exports. This included coal for 'ship's use', which was exported without duty. Coal was important for the Western powers in East Asia for a combination of military, political and commercial reasons.

As we have already seen, the United States needed coaling depots and ports of refuge for vessels engaged in the China trade and in whaling in the northern Pacific.[1] Russia had for some time regarded control of Sakhalin as a step towards the establishment of commercial relations with Japan. On discovering in 1851 that there were deposits of coal on the island, the Russians investigated their location and accessibility. Sakhalin thus gradually became a place of strategic importance in Russia's East Asia policy.[2] The Netherlands was also interested in Japanese coal and the opportunity it offered for restoring its trade with Japan at Nagasaki. Kattendyke, who had come to Japan as a naval instructor for the Nagasaki Naval Training School, was confident that good-quality coal could be produced in the neighbourhood of Nagasaki. He therefore suggested the introduction of coal-mining machinery.[3]

Britain's interest in Japanese coal was primarily military and resulted from the increase in political tension towards Russia after the Crimean War (1853–6). In 1860 Britain made a strong request for permission from the Bakufu to dispatch mining engineers to Japan to investigate coal mines in northern Kyūshū, but met with a prompt refusal.[4] Again, towards the end of that decade a British consul complained of the slow development of the Japanese coal industry, and suggested the introduction of foreign capital and Western technology to increase production.[5] This concern on the part of the consul seems to reflect British anxiety about the increasing Russian commitment to East Asia, which had been strengthened by the Russian landing on the island of Tsushima in 1861.[6] In 1867 Harry Parkes, the British Minister to Japan, wrote about Japanese coal:

> The demand for fuel is constantly increasing, and our interests (*sic*) in obtaining supplies upon the spot is second only to that which it may be presumed is felt by Japan itself. The competition, however, which may thus be created with the mining operations of the Russians in the neighbouring island of Saghahe [Sakhalin], where coal of good quality is also found, will perhaps account for their [the Russians] not viewing these efforts of the Japanese Government with similar favour.[7]

Of course, shipping companies were also interested in coal. It was important for them to have supplies for the steamers which they had engaged in regular services. British shipowners usually entered into yearly contracts with specific large coaling agents and contractors who had facilities for steamers in most of the coaling stations of the world.[8] Steamers were more costly than sailing ships in terms of both construction and transportation and therefore required large cargoes in order to make profitable voyages. However, since the early steamers consumed enormous amounts of fuel and needed large bunker coal for ocean shipping, they had limited cargo space. This combination of factors led to high freight rates. In practical terms, their use was therefore confined to a limited number of highly subsidized mail and passenger services. In most later steamers the space for coal and for cargo was interchangeable, and any space not taken up by cargo was filled with coal.[9] This improved profitability. Steamers were taking part in the China trade in the early 1860s but were still more costly to run than sailing ships and there was little or no prospect that it would become profitable to operate them on such long routes.[10] The shift from sailing ships to steamers did, however, come and was hastened by the fall in running costs brought about by continuous improvements in marine technology, such as the development of the compound and triple-expansion engines. In the 1880s steamers actually replaced sailing ships,[11] and the reduced rate of fuel consumption made it possible to go from London to Japan without stopping for coal. Fresh supplies were still needed, however, for the voyage home. By around 1880 coal supplies from Britain to Singapore were being brought by steamer, but most of the coal sent from Britain to Hong Kong was being transported by swift sailing ships specially built for that purpose.[12]

For the Peninsular and Oriental Steam Navigation Co. transportation of coal and related expenses between 1856 and 1865 amounted to an annual average of £525,000, 27 per cent of their total annual average costs of £1,946,295. They usually kept about 90,000 tons of coal in stock at their different coaling stations in the following proportions:[13]

Southampton	2,000 tons	Calcutta	4,000 tons
Malta	5,000 tons	Singapore	8,000 tons
Alexandria and Suez	6,000 tons	Hong Kong	10,000 tons
Aden	20,900 tons	Shanghai	6,000 tons
Bombay	8,000 tons	Yokohama	2,200 tons
Point de Galle	12,000 tons	King George's Sound	4,000 tons
Madras	500 tons	Sydney	1,200 tons

P & O extended their regular service to Shanghai in 1850, but in 1853 and 1854 the rapid rise in the price of bunker coal and the high cost of shipping coal to East Asia threatened the profitability of that service. P & O agents found a partial solution to this matter by opening up new coal fields which had been discovered in Labuan and Formosa, and by purchasing steamers specifically to transport coal to their Eastern depots. Nevertheless, the maintenance of coal depots and supplies remained a heavy charge for them. Until the mid-1870s, in addition to owning two ships which they used exclusively to carry out machinery and stores, P & O also chartered an annual average of 170 sailing ships to carry coal to their Eastern depots.[14]

The expansion of the East Asian trade, particularly after the opening of the Suez Canal in 1869, led to an increase in the number of vessels engaged in trade and consequently in the demand for coal as fuel for steamers. The major ports for ocean trade in Southeast and East Asia were Singapore, Hong Kong and Shanghai. Table 6-1 shows the number and tonnage of vessels entering these three ports. Both the number and tonnage of vessels, especially of steamers, steadily increased after the mid-1870s. The Hong Kong coal market is clearly the largest of the three. In 1895 the average size of ship for Singapore was 825 tons and for Shanghai 1,193 tons, while for Hong Kong it was 1,270 tons.

The Structure of the Shanghai Coal Market

As one of the two commercial centres of China's foreign and coastal trade, Shanghai was a major coaling station for East Asia.[15] Imports of foreign coal and deliveries of Chinese coal to Shanghai are shown in Table 6-2. Imports were small before 1861, with an annual average of 43,502 tons for 1858-61, but they began to increase after 1862. In 1865, 51 per cent of the 93,779 tons of coal imported from abroad came from Britain and 29 per cent from Australia. The British share dropped to 43 per cent in 1866, however, since 'The Excessive dearness of English and American Coals has led, naturally, to the use by Steamer owners of Coal procurable from [the] nearest sources, and at a cheaper rate, although of inferior quality.'[16] In that year the increase in imports from Australia, Japan and Formosa signalled a change in the structure of the Shanghai coal market. The British consul predicted that 'Australia and Japan coals are now likely to monopolize the market on account of their cheapness.'[17]

In fact, the late 1860s to early 1870s saw a transition from British to Japanese supremacy in the Shanghai coal market. During this period there was keen competition between imports from Britain, the United States, Australia, Japan, and Formosa. Since, as Table 6-2 makes clear, total imports of coal into Shanghai remained stagnant until the late 1870s, a detailed review of conditions – such as fluctuations in price and freight rates – is required for an understanding of the competition among the various coals during this period.[18] A report on trade by the Chinese Imperial Maritime Customs for 1865 had already pointed out the increase in Japanese coal and the

Table 6-1 The Asian Coal Market, 1870–1900
(in thousand tons for both coal imports and tonnage)

Year	Shanghai			Hong Kong			Singapore		
	Coal imports	Vessels entered		Coal imports	Vessels entered		Coal imports		
		No. of vessels	Total tonnage		No. of vessels	Total tonnage		No. of vessels	Total tonnage
1870	80	1,643	882	93	2,400	1,328	63	1,604	668
1875	148	1,947(1,393)	1,300(1,154)	137	2,609	1,952	94	2,261(1,275)	1,284(1,047)
1880	205	2,288(1,755)	1,684(1,543)	181	2,881	2,536	171	2,120(1,753)	1,693(1,427)
1885	271	2,426(1,948)	1,976(1,856)	375	3,428	3,867	328	3,088(2,751)	2,533(2,306)
1890	305	2,942(2,555)	2,729(2,615)	419	4,114	4,894	311	3,646(3,548)	2,989(2,906)
1895	488	3,427(2,990)	3,710(3,568)	609	4,546	5,772	461	4,437(4,347)	3,784(3,715)
1900	594	3,667(3,273)	4,726(4,596)	677*	5,473	7,022	662	4,652(4,579)	4,836(4,810)

Sources: (1) For Shanghai, IMC, *Returns of Trade at the Treaty Ports in China* and *Returns of Trade at the Treaty Ports in China and Trade Reports*, corresponding years.
(2) For Hong Kong, calculated from the *Overland China Mail*, CS: *Blue Book of Statistics*, corresponding years.
(3) For Singapore, Straits Settlements, *Blue Book of Statistics*, corresponding years.
Notes: (1) Figures in parentheses are for steamers. (2) 'Chinese junks' and 'Native crafts' are excluded. (3) * 1899.

Table 6-2 Annual Averages of Coal Imports into Shanghai, 1861–99
(in tons)

Period	Britain	%	USA	%	Australia	%	Japan	%	Others	%	Foreign coal total	%	China	%	Total	%
1861/65											115,956				n.a.	
1866/70	42,785	(35.0)	8,453	(6.9)	42,989	(35.2)	16,253	(13.3)	1,873	(1.5)	112,353	(91.9)	9,938	(8.1)	122,291	(100)
1871/75	20,120	(15.0)	3,981	(3.0)	35,966	(26.9)	51,824	(38.7)	2,955	(2.2)	114,846	(85.8)	19,084	(14.2)	133,929	(100)
1876/80	9,784	(5.6)			29,094	(16.6)	104,179	(59.3)	15,519	(8.8)	158,578	(90.3)	17,056	(9.7)	175,633	(100)
1881/85	8,143	(3.3)			25,095	(10.2)	174,485	(71.0)	14,176	(5.8)	221,898	(90.3)	23,784	(9.7)	245,682	(100)
1886/90	2,497	(0.8)			20,772	(6.6)	242,674	(77.1)	16,109	(5.1)	282,052	(89.6)	32,757	(10.4)	314,809	(100)
1891/95	16,256	(3.7)	218	(0.1)	23,318	(5.4)	318,682	(73.1)	24,195	(5.6)	382,669	(87.8)	53,139	(12.2)	435,808	(100)
1896/99	16,385	(2.7)	–		14,951	(2.5)	398,307	(65.9)	55,317	(9.2)	497,438	(82.3)	106,897	(17.7)	604,335	(100)

Sources: (1) 1861–5, 1867–73: John Thorne (Coal Circular), Shanghai, 6 January 1866: John Thorne & Co.'s Shanghai Coal Market Report, 4 January 1871, 4 January 1872, 15 January 1873; Thorne, Rice & Co.'s Shanghai Coal Market Report. 14 January 1874. in JMA, PCMR 46. 74. 75. 76. 77. (2) 1866: IMC. Report on Trade at the Ports in China. (3) 1874, 1875: CR, Shanghai. (4) 1876, 1877: IMC. Reports on Trade at the Treaty Ports. (5) 1878, 1879: China Overland Trade Report. Nos 2–25 (1878) and Nos 1–5, 7–15, 18–26 (1879). (6) 1880, 1882, 1883, 1885–7: Japan Daily Mail. 21 January 1888, in Nōshōmushō, Nōshōkō kōhō, No. 36, 15 February 1888. p. 1413. (7) 1881, 1884, 1888–99: NCH. CI, corresponding years. (8) Totals of foreign and Chinese coal for 1870–81, IMC. Returns of Trade at the Treaty Ports, Pt II. Shanghai, corresponding years, and those for 1882–99, IMC. Reports of Trade and Trade Reports, Pt II, Shanghai. corresponding years.

Notes: (1) Figures for distribution of coal imports by country are not consistent with total figures owing to different sources. (2) Totals of foreign coals include imports of foreign coals from Chinese ports and Hong Kong. (3) Totals of Chinese coal for 1871–86 are calculated from figures in piculs. taking a picul as 60.5 kg. (4) Figures for 1878 and 1879 exclude some periods owing to unavailability of materials.

decrease in British coal, and attributed the decline in imports of coal from Britain to various causes:

> This falling off is more particularly notable in English coal. . . This has its source in several causes combined: the decrease in the number of Steamers employed on the Yang-tze and on the Coast; the competition of other Coals, more particularly those of Japan and Australia; and above all, the small number of vessels dispatched from Great Britain to China. The Coal trade could not of itself establish and sustain a direct line of navigation between Europe and the Far East.[19]

Figure 6 shows the average prices of the various kinds of coals on the Shanghai coal market. Throughout the period Cardiff and American coal were the most expensive, followed by English and Australian coal, with Japanese and Formosan coal the cheapest. It should be noted that the price of Japanese coal during this period of keen competition remained constant, and at a lower level even than Formosan coal except for the second half of 1871. This was particularly significant in the early 1870s, when the prices of British, American and Australian coal rose from the trough of 1870. A British consular report stated that 'by its cheapness and quantity, the Japanese coals should be established in the eastern markets before supplies are also produced from China.'[20] Competition was intensified by the advance of Japanese coal into the Shanghai market, and towards the end of the 1860s cheaper coal from Australia, Japan and Formosa was widely used.[21] In the second half of the 1870s, as imports of Japanese coal increased, the market price in Shanghai became strongly influenced by the price of Japanese coal. This meant that the Shanghai coal market became very sensitive to fluctuations in the quantity of supply and the price of Japanese coal.[22]

The principal factor in determining the intensity of competition was the cost of power per unit, which depended on the price of coal and its efficiency. Freight rates were the prime factor in improving or worsening competitiveness.[23] Table 6-3 shows the distances between the main coal-producing countries and the Eastern coal market. Coal was a bulky cargo, and the cost of transporting it from Britain made it too expen-

Figure 6 Price Fluctuations of Imported Coal in the Shanghai Coal Market, 1866–99 (per ton)

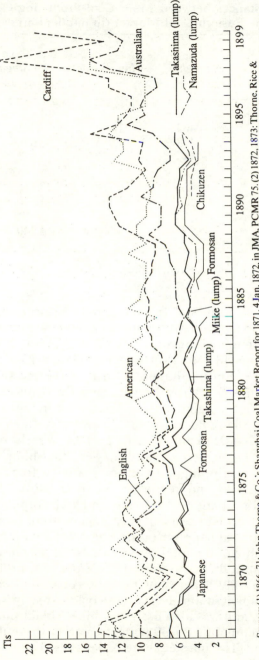

Sources: (1) 1866–71: John Thorne & Co.'s Shanghai Coal Market Report for 1871. 4 Jan. 1872, in JMA, PCMR 75. (2) 1872, 1873: Thorne. Rice & Co.'s Shanghai Coal Market Report for 1873. 14 Jan. 1874, in JMA, PCMR 77. (3) 1874, 1875: CR. Shanghai for 1875, p. 23. (4) 1876–June 1878. Dec. 1881–1899: *NCH*, CI. Nos. 475, 502, 529, 554, 580, 759, 784, 808, 835, 860, 886, 912, 937, 963, 988, 1014, 1039, 1064, 1091, 1116, 1143, 1168, 1195, 1221, 1247, 1273, 1299, 1325, 1351, 1377, 1403, 1429, 1455, 1481, 1507, 1535, 1559, 1587, 1612, 1638, 1664, 1689. (5) Dec. 1878–June 1881: *China Overland Trade Report*, 4 Jan. 1879, 1 July 1879, 31 Dec. 1879, 28 June 1880, 29 Dec. 1880, 23 June 1881.
Notes: (1) 1866–75: Average prices for the 6 months ending 30 June or 31 Dec. (2) 1876–99: Quotations available close to the end of June or December. (3) For Australian coal from June 1876 to June 1895, the averags between the lowest and the highest prices of Sydney and Newcastle coal. (4) Takashima coal price for Dec. 1880 is for dust coal.

Table 6-3 Distances between Main Coal-Producing Countries and the Eastern Coal Market (in nautical miles)

To From	Shanghai	Hong Kong	Singapore
Japan			
Nagasaki	462	1,074	2,421
Kuchinotsu	478	1,085	n.a.
Moji	547	1,179	2,537
Britain			
Cardiff	10,470	9,718	8,188 (via Suez)
			11,520 (via Cape)
Australia			
Sydney	5,030	4,500	4,240

Source: Imperial Japanese Navy, Hydrographic Department, *The Distance Tables* (1937).

sive to compete with coal from Japan and Formosa, which was supplied in large quantities and at a moderate price.[24] The average coal freight charged per ton from Wales to Shanghai during the years 1869 to 1871 was 41s. The average price of Cardiff coal per ton in Shanghai during the same years was 9.1 taels, equal to 59s.11d.[25] Freight rates thus constituted 68 per cent of the Shanghai selling price. The freight between Nagasaki and Shanghai was naturally far lower. In 1872 it was 2.25–3 dollars, equal to only 10s.2d.–13s.6d.[26] Vessels for carrying coal from Japan were usually chartered at Shanghai with 'the privilege of shipping cargo from Shanghai free'.[27] Moreover, 'proximity to and ready access from China' made it much easier for Japanese coal to respond to the rapid increase in steamer demand. In consequence, Japanese coal continued 'to be the principal supplier of the Shanghai coal market'.[28]

Britain's share of the total of imported coal decreased from 33–37 per cent in the late 1860s to 22–28 per cent in the early 1870s, and to only 9 per cent in 1873. Australian coal was mixed with Japanese and Formosan coal for use in steamers and warships, and was also used by Chinese blacksmiths.[29] It was able to maintain a 24–39 per cent market share throughout this period. The market share of Japanese coal increased from below 10 per cent in the late 1860s (with the exception of 1867) to 25–29 per cent at the beginning of the 1870s. However, since the supply was irregular, there remained a possibility that 'foreign coals will continue to be sent to supply the deficiency [of Japanese coal].'[30]

Given that consumption remained constant in the early 1870s, it was clear that the deficiencies of British coal – high price and insufficient supply – were made good by the nearer countries of Australia, Japan and Formosa.[31] Japanese coal gradually became more and more important in the Shanghai market. It superseded British coal in 1870 and then entered largely into competition with Australian and other kinds.[32] In 1873 Japanese coal gained 41 per cent of the market, and reached 53 per cent in 1875. A British consular report for Shanghai stated:

> The most noticeable feature in this [coal] trade is the large and annually increasing amount of Japanese coal imported. Of all the coal imported into Shanghae (*sic*) more than one-half comes from Takasima (*sic*) mines near Nagasaki... Of course this large supply of Japanese coal tends to drive other sorts out of market. English, American, Australian, and Formosan coals all show a marked falling off.[33]

Thus Japanese coal, along with Formosan, was 'slowly but surely forcing English and Australian coal from the market'.[34] The *Japan Mail* commented: 'Nor indeed does there seem any good reason why Japan should not supply the whole of the East with fuel – at least as far as India, if not even India.'[35] This is what in fact happened in the late nineteenth century.

Japanese coal was widely used for many purposes, depending on its quality and price.[36] In the early 1870s most of the Japanese coal in the Shanghai market came from Takashima and Karatsu.[37] Takashima coal had been noted soon after the opening of the ports to be well adapted for steamers, and was even said to be the best type of coal for them. Its screened coal was used 'by some of the fast steamers on their voyages from China to London with the first teas of the season'.[38] P & O and Messageries Maritimes used Takashima large coal extensively for their Eastern agencies.[39] The coal produced at Karatsu, about 120 miles north of Nagasaki, came to be 'exported to Shanghae (*sic*) in large quantities, where it finds a ready sale when English coal cannot be obtained.' However, it was said to work badly in steamers.[40] Since the quality of all coal shipped from Japan during this period – apart from that produced in Takashima – was of a very inferior and mixed description, Japanese coal came to lose its reputation among consumers in China. In consequence, demand became irregular and rates unstable.[41] Until 1873, Japanese coal had been in demand and sold on Chinese account, while all other foreign coals were delivered only on order.[42] After 1874, however, it was imported on a contract basis. Takashima coal was contracted on a large scale from the mid-1870s, and a contract for Miike coal of 65,000 tons a year was made in 1881.[43] From then onwards, deliveries of Takashima and Miike coal were mostly brought to Shanghai 'in fulfilment of contracts'.[44] In 1891 the circular of a Shanghai coal dealer commented:

> The Miike mine has made a contract with one of the mail lines for the supply of their coals for several years, this mine has now contracted for almost their total outport [output] for this year, only a margin being kept for supplies to outside steamers.[45]

The annual average imports of Japanese coal increased from 174,485 tons for 1881 to 1885 to 242,674 tons for 1886 to 1890, and 318,682 tons for 1891 to 1895; while it kept a constant market share of from 61 to 81 per cent after 1880. There was an overall decline in freight rates in the years up to 1885. From then until 1889 the freight market was stable, with rates ranging from 1 to 1.85 dollars per ton.[46] Freight constituted around 30 per cent of the selling price of Japanese coal in Shanghai, and the decrease in freight rates helped to keep its price down.[47] From 1890, however, the decline in freight rates became so steep that shipping dealers could no longer make a profit on deliveries of Japanese coal, and this led to a decrease in imports to Shanghai. The actual decrease was from 1–1.75 dollars in 1889 to 0.90–1.55 dollars in 1890, 0.70–1.50 dollars in 1891 and 0.70–1.40 dollars in 1892 and 1893. The low freight rates brought the market to 'a perfect standstill' and made Japanese coal unsaleable, prices reaching 'Bed Rock' in mid-

1892. The low prices in turn led to the closure of small and medium-sized Japanese coal mines. Although the price rose in 1893, this was neutralized by the continuing low freight rates.[48]

By around September 1893, these market conditions in Shanghai meant that Japanese coal was now in a position to meet the demand which had arisen in ports to the south and west. Large quantities were sent as far as Singapore in order to benefit from higher prices.[49] In early 1894 even first-class Japanese coal, such as that from Miike, started to be sent to Singapore in large quantities at 'extraordinarily good prices'.[50] Miike coal, together with Takashima coal, had been one of the leading Japanese coals on the Shanghai market, but the quantity sent to Shanghai decreased after 1893. Instead increasing amounts of the cheaper, more abundant Chikuhō coal were dispatched there. The beginning of the Sino–Japanese War in 1894, however, saw a sudden increase in the demand for coal.[51] Freight rates between Japan and Shanghai also rose rapidly, and led not only to a rise in the price of Japanese coal but also to a situation in the Shanghai coal market such that 'No steamers calling here [Shanghai] seem to require bunker coals, as they can be procured so very much cheaper in Japan.'[52] After the end of the war in 1895 freights between Japan and Shanghai went down again, making it possible to import Japanese coal to Shanghai in large quantities and at a lower price. In September 1896 coal freight reached its lowest level of 0.60 dollars per ton. In market reports on coal in Shanghai after 1894, Takashima, Namazuda (one of the Chikuhō mines) and Miike coal were mentioned as 'All contracted for' or 'None for Sale', and quotations disappeared.[53]

Chinese coal accounted for only about 10 per cent of the total coal imports to Shanghai until 1893. Formosan coal was the main Chinese coal. Coal exports from Formosa were 23,754 tons on an annual average for 1865 to 1880[54] and annual average deliveries of Formosan coal to Shanghai amounted to 10,205 tons (66 per cent of total Chinese coal imports) for 1865 to 1880 and 9,778 tons (35 per cent) for 1881 to 1890. This situation continued until Formosan coal was replaced by Kaiping coal in the early 1890s. From the mid-1890s deliveries of Kaiping coal increased dramatically; it gradually came to threaten the established market for Japanese coal and actually replaced

Australian coal. Kaiping coal was supplied to the Shanghai market at prices equivalent to Japanese coal, ranging from 6 to 8 taels per ton at the end of 1898.[55]

The Structure of the Hong Kong Coal Market

Hong Kong emerged as a major centre of East Asian trade in the 1850s in association with the development of shipping along the China coast.[56] As Table 6–1 clearly shows, the Hong Kong coal market was the biggest of the three main markets in Southeast and East Asia. As Hong Kong was a free port, there are no official trade figures.[57] It is, however, possible to reconstruct the figures for coal using the information on coal arrivals at Hong Kong given in the commercial summaries of the *Overland China Mail* (although small amounts seem to have been omitted), together with Japanese consular reports and other sources.[58] Table 6–4 shows the distribution of coal imports into Hong Kong by country. The annual average imports of coal to Hong Kong increased from 138,022 tons for 1871 to 1875 to 278,186 tons for 1881 to 1885, and to 500,410 tons and 704,120 tons in the first and second halves of the 1890s respectively.

Between 1870 and 1875, an average 93 per cent of the coal imported into Hong Kong came from Britain and Australia.[59] The British share of the Hong Kong coal market decreased slightly from 50 per cent in 1878 to 44 per cent in 1882, and then rapidly lost importance. In the early 1870s Australian coal was most in demand and the decrease in British coal was thus made up in part by imports from Australia, from Newcastle (NSW), Sydney and the Bulli mine.[60] Australian coal maintained a market share of from 22 to 41 per cent between 1877 and 1886, but was mostly reshipped from Hong Kong to Shanghai.[61] The main reason for the decline in imports of British coal – and for the similar decline in Australian coal from the mid-1880s – was obviously the intensified competition caused by the rapid increase in imports of Japanese coal. It was a replay of what had happened in Shanghai from the late 1860s to the early 1870s.

Japanese coal was first brought to Hong Kong in the early 1870s. Takashima coal, which arrived in 1873, was acknowledged to be equal to the best English coal and sold at a price

Table 6-4 Annual Averages of Coal Imports into Hong Kong, 1871–99
(in tons)

Period	Britain %	USA %	Australia %	Japan %	Formosa %	Hongay, Halong Bay, Kebao etc. %	Total (with others) %
1871/75	64,832(47.0)	2,340(1.7)	63,660(46.1)	2,538(1.8)	4,652(3.4)	–	138,022(100)
1876/80*	78,900(44.1)	825(0.5)	61,223(34.2)	25,575(14.3)	9,683(5.4)	–	178,985(100)
1880/85	84,063(30.2)	774(0.3)	91,259(32.8)	90,291(32.5)	11,799(4.2)	–	278,186(100)
1886/90	32,495(9.0)	890(0.2)	47,584(13.2)	275,934(76.3)	3,017(0.8)	350(0.1)†	361,410(100)
1891/95	30,196(5.6)	n.a.	16,277(3.0)	432,371(79.9)	n.a.	52,742(9.7)	541,299(100)
1896/99	59,372(8.1)	n.a.	27,260(3.7)	526,971(72.1)	n.a.	108,763(14.9)	730,466(100)

Sources: (1) 1870–4: Bottomley & Hughes' Market Report, No. 34 (5 January 1875), in JMA, PCMR 64.
(2) 1875: W. Kerfoot Hughes' Market Report, Nos 82–4 (14, 21, 28 December 1875), in JMA. PCMR 64.
(3) 1877–91, 1899: *Overland China Mail*, CS, corresponding years.
(4) 1892–4: Nōshōmushō, Nōmukyoku, *Yushutsu jūyōhin yōran*, Kōzan-no-bu, Sekitan (1896), pp. 4–5.
(5) 1895–8: Gaimushō, *Tsūshō isan*, No. 91, pp. 6–7; No. 123, pp. 33–4.

Notes: (1) * 1877–80. (2) † 1890 only.

of 12–12.50 dollars per ton.[62] In the mid-1870s it was tested in steamers with favourable results.[63] Imports of Japanese coal tripled from 9,785 tons in 1878 to 31,229 tons in 1879. Over the same period its share in the total coal imports to Hong Kong increased from 5 to 23 per cent. The increase in imports of Japanese coal received the following comment in a market report on coal in the *Overland China Mail*:

A new feature in our market is the increased import of Takasima (*sic*) Coals to different Consignees, causing a competition which has not heretofore existed. The effect of this is not apparent, but doubtless, if the price at which it can be sold be low, consumers will eventually be found.[64]

Figure 7 shows the fluctuations in coal prices for the last available complete week in June and December of each year from 1874 to 1899. It should be noted that coal was cheaper in Hong Kong than in Shanghai. Cardiff coal was always the most expensive imported coal. Australian coal was cheaper than Takashima coal until 1878, when the price of Japanese coal suddenly declined from 8 to 6 dollars per ton. This implies that the advance of Japanese coal into the Hong Kong market, which became marked in 1879, was supported by lower prices. Japanese coal was thereafter fixed at a lower level than the other major foreign coals, and was thus able to overcome the keen competition.

The average coal freight from Wales to Hong Kong during the years 1872 to 1874 was 35s.5d. per ton, equivalent to 8 dollars.[65] The annual average price of Cardiff coal during these years ranged from 11.25 to 14.25 dollars.[66] If we therefore take 12.75 dollars as the average price over all three years, it is clear that freight rates constituted as much as 64 per cent of the selling price of Cardiff coal in Hong Kong. By contrast, the coal freight between Nagasaki and Hong Kong in 1873 was 3 dollars per ton and the average price of Japanese coal was 7.75 dollars.[67] For both coals, however, the difference between the selling price and the freight rate was 4.75 dollars.

A few more years were required after 1879 before Japanese coal overcame the competition completely and was able to establish a dominant position in the market. Imports of Japanese coal increased to 86,050 tons in 1883, superseding

Figure 7 Price Fluctuations of Imported Coal in the Hong Kong Market, 1874–99 (per ton)

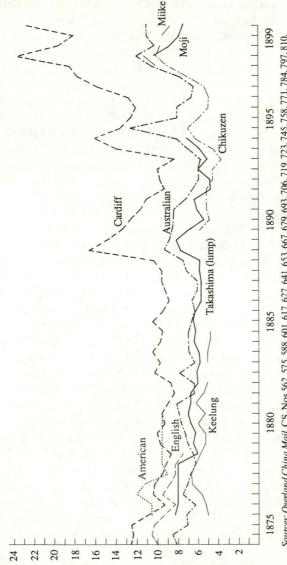

dollars

Sources: *Overland China Mail*, CS. Nos 562, 575, 588, 601, 617, 627, 641, 653, 667, 679, 693, 706, 719, 723, 745, 758, 771, 784, 797, 810, 824, 841, 866, 892, 919, 943, 970, 994, 1021, 1043, 1070, 1092, 1119, 1145, 1175, 1197, 1121, 1249, 1275, 1293, 1349, 1377, 1407, 1433, 1457, 1485, 1511, 1534, 1560, 1588, 1614.

Notes: (1) Quotations are the average prices between the lowest and the highest available close to the end of June and December each year.

(2) Prices of Australian coal for 1875–80 are the average of average prices of hard and soft coal.

(3) Takashima coal price for December 1875 is for Japan coal, and during the period from December 1889 to June 1892 seems to include dust coal.

(4) Chikuzen coal prices for December 1894 and June 1896 are for Moji coal.

British coal, and its share in the market also increased from 18 per cent in 1882 to 32 per cent in 1883. In the following year imports of Japanese coal increased to 124,644 tons, and finally exceeded Australian coal. Since the market shares of British, Australian and Japanese coal were 31 per cent, 32 per cent and 35.5 per cent respectively, British and Australian coal combined still held over 60 per cent of the Hong Kong market. In 1885, however, imports of Japanese coal reached 182,057 tons, a 48.5 per cent market share, which was the same as that of Britain and Australia together. In 1886 the Japanese share increased to 57 per cent, and Japanese coal had established a predominant position in the Hong Kong market. This rapid growth can be ascribed both to continuing low prices and to increases in supply following the introduction of mechanized mining technology, as we shall see later.

The production of Takashima coal was limited and its infrequent supply tended 'to sustain the value of Australian [coal imports]'.[68] This increased the relative importance of Miike coal. Said to be inferior in quality to Takashima coal, Miike coal had first been brought to Hong Kong in 1880.[69] As increasing amounts were imported, it played a crucial role in sustaining the demand for Japanese coal. Except for December 1881 and December 1892, Japanese coal continued to be cheaper even than Australian coal. The difference in price was comparatively small, however, ranging from only 0.10 to 1.70 dollars per ton during the years 1879 to 1887. Prices were influenced in part by the decline in silver value against gold, but the potential quantity of supply was also important, particularly in overcoming the keen competition from Australian coal. From the early 1880s Takashima coal was sold on a large scale, both on a contract basis and at a fixed price.[70] Miike coal was cheaper than Takashima, and by the mid-1880s had largely replaced it. In the 1890s even Miike coal was unable to meet the demand at Hong Kong, and it was largely replaced by Moji coal. This came mainly from the rapidly developing Chikuhō coal fields and was said to be inferior in quality even to Miike coal, but it had a large supply potential.

Prices started to fluctuate widely from the mid-1890s, possibly reflecting uncertainty in the Hong Kong coal market itself. Formosan coal had less than 10 per cent of the market and American anthracite was of negligible importance here. The 'main feature of the Hong Kong coal market in the 1890s was the increase in imports of Tongking coal, in particular from the Hongay coal mine which was opened in 1891 by the Société Française des Charbonnages du Tonkin. Hongay coal was supplied to steamers on the China coast, and its bricquettes were largely used by French men-of-war and by the Messageries Maritime.[71] The yearly increase in Tongking coal threatened the established market for Japanese coal, but Hongay coal had a large dust content and the failure to develop methods of using dust coal for steamers limited the expansion of its markets.[72]

The Structure of the Singapore Coal Market

Singapore was a commercial centre of the highest importance in both intra-Asian trade and trade between Europe and Asia.[73] It also had a vital strategic role. As the final report of the Carnarvon Commission pointed out, in addition to being 'one of our [British] chain of coaling stations, dividing the distance between those of Hong Kong and Ceylon, it also occupies a most important strategic position with respect to the command of the waters of the Eastern Archipelago.'[74]

Table 6–5 gives the imports of coal into Singapore by country, and their market share from 1881–5 to 1895–1900. The annual average of coal imports to Singapore increased from 309,194 tons in 1881–5 to 382,418 tons in 1891–5, and 540,400 tons in 1895–1900. Compared to Shanghai and Hong Kong the Singapore coal market was small, its expansion slow, and its selling prices high. As Table 6–1 shows, the average size of steamers entering Singapore was also small by comparison with Shanghai and Hong Kong. This implies that large steamers were able to travel to and from East Asia without having to stop to replenish their coal supplies in Singapore. In the 1880s, over 70 per cent of all coal imports to Singapore came from Britain. As imports from Australia and Japan increased, however, Britain's market share gradually declined: from 92 per cent in 1886 to 60 per cent in 1890.

Japanese coal was first imported into Singapore in 1883, but until 1892 its market share was less than 18 per cent. In the 1880s Miike coal was the major Japanese imported coal, with 31,620 tons in 1888, compared to 8,425 tons for Takashima

Table 6-5 Annual Averages of Coal Imports into Singapore, 1881–1900
(in tons)

Period	Britain	%	Australia	%	Japan	%	India	%	Labuan	%	Sarawak	%	Total (with others)	%
1881/85	286,797	(92.8)	17.534	(5.7)	2,215	(0.7)	–		114	(0.0)	1,914	(0.6)	309,194	(100)
1886/90	246,317	(75.5)	32.750	(10.0)	37.800	(11.6)	3,256	(1.0)	1,105	(0.3)	4,716	(1.4)	326,422	(100)
1891/95	174,145	(45.5)	49,990	(13.1)	122,650	(32.1)	9,529	(2.5)	11,729	(3.1)	12,163	(3.2)	382,418	(100)
1896/1900	82,305	(15.2)	54,551	(10.1)	301,234	(55.7)	62,378	(11.5)	11,856	(2.2)	20,949	(3.9)	540,400	(100)

Sources: Straits Settlements, *Blue Book.* 1881–1900.

coal.[75] Although the decline in British coal and the rapid increase in Japanese coal had already attracted notice in 1890,[76] it was only after 1893 that Japanese coal took an important position in the Singapore market. In 1893, when the market share of British coal had fallen to 44 per cent, imports of Japanese coal increased to 118,380 tons (Takashima 16,897 tons, and Miike 69,540 tons) and its market share thus reached 36 per cent.[77] During this period, if a vessel engaged in trade between Europe and China and Japan could not find any suitable return cargo in Japan, it was common practice to carry Japanese coal to Hong Kong or Singapore.[78]

Figure 8 shows the price fluctuations of imported coal at Singapore from 1880 to 1900. It is important to note that prices in the Singapore market were higher than those in Shanghai and Hong Kong. While British coal was the most expensive, the others competed against each other in terms of price. Labuan and Sarawak coal grew cheaper after 1891, but were irregular in supply. From 1887 to 1896 the price movements of Australian, Japanese and Indian coal were complex, but after this time Japanese coal emerged supreme, being available in large quantities to meet demand at Singapore. The factor which made Japanese coal relatively cheaper, and therefore facilitated its import, was the worldwide decline in the value of silver relative to gold.[79]

The British coal strike of 1893 gave Japanese coal a temporary advantage, but the fundamental trend was also in Japan's favour. In 1894 imports of Japanese coal amounted to 192,409 tons and reached a market share of 44 per cent, surpassing the 42 per cent of British coal (182,839 tons). The Straits Settlements *Annual Report for the Year 1894* stated:

> Coal importations increased by over 100,000 tons, of which excess about one-third was contributed by the United Kingdom, but the feature of note is the position now taken by Japan, which has supplanted the United Kingdom as the principal seller.[80]

British coal suffered not only from the fall in silver value but also from a rise in price caused by a further miners' strike in 1898.[81] Its share of the market continued to decrease, falling to 12 per cent in 1900. Imports of Australian coal did not increase markedly, and the Australian market share varied

**Figure 8 Price Fluctuations of Imported Coal in the
Singapore Coal Market, 1880–1900 (per ton)**

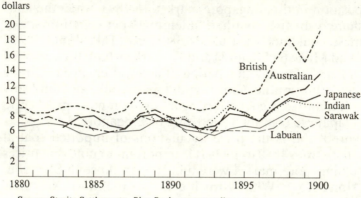

Source: Straits Settlements, *Blue Book*, corresponding years.

from 6 to 23 per cent between 1887 and 1900. While Welsh
coal was used for British and other warships, Japanese coal
was chiefly used for mail steamers.[82] Annual imports of
Japanese coal reached an average of 241,610 tons between
1894 and 1899. Japan enjoyed a consistently dominant share
of over 50 per cent after 1896, and took a 67 per cent share
(442,972 tons) of the Singapore market in 1900. As Table 6–5
shows, however, Japanese coal was not entirely without rivals
in the Singapore market and faced competition from increasing
imports of Indian coal after 1897. Coal production in India
increased from 1.2 million tons for 1881–5 to 1.8 million for
1886–90, 2.8 million for 1891–5, and 4.8 million for 1896–1900;
exports of Indian coal reached 53,665 tons in 1894–5.[83]

The smallness of the market and its relatively high prices
made it possible for Japanese coal to compete with other coals
here on easier terms than in Shanghai and Hong Kong. This
was also true, however, for the other coals. As long as there
was a sufficient supply and its price was reasonable, Japanese
coal was able to maintain a strong market position in Singapore,
but this position was always somewhat precarious. Japanese
coal maintained a 60–70 per cent share of the market between
1900 and 1904, but this decreased to 44 per cent in 1905.[84]

The Development of the Coal Industry in Japan

As the previous sections have shown, Japanese coal exports developed after 1859 in the midst of an overall expansion in the East Asian coal market which reflected the rapid increase in East Asian trade. In this section I shall examine the internal factors which affected the competitiveness of Japanese coal on overseas markets.

Table 6–6 gives figures for Japanese coal output and exports. Coal production in the 1860s was estimated at 390,000 tons;[85] from the late 1870s onwards it steadily increased, reaching 5 million tons in 1896 and 7.5 million in 1900. The annual average of coal exports also increased, from 118,000 tons in the period 1871 to 1875, to 924,000 in 1886–90, and 2,464,000 in 1896–1900. In 1886 the three large mines of Takashima, Miike and Chikuhō were supplying 63 per cent of the total coal production. Between 1875 and 1899, an average 39 per cent of all Japan's coal production was exported, with a peak average of 46 per cent being reached in 1884–90. If one were to include in these figures coal loaded at treaty ports for the use of steamers, the percentages would be higher still. Increasing amounts of Japanese coal were used in this way after 1869, when such coal ceased to be treated as export coal and was thus freed from export duties.[86]

Because of its geographical situation Nagasaki naturally became the coal-exporting centre, shipping an average of 97 per cent of all coal exports between 1867 and 1880. The number and total tonnage of vessels entering Nagasaki increased from 108 vessels (a total of 39,497 tons) in 1860 to 296 vessels (276,415 tons) in 1875 and 997 vessels (1,168,489 tons) in 1890. Steamers replaced sailing vessels rapidly after 1871 and accounted for 925 vessels (1,140,308 tons) out of the 1890 total.[87] There was a parallel increase in the demand for coal at the port, both for direct use in steamers and for export to Shanghai. A British consular report in the mid-1860s mentioned bright prospects for the Nagasaki coal trade:

This mineral [coal] is evidently destined to become of great importance, and is likely to form an important feature in the export trade of this port. . . These [Takashima, Karatsu, Hirado, and Hizen] mines have hitherto been worked by

Table 6-6 Annual Output and Exports of Japanese Coal, 1861–1900
(in thousand tons)

Period	Output				Export				
	Takashima	Miike	Chikuhō[1]	Total (with others) (A)	Lump & dust	Ships' use	Total (B)	(B)/(A) %	Export price per ton yen
1861/65						12	12	–	
1866/70						31	31	–	
1871/75	125[2]	43[3]	n.a.	388[4]	36	82	118	30.4	5.31[5]
1876/80	153	95	n.a.	693	97	105	202	29.1	4.97
1881/85	245	188	n.a.	1,058	151	271	422	40.4	4.27
1886/90	277	383	544	2,028	465	459	924	45.6	3.55
1891/95	205	594	1,408	3,752	1,106	412	1,518	40.5	3.71
1896/1900	171	704	4,087	6,235	1,873	591	2,464	39.5	5.71

Sources: For output, Nihon Kōgakukai, *Meiji kōgyō-shi: Kōgyō-hen* (1930), pp. 656–9; Takanoe Mototarō, *Nihon tankō-shi* (1908), pp. 172–3. For coal exports for 1861–7, CR, corresponding years, and for 1868–1900, *Nihon bōeki seiran* (1935), p. 106.
Notes: (1) Figures for Chikuhō are the totals of coal sent from the five major coal districts. (2) 1875 only. (3) 1873–5. (4) 1874–5. (5) 1868–70.

manual labour, but as soon as the proposed machinery has been introduced and placed in working order it is expected that they will produce a sufficient supply for the China and Japan ports, and I have no doubt will be considerably used by Her Majesty's ships on this station. The average price is from 5 to 6½ dollars per ton, whereas the English cannot be laid down for less than 18 to 20 dollars per ton.[88]

Coal prices at Nagasaki fluctuated in accordance with the price fetched by Japanese coal at Shanghai, where its value was influenced by other foreign coals. Of the 117,499 tons sent to Nagasaki in 1872, 48,000 tons (41 per cent of the total) were shipped to Shanghai; 6,000 (5 per cent) to Northern Chinese ports; 12,000 (10 per cent) to Yokohama (for use by Pacific Mail steamers); 27,499 (23 per cent) was actually sold on the spot to the Pacific Mail Co.; and 12,000 (10 per cent) was sold to other steamers and to men-of-war respectively.[89] As the coal exported to Chinese ports was probably used for steamers, it can be said that most of the coal disposed of in Nagasaki was destined for this purpose. Even as late as 1895, 80 per cent of the coal exported from Japan was for use in steamers.[90]

The Takashima and Miike mines were the main Japanese coal mines in the 1870s and 1880s, both producing bituminous coal. They accounted for 28 to 44 per cent of the total Japanese output during this period, and played a leading role in the development of the Japanese industry. Other mines were generally small, poorly equipped and capable of producing only inferior coal, which was mainly used in domestic salt manufacture.

Soon after the opening of the ports, engineers from both men-of-war and merchant steamers expressed the opinion that Takashima coal 'is well adapted for sea going steam vessels' when 'mixed with Welsh coal'.[91] It was estimated that 25 tons of the best Japanese coal, such as Takashima, would give the same result for steaming purposes as 20 tons of Welsh or English coal.[92] Screened coal from Takashima was widely used by men-of-war of the French, American, Russian and German navies; small or dust coal was used by shipping companies such as Pacific Mail, P & O and the Occidental and Oriental Steamship Co., and by Mitsubishi mail steamers.[93]

Until 1868 Takashima coal was worked 'on too limited a

scale' and 'produced but a small quantity of coal, owing to the defective system of mining pursued by the natives'.[94] Only after 1868 was the mine developed as a modern colliery using Western mining technology, following an agreement between Glover & Co. and the domain of Saga. Apparently, 'Glover & Co. obtained a joint lease of the property, in partnership with the Prince of Hizen [Saga], and sank a shaft of 150 feet deep on the opposite side of the island, where they struck the 8 ft. seam.'[95] When Glover & Co. went into bankruptcy in 1870, the Netherland Trading Society took over operation of the mine. It was purchased by the Meiji government in 1874, and sold to Gotō Shōjirō in the same year.[96] Takashima was only about five miles from Nagasaki, and the coal mined there was carried to the port in fleets of from 60 to 80 barges towed by one small steamer.[97] It is said that 300–400 labourers were employed at the mine in 1868, but in the mid-1870s it faced a labour shortage, particularly after the beginning of the Satsuma Rebellion in 1877.[98] Convicts were employed to make good these shortages, and the labour organization system (*naya-seido*), according to which the company relied on self-employed contractors to supply labour, was adapted so that the former contractors were employed by the company as heads of the labour organizations.[99] The annual output of coal at Takashima increased from 35,000 tons in 1869 to 125,000 in 1875 and to 230,000 in 1880. An American consular report stated: 'The Takashima Coal has been gradually coming more and more into favour as a steam Coal, both for vessels of war and merchant steamers.'[100]

The Miike coal mine was

> situated in the south-east corner of the province of Chikugo [Fukuoka], on the east of the Shimabara Gulf. This coal-field forms a strip of about four miles wide, from east to west, and runs a few miles from north to south. . . There are two seams of excellent bituminous coal, the upper one exceeding 6 feet in thickness, and separated from the lower seam, which averages 5 feet, by a parting of stone 6 feet thick.[101]

The mine was purchased by the government in 1873 and remained under government direction until 1888. Western technology was introduced to modernize its operations, in accordance with government policy to encourage exports such as coal as a way of obtaining foreign exchange. In 1876 the government sent samples of Miike coal to Shanghai to investigate the demand for it there. Shinagawa Tadamichi, then Japanese consul to Shanghai, suggested that a market for Miike coal might exist if it were sold at a low price. In the same year, Mitsui Bussan Kaisha was appointed sole agent for Miike coal and opened a branch in Shanghai in order to facilitate coal exports.[102] This signified the breakthrough by a Japanese firm into the existing export system in Japan as controlled by Western merchants under the 'unequal' treaties.

Miike coal was sold to consumers in China such as Jardine, Matheson & Co., Butterfield & Swire, and the China Merchant Steam Navigation Co. through Western coal dealers who bought it from the Shanghai branch of Mitsui Bussan.[103] Exports were facilitated in 1878 by the establishment of Kuchinotsu, at the southern extremity of the Shimabara peninsula, as the special port for the shipment of Miike coal, and by the government's loan of a sailing vessel to Mitsui Bussan for transportation of coal. After this most Miike coal was shipped from Kuchinotsu rather than from Nagasaki.[104] According to Table 6-7, which shows the distribution of shipments and sales of Miike coal, the first half of the 1880s saw a shift in its main market from Japan itself to overseas, and to Shanghai in particular until 1884. Coal exports became an important source of revenue for Mitsui Bussan.[105] The overseas demand encouraged the development of the mine, and the production system was organized with the overseas market in mind.[106] The employment of convicts, which began on a large scale in 1876, was intended to overcome the difficulties of recruiting skilled miners from the adjacent agricultural areas, but it also made it possible to maintain low costs and thus overcome competition on the Shanghai market.[107]

As we have already seen, by 1880 Japanese coal had established a dominance in the Shanghai coal market. As the more plentiful Miike coal became the main coal exported from Japan, Takashima coal lost its position and began to be exported to Hong Kong. Table 6-8 shows the shipments and sales of Takashima coal between 1875 and 1893. Since the ratio of coal

Table 6-7 Shipments and Sales of Miike Coal, 1877–93
(in thousand tons)

Year	Exported to					Sold to the domestic market	Total output
	Shanghai	Hong Kong	Singapore	Other ports	Total		
1877	0	–	–	0	0	56	55
1880	62	1	–	8	70	86	118
1885	82	85	–	13	180	50	248
1890	96	141	25	31	294	172	495
1893	100	225	70	35	430	213	599

Sources: (1) Exports: Ueda Jushirō, 'Ueda Yasusaburō nenpu' (1973), pp. 318–19; Sumiya Mikio, *Nihon sekitan sangyō bunseki* (1968), p. 265.
(2) Sales to the domestic market: Tanaka Osamu, 'Kōbushō shokan jigyō no haraisage to Miike tankō no haraisage' (1968), p. 81; Kasuga Yutaka, 'Kanei Miike tankō to Mitsui Bussan' (1976), p. 230; Sumiya, *ibid*, p. 265.
(3) Total output: Nihon Kōgakukai, *Meiji kōgyō-shi: Kōgyō-hen* (1930), pp. 658–9; 'Mitsui kōzan gojūnen shikō', quoted by Kasuga Yutaka, 'Mitsui zaibatsu ni okeru sekitangyō no hatten kōzō' (1977), p. 121.

exports to the total shipments and sales was 44 per cent, it is clear that the main market for Takashima coal lay within Japan, at Nagasaki and Yokohama, rather than overseas. From 1883 to 1891, around 60 per cent of exported Takashima coal was destined for Hong Kong. In 1882 the price of one ton of Takashima lump coal at Shanghai was 4.25 taels. The combined charges for items such as freight, export duty, landing and storing, and commission at 2.5 per cent came to 1.73 taels per ton; once this was deducted, sales of Takashima lump coal showed a profit of 2.52 taels per ton, equivalent to 3.46 dollars.[108]

Takashima coal faced severe competition overseas, both from Miike coal and from non-Japanese coals. To compensate for the grave disadvantage of its limited supply, Takashima coal was forced to seek more distant markets where it would not have to compete with other more abundant Japanese coals. The Takashima colliery was transferred to Mitsubishi in 1881, but until 1888 there were no attempts to introduce new machinery or to expand existing equipment.[109]

Table 6-8 Shipments and Sales of Takashima Coal, 1875–93
(in thousand tons)

| Year | Exported to | | | | | Shipped to Yokohama & other Japanese ports | Sold at Nagasaki | Total | Stock (at the end of the year) | Total output |
	Shanghai	Hong Kong	Singapore	Other ports	Total					
1875	25	13	–	5	43	2	79	124	–	125
1880	n.a.	n.a.	n.a.	n.a.	105	5	113	223	23	210
1885	43	59	–	4	106	37	127	270	21	286
1890	54	111	–	36*	202	70	139	411	9	404
1893	49	50	17	5	120	35	132	287	3	252

Sources: CR, Nagasaki, corresponding years.
Notes: (1) Figures for total output after 1885 include coal produced at Nakanoshima.
(2) * These figures include Singapore and Japanese ports other than Yokohama and Nagasaki.

Under Mitsubishi management the *naya-seido* was reinforced as a way of fighting competition by raising labour productivity. Labour was intensified around 1885 and 1886, and reached a peak in 1887. The following year the treatment of the Takashima labour force was exposed by the periodical *Nihonjin* as a major social problem.[110]

Even though Japanese coal had been able to establish dominance in Shanghai by 1880, it was not easy for it to enter the Hong Kong market because it was not available in sufficient quantities and at a competitive price. Thus, when Miike coal first tried to advance into Hong Kong in 1882, insufficient supplies meant that it was unsuccessful. Under pressure from Mitsui Bussan to remedy this problem the Miike mine developed new pits, increased its dependence on convict labour, and mechanized the production process. In 1878 Ōura pit was the site of the first winch to be set up in the mine; drainage pumps were introduced in 1882 and ventilation fans in 1884.[111] Mitsui Bussan, for its part, increased its coal-carrying ships from three vessels with a total tonnage of 2,221 tons in 1880 to six with 4,050 tons in 1890 and seven with 19,635 tons in 1900.[112] The firm's Hong Kong branch, which had been set up in 1878 for currency exchange and closed in 1881, was reopened in 1886 for the sale of coal.[113]

In contrast with the rapid introduction of modern processes in some areas of mining, there was no mechanization at the coal face itself and convicts continued to be employed on a large scale. In 1879 the number of convicts employed in the Miike colliery reached 631, or 41 per cent of a total of 1,659 employees, and from around 1882–3 they became even more important. As well as providing an answer to the labour shortage, they helped to keep down the wages of non-convict labourers and thus played an important role in the fight to overcome foreign competition and expand the market for Miike coal in Hong Kong which had been going on since the late 1870s.[114] The average daily wage was lower at Miike (14–16 sen in 1882–7) than at Takashima (15–30 sen around 1885) and Chikuhō (22–26 sen around 1887).[115] Since Miike itself had no power to reduce freight rates, it could strive to become more competitive only through increasing production and keeping wages low. The low wages helped to bring about a decline in the cost per ton of Miike coal, particularly after 1883, but only at the expense of intensifying labour at the unmechanized coal face, as Table 6-9 shows. It is this less pleasant side to the policy which was doubtless the cause of the miners' riots of 1883, 1884, 1885 and 1887.[116]

Freight rates declined too, as a result of the increase in the number of coal-carrying ships possessed by Mitsui Bussan. This meant that they could lower their rates without reference to fluctuations in the freight market. The average cost for freight per ton of coal between Shanghai and Kuchinotsu decreased from 2.82 dollars in 1881 to 2 in 1884 and 1.78 in 1887. Declining costs in both mining and transport allowed for a rapid fall in the selling price of Miike coal.[117]

In 1886 the market situation in Singapore was surveyed in order to investigate a possible demand for Miike coal there and thus solve the glut caused by the depression from which the domestic Japanese coal market was then suffering. As a result, sales to Singapore began, and were successful. In 1888 – around the time of the transfer of the colliery from the government to Mitsui – Ueda Yasusaburō, manager of the Shanghai branch of Mitsui Bussan, expressed the hope of opening a Singapore branch in consequence of the great increase in demand for Miike coal there. This had been hastened by a combination of a decrease in supplies of Takashima coal and a shortage caused by a miners' strike in Australia.[118] Miike coal came to replace Takashima coal in the overseas markets, and increased its exports from 193,000 tons in 1887 to 294,000 in 1890, and 430,000 in 1893.[119]

Chikuhō coal, produced in northern Kyūshū, was mainly in demand for domestic salt manufacture until the late 1880s, when developments in coal utilization widened the market for coarse and dust coal. Some of the better mines in the Chikuhō area were mechanized through the introduction of winches and drainage pumps around that time. Exports of Chikuhō coal were facilitated by the abolition of the export duty on coal in 1888, the establishment of Moji (at the extreme end of Japan proper) as a special export port in 1889, and the completion of the railway between the Chikuhō region and Moji in 1893. In addition, the shortage caused by the 1888 miners' strike in Australia and the consequent price rises on the Hong Kong and Singapore markets encouraged big enterprises such as Mitsubishi to consider investing in the Chikuhō mines.[120]

Table 6-9 Production Costs of Miike Coal, 1880–87
(per ton)

Financial Year	Total expenses		Costs of actual face-work	
	yen		yen	
1880	1.98	(100)	1.76	(100)
1881	2.10	(106)	1.85	(105)
1882	2.83	(143)	2.07	(118)
1883	1.93	(97)	1.36	(77)
1884	1.37	(69)	1.02	(58)
1885	1.28	(65)	0.82	(47)
1886	1.10	(56)	0.77	(44)
1887	1.04	(53)	0.64	(36)

Source: Kasuga Yutaka, 'Kanei Miike tankō to Mitsui Bussan', *Mitsui bunko ronsō*, no. 10 (1976), p. 304.
Note: Figures in parentheses are indices calculated by the author.

Many coal mines were opened in Chikuhō during the 'coal fever' of 1887 to 1890. A British consular report for 1891 described the results of this 'fever':

> Simultaneously with the increased production, lower prices ruled at Nagasaki and elsewhere. The coal had to be sold or shipped on some terms so as to secure funds to continue working, with the result that at Hong-Kong, Manila, and Shanghai, Japan coals (outside of Takashima and the coal from the other mines of the Mitsu Bishi Company) can hardly be given away in these times of depression. The small mine owners are in financial difficulties, and no doubt many of them will have to close up. These mines will then probably fall into the hands of the Mitsu Bishi Company and other large companies, who will work them on business methods and regulate production so as to keep prices on a paying level.[121]

As this report relates, the 'coal fever' led to a depression in the coal trade due to over-production. Prices dropped, and the market was flooded with Japanese coal of inferior quality. This encouraged a further fall in prices. The outbreak of the Sino–Japanese War in 1894, however, provided the impetus for further large-scale development of mining in the Chikuhō area, since the increased political tension led to a jump in demand for coal and therefore higher prices.[122]

Mitsui Bussan established a special coal department in 1894 and made offers of financial assistance in exchange for distribution rights to coal-mining enterprises in the Chikuhō area which produced good-quality coal but suffered from lack of capital. Mitsui intended to establish themselves as the leading firm in the coal industry and to exert pressure on Miike coal by gaining control of other good-quality coals which might provide competition.[123]

In 1897 there were ninety collieries in the Chikuhō area, employing a total of 23,184 miners and producing 2,726,000 tons, 50 per cent of total Japanese coal output. Along with the growth in output from Chikuhō, in the 1890s there was a shift in the location of the main coal exporting ports, from Nagasaki (near the Takashima mine) and Kuchinotsu (near Miike) to Moji and Wakamatsu, which were both near Chikuhō.[124]

The post Sino–Japanese War period saw a rapid growth in domestic Japanese coal consumption, which reflected the pace of the economic development being encouraged by the government. Table 6-10 shows the distribution of coal consumption in Japan at this time. Factory demand increased at a faster rate than steamer demand, and reached 50 per cent of total demand in 1896.[125] The development of the industry was also encouraged by the rapid expansion of the overseas market. The increase in political tension in East Asia made the coal market unstable, however, because it caused an imbalance between supply and demand. When there was a sudden release on to the East Asian market of surplus coal of a superior type which had originally been imported for military purposes, inferior Japanese coal had to be sold at a loss. For example, the sudden tension caused by German acquisition of a lease on Kiaochow in 1898 led to an increase in available supplies of good-quality British coal, which had an adverse effect on the East Asian market for inferior coals. Good-quality Japanese coal was not, however, affected, since it was

Table 6-10 Coal Consumption in Japan, 1886–1900
(in thousand tons)

Year	Steamers	Railways	Factories	Salt manufacturing	Total
	%	%	%	%	%
1886	237 (27.6)	18 (2.1)	147 (17.1)	456 (53.1)	858 (100)
1890	461 (32.2)	69 (4.8)	424 (29.7)	477 (33.3)	1,430 (100)
1895	747 (27.8)	223 (8.3)	1,198 (44.5)	522 (19.4)	2,689 (100)
1900	1,464 (27.8)	507 (9.6)	2,653 (50.4)	639 (12.1)	5,262 (100)

Source: Sumiya Mikio, *Nihon sekitan sangyō bunseki* (1968), pp. 190, 244, 345.

purchased on a contract basis. Speculation further exacerbated price fluctuations.[126]

The increasing domestic consumption eventually led to a shortage of coal for export and a subsequent rise in domestic prices. This in turn led to a rise in the selling price of Japanese coal on overseas markets and made the competition with Chinese and Australian coal fiercer. Japanese coal found itself more and more at a disadvantage on overseas markets, particularly after the adoption of the gold standard in 1897, since this removed the favourable effect of a steady decrease in silver value. The shift to the domestic market was therefore further accelerated.[127]

Japan's Coal Exports and the Eastern Coal Market

Japanese merchants found that it was much easier to break into the overseas coal market than into the overseas raw silk and tea markets. In 1896 they were handling 91 per cent of Japan's total coal exports.[128] This was partly because it was neither profitable nor convenient for Western merchants to deal in such a bulky cargo. Even so, as Table 6–11 shows, in 1896 foreign shipping companies clearly found coal profitable in view of the high freight rates involved, and 88 per cent of coal exports were carried by foreign vessels.

Table 6-11 Coal Exports by Destination and by Ship in 1896

To	By Japanese vessels	By foreign vessels	Total
Asia	tons	tons	tons
China	45,086	625,726	670,812 (42%)
Hong Kong	128,325	476,772	605,097 (37%)
British India	11,201	231,261	242,462 (15%)
Others	11,005	43,137	54,142 (3%)
Europe	–	4,400	4,400 (0%)
USA	–	26,512	26,512 (2%)
Others	551	10,748	11,299 (1%)
Total	196,168 (12%)	1,418,556 (88%)	1,614,724 (100%)

Source: Naikaku Tōkeikyoku, *Nihon teikoku tōkei nenkan* (for 1896), pp. 609–10.
Note: Coal for ships' use is excluded.

Within Japan, coal for steamer use was transacted in the following straightforward way. A seller and a buyer would come to an agreement over price and quantity on the basis of samples, and then exchange contracts or make a verbal agreement. Payment was made on completion of the transaction.[129] When Japanese coal dealers received instructions from consumers overseas, they fixed their quotations in accordance with the price at the port of destination and with the relevant freight rate, and made arrangements for transportation. When the coal was loaded on to the ship, the dealer would get the captain to write an invoice for it. On the basis of this invoice the buyer would pay 80–95 per cent of the value in advance of receipt. Final settlement of accounts would follow checks on the amount of coal when it arrived at the port of destination. The buyer paid separately for items such as marine insurance and the wages of those involved in unloading.[130]

Table 6–12 shows the relationship between Japan's coal

Table 6-12 Japan's Coal Exports and the Eastern Coal Market, 1871-99

Year	Average export price from Japan (A)		Shanghai				Hong Kong				Singapore			
	¥ (A)	$	Freight to (B) $	Average selling price (C) $	(A)/(C) %	(B)/(C) %	Freight to (D) $	Average selling price (E) $	(A)/(E) %	(D)/(E) %	Freight to (F) $	Average import price (G) $	(A)/(G) %	(F)/(G) %
1871	5.34	5.46	-	8.05	68	-								
1875	4.16	4.04	2.25	6.96	58	32	1.85	8.25	49	22				
1880	3.49	3.49	2.88	6.31	55	46	2.35	6.25	56	38				
1885	3.27	3.29	1.43	5.32	62	27	1.53	5.65	58	27	-	8.00	41	-
1890	3.63	3.64	1.23	6.74	54	18	1.50	6.13	59	24	2.00	7.16	51	28

Table 6-12 continued

1895	3.93	3.87	1.88	6.89	56	27	2.00	5.75	67	35	2.63	8.16	47	32
1899	5.85	6.10	2.03	–	–	–	2.53	8.25	74	31	3.03	10.04	61	30

Sources: (A) Tōyō Keizai Shinpōsha (ed.), *Nihon bōeki seiran* (1935), p. 106; *Yokohamashi-shi*, vol. 3, Pt II (1963), pp. 285, 359; Nihon Tōkei Kenkyūjo (ed.), *Nihon keizai tōkei-shū* (1958), p. 171; Hsiao, *China's Foreign Trade Statistics* (1974), pp. 190–91. (B) *NCH*, CI. (C) See sources in Figure 6. (D) *Overland China Mail*, CS. Figures for 1875 and 1880, *NCH*, CI. (E) See sources in Figure 7. (F) *Overland China Mail*, CS. Figures for 1890, *NCH*, CI. (G) See sources in Table 6-5.

Notes: (1) Figures in (A) are calculated on the basis of the Mexican dollar-yen exchange rates. (2) Freight rates are the average between the highest and lowest rates available in each year. Quotations are mainly nominal rates and exclude rates without mentioning 'coal' freight. (3) Figures in (B) are from Nagasaki or Kuchinotsu to Shanghai until 1890, and from Moji to Shanghai for 1895 and 1899. (4) Figures in (C) are calculated from those in taels on the basis of the exchange rates in Hsiao, op. cit; CR, Summary of Commercial Reports in Japan for 1876, pp. 40–41; and Nihon Ginkō Tōkeikyoku, *Honpō shuyō keizai tōkei* (1966), p. 318. (5) Figures in (C) after 1880 and (E) are the average between the highest and lowest prices in June and December in each year. (6) For 1899, no quotations are available for coal from the main Japanese mines to Shanghai.

exports and the Eastern coal market, in terms of price and freight rates. Between 1871 and 1897 the ratio of the average Japanese export price to the market price in Shanghai was 56 per cent. Freight rates played a crucial role in the cost structure, since they moved independently of export prices. They fluctuated from year to year, but after 1883 variations became smaller. At this point a tendency to decline appeared, and freight rates steadily became less of a factor in the final price of Japanese coal in Shanghai. When the Japanese export price jumped to 3.83 dollars per ton in 1889 it was possible to offset this rise until 1893 as freight rates were declining. The price of Japanese coal in Hong Kong changed in the same way as on the Shanghai market. Between 1875 and 1899 the ratio of the Japanese export price to the market price in Hong Kong was 59 per cent. Freight rates were, of course, slightly higher than those to Shanghai.

In 1897 a British consular report, commenting on the export market for Takashima coal, pointed out that 'a particular feature of the business was that this coal was sought after from more distant ports than has hitherto been the case.'[131] The greater the distance from Japan, however, the greater the competition from other coals. In San Francisco, for instance, Japanese coal was unable to compete in price against British and Australian coal.[132] It is therefore necessary to review the competition between coals in terms of their differing market prices, and I shall do so through a review of the coal market in Singapore, where British and Australian coal were major competitors of Japanese coal.

Table 6–13 shows the price structure of the coal imported into Singapore from Britain, Australia and Japan between 1880 and 1899. Average export prices from Britain were lower than those from Japan until 1888, while Australian and Japanese prices were almost equal from the early 1880s until 1896. From this table it is obvious that the major factor behind differences in import prices in Singapore was different freight rates. Japanese coal was cheaper largely because of lower freight charges. As imports from Japan increased, therefore, British and Australian coal, with their relatively high freight rates, became non-competitive and were forced to withdraw from the Singapore market. Despite its overall dominance, however, Japanese coal could not replace high-quality British coal imported for the British navy.

Table 6-13 Price Structure of Coal imported into Singapore from Britain, Australia and Japan, 1880–99

	Britain					Australia					Japan				
Year	Average export price from Britain (A)	Freight to (B)	Average import price (C)	(A)/(C)	(B)/(C)	Average export price from NSW (D)	Freight to (E)	Average import price (F)	(D)/(F)	(E)/(F)	Average export price from Japan (G)	Freight to (H)	Average import price (I)	(G)/(I)	(H)/(I)
	s d $	s d $	$	%	%	s d $	s d $	$	%	%	$	$	$	%	%
1880	9.5(2.48)	22.0(5.80)	9.45	26	61	9.3(2.44)	17.3(4.55)	7.85	31	58	3.49	n.a.			
1885	9.4(2.68)	18.6(5.31)	8.65	31	61	11.0(3.16)	10.3(2.94)	6.24	51	47	3.29	n.a.	8.00	41	–
1890	13.3(3.93)	17.8(5.24)	10.24	38	51	10.2(3.02)	14.6(4.30)	7.83	39	55	3.64	2.00	7.16	51	28
1895	9.9(4.56)	10.6(4.91)	10.99	41	45	7.6(3.51)	9.3(4.33)	8.59	41	50	3.87	2.63	8.16	47	32
1899	11.3(5.72)	14.9(7.50)	15.27	37	49	8.0(4.07)	14.0(7.12)	11.71	35	61	6.10	3.03	10.04	61	30

Sources: (A) B.R. Mitchell and P. Deane, *Abstract of British Historical Statistics* (1962), pp. 121, 304–5. (B) E.A.V. Angier, *Fifty Years' Freights, 1869–1919* (1920). (C), (F), (I) Straits Settlements, *Blue Book*, corresponding years. (D), (E), K.H. Burley, 'The Overseas Trade in New South Wales Coal and the British Shipping Industry, 1860–1914', *Economic Record*, vol. 36, no. 75 (1960). p. 413. (G) *Nihon bōeki seiran* (1935). p. 106. (H) For 1890, *NCH*, CI; for 1895 and 1899, *Overland China Mail*, CS.

Notes: (1) Figures in Mexican dollars in parentheses are calculated on the basis of the Mexican dollar–sterling exchange rates in Hsiao, *China's Foreign Trade Statistics* (1974), pp. 190–1. Figures for 1880 are calculated on the basis of the Mexican dollar–sterling exchange rates in each year. Figures for 1880 are calculated on the assumption that 5s. 9 5/8d. was equivalent to 1.53 Mexican dollars. (2) Freight rates are the average between the highest and the lowest rates available in each year. (3) Figures in (B) are freight rates from Wales (Cardiff) to Singapore. (4) Figures in (G) are calculated on the basis of the Mexican dollar–yen and Mexican dollar–sterling exchange rates in Nihon Tōkei Kenkyūjo (ed.), *Nihon keizai tōkei-shū* (1958). p. 171. and Hsiao, op. cit., pp. 190–1.

Also of importance in determining the price – and therefore the competitiveness – of any coal on the overseas market were labour productivity, wages, and technological developments in the producer country.[133] British coal, for example, came mainly from Wales. In the second half of the nineteenth century, demand expanded rapidly and coal was the most important element in Britain's trade with Europe.[134] The gradually expanding market for coal stimulated technological innovation in the industry in the middle decades of the century. Despite improvements in ventilation, shaft construction, winding machinery, and in the methods of transporting coal from the coal face to the surface, however, pick and shovel mining remained the rule as late as 1913.[135] Labour productivity rose, as did wages, but since productivity was rising quickly enough to offset wage increases, it was the former which played the leading role in shaping the industry until the late 1880s. After that time, however, productivity began to fall, and the continuing upward trend in wage rates began to have a direct – and increasingly unfavourable – effect on the profitability of the British coal-mining industry.[136]

Table 6–14 shows the development of the South Wales coal industry in the second half of the nineteenth century. By the mid-1860s coal for use in steamers had become a significant part of the output of the South Wales coal fields, which were producing 8–17 per cent of Britain's total output. In 1860, only 16 per cent of the total South Wales output of 10.8 million tons was exported, but this increased to 33 per cent in 1880 and 47 per cent in 1900. The ratio of coal exports from South Wales to coal exports from the whole of Britain also increased, from 24 per cent in 1860 to 38.5 per cent in 1880 and 42 per cent in 1900.[137] In 1880 there were 343 working collieries in South Wales, and forty-nine coal exporters in Cardiff were buying coal for steamers. Sixty to seventy per cent of all such coal was normally sold by annual contract. The total number of coal shippers in Cardiff increased from forty-six in 1882 to sixty-four in 1886 and sixty-nine in 1889.[138]

If one looks at figures for the distribution of British coal exports in the second half of the nineteenth century, over three quarters went to Europe and only 3.0–6.8 per cent to Asia and Oceania. Figures for exports from ports in South Wales suggest that exports of Welsh coal to India and the 'East Indies'

Table 6-14 South Wales Coal Industry, 1856–1900

Period	Annual average output	Labour productivity (annual output per man above & below ground)	Wage rate index (1879=100)	Export price index for Welsh coal (f.o.b.) (1880=100)	Total coal exports from Britain
	mil. tons	tons			mil. tons
1856/60	8.9		109	104	6.4
1861/65	11.4		108	103	8.2
1866/70	13.6		110	101	10.3
1871/75	14.8	239	128	191	12.9
1876/80	18.1	275	105	107	15.8
1881/85	24.0	306	108	112	21.1
1886/90	27.0	289	109	114	25.4
1891/95	31.5	262	124	130	29.9
1896/1900	35.1	267	117	129	37.7

Sources: R.H. Walters, *The Economic and Business History of the South Wales Steam Coal Industry, 1840–1914* (1977), pp.6, 327, 355, 360–1; B.R. Mitchell and P. Deane, *Abstract of British Historical Statistics* (1962), p. 121.

(which presumably included East and Southeast Asia) amounted to 450,000–750,000 tons between 1880 and 1900, 3.1–7.4 per cent of all the coal exported from South Wales ports.[139] This non-Asian bias of the market for British coal helped Japanese coal to compete on favourable terms in East and Southeast Asia. Since the main use for coal in this region was in steamers, the rapid increase in coal exports from Japan was closely connected with the increase in the number of steamers engaged in trade on the China and Japan coasts, particularly after the opening of the Suez Canal.

Australian coal production also showed a rapid increase in the latter half of the nineteenth century, from 501,920 tons in 1861–5 to 2,530,148 in 1881–5 and 5,362,741 in 1896–1900 (Table 6–15). New South Wales was the major coal-producing district, accounting for 90 per cent of total Australian output. K. H. Burley observed:

Table 6-15 Production and Exports of Australian (NSW) Coal, 1861–1900 (in thousand tons)

Period	Annual average production in Australia	Annual average production in NSW	Major markets of coal exports					
			New Zealand	Pacific Isles	Asia	North America	Central & South America	Total (with others)
1861/65	502	477	54	8	49	15	2	138
1866/70	890	857	90	21	130	53	6	304
1871/75	1,188	1,148	117	44	162	106	3	441
1876/80	1,544	1,478	159	50	161	106	6	487
1881/85	2,530	2,406	166	83	257	194	50	764
1886/90	3,453	3,135	156	96	238	339	131	970
1891/95	4,117	3,702	163	137	182	289	266	1,057
1896/1900	5,363	4,621	171	235	267	235	449	1,374

Sources: Z. Kalix *et al.* (eds), *Australian Mineral Industry: Production and Trade, 1842–1964* (1966), p. 92; K.H. Burley, 'The Overseas Trade in New South Wales Coal and the British Shipping Industry, 1860–1914', *Economic Record*, 36, 75 (1960), p.411; Burley, 'The Organization of the Overseas Trade in New South Wales Coal, 1860 to 1914', *Economic Record*, 37, 79 (1961), p. 381.

A major factor in the successful disposal of N.S.W. coal overseas was its landed cost in relation to that of competing coals in foreign markets. The cost advantage enjoyed by N.S.W. coal ... derived from the cheap coal freights secured from its association with the British shipping industry.'[140]

However, the figures in Table 6-13 suggest that Australian coal was unable to compete in the Asian market with Japanese coal, largely because of higher freight rates. It was therefore forced to move out of Asia, as Table 6-15 shows. Asia's share in Australian exports decreased from 43 per cent in 1866-70 to 19 per cent in 1896-1900, and that of New Zealand from 33 per cent in 1876-80 to 12 per cent in 1896-1900; while that of Central and South America increased from 1 per cent in 1876-80 to 33 per cent in 1896-1900. Thus, in the late nineteenth century, the main export markets for New South Wales coal shifted from Asia and New Zealand to North, Central and South America.

In Singapore, as we have seen, although the smallness of the market and the relatively high price of coal favoured an increase in Japanese coal imports, Japanese coal had to be supplied in large and secure quantities at a low price to overcome the competition. The 1890s increase in demand for coal was caused by the rising political tension in East Asia. Although high-quality Japanese coal kept its established markets, because transactions were mainly carried out on a contract basis, the increase in imports of British coal for naval use had an adverse effect on ordinary and inferior Japanese coal in Hong Kong. However, since the rise in the price of Japanese coal was offset by a decline in freight rates between 1896 to 1898 and the 1898 British coal strike prevented imports of British coal from increasing, Japanese coal was able to maintain its dominant position in the Hong Kong market. None the less, the increase in domestic coal consumption and the consequent rise in production costs meant that 'but a small margin of difference is left between the cost at which coal can be laid down in Manila, Singapore, and Hong-Kong from Australia and from Japan', making Australia coal more competitive.[141]

Exports of Japanese coal developed an interesting market pattern. It was Takashima, the highest-quality Japanese coal, that opened up new markets. Takashima coal always acted as a spearhead in defeating other foreign coals and paved the way for lower-quality Japanese coals such as Miike. Takashima coal had ousted British and Australian coal from the Shanghai market by 1873. When Takashima coal exports were shifted to Hong Kong, partly by strong competition from Miike coal, the latter took over the Shanghai market and by 1880 had established a dominant position against a general increase in demand for coal for both steamers and factories in China. Miike coal was exported to Hong Kong from the mid-1880s onwards, leaving the Shanghai market to the inferior Chikuhō coal. On the Hong Kong market Takashima coal competed strongly against British and Australian coal, supported by the supply of Miike coal in large quantities; Japanese coal gained control of the Hong Kong coal market in 1886. Chikuhō coal reached Singapore in the 1890s and played a major role in establishing the market for Japanese coal there.

Increased production and proximity to the market allowed Japanese coal exports to increase and to replace British and Australian coal in the Asian market. However, the increasing domestic consumption of coal and the development of coal industries in other Asian countries which had easier access to the market, such as China and India, gradually forced Japanese coal to withdraw from Asia, and in 1923 Japan became a net coal importer.[142]

7
Conclusion

Japan's success at industrializing in the nineteenth century draws our attention both because of its speed and because it was a success which eluded all other non-Western countries until much later. In this book I have looked at how this industrialization was possible and at the circumstances which made it possible, paying attention to changes in the international economic and political environment as well to internal factors. I have analysed the links between the two with special reference to the raw silk, tea and coal export industries. Throughout I have tried to bear in mind the links between this rapid industrialization and Japan's economic and military advance into Asia.

Japan was opened to foreign trade in 1859 following the commercial treaties which she had reluctantly signed with the Western powers the previous year. Like China's before her, Japan's opening to trade was the result of changes in the structure of the world economy brought about by the formation of a world market by the countries of the West, led by Great Britain. The industrialization of the European countries and of the United States transformed the pattern of worldwide supply and demand. Japan's exports developed in connection with overseas markets, supported by the rapid development of export industries and by the favourable international economic situation provided by this expansion of world trade and the rapidly changing world economic structure. Although the changing structure of the world economy in the second half of the nineteenth century set the framework for Japan's industrialization, her role was one of positive adaptation rather than passive response.

Throughout the second half of the nineteenth century, the countries of East Asia were exposed to constant pressure from the West. The direction of Japanese economic development was clearly governed by the existence of this external pressure, and no analysis of Japan's industrialization which avoids consideration of this factor can hope to be successful. By placing too much attention on the West, however, many writers – and this includes both advocates of the 'imperialism of free trade' and dependency theorists – have tended to portray non-Western countries in a wholly passive role and to see their history purely as a process of 'response to the West'. To a greater or lesser extent, such writers assume that the Western powers were powerful – even omnipotent – throughout the world. From this they are bound to infer that Japan was able to industrialize only because it was strong enough to keep the Western powers at bay. They therefore show a very high appreciation of the importance of the Meiji Restoration and the role of the Meiji government.

I began my analysis with an examination of the political, economic and military presence in East Asia of Britain, the dominant Western power in the area during the period in question – an examination in which I laid emphasis on the role of Britain's domestic politics and economy. The 1860s were a turning point for British policy in East Asia, largely as a result of constraints imposed by the domestic political and economic situation. From the 1860s through into the mid-1880s the activities of the British China Squadron were severely limited, first by reductions in the number of vessels and personnel and a general need to economize because of problems over military expenditure; secondly because of difficulties in ensuring an adequate supply of coal. Consequently British military power in East Asia was barely sufficient for defence of the treaty ports. Any attempt by Britain to extend her territory or influence in the area through military action might have produced short-term gains, but long-term colonization would have been completely out of the question.

In spite of its limitations, however, British military power was still much greater than that of any other nation, particularly in naval terms, and was endorsed by Britain's accompanying economic dominance. Thus the countries which were facing the Western threat were not necessarily able to see through to the weakness behind the façade. In Japan, Western pressure induced a feeling of crisis which acted as a catalyst for internal development. It can be argued that at first Britain's dominance in the area actually brought stability in international relations, but from the second half of the 1880s the growing confidence with which Japan was able to pursue a political and economic advance into Korea and China gradually exposed the gap between the image of British dominance and limited British capability.

Japan was able to industrialize as a result of a fortuitous combination of external and internal factors. As far as the external situation was concerned, there was the 'perception gap' between image and reality referred to above. The West could exert pressure on Japan, but only pressure of a limited kind, and it was never in a position to colonize or subjugate her; the Meiji leaders were therefore driven by a sense of crisis which was much greater than in reality it need have been. Internally, while economic development in the late Tokugawa period had not yet reached the stage where Japan was in a position to industrialize spontaneously, she was ready to do so as soon as some stimulus was provided. The most significant contribution came not from the production sector, where commercial agriculture already existed, but from the distribution sector, where a nationwide market and several regional economies had formed as a result of the development of a credit system based on money exchange dealers. In other words, the Japanese economy already had an independent domestic commercial and distribution network.

For Japan, the commercial treaties of 1858 and the subsequent opening of the ports signified her incorporation into the world economy and a shift in her economic structure from closed to open. The commercial treaties were 'unequal'. As with China, trade was based upon the treaty port system and the activities of foreign merchants were limited to the areas of the treaty ports. Although the treaties guaranteed that the countries of the West had access to 'free trade', in Japan (and China) the system had unforeseen results. Internally, the existing commercial and distribution network linked up with a trading system formed by indigenous export and import merchants at the treaty ports, and in effect hindered attempts by Western capital and trade to enter, infiltrate, or expand into domestic distribution. Externally, not only did the agency house system according to which Western merchants operated prove inefficient, but the Western powers did not have the military capability to force Japan to observe the requirements of 'free trade'. Thus both internal and external factors operated in such a way that even with the low tariffs stipulated by the 'unequal' treaties, the treaty port system as a whole functioned as a non-tariff barrier in Japan's favour. Western merchants were prevented from extending their activities beyond the treaty ports, and Japan's domestic markets were protected from an excessive influx of foreign capital. The abolition of the system in 1899 had little effect on these business methods, which had by then become well entrenched.

Japan's industrialization in the late nineteenth century thus took place against a background of various external and internal factors: the changing world economy, a limited Western military and commercial impact, a high degree of economic and commercial development before the opening of the ports, the treaty port system, and also the existence of a unified government which wanted to encourage industrialization. Having described this background I went on to review the development of Japan's three main exports – raw silk, tea, and coal – in the context of the changing world economy in the second half of the nineteenth century.

The advent of foreign trade caused radical changes in the Tokugawa economic system, particularly in export-related industries and in the structure of prices, which had to adjust to international levels. In raw silk and tea, Japan had to challenge Chinese dominance and compete with Chinese products on the European and the American markets. Silk provides an example of the way Japan was able to increase its exports through change and adjustment to overseas demand. Tea provides a contrasting example where Japan was unable to increase its exports in the face of fierce competition, although tea exports did play an important role until the late 1880s.

Table 7–1 shows the position of the major types of Japanese silk in the overseas market. After the opening of the ports Japanese silk was exported to the European market, which had been badly affected by the silkworm disease *pebrine*. Exports increased to offset the deficiency of Chinese silk, and were facilitated by the opening of regular shipping services in the mid-1860s. The continuing increase in demand for Japanese silk overseas stimulated the development of the silk industry,

Table 7-1 Japanese Raw Silk in the Overseas Markets

Market Period	Europe	USA
1860s	Hanks (F,G,N)	
1870s	Hanks (F)	Hanks (G,N)
1880s	Hanks (F)	Re-reels (G)	Filatures (N)
1890s		Re-reels (F,G)	Filatures (N)
1900s		Filatures (N)

Source: Compiled from Chapter 4.
Note: F: Fukushima, G: Gunma, N: Nagano

both in production methods and in the adoption of improved technologies in sericulture and silk reeling. Traditional reeling machines were gradually replaced by improved reeling machines. Overseas demand for Japanese raw silk remained high because of the continuing poor cocoon harvests in the main European silk-producing countries. At first Japanese silk was able to command high prices in Europe, but these fell as the consequent rise in the price which raw silk for export fetched in Japan encouraged producers to concentrate on quantitative expansion of production rather than on the maintenance of quality. In the late 1860s the market for Japanese silk became restricted due to both an increase in competition between various Asian and European silks – particularly after the opening of the Suez Canal – and to the decline in the quality of Japanese silk itself. In the early 1870s both the private sector and the government embarked on attempts to improve quality through establishing modern Western-style filatures. These ventures did not prove financially viable, but they played a significant role through diffusing improved machine reeling methods and technologies.

Faced with difficulty in expanding her European market in the early 1870s, Japan found a temporary solution by shifting her silk exports from Europe to the United States, which had emerged as a silk-manufacturing country. This was facilitated by the completion of the Trans-Continental Railway in 1869. Table 7–2 shows the position of Japanese silk in the United States market. As the American silk industry developed in the 1870s, exports of Japanese silk increased rapidly. In Nagano particularly, many small filatures were established with modified Western-style reeling machines. However, the diffusion of the power loom in the American industry adversely affected the increase in exports from Japan, since American factories required threads of superior quality, uniformity and strength. In the 1880s – as a result of the increase in superior Italian and French silk for the warp – Japanese silk was gradually ousted from the warp market to the weft market, where it replaced the inferior Chinese silk. The old silk-producing districts such as Gunma and Fukushima increased production without any fundamental changes in reeling methods, simply by unifying the re-reeling and/or finishing processes. In Nagano in the mid-1880s joint re-reeling factories were established to produce large quantities of standardized silk at a reduced cost and with strict quality control. In the 1890s, however, a continuous deterioration in quality caused the virtual departure of all Japanese silk from the warp market to the weft market, where it completely expelled Chinese silk. In other words Japan adjusted her raw silk exports, changing her main market from the warp to the weft. Coming between European and Chinese silk both in quality and in price, Japanese silk was thus able to remain competitive on the United States market. The decline in quality in the 1890s, however, signalled the urgent need for Japanese silk manufacturers in re-reel-producing districts to reorganize their production methods.

Since the sericulture and silk reeling industries throughout the world were based on seasonal and intensive manual labour, the difference in productivity between Japan and the advanced silk producing countries, France and Italy, was small by comparison with that in the cotton industry. The highly developed nature of the silk industry in Japan therefore made it possible for Japanese silk to compete with French and Italian silk of superior quality in the international market, soon after the opening of the ports in 1859. But in the same way, the small gap in productivity and technology meant that Japanese silk

Table 7-2 Japanese Raw Silk in the United States Market

Period	*Use* *Warp*	*Weft*	*Machine twist and sewing silk*
1870s	Japanese	Chinese	
1880s	French, Italian → Japanese	Chinese	
1890s	French, Italian, Chinese (filature)	Japanese	Chinese

Source: Compiled from Chapter 4.

had to face severe competition from Chinese and Bengali silk, despite their inferior quality.

As the world silk trade expanded with the increasing demand for silk fabrics, there was considerable geographical specialization between raw silk-producing and raw silk-consuming countries. By the end of the nineteenth century Chinese raw silk had become specialized in meeting French manufacturing requirements, while Japan catered for the United States. Japan took advantage of market conditions, changing the quality of her exported raw silk from hanks, which were produced by sedentary reeling machines, to re-reels and filatures, thus improving her reeling technology to meet overseas demand. From the first decade of the twentieth century, Japan's silk exports became to a great extent dependent on the United States market. This meant that she was vulnerable to fluctuations in the American economy: the 1929 economic depression dealt her exports a severe blow.

Green tea, sent to Britain until 1865, was another of Japan's main export articles. After 1865 it was exported exclusively to the American market, depriving China of its dominance there. The rapid increase in tea exports inevitably caused a deterioration in quality after the early 1870s, as a consequence of hurried and careless preparation. However, the American green tea market remained relatively small, and Japanese tea had ousted Chinese tea by the mid-1870s. Nevertheless, it still had to face competition from alternatives such as black tea (from India, Ceylon and China), coffee and cocoa. In the mid-1870s Japanese tea began to lose its former popularity among American consumers, as quality deteriorated as a result of overproduction. This deterioration continued throughout the 1880s and 1890s. Despite efforts by tea producers and strenuous encouragement and support from the government, Japan's tea exports did not develop. Although Japanese tea was able to maintain its export market in the 1880s, the shift in consumption from green to black tea in the American market and the price rises caused by increasing production costs in Japan made it harder to maintain a competitive market price in the States. The severe competition in the States led Japanese tea to shift its export market gradually to Canada. Exports of Japanese green tea to both markets suffered a severe blow in the 1890s because of the increasing competition from coffee and black tea, deteriorating quality, and sharply rising prices.

Unlike raw silk and tea, Japanese coal exports developed in the East Asian market, competing with British and Australian coals, helped by the depreciation in the value of silver. The coal market in East and Southeast Asia was formed in the mid–nineteenth century, facilitated by the evolution of marine transporation and communication which took place particularly after the opening of the Suez Canal in 1869. The coal industry in Japan developed to supply coal to steamers engaged in the Eastern trade. This development was achieved by the introduction of Western mining technology, the intensification of labour, and the reduction of freight rates. Coal exports from Japan increased rapidly, because they were suitable for use in both steamers and in factories and could be supplied at a low price as against other imported coals. Japanese coal was therefore able to overcome severe competition and to establish a dominant position in the Eastern market.

Table 7-3 shows the position of Japanese coal in the Eastern market. Japanese coal gained control over the Shanghai market in the mid-1870s, the Hong Kong market in the mid-1880s, and the Singapore market in the mid-1890s. The advance of Japanese coal exports into the Asian market was in line with a gradual change in the pattern of Japan's foreign trade as a

Table 7-3 Japanese Coal in the Eastern Market

Market	Period of keen competition with other coals	Year when Japanese coal took the main share	Year when Japanese coal took over 50% share
Shanghai	1870–73	1873	1875
Hong Kong	1879–86	1884	1886
Singapore	1888–96	1894	1896

Source: Compiled from Chapter 6.

whole from Europe and the United States to Asia. The greater the distance from Japan, the longer it took for dominance over other coals to be gained. Japan was, however, able to overcome keen competition and expand coal exports by maintaining low production costs and reducing freight rates. After the Russo–Japanese War (1904–5) increasing domestic consumption led to a shortage of coal for export and a subsequent price rise. This in turn led to a rise in the selling price of Japanese coal on the overseas markets and made competition with Chinese and Australian coals fiercer. Japanese coal found itself at more and more of a disadvantage on the overseas markets and was gradually directed solely towards the domestic market.

While the trade in silk and tea was exclusively in the hands of Western merchants and shipping lines, the development of Japan's coal industry and maritime coal transportation was closely connected with the formation of the zaibatsu, especially Mitsubishi and Mitsui. Mitsubishi's interest in the Takashima coal mine arose from its shipping concerns and expanded to the Chikuhō mines in the 1890s. Mitsui was given the opportunity to become involved in coal exports and the coal industry by Mitsui Bussan's appointment in 1876 as sole agent for Miike coal. Its involvement was increased by its purchase of the Miike mine in 1888, in order to compete with Mitsubishi. In any case, the coal industry became a very important field of activity for both firms. It would be no exaggeration to say that coal exports played an important and strategic role in the nineteenth century industrialization of Japan.

Quality and price are the two most crucial factors in

competitiveness. The analysis of Japan's export trade suggests that the most important factor in its expansion was a relative strength in competitiveness on the overseas markets. Entrance into established markets and increases in exports were achieved by keeping prices at a relatively low level. This was mainly due to maintenance of or reductions in production costs. Low wages, however, did not constitute the only or even the most important element. In raw silk production, competitiveness was achieved by low cocoon prices and technological developments in sericulture and silk reeling. Coal exports increased because of the reduction in production costs obtained through introducing high-productivity machinery, togehter with a decline in freight rates and the depreciation in the value of silver. However, the competitiveness of Japanese tea was rapidly weakened by unfavourable overseas market conditions and increases in production costs.

Exports of products of traditional industries and of mining played an important role in Japan's industrialization, representing significant initiatives in themselves and earning foreign exchange. The latter brought about conditions favourable to stable domestic economic development, through restraining the outflow of specie while at the same time limiting the potential entry of foreign capital, keeping the imbalance of international payments to a minimum, and increasing import capacity. By the mid-1890s Japan had passed through the initial stages of industrialization. Her trade pattern had become increasingly independent, comprising trade with both the industrialized countries of Europe and the United States and with the primary countries of Asia. This process was inevitable, for Japan, as a latecomer country, could achieve industrialization only through adjusting to the international economic structure and turning it to her advantage.

The same basic pattern continued into the twentieth century, with World War I providing a particular opportunity for Japan to expand her trade and further her industrial development. Raw silk exports remained important, but the rapid development of domestic light industries such as cotton, and the start of new ventures in heavy industry such as iron and steel and machinery, caused changes in Japan's trade pattern which took coherent shape as a result of World War I. The dependent colonial trade structure gave way to a more complex pattern with two contrasting faces. In her trade with Europe and the United States Japan still played the role of a backward country, exporting primary and semi-manufactured products such as raw silk and silk manufactures and importing manufactured goods such as machinery. In her trade with Asia, however, she now played the role of an industrialized country, exporting light manufactured goods such as cotton products and importing raw materials. Thus Japan's industrial development continued to take place in the context of its interaction with a constantly changing world economy.

Appendix Tables

Table A-1 Annual Averages of Japan's Foreign Trade by Commodity Category, 1868-1935
(in million yen at current prices)

Exports

Period	Foodstuffs	Raw materials	Semi-manufactured goods	Finished goods	Others	Total
	%	%	%	%	%	%
1868/1870	4(31)	4(25)	6(41)	0(1)	0(2)	14(100)
1871/1875	7(39)	3(18)	7(37)	1(3)	1(4)	19(100)
1876/1880	10(38)	3(12)	11(41)	1(5)	1(4)	27(100)
1881/1885	11(31)	4(12)	16(46)	3(8)	1(3)	35(100)
1886/1890	16(26)	7(12)	26(45)	8(13)	2(4)	59(100)
1891/1895	19(19)	10(10)	46(45)	24(23)	4(4)	102(100)
1896/1900	22(13)	20(12)	81(47)	45(26)	5(3)	173(100)
1901/1905	35(12)	27(9)	133(46)	85(30)	8(3)	288(100)
1906/1910	47(11)	39(9)	197(47)	132(31)	6(2)	421(100)
1911/1915	63(11)	45(8)	287(49)	178(31)	8(1)	581(100)
1916/1920	156(9)	98(6)	722(41)	737(42)	35(2)	1,748(100)
1921/1925	107(6)	103(6)	809(48)	650(38)	22(1)	1,690(100)
1926/1930	149(8)	105(5)	811(42)	825(43)	36(2)	1,925(100)
1931/1935	147(8)	75(4)	534(29)	1,012(56)	49(3)	1,818(100)

Imports

Period	Foodstuffs	Raw materials	Semi-manufactured goods	Finished goods	Others	Total
	%	%	%	%	%	%
1868/1870	10(44)	1(4)	4(19)	7(31)	0(2)	22(100)
1871/1875	4(14)	1(4)	6(21)	15(57)	1(4)	26(100)
1876/1880	4(13)	1(4)	8(28)	16(52)	1(3)	31(100)
1881/1885	6(19)	1(4)	9(29)	14(46)	1(2)	30(100)
1886/1890	11(20)	4(7)	17(29)	25(42)	1(2)	58(100)
1891/1895	20(22)	20(21)	19(20)	33(35)	2(3)	94(100)
1896/1900	55(23)	63(27)	42(18)	73(31)	3(1)	235(100)
1901/1905	84(25)	112(33)	53(16)	86(25)	5(1)	341(100)
1906/1910	65(15)	175(40)	82(19)	116(26)	4(1)	442(100)
1911/1915	72(12)	311(52)	109(18)	102(17)	4(1)	598(100)
1916/1920	164(10)	841(53)	388(24)	190(12)	11(1)	1,594(100)
1921/1925	298(14)	1,048(50)	371(18)	371(18)	14(1)	2,103(100)
1926/1930	290(14)	1,152(55)	336(16)	308(15)	16(1)	2,103(100)
1931/1935	172(9)	1,125(60)	319(17)	237(13)	14(1)	1,868(100)

Source: Nihon Ginkō, Tōkeikyoku, *Meiji-ikō honpō shuyō keizai tōkei* (1966), pp. 280–1.

Notes: (1) Trade returns with Korea, Formosa and South Sakhalin are not included. (2) 'Semi-manufactured goods' are manufactures for further use such as raw silk and cotton yarn.

Table A-2 Annual Average Shares of Japan's Foreign Trade by Region, 1873–1935 (in per cent)

Exports to

| Period | Asia | | | North America | Europe | | | | S America, Africa & Oceania |
	China	India	Total	Total	UK	France	Germany	Total	
1873/1875	22	–	22	32	19	17	0	42	–
1876/1880	22	3	25	30	18	22	0	44	1
1881/1885	19	1	21	39	12	24	1	38	1
1886/1890	15	1	24	40	10	19	2	33	1
1891/1895	8	3	28	40	6	19	2	29	1
1896/1900	16	4	43	31	6	13	2	24	2
1901/1905	22	3	44	31	5	11	2	22	2
1906/1910	24	3	43	32	6	10	2	22	2
1911/1915	27	5	44	32	6	8	2	20	3
1916/1920	25	8	47	33	8	5	0	14	6
1921/1925	25	7	43	44	3	3	0	7	5
1926/1930	23	8	44	43	3	2	1	7	6
1931/1935	22	11	51	27	5	2	1	10	13

Imports from

Period	Asia			North America Total	Europe				S America, Africa & Oceania
	China	India	Total		UK	France	Germany	Total	
1873/1875	33	–	33	5	46	10	4	60	–
1876/1880	19	4	22	7	54	11	3	70	0
1881/1885	21	9	30	9	46	6	5	60	0
1886/1890	15	11	34	9	39	5	8	55	0
1891/1895	17	9	42	8	33	4	8	48	1
1896/1900	12	14	40	16	26	3	9	42	1
1901/1905	13	19	45	18	20	1	9	35	2
1906/1910	15	16	42	16	23	1	10	39	2
1911/1915	15	24	48	18	17	1	8	29	4
1916/1920	20	17	46	36	8	0	0	9	8
1921/1925	17	16	42	30	11	1	5	21	6
1926/1930	17	13	41	32	7	1	6	18	8
1931/1935	15	11	35	35	4	1	5	14	14

Table A-3 Annual Average Balance of Payments by Region, 1873–
1935 (*=minus, in million yen)

Period	Asia	North America	Europe	South America	Africa	Oceania	Total
1873/1875	*4.7	4.9	*8.1	–	–	–	*7.9
1876/1880	*0.4	5.7	*9.8	*0.0	–	0.1	*4.5
1881/1885	*1.7	10.8	*4.8	*0.0	–	0.2	4.6
1886/1890	*5.6	17.5	*13.2	*0.0	–	0.4	*1.0
1891/1895	*10.8	32.5	*15.8	*0.0	–	0.7	6.2
1896/1900	*22.3	14.8	*58.0	*0.0	*0.6	1.4	*66.0
1901/1905	*26.3	28.8	*53.4	0.0	*2.1	2.5	*52.7
1906/1910	*7.0	66.7	*76.8	*0.9	*3.4	3.5	*20.4
1911/1915	*28.3	77.9	*54.2	*1.4	*4.7	*0.5	*16.8
1916/1920	85.0	1.1	99.8	3.0	*17.4	0.6	154.0
1921/1925	*156.6	103.3	*308.0	4.5	2.0	*57.5	*412.4
1926/1930	*13.2	137.8	*242.1	8.5	15.9	*73.3	*177.6
1931/1935	263.0	*168.8	*93.0	19.4	81.0	*123.5	*50.0

Appendix Tables 2 and 3
Source: Nihon Ginkō, Tōkeikyoku, *Meiji-ikō honpō shuyō keizai tōkei* (1966),
pp. 290–7
Notes: (1) Before 1914 the figures represent the totals for the main
countries only.
(2) The totals in Table 3 are not consistent because of different original
sources.

Notes

1: Introduction

1. Throughout this book I use the word 'industrialization' in the straightforward sense of the process by which an agricultural society is transformed into one centred on industrial production.
2. For instance, N. Charlesworth, *British Rule and the Indian Economy, 1800–1914* (1982), *passim*; T. Kemp, *Industrialization in the Non-Western World* (1983), ch. 2; B.R. Tomlinson, 'Writing History Sideways: Lessons for Indian Economic Historians from Meiji Japan', *Modern Asian Studies*, 19, 3 (1985).
3. R. Nurkse, *Problems of Capital Formation in Underdeveloped Countries* (1953), pp. 75, 90–1, 143, 148–9; A.O. Hirschmann, *The Strategy of Economic Development* (1958); P. Baran, *The Political Economy of Growth* (1957), pp. 151–61; A.G. Frank, *Capitalism and Underdevelopment in Latin America* (1967), pp. 56–7, 94–5, and *Latin America* (1969), p. 11; S. Amin, *Accumulation on a World Scale* (1974), pp. 464–5.
4. For instance, see J.K. Fairbank, E.O. Reischauer, and A.M. Craig (eds), *East Asia: Tradition and Transformation* (1973). See also P.A. Cohen, *Discovering History in China* (1984).
5. See W. Lipman, *Public Opinion* (1922), ch. 1; B. Porter, *Britain, Europe and the World, 1850–1982* (1983).
6. For a summary of this debate, see M. Sumiya and K. Taira (eds), *An Outline of Japanese Economic History, 1603–1940* (1979), pp. 6–9, 270–4, 290–1; G. Hoston, *Marxism and the Crisis of Development in Prewar Japan* (1986). E.H. Norman was among those who denied the revolutionary nature of the Restoration; see his *Japan's Emergence as a Modern State* (1940).
7. For the findings of the modernization theorists, see the following Princeton series on modern Japan: M.B. Jansen (ed.), *Changing Japanese Attitudes toward Modernization* (1965); W.W. Lockwood (ed.), *The State and Economic Enterprise in Japan* (1965); R.P. Dore (ed.), *Aspects of Social Change in Modern Japan* (1967); R.E. Ward (ed.), *Political Development in Modern Japan* (1968); D.H. Shively

(ed.), *Tradition and Modernization in Japanese Culture* (1971). As one might expect, the re-evaluation of the Tokugawa period implicit in this approach has had a great impact in Japan.

8. W.W. Rostow, *The Stages of Economic Growth* (2nd edn, 1971), *passim*.

9. For example, see K. Ohkawa and M. Shinohara (eds), *Patterns of Japanese Economic Development* (1979); R. Minami, *The Economic Development of Japan* (1986). Simon Kuznets has pointed to the need for comparative surveys of cultural and social conditions in Asia as well as in Western countries (*Modern Economic Growth* (1966), pp. 290–4, 458–60).

10. Hayami Akira, *Nihon ni okeru keizai shakai no tenkai* (1973); Shakai Keizaishi Gakkai (ed.), *Atarashii Edo jidaishi-zō o motomete* (1977); Shinbo Hiroshi, *Kinsei no bukka to keizai hatten* (1978); Umemura Mataji, 'Bakumatsu no keizai hatten', *Kindai Nihon kenkyū*, 3 (1981); Harada Toshimaru and Miyamoto Matao (eds), *Rekishi no naka no bukka* (1985); S.B. Hanley and K. Yamamura, *Economic and Demographic Change in Preindustrial Japan, 1600–1868* (1977), pp. 28, 320.

11. R. Toby, *State and Diplomacy in Early Modern Japan* (1984); Tashiro Kazui, *Kinsei Nitchō tsūkō bōeki-shi no kenkyū* (1981).

12. A. Gerschenkron, *Economic Backwardness in Historical Perspective* (1962), pp. 26–7.

13. G. Myrdal, *Asian Drama* (1968), 3 vols, chs. 1, 4.

14. W.W. Lockwood, 'Japan's Response to the West', *World Politics*, 9, 1 (1956), and *The Economic Development of Japan* (expanded edn, 1968), viii, p. 185.

15. P. Deane and W.A. Cole, *British Economic Growth, 1688–1959* (2nd edn, 1969), pp. 28–30, 309–12; D.C. North, *The Economic Growth of the United States, 1790–1860* (1961), pp. 64–77; W.A. Lewis, *Tropical Development, 1880–1913* (1970), ch. 1; M.H. Watkins, 'A Staple Theory of Economic Growth', *Canadian Journal of Economics and Political Science*, 24, 2 (1963); R.F. Emery, 'The Relation of Exports and Economic Growth', *Kyklos*, 20, 2(1967), p. 483.

16. Nōshōmushō, 'Meiji jūsannen mentō kyōshinkai hōkoku', No. 2 (1880), pp. 1–2.

17. See Nakamura Takafusa, *Senzenki Nihon keizai seichō no bunseki* (1971), ch. 2.

18. A similar approach is suggested by R.M. McInnis in W. Fischer, R.M. McInnis and J. Schneider (eds), *The Emergence of a World Economy, 1500–1914*, vol. II (1986), ch. 1.

2: East Asia in the World Economy

1. B. Semmel, *The Rise of Free Trade Imperialism* (1970), pp. 146–50, 176–81.
2. P. Mathias, *The First Industrial Nation* (2nd edn, 1983), p. 229.
3. W. Schlote, *British Overseas Trade from 1700 to the 1930s* (1952), pp. 52–4.
4. Ibid., pp. 68–75.
5. W. Ashworth, *A Short History of the International Economy since 1850* (3rd edn, 1975), pp. 150–1, 210–11, 217–19.
6. A.H. Imlah, *Economic Elements in the Pax Britannica* (1958), p. 189.
7. W.W. Rostow, *The World Economy* (1978), p. 67; Schlote, op. cit., p. 42.
8. League of Nations, *Industrialization and Foreign Trade* (1945), p. 13.
9. D.K. Fieldhouse, *Economics and Empire, 1830–1914* (1973), p. 11.
10. S.B. Saul, *Studies in British Overseas Trade, 1870–1914* (1960), p. 62; A.G. Kenwood and A.L. Lougheed, *The Growth of the International Economy, 1820–1960* (1971), pp. 103–4.
11. Ashworth, op. cit., pp. 215–16; League of Nations, op. cit., p. 157.
12. S. Kuznets, 'Quantitative Aspects of the Economic Growth of Nations: X. Level and Structure of Foreign Trade', *Economic Development and Cultural Change*, 15, 2, Pt II (1967), pp. 33, 38.
13. Imlah, op. cit., p. 170.
14. League of Nations, op. cit., pp. 166–7.
15. W. Ashworth, *An Economic History of England, 1870–1939* (1960), pp. 147–9, and *A Short History of the International Economy since 1850*, p. 216. For the importance of Asian and African countries in the nineteenth century world economy, see A.J.H. Latham, *The International Economy and the Underdeveloped World, 1865–1914* (1978); W.A. Lewis, *Growth and Fluctuations, 1870–1913* (1978), pp. 167–72; J.R. Hanson, Jr, *Trade in Transition* (1980).
16. D.H. Aldcroft and H.W. Richardson, *The British Economy, 1870–1939* (1969), p. 116.
17. Ibid., pp. 71–4; M. Simon, 'The Pattern of New British Portfolio Foreign Investment, 1865–1914', in A.R. Hall (ed.), *The Export of Capital from Britain, 1870–1914* (1968), pp. 39–40.
18. A.O. Hirschmann, 'The Commodity Structure of World Trade', *Quarterly Journal of Economics*, 57, 4 (1943), p. 590.

19. D.H. Aldcroft (ed.), *The Development of British Industry and Foreign Competition, 1875–1914* (1968), p. 23.
20. W.A. Lewis, 'World Production, Prices and Trade, 1870–1960', *Manchester School*, 20, 2 (1952), p. 117; S.B. Saul, *The Myth of the Great Depression, 1873–1896* (2nd edn, 1985), pp. 30, 54.
21. Imlah, op. cit., Table 4, pp. 70–5.
22. For British interests in East Asia in the nineteenth century, see E.M. Gull, *British Economic Interests in the Far East* (1943); N.A. Pelcovits, *Old China Hands and the Foreign Office* (1948); W.G. Beasley, *Great Britain and the Opening of Japan, 1834–1858* (1951); B. Dean, *China and Great Britain* (1974); P. Lowe, *Britain in the Far East* (1981).
23. D.A. Farnie, *The English Cotton Industry and the World Market, 1815–1896* (1979), p. 91. See also A. Redford, *Manchester Merchants and Foreign Trade*, vol. 2 (1956), pp. 79–89.
24. R.E. Tyson, 'The Cotton Industry', in Aldcroft (ed.), op. cit., pp. 108–15, 125–6.
25. T. Ellison, *The Cotton Trade of Great Britain* (1886), pp. 317–24; Redford, op. cit., pp. 36–8.
26. Tyson, op. cit., pp. 104–8. See also Farnie, op. cit., pp. 173, 187–205.
27. Ellison, op. cit., p. 152.
28. Ellison, ibid., p. 69; Farnie, op. cit., pp. 101–2; MCC, *Monthly Record* (June 1901), pp. 138–9.
29. C.H. Feinstein, 'Home and Foreign Investment: Some Aspects of Capital Formation, Finance and Income in the United Kingdom, 1870–1913' (unpublished Ph.D. thesis, University of Cambridge, 1959), p. 121.
30. Saul, *Studies in British Overseas Trade*, pp. 44–5, 60; F.E. Hyde, *Far Eastern Trade, 1860–1914* (1973), ch. 9.
31. See DCRTF, No. 1266, Shanghai for 1892, p. 14; No. 1605, Shanghai for 1894, p. 14; No. 1786, Hyōgo and Ōsaka for 1895, pp. 46–7.
32. Ōkurashō, 'Kahei seido chōsakai hōkoku' (1895), pp. 1–2, 198 ff.
33. J. Gallagher and R. Robinson, 'The Imperialism of Free Trade', *Economic History Review*, 2nd series, 6, 1 (1953), pp. 1–15, reprinted in W.R. Louis (ed.), *Imperialism: The Robinson and Gallagher Controversy* (1976). See also R. Robinson and J. Gallagher, with A. Denny, *Africa and the Victorians: The Official Mind of Imperialism* (2nd edn, 1981); R. Robinson and J. Gallagher, 'The Partition of Africa', in *The New Cambridge Modern History*, vol. XI (1962).
34. For a general survey of the debate, see Louis (ed.), op. cit., pp. 2–51; P.J. Cain, *Economic Foundations of British Overseas Expansion, 1815–1914* (1980); D.K. Fieldhouse, ' "Imperialism": An His-

toriographical Revision', *Economic History Review*, 2nd series, 14, 2 (1961).

35. C.C. Eldridge (ed.), *British Imperialism in the Nineteenth Century* (1984), introduction, pp. 11–12. See also the chapter by P. Kennedy, 'Continuity and Discontinuity in British Imperialism, 1815–1914'.

36. D.C.M. Platt, 'The Imperialism of Free Trade: Some Reservations', *Economic History Review*, 2nd series, 21, 2 (1968), p. 305, and 'Further Objections to an "Imperialism of Free Trade", 1830–60', *Economic History Review*, 2nd series, 26, 1 (1973), p. 87.

37. C.C. Eldridge, *Victorian Imperialism* (1978), pp. 5, 145.

38. P.J. Cain and A.G. Hopkins, 'The Political Economy of British Expansion Overseas, 1750–1914', *Economic History Review*, 2nd series, 33, 4 (1980), pp. 463, 466, 489. See also P.J. Cain and A.G. Hopkins, 'Gentlemanly Capitalism and British Expansion Overseas II: New Imperialism, 1850–1945', *Economic History Review*, 2nd series, 40, 1 (1987).

39. R. Robinson, 'Non-European Foundations of European Imperialism: Sketch for a Theory of Collaboration', in R. Owen and B. Sutcliffe (eds), *Studies in the Theory of Imperialism* (1972). See Robinson and Gallagher, *Africa and the Victorians*, p. 484.

40. Gallagher and Robinson, 'The Imperialism of Free Trade', in Louis (ed.), op. cit., p. 65.

41. Platt, 'Further Objections to an "Imperialism of Free Trade" ', p. 88.

42. D.C.M. Platt, *Finance, Trade and Politics in British Foreign Policy, 1815–1914* (1968), pp. 263–5, 367–8.

43. B. Dean, 'British Informal Empire: The Case of China', *Journal of Commonwealth & Comparative Politics*, 14, 1 (1976), pp. 74, 75.

44. Ibid., p. 76–7.

45. Robinson, op. cit., p. 127.

46. For the development of dependency theory, see T. dos Santos, 'The Crisis of Development Theory and the Problems of Dependence in Latin America', in H. Bernstein (ed.), *Underdevelopment and Development* (1973); G. Palma, 'Dependency and Development: A Critical Overview', in D. Seers (ed.), *Dependency Theory* (1981). Several hypotheses of dependency theory have yet to receive statistical and historical proof. I do not, however, agree with Patrick O'Brien's rather one-sided stress on the 'peripheral' contribution of the periphery to the growth of output and capital formation at the core ('European Economic Development: The Contribution of the Periphery', *Economic History Review*, 2nd series, 35, 1 (1982)).

47. F.V. Moulder, *Japan, China, and the Modern World Economy* (1977). See also Frank, *Latin America*, pp. 9–11, and *Capitalism and Underdevelopment in Latin America*, pp. 11, 56–7, 94–5. For a critique of Moulder, see Cohen, *Discovering History in China*, pp. 111–25.

48. Moulder, ibid., pp. 200–201.

49. C.J. Bartlett, *Great Britain and Sea Power, 1815–1853* (1963); G.S. Graham, *The Politics of Naval Supremacy* (1965), ch. 4; P.M. Kennedy, *The Rise and Fall of British Naval Mastery* (1976), p. 169–73; W. Ashworth, 'Economic Aspects of Late Victorian Naval Administration', *Economic History Review*, 2nd series, 22, 3 (1969).

50. G. Fox, *British Admirals and Chinese Pirates* (1940), p. 25; G.S. Graham, *The China Station* (1978), p. 267.

51. See Fox, ibid.

52. F.W. Hirst, *Gladstone as Financier and Economist* (1931), ch. 11.

53. Calculated from B.R. Mitchell and P. Deane, *Abstract of British Historical Statistics* (1962), pp. 393, 397.

54. 'Copy of Report of the Committee on Expense of Military Defences in the Colonies', p. 4, in *BPP* (1860).

55. See W.L. Clowes, *The Royal Navy*, vol. 7 (1903, reprint 1966), p. 12.

56. Pelcovits, op. cit., chs. 1, 2; Fox, op. cit., pp. 67–71.

57. Lord Clarendon to H.S. Parkes, 9 April 1866 (FO 46/63). See also G. Daniels, 'The British Role in the Meiji Restoration', *Modern Asian Studies*, 2, 4 (1968); G. Fox, *Britain and Japan, 1858–1883* (1969), chs. 7, 8; Ishii Takashi, *Meiji ishin no kokusaiteki kankyō* (expanded and revised edn, 1973), vol. 2, pp. 556–63, vol. 3, pp. 772–84.

58. C.J. Bartlett, 'The Mid-Victorian Reappraisal of Naval Policy', in K. Bourne and D.C. Watt (eds), *Studies in International History* (1967), pp. 192–8, 200–1, 204–8.

59. For the Kagoshima bombardment, see File 'Expedition to Kagoshima' in ADM 1/5825; *London Gazette*, 30 October 1863; Clowes, op. cit., pp. 193–202. Much of the correspondence respecting the indemnity is reprinted in *BPP* (1864).

60. A.L. Kuper to Admiralty, Euryalus at Yokohama, 14 April 1863 (ADM1/5824).

61. A.L. Kuper to Admiralty, Euryalus at Yokohama, 28 April 1863 (ADM1/5824). See also A.L. Kuper to E. St. J. Neale, Euryalus at Yokohama, 28 July 1863 (ADM1/5825).

62. 'Memorandum by the Inspector-General of Fortifications, on the Defenceless Condition of the Commercial Harbours at Home, and of Coaling Stations Abroad' (PRO 30/6/122);

'Position of Cruising Ships for Protection of Trade', by A. Milne, December 1874 (PRO 30/6/131); 'Memorandum by the Defence Committee at their Meeting of the 5th of June 1877 with reference to the Defence of Commercial Harbours at Home, and of Coaling Stations Abroad' (PRO 30/6/122); 'Memorandum on the Relative Importance of Coaling Stations' by C.H. Nugent, 1 April 1877 (PRO 30/6/123).

63. *London Gazette*, 12 September 1879. See also *First Report of the Royal Commissioners appointed to inquire into the Defence of British Possessions and Commerce abroad* (3 September 1881) (hereafter *First Report of Carnarvon Commission*) (CAB 7/2).

64. *First Report of Carnarvon Commission*, Adm. Sir A. Cooper Key's statement 1618, p. 61 (CAB 7/2).

65. *Final Report of Carnarvon Commission* (22 July 1882), N. Barnavy's statement, p. 603, and Appendix, No. 1, p. 38 (CAB 7/4); *Second Report of Carnarvon Commission* (23 March 1882), p. 4 (CAB 7/3).

66. *Final Report of Carnarvon Commission*, p. 28.

67. Admiralty, *Navy List*, June 1870, pp. 127–200; Admiralty to Commander-in-Chief, China Station, London, 28 February 1902, Enclosure (D) (ADM 125/56).

68. B. Ranft, 'The Protection of British Seaborne Trade and the Development of Systematic Planning for War, 1860–1906', in B. Ranft (ed.), *Technical Change and British Naval Policy, 1860–1939* (1977).

69. 'An Account for Five Years ending the 31st day of December 1859 of the Quantity of Steam Coal, Annually Purchased for the Use of Her Majesty's Navy, and Supplied to the Several Depôts Abroad', in *BPP* (1860), pp. 2–3.

70. 'A Return of the Quantity of Coal purchased by the Government for the Use of Her Majesty's Navy in the Years 1857, 1858, and 1859, distinguishing Welsh from Hartley Coal', in *BPP* (1860).

71. 'List of Coaling Stations now used by Her Majesty's Ships, and Remarks on Coaling Stations required in time of War', pp. 35–7 (CAB 7/4). 'Memorandum on the Relative Importance of Coaling Stations' by Nugent shows a different classification: primary Admiralty coaling stations were Singapore, Hong Kong and Shanghai; secondary Admiralty coaling stations were Amoy, Nagasaki and Hyōgo; and mercantile coaling stations were Yokohama, and King George Sound in Australia (Plate III, in PRO 30/6/123).

72. Admiralty to Commander-in-Chief, China Station, London, 28 February 1902, Enclosure (D) (ADM 125/56).

73. Vice-Admiral, China Station, to Admiralty, 8 August 1901 (ADM 125/56).

74. G.O. Willes to Admiralty, Coal Supply on the China Station, 26 June 1881, and Admiralty to G.O. Willes, 7 October 1881, both in ADM 125/84.
75. Admiralty to G.O. Willes, 7 October 1881 (ADM 125/84).
76. Admiralty to all Commanders-in-Chief, Senior Officers, Captains, Commanders, and Commanding Officers of Her Majesty's Ships and Vessels, 28 April 1882 (ADM 125/84).
77. Admiralty to G.O. Willes, 12 October 1883 (ADM 125/84). See 'Reports of Trial of Takashima and Welsh or Patent Fuel' (ADM 125/84).
78. Admiralty to G.O. Willes, 7 October 1881 (ADM 125/84).
79. Admiralty to G.O. Willes, 26 November 1881 (ADM 125/84). The coal depot in Hyōgo was, however, abolished in December 1881.
80. Admiralty to Commander-in-Chief, China Station, 28 February 1902, Enclosure (D) (ADM 125/56).
81. Vice-Admiral, China Station, to Admiralty, 8 August 1901 (ADM 125/56, No. 363). See also 'China Station, Coal Requirements for 1902–1903', Commander-in-Chief, China, to Admiralty, 9 September 1901 (ADM 125/56, No. 365).
82. For subsequent developments in British naval strategy in East Asia, see A.J. Marder, *British Naval Policy, 1880–1905* (1940), chs. 7, 8, 14, 21. The United States Navy was similarly unable to commit itself to anything more than the defence of the treaty ports: see R.E. Johnson, *Far China Station* (1979), pp. 267–8.

3: Japan's Incorporation into the World Economy

1. See Fairbank, Reischauer and Craig, *East Asia: Tradition and Transformation*, pp. 485–90; Yokohamashi (ed.), *Yokohamashi-shi*, vol. 2 (1959), pp. 1–50.
2. For the commercial treaties and additional trade regulations, see Gaimushō, *Jōyaku isan* (1884), pp. 418–41, 727–51; C. Parry (ed.), *The Consolidated Treaty Series*, vol. 119 (for 1858) (1969), pp. 254–80, 314–32, 338–47, 402–12, and vol. 120 (for 1858–9) (1969), pp. 8–20. Trade at Niigata was negligible and the opening of Hyōgo and Ōsaka was later postponed until 1868.
3. Duties on cotton and woollen manufactures, major British export articles, were at 20 per cent in the trade regulations drawn up by Japan with the United States, but were revised to 5 per cent in the regulations with Britain.
4. See A.P. Andrew, 'The End of the Mexican Dollar', *Quarterly Journal of Economics*, 18 (1904); 'Report made by the late Mr. Arbuthnot to the Lords of the Treasury on the Subject of Japanese Currency', in *BPP* (1866).

5. Gaimushō, *Jōyaku isan*, pp. 442–4; 'Correspondence respecting the Revision of the Japanese Commercial Tariff', in *BPP* (1867). For the political background, see W.G. Beasley, *Select Documents on Japanese Foreign Policy, 1853–1868* (1955), Introduction.

6. Yamazawa Ippei and Yamamoto Yūzō, *Bōeki to kokusai shūshi* (LTES, vol. 14) (1979), p. 77.

7. For the treaty revision process, see F.C. Jones, *Extraterritoriality in Japan and the Diplomatic Relations Resulting in its Abolition, 1853–1899* (1931), chs 5–8; Yamamoto Shigeru, *Jōyaku kaisei-shi* (1943). For changes in tariff rates by commodity, see Ōkurashō, *Nihon kanzei zeikan-shi shiryō*, vol. 2 (1958).

8. J. Rabino, 'The Statistical Story of the Suez Canal', *Journal of the Royal Statistical Society*, 50, Part III (1887), pp. 526, 527.

9. A.W. Kirkaldy, *British Shipping* (1914), pp. 317–8; C.K. Harley, 'The Shift from Sailing Ships to Steamships, 1850–1890', in D.N. McCloskey (ed.), *Essays on a Mature Economy* (1971), p. 224.

10. *First Report of Carnarvon Commission*, p. 22, and A. Holt's statements 380, 381, in ibid., p. 14 (CAB 7/2); Rabino, op. cit., p. 531. For the significance of the opening of the Suez Canal, see M.E. Fletcher, 'The Suez Canal and World Shipping, 1869–1914', *Journal of Economic History*, 18, 4 (1958).

11. B. Cable, *A Hundred Year History of the P. & O., 1837–1937* (1937), pp. 105, 173; M. Medzini, *French Policy in Japan during the Closing Years of the Tokugawa Regime* (1971), p. 109; H.A. Innis, *A History of the Canadian Pacific Railway* (1923), p. 138; G. Musk, *Canadian Pacific, 1883–1968* (revised edn, 1968), p. 2; G.C. Allen and A.G. Donnithorne, *Western Enterprise in Far Eastern Economic Development* (1954), p. 124.

12. For shipping conferences in regard to East Asia, see F.E. Hyde, *Blue Funnel* (1956), ch. 4, and *Far Eastern Trade*, pp. 24–41; S. Marriner and F.E. Hyde, *The Senior, John Samuel Swire, 1825–98* (1967), chs 8, 9; B.M. Deakin (with T. Seward), *Shipping Conferences* (1973), pp. 29–36.

13. J. Ahvenainen, *The Far Eastern Telegraphs* (1981); Allen and Donnithorne, op. cit., p. 269.

14. CR, Shanghai for 1872, p. 149; Hyde, *Far Eastern Trade*, pp. 62–3.

15. See M. Greenberg, *British Trade and the Opening of China, 1800–42* (1951).

16. There is a brief description of the China trade in the mid-nineteenth century in Yen-p'ing Hao, *The Comprador in Nineteenth Century China* (1970), pp. 15–23.

17. In 1880 the number of Western trading firms located in major cities in Southeast Asia was 38 in Singapore, 38 in Manila, 16 in Iloilo, 11 in Bangkok and 10 in Saigon. In Hong Kong in the

same year, there were 60 major Chinese merchants in addition to 37 Chinese commission agents (Hongkong Daily Press, *The Chronicle and Directory for China, Japan and the Philippines,* for 1880).

18. In Hong Kong, out of the 111 firms which existed in 1865, only 55 firms survived into 1870. 56 firms had disappeared, to be replaced by the 55 new firms which were listed in 1870. In Shanghai the 90 firms which existed in 1865 had decreased to 48 in 1870, while 48 new firms were listed. In Yokohama, the life expectancy of firms was even worse than Hong Kong and Shanghai, with only 19 firms surviving in 1870 out of the 51 firms which existed in 1865 (calculated from *The Chronicle and Directory for China, Japan, and the Philippines,* for 1866 and 1871). If one added the firms which were established and disappeared between 1865 and 1870, the rates would be higher still. Almost all firms with large capital, such as Jardine, Matheson & Co., Gibb Livingston & Co., Lane, Crawford & Co., David Sassoon & Co., Russell & Co., Augustine Heard & Co., and Olyphant & Co., but with the exception of Dent & Co., survived the 1866 Overend Gunney crisis. This suggests, as one would expect, that it was the more numerous medium and small-sized firms which tended to be unstable, but even the large firms must have experienced stress.

19. A.S.J. Baster, *The Imperial Banks* (1929), pp. 88–112, 133 ff., 266–8, and 'The Origins of the British Exchange Banks in China', *Economic History, A Supplement to the Economic Journal,* 3, 9 (1934); M.S. Collis, *Wayfoong* (1965), ch. 2; Ishii Kanji, 'Igirisu shokuminchi ginkō-gun no saihen' (1), *Keizaigaku ronshū,* 45, 1 (1979), p. 22. The number of branches and sub-branches of British imperial banks in India and East Asia was 17 in 1855, 95 in 1865, 41 in 1875, 42 in 1885, and 40 in 1895 (Baster, *The Imperial Banks,* p. 269).

20. S. Sugiyama, 'Thomas B. Glover: A British Merchant in Japan', *Business History,* 26, 2 (1984).

21. S. Marriner, *Rathbones of Liverpool, 1845–73* (1961), pp. 37, 68–73, 112; S.C. Lockwood, *Augustine Heard and Company, 1858–1862* (1971), pp. 118–19; E. LeFevour, *Western Enterprise in Late Ch'ing China* (1968), p. 48; C.F. Remer, *The Foreign Trade of China* (1926), p. 41.

22. C. Mackenzie, *Realms of Silver* (1954), pp. 93–100.

23. Collis, op. cit. (1965), p. 48; Mackenzie, ibid., p. 99.

24. Ishii Kanji, 'Igirisu shokuminchi ginkō-gun no saihen' (1), p. 23.

25. CR, General Report on the Trade of Japan for the Year 1884, p. 116. Figures are also available for 1882 and 1883, but the number

of firms at Nagasaki is said to be 19 for both years, which seems implausible by comparison with figures of 53 and 56 in Hyōgo and Ōsaka respectively (CR, Annual Summary of the Foreign Trade of Japan for the Year 1882, p. 42; CR, Summary of the Foreign Trade of Japan for the Year 1883, p. 196).

26. G.S. Fisher to W.H. Seward, No. 221, 18 October 1866, in USA, *Despatches from the United States Consuls in Kanagawa,1861-1897,* vol. 3.
27. *Yokohamashi-shi,* vol. 5, Pt I (1971), p. 212.
28. DCRTF, No. 754, Yokohama for 1889, pp. 37–8.
29. Minutes of Meeting of British Subjects, Nagasaki, 1 March 1861, Enclosure 2 of G.S. Morrison to R. Alcock, Nagasaki, 2 March 1861 (FO 262/29); CR, Nagasaki for 1862, pp. 226, 230. There are very few studies on Chinese business activities in Japan. See, however, Uchida Naosaku, *Nihon kakyō shakai no kenkyū* (1949); Shiba Yoshinobu, 'Meiji-ki Nihon raijū kakyō ni tsuite', *Shakai keizai shigaku,* 47, 4 (December 1981).
30. *Nagasaki Express,* 19 March 1870, 26 March 1870.
31. Ōsaka Shiyakusho (ed.), *Meiji Taishō Ōsakashi-shi* (1933), vol. 3, pp. 65 ff., 191.
32. CR, Hyōgo and Ōsaka for 1875, pp. 13–14; for 1876, p. 11; for 1877, p. 21.
33. Yamazawa and Yamamoto, op. cit.
34. *Nihon bōeki seiran,* pp. 42, 45–6.
35. Regarding these problems, see Yamaguchi Kazuo, *Bakumatsu bōeki-shi* (1943), pp. 10–24; Ohkawa *et al.* (eds), *Kokumin shotoku* (LTES,vol. 1) (1974), pp. 97–105.
36. CR, Nagasaki for 1862, pp. 225–6.
37. CR, Kanagawa, Nagasaki, and Hakodate, for 1859–67; Katsu Kaishū, *Kaigun rekishi* (1928), pp. 443–55.
38. CR, Nagasaki for 1865, p. 22; CR, Hakodate for 1865, p. 7.
39. CR, Kanagawa for 1863, p. 160; CR, Nagasaki for 1865, p. 23.
40. *Nihon bōeki seiran,* pp. 41–2, 45–6; M. Baba and M. Tatemoto, 'Foreign Trade and Economic Growth in Japan: 1858–1937', in L. Klein and K. Ohkawa (eds), *Economic Growth: The Japanese Experience since the Meiji Era* (1968), pp. 166–7; Ohkawa *et al.* (eds), *Kokumin shotoku,* pp. 97–105; Yamazawa and Yamamoto, op. cit.
41. Ishii Takashi, *Bakumatsu bōeki-shi no kenkyū* (1944), ch. 1.
42. CR, Summary of Foreign Trade in Japan for the Year 1878, p. 25.
43. M. Paske-Smith, *Western Barbarians in Japan and Formosa in Tokugawa Days, 1603–1868* (Kōbe, 1930), p. 303.
44. If one compares the figures for 1869 in the commercial reports with the official Japanese statistics, it is clear that the exchange

rate is 1.12 yen per dollar for exports and 1.20 yen per dollar for imports. The fact that this is not entirely consistent with the annual average exchange rate of 1.24 yen per dollar does not cause difficulties since, as I have already pointed out, the figures prior to 1868 are also generally undervalued. (Calculated from Hora Tomio, *Bakumatsu ishin-ki no gaiatsu to teikō* (1977), p. 178.)

45. Shinbo, *Kinsei no bukka to keizai hatten*, pp. 279–300, 324–331, and 'Bakumatsu Meiji-ki no kakaku kōzō', *Shakai keizai shigaku*, 33, 1 (1967), p. 17; J.R. Huber, 'Effect on Prices of Japan's Entry into World Commerce after 1858', *Journal of Political Economy*, 79, 3 (1971), pp. 616–19.

46. For developments in Japanese domestic politics, see Oka Yoshitake, *Kindai Nihon seiji-shi*, I (1967); W.G. Beasley, *The Meiji Restoration* (1973).

47. See A.E. Tiedemann, 'Japan's Economic Foreign Policies, 1868–1893', in J.W. Morley (ed.), *Japan's Foreign Policy, 1868–1941* (1974), pp. 132–8.

48. See J.K. Fairbank, 'The Creation of the Treaty System', in Fairbank (ed.), *The Cambridge History of China*, vol. 10 (1978).

49. The Jardine Matheson Archive is deposited at the University Library, Cambridge. See bibliography, p. 273.

50. Japanese scholars have tended to see these as important examples of the economic penetration of foreign capital. (For instance, see Unno Fukuju, 'Meiji shonen no bōeki mondai', in *Iwanami kōza: Nihon rekishi*, vol. 15 (1962), pp. 128–9; Nakamura Satoru, 'Kaikō', in Rekishigaku Kenkyūkai and Nihonshi Kenkyūkai (eds), *Kōza Nihonshi*, vol. 5 (1970), pp. 66–7; *Yokohamashi-shi*, vol. 2, pp. 711–2.) However, further examination seems to be required to provide evidence based on substantial and detailed case studies rather than on assumptions about the 'colonising' intentions of the Western powers.

51. *Yokohamashi-shi*, vol. 2, pp. 706–27.

52. Kajinishi Mitsuhaya, 'Shihonshugi no ikusei', in *Iwanami kōza: Nihon rekishi*, vol. 16 (1962), p. 14; Ishii Kanji, 'Ginkō sōsetsu zengo no Mitsui-gumi', *Mitsui bunko ronsō*, 17 (December 1983), pp. 34–9.

53. Nakamura Satoru, 'Kaikō', p. 68.

54. CR, Nagasaki for 1867; 'Reports on the Production of Tea of Japan', p. 9, in *BPP* (1873).

55. Sugiyama, op. cit., pp. 127 ff.

56. J. McMaster, 'The Takashima Mine: British Capital and Japanese Industrialization', *Business History Review*, 37, 3 (1963); Ishii Kanji, *Kindai Nihon to Igirisu shihon* (1984), ch. 3.

57. Ariizumi Sadao, 'Kikai seishi bokkō-ki ni okeru ichi seishi

burujoajii no shōgai', Kyōto Daigaku Dokushikai (ed.), *Kokushi ronshū*, no. 2 (1959), pp. 1596–9.

58. E. Whittall to W. Keswick, Yokohama, 12 July 1869 (JMA, B10/9/ 974). For Adams' reports, see 'Report on the Central Silk Districts of Japan', in *BPP* (1870); 'Further Report on Silk Culture in Japan', in *BPP* (1870).

59. E. Whittall to F.B. Johnson, Yokohama, 28 August 1869 (JMA, B10/9/1047); E. Whittall to W. Keswick, Yokohama, 18 September 1869 (JMA, B10/9/1090).

60. H. Smith to R.A. Houston, Yokohama, 7 June 1870 (JMA, B10/9/ 1481).

61. C.S. Hope to W. Keswick, Yokohama, 28 February 1866 (JMA, B10/9/579). Takasuya Seibei came from Isshiki Village, Hazu Country in Sanshū (now Aichi Prefecture) and started an export and import business in Yokohama in 1859 (*Yokohamashi-shi*, vol. 2, Appendix p. 14; 'Eishō Gower wagashō Takasuya ni kakaru kiito hanbai iyaku ikken', [321], in *Zoku tsūshin zenran*, Ruishū-no-bu, Soshō-mon, reprinted in *Yokohamashi-shi*, Shiryō-hen, vol. 4 (1967)). This case is also mentioned in *Yokohamashi-shi*, vol. 2, pp. 711–15; Ishii Kanji, *Kindai Nihon to Igirisu shihon*, pp. 31–42.

62. W. Keswick to J. Whittall, Yokohama, 20 June 1860 (B4/5/P17), and 26 June 1860 (B4/5/P19).

63. S.J. Gower to C.A. Winchester, Yokohama, 30 April 1864 (JMA, B10/9/375).

64. S.J Gower to J. Whittall, Yokohama, 25 March 1863 (JMA, B10/9/ 229).

65. S.J. Gower to C.A. Winchester, Yokohama, 30 April 1864 (JMA, B10/9/375).

66. S.J. Gower to J. Whittall, Yokohama, 27 May 1863 (JMA, B10/9/ 253).

67. Ibid., 24 May 1862 (JMA, B10/9/166).

68. Ibid., 27 December 1862 (JMA, B10/9/197); ibid., 31 December 1862 (JMA, B10/9/200). According to the former, best Ōshū cost 480 dollars and common 400 dollars, and the rates of country purchase were cheaper by 25–30 dollars per picul.

69. Ibid., 7 February 1863 (JMA, B10/9/217); ibid., 30 March 1863 (JMA, B10/9/230); ibid., 27 May 1863 (JMA, B10/9/253).

70. S.J. Gower to A. Perceval, Yokohama, 4 February 1863 (JMA, B10/9/215).

71. S.J. Gower to J. Whittall, Yokohama, 25 March 1863 (JMA, B10/ 9/229); ibid., 27 May 1863 (JMA, B10/9/253).

72. S.J. Gower to A. Perceval, Yokohama, 26 May 1863 (JMA, B10/9/ 250); S.J. Gower to J. Whittall, Yokohama, 27 May 1863 (JMA, B10/9/253).

73. C.A. Winchester to R. Alcock, Kanagawa, 29 April 1864 (FO 262/80).
74. W. Keswick to A. Perceval, Yokohama, 3 June 1863 (JMA, B10/9/256).
75. Ibid., 10 June 1863 (JMA, B10/9/260).
76. 'Eishō Gower wagashō Takasuya ni kakaru kiito hanbai iyaku ikken', [311] C.A. Winchester to Kanagawa Chindai, 14 November 1863, and [313] Ōkubo Kii-no-kami and Hori Gunai to C.A. Winchester, December 1863; C.A. Winchester to R. Alcock, Kanagawa, 29 April 1864 (FO 262/80).
77. 'Eishō Gower wagashō Takasuya ni kakaru kiito hanbai iyaku ikken', [316] Gaikoku Bugyō to Kanagawa Bugyō, April 1864.
78. W. Keswick to S.J. Gower, Shanghai, 10 October 1863 (JMA, B7/37/2508).
79. S.J. Gower to W. Keswick, Yokohama, 31 October 1863 (JMA, B10/9/319); C.A. Winchester to S.J. Gower, Kanagawa, 29 October 1863 (JMA, B10/9/316).
80. S.J. Gower to A. Perceval, Yokohama, 16 November 1863 (JMA, B10/9/322).
81. S.J. Gower to W. Keswick, Yokohama, 16 November 1863 (JMA, B10/9/324).
82. S.J. Gower to A. Perceval, Yokohama, 1 December 1863 (JMA, B10/9/327).
83. C.A. Winchester to S.J. Gower, Kanagawa, 11 December 1863 (JMA, B10/9/334); 'Eishō Gower wagashō Takasuya ni kakaru kiito hanbai iyaku ikken', [313] Ōkubo Kii-no-kami and Hori Gunai to C.A. Winchester, December 1863; C.A. Winchester to R. Alcock, Kanagawa, 29 April 1864 (FO 262/80).
84. S.J. Gower to W. Keswick, Yokohama, 17 December 1863 (JMA, B10/9/337).
85. W. Keswick to S.J. Gower, Shanghai, 20 December 1863 (JMA, B7/37/2637).
86. According to a Japanese document, in January 1864 Gower officially informed the Governor of Kanagawa through the British Consul that Jardines was willing to give Takasuya time if the Customs House would guarantee his repaying ('Eishō Gower wagashō Takasuya ni kakaru kiito hanbai iyaku ikken', [314] C.A. Winchester to Kanagawa Bugyō, Kanagawa, 12 January 1864).
87. W. Keswick to S.J. Gower, Shanghai, 18 April 1864 (JMA, B7/37/2763).
88. R. Alcock to C.A. Winchester, Yokohama, 30 April 1864 (copy) (JMA, B10/9/375); 'Eishō Gower wagashō Takasuya ni kakaru kiito hanbai iyaku ikken', [315] R. Alcock to Gaikoku Bugyō, 30 April 1864.

89. 'Eishō Gower wagashō Takasuya ni kakaru kiito hanbai iyaku ikken', [316] Gaikoku Bugyō to Kanagawa Bugyō, April 1864, [317] Gaikoku Bugyō to [Kanagawa Bugyō], 22 June 1864, and [318] Itakura Suō-no-kami, Inoue Kawachi-no-kami and Makino Bizen-no-kami to [Gaikoku Bugyō], November 1865.

90. Ibid., [321] Hayakawa Noto-no-kami and Mizuno Wakasa-no-kami to [Gaikoku Bugyō], November 1865.

91. C.A. Winchester to C.S. Hope, Kanagawa, 23 June 1864 (JMA, B10/9/394).

92. C.S. Hope for S.J. Gower to W. Keswick, Yokohama, 27 June 1864 (JMA, B10/9/398). See also C.S. Hope for S.J. Gower to J.M. & Co. (Hong Kong), Yokohama, 27 June 1864 (JMA, B10/9/396).

93. S.J. Gower to J.M. & Co. (Hong Kong), Yokohama, 9 August 1864 (JMA, B10/9/408); 'Eishō Gower wagashō Takasuya ni kakaru kiito hanbai iyaku ikken', [319] Kanagawa Bugyō to Gaikoku Bugyō, 28 June 1864.

94. C.S. Hope to J.M. & Co. (Shanghai), Yokohama, 11 August 1864 (JMA, B10/9/541).

95. W. Keswick to S.J. Gower, Shanghai, 14 June 1864 (JMA, B7/37/2834).

96. S.J. Gower to W. Keswick, Yokohama, 20 August 1864 (JMA, B10/9/414).

97. Ibid., 25 August 1864 (JMA, B10/9/419). See also S.J. Gower to J. Whittall, Yokohama, 25 August 1864 (JMA, B4/5/P53).

98. S.J. Gower to J.M. & Co. (Hong Kong), Yokohama, 12 September 1864 (JMA, B10/9/421).

99. S.J. Gower to J. Whittall, Yokohama, 1 September 1864 (JMA, B4/5/P54); S.J. Gower to W. Keswick, Yokohama, 12 September 1864 (JMA, B10/9/423).

100. W. Keswick to S.J. Gower, Shanghai, 15 September 1864 (JMA, B7/37/2972).

101. S.J. Gower to W. Keswick, Yokohama, 30 September 1864 (JMA, B10/9/430); Cash Book, Yokohama Branch (JMA, Accounts, Box 7).

102. S.J. Gower to W. Keswick, Yokohama, 11 October 1864 (JMA, B10/9/434).

103. Ibid., 17 October 1864 (JMA, B10/9/439).

104. W. Keswick to S.J. Gower, Shanghai, 2 November 1864 (JMA, B7/37/3050).

105. S.J. Gower to W. Keswick, Yokohama, 10 March 1865 (JMA, B10/9/503).

106. C.S. Hope to W. Keswick, Yokohama, 13 April 1865 (JMA, B10/9/517).

107. Ibid., Yokohama, 12 July 1865 (JMA, B4/5/P61).

108. 'Eishō Gower wagashō Takasuya ni kakaru kiito hanbai iyaku

ikken', [321] Kanagawa Bugyō to [Gaikoku Bugyō], November 1866.
109. E. Satow to C.S. Hope, Kanagawa, 13 January 1866 (JMA, B10/9/570).
110. C.S. Hope to W. Keswick, Yokohama, 15 March 1866 (JMA, B10/9/580); 'Eishō Gower wagashō Takasuya ni kakaru kiito hanbai iyaku ikken', [321] Kanagawa Bugyō to [Gaikoku Bugyō], November 1866.
111. C.S. Hope to [W. Keswick], Yokohama, 27 August 1866 (JMA, B10/9/619); F.G. Myburgh to H.S. Parkes, Kanagawa, 18 October 1866 (FO262/117); 'Eishō Gower wagashō Takasuya ni kakaru kiito hanbai iyaku ikken', [320] H.S. Parkes to Gaikoku Bugyō, Edo, 23 November 1866.
112. H.P. Austin to W. Keswick, Yokohama, 28 July 1867 (JMA, B10/9/670).
113. Ibid., 15 October 1867 (JMA, B10/9/681).
114. H.P. Austin to W. Keswick, Yokohama, 14 December 1868 (JMA, B10/9/774).
115. H. Smith to W. Keswick, Yokohama, 28 September 1870 (JMA, B10/9/1632).
116. E. Whittall to W. Keswick, Yokohama, 7 October 1870 (JMA, B10/9/1642).
117. E. Whittall to J. Whittall, Yokohama, 31 December 1870 (JMA, B10/9/1709).
118. J.M. & Co. to J.M. & Co. (Hong Kong), Yokohama, 5 February 1872 (JMA, B10/9/1946).
119. S.J. Gower to E. Whittall, Yokohama, 17 January 1865 (JMA, B10/9/484).
120. S.J. Gower to J.M. & Co. (Hong Kong), Yokohama, 30 November 1864 (JMA, B10/9/460); S.J. Gower to J. Whittall, Yokohama, 31 January 1865 (JMA, B4/5/P56).
121. W. Keswick to S.J. Gower, Shanghai, 24 January 1865 (JMA, B7/37/3176). See also S.J. Gower to W. Keswick, Yokohama, 15 February 1865 (JMA, B10/9/492).
122. S.J. Gower to E. Whittall, Yokohama, 17 January 1865 (JMA, B10/9/484); S.J. Gower to W. Keswick, Yokohama, 12 March 1865 (JMA, B10/9/504); C.S. Hope to W. Keswick, Yokohama, 15 March 1866 (JMA, B10/9/580).
123. C.S. Hope to W. Keswick, Yokohama, 27 May 1865 (JMA, B10/9/526); 'Eishō Gower wagashō Takasuya ni kakaru kiito hanbai iyaku ikken', [356] H.S. Parkes to Gaikoku Bugyō, 23 November 1866. In March 1867 the Nanbu domain agreed to repay the total debt of 27,378 dollars including interest over two years as follows: an initial amount of 10,667 dollars by October 1867 and the remaining balance of 16,711 dollars either in 1867 or in 1868.

See 'Eishō Gower wagashō Takasuya ni kakaru kiito hanbai iyaku ikken', [362] Kanagawa Bugyō to Gaikoku Bugyō, March 1867; also H.P. Austin to J.M. & Co. (Shanghai), Yokohama, 1 May 1868 (JMA, B10/9/710).

124. C.S. Hope to E. Whittall, Yokohama, 15 December 1866 (JMA, B10/9/637).

125. S.J. Gower to J.M. & Co. (Hong Kong), Yokohama, 16 November 1863 (JMA, B10/9/323).

126. S.J. Gower to J.M. & Co. (Hong Kong), Yokohama, 16 February 1864 (JMA, B10/9/350). Gower was strongly prohibited by A. Perceval from making advances to 'natives' for purchases of raw cotton for export (S.J. Gower to W. Keswick, Yokohama, 16 November 1863 (JMA, B10/9/324)).

127. H.P. Austin to J.M. & Co. (Shanghai), Yokohama, 1 May 1868 (JMA, B10/9/710).

128. JMA, Accounts, Boxes 7 and 8.

129. Transactions of the following amounts are found in the Jardine Matheson Archive Accounts for the year from July 1864 to June 1865 (except January 1865): 79,873 dollars with Sugimuraya, 66,699 dollars with Eikiya, 65,848 dollars with Nozawaya, 54,884 dollars with Kobashiya, and 50,861 dollars with Yoshimuraya. See also Ishii Kanji, *Kindai Nihon to Igirisu shihon*, pp. 49–54.

130. CR, Foreign Trade in Japan for 1878, p. 26.

131. *Nihon bōeki seiran*, pp. 230, 239. British cotton yarn exports reached a peak in 1884 (271 million lb) and then declined, but in the mid-1890s Japan was the next most important buyer after India of cotton yarn from Britain ('European and American Exports of Cotton Yarns and Piece Goods to Africa and the East', *Board of Trade Journal*, August 1896, p. 141).

132. For instance, see Kawakatsu Heita, 'Jūkyū-seiki matsuyō ni okeru Eikoku mengyō to higashi-Ajia shijō', *Shakai keizai shigaku*, 47, 2 (1981).

133. F.O. Miscellaneous Series, No. 7, 'Report on the Import Trade of Great Britain with Japan', in *BPP* (1887); No. 49, 'Reports on the Native Cotton Manufactures of Japan', in *BPP* (1887); CR, Kanagawa for 1875, p. 40; MCC, Proceedings, 7 June 1882, 25 June 1884, 28 September 1886 and 24 November 1886 (MCC Archives M8/2/9, 2/10). See also S. Sugiyama, 'The Impact of the Opening of the Ports on Domestic Japanese Industry', *Economic Studies Quarterly*, 38, 4 (1987), pp. 343–46.

134. F.O. Miscellaneous Series, No. 7, 'Report on the Import Trade of Great Britain with Japan', p. 8.

135. CR, Nagasaki for 1870, p. 60. For more information about Chinese competition, see CR, Hyōgo and Ōsaka for 1875, p. 13; for 1876, p. 11; for 1877, p. 21.

136. E. Whittall to W. Keswick, Yokohama, 9 August 1869 (JMA, B10/9/1016).
137. H. Smith to J.M. & Co. (Hong Kong), Yokohama, 23 August 1869 (JMA, B10/9/1026); H. Smith to Murdoch's Nephews, Yokohama, 18 September 1869 (JMA, B10/9/1087); H. Smith to Schuster Son & Co., Yokohama, 12 February 1870 (JMA, B10/9/1280).
138. H. Smith to F.B. Johnson, Yokohama, 10 July 1869 (JMA, B10/9/968).
139. CR, Kanagawa for 1872, p. 34.
140. The following is based on market reports from the Yokohama branch (JMA, B10/9/1229–1705).
141. H. Smith to J.M. & Co. (Hong Kong), Yokohama, 15 January 1870 (JMA, B10/9/1242).
142. H. Smith to J.M. & Co. (Hong Kong), Yokohama, 7 April 1869 (JMA, B10/9/873); ibid., 15 January 1870 (JMA, B10/9/1242).
143. H. Smith to J.M. & Co. (Hong Kong), 7 April 1869 (JMA, B10/9/873). He also advised Kraentler & Mieville, a direct shipper in London, on the types of blanket suitable for the Japanese market: 'The favorite Colors amongst the Dealers at present are Scarlet Brown & Green . . . the Blue will I fear prove difficult of sale . . . 6 and 7 lbs goods are not so easy of sale as 8 lb weight' (H. Smith to Kraentler & Mieville, 23 August 1869 (JMA, B10/9/1028)).
144. J.M. & Co. to J.M. & Co. (Hong Kong), Yokohama, 8 December 1871 (JMA, B10/9/1921).
145. H. Smith to F.B. Johnson, Yokohama, 8 June 1869 (JMA, B10/9/935).
146. CR, Nagasaki for 1874, p. 15; CR, Kanagawa for 1874, p. 30.
147. J.S. Swire to [Butterfield & Swire] (China), London, 18 June 1888 (JSSI 1/8). See also E. Whittall to W. Keswick, Yokohama, 26 February 1872 (JMA, B4/5/P123).
148. F.O. Miscellaneous Series, No. 49, 'Reports on the Native Cotton Manufactures of Japan', p. 16. See also 'Development of German Trade in the Far East', *Board of Trade Journal*, April 1898; Diplomatic and Consular Report, Miscellaneous Series, No. 564, 'Japan: Notes on the Foreign Trade and Shipping of Japan, 1872–1900', in *BPP* (1902), pp. 4–6.
The overseas marketing performance of British business before World War I has been given a high rating by S.J. Nicholas, who criticizes the over-reliance of economic historians on consular reports ('The Overseas Marketing Performance of British Industry, 1870–1914', *Economic History Review*, 2nd series, 37, 4 (1984), pp. 489–506). However, it seems to me that business archives are less likely than consular reports to reflect an objec-

tive long-term view. Moreover, the fact that they dealt in a variety of goods does not necessarily mean that British firms functioned efficiently. If performance had been efficient, there would have been no call for the repeated complaints about the inefficiency of British trading methods in the face of foreign competition. In fact, the British system of separating production and marketing seems to have been efficient only in the areas where British goods were competitive anyway (see 'Foreign Trade Competition: Opinions of H.M. Diplomatic and Consular Officers on British Trade Methods', in *BPP* (1899); 'British Economic Mission to the Far East', MCC, *Monthly Record*, April 1931, pp. 113–14; 'Lancashire and the Future', ibid., June 1937, pp. 253–4).

149. For instance, see Hayashi Reiko, 'Kokunai shijō seiritsu-ki ni okeru shūsanchi tonya', in Sakasai Takahito *et al.* (eds), *Nihon shihonshugi* (1978), pp. 19–35; Chōgin-shi Kenkyūkai (ed.), *Henkaku-ki no shōnin shihon* (1984).

150. Yokohama Shiyakusho, *Yokohamashi shikō: Sangyō-hen* (1932), pp. 135–7.

151. For instance, see Chōgin-shi Kenkyūkai (ed.), op. cit., pp. 280–5.

152. Nakamura Satoru, *Meiji ishin no kiso kōzō* (1968), pp. 246–8; Takamura Naosuke, *Nihon bōsekigyō-shi josetsu*, vol. 1 (1971), pp. 322–3.

153. Tsūshō Sangyōshō (ed.), *Shōkō seisaku-shi*, vol. 5 (1965), pp. 250–60; Takamura, ibid., pp. 32–3; CR, Hyōgo and Ōsaka for 1875, p. 14; for 1877, p. 19.

154. Iwata Jin, 'Nihon shihonshugi seiritsu katei ni okeru haikyū soshiki no henkaku', *Mita gakkai zasshi*, 32, 7 (1938); Higuchi Hiroshi, *Nihon tōgyō-shi* (1956), pp. 483–530.

155. Miyamoto Mataji, *Zoku Nihon kinsei tonyasei kenkyū* (1954), pp. 153–55, 159 ff.; Kitajima Masamoto (ed.), *Edo shōgyō to Ise-dana* (1962), pp. 658–9. For a Western view of Japanese guilds, see 'Memorandum by Mr Aston on the Commercial System of Osaka', in CR for 1870, pp. 95–9.

156. For the Treaty of Tientsin, see Parry (ed.), *The Consolidated Treaty Series*, vol. 119, pp. 164–87, 190–206; J.K. Fairbank, *Trade and Diplomacy on the China Coast* (1953).

157. See Blackburn Chamber of Commerce, *Report of the Mission to China, 1896–97* (1898); Hao, *The Comprador in Nineteenth Century China*; Miyata Michiaki, 'Shin-matsu ni okeru gaikoku bōekihin ryūtsū kikō no ichi-kōsatsu', *Sundai shigaku*, 52 (1981).

158. G.W. Skinner, 'Marketing and Social Structure in Rural China', *Journal of Asian Studies*, 24, 1, 2 (1964, 1965).

159. R. Murphey, *The Outsiders* (1977), chs 7–12; T.G. Rawski,

'Chinese Dominance of Treaty Port Commerce and Its Implications, 1860–1875', *Explorations in Economic History*, 7, 4 (1970), p. 472.
160. See the accounts for 'Piece Goods from England' in JMA A7/200; Marriner and Hyde, op. cit., p. 191; *Tōkyō keizai zasshi*, 4 March 1882, p. 282.
161. F.O. Miscellaneous Series, No. 49, 'Reports on the Native Cotton Manufactures of Japan', pp. 11, 28. See also *Tōkyō keizai zasshi*, 3 March 1883, p. 260.
162. 'Bombay and Lancashire Cotton Spinning Inquiry', *Board of Trade Journal* (January 1889); Redford, *Manchester Merchants and Foreign Trade*, vol. 2, p. 35.
163. 'British Trade Abroad: Yokohama', *Board of Trade Journal* (August 1904), p. 260.

4: The Development of the Silk Industry

1. F.R. Mason, *The American Silk Industry and the Tariff* (1910), p. 171; F.W. Taussig, *Some Aspects of the Tariff Question* (1931), p. 237.
2. The term 'silk' generally comprises raw silk, waste silk, floss silk, dupion, cocoons, and silkworm eggs, but not silk piece goods. Raw silk of coarse quality was also imported into Japan from China for manufacturing domestic silk goods, but amounts were small.
3. *Nihon bōeki seiran*, pp. 3, 52, 53, 55.
4. Holdsworth's Silk Circular, Shanghai, 4 July 1866, in JMA, PCMR 46; G.S. Fisher to W.H. Seward, No. 19, 1 October 1862, and No. 41, 1 October 1863, both in USA, *Despatches from United States Consuls in Kanagawa, 1861–1897*, vol. 1.
5. For French policy towards Japan, see Medzini, *French Policy in Japan during the Closing Years of the Tokugawa Regime*; Ishii Takashi, *Meiji ishin no kokusaiteki kankyō*, vol. 2, pp. 615–58, 713–18; Shibata Michio and Shibata Asako, 'Bakumatsu ni okeru Furansu no tainichi seisaku', *Shigaku zasshi*, 76, 8 (1967); Gonjō Yasuo, 'Furansu shihonshugi to kaikō', in Ishii Kanji and Sekiguchi Hisashi (eds), *Sekai shijō to bakumatsu kaikō* (1982), pp. 158–65. See also Fieldhouse, *Economics and Empire, 1830–1914*, pp. 203–6, 210.
6. CR, Kanagawa for 1865, p. 244.
7. Japan, Imperial Department of State for Agriculture and Commerce, *General View of Commerce and Industry in the Empire of Japan* (1900), p. 131.

The silk industry can be divided into three sectors: sericulture, reeling, and weaving (manufacturing). Silk reeling in Japan consisted of three main processes: reeling, re-reeling and finishing (dressing and packing). For a detailed description of silk reeling methods, see Imperial Japanese Silk Conditioning House (Honda Iwajirō), *The Silk Industry in Japan* (1909), pp. 132–42, and, for dressing of silk, pp. 160–2.

The estimated fineness of raw silk is indicated by the unit of weight for silk yarn called 'denier'. The Lyons standard of denier measurement was based on the weight of a length of yarn of 476 metres. 476 metres of silk yarn of 1 denier weighed 0.05313 g. Japan used this criterion until 1905, when it adopted a new standard according to which 1 denier signified silk yarn which weighed 0.05 g at 450 metres.

Generally speaking, 'fine yarn' meant less than 11.5 deniers, 'medium yarn' from 11.5 to 13.5 deniers, 'coarse yarn' from 13.5 to 17 deniers, and 'super coarse yarn' over 17 deniers. In the Yokohama market, however, 'fine yarn' meant less than 12.5 deniers and 'coarse yarn' over 21.5 deniers (Hayakawa Naose, *Kiito to sono bōeki*(revised edn, 1928), pp. 113–14).

 8. *Yokohamashi-shi*, vol. 4, Pt I, pp. 82–3, 87 ff; Furushima Toshio, *Sangyō-shi* (1966), p. 377.
 9. CR, Summary of the Foreign Trade of Japan for 1876, p. 31.
10. *Yokohamashi-shi*, vol. 3, Pt I, p. 514.
11. Yamaguchi Kazuo (ed.), *Nihon sangyō kinyū-shi kenkyū: Seishi kinyū-hen* (1966), pp. 20–1.
12. Ōkurashō, *Shōkyō nenpō* (for 1879/80), No. 5, p. 9.
13. See Nōshōmushō, *Yushutsu jūyōhin yōran*, Sanshi (1896), pp. 82–3; *Yushutsu jūyōhin yōran*, Sanshi (1901), pp. 108–9; Hara Gōmei Kaisha, *Ōbei sangyō ippan* (1900), p. 7; Imanishi Naojirō, *Ōbei sanshigyō shisatsu fukumeisho* (1902), p. 73; J. Chittick, *Silk Manufacturing and Its Problems* (1913), ch. 3.
14. See L.G. Sandberg, 'Movements in the Quality of British Cotton Textile Exports, 1815–1913', *Journal of Economic History*, 28, 1 (1968).
15. IMC, *Decennial Report, 1882–1891*, p. 554; IMC, *Silk* (Special Series, No. 3, 1881), p. 148.
16. Tōa Kenkyūjo, *Shina sanshigyō kenkyū* (1943), pp. 13–14, 121, 183. For the development of the silk industry and silk trade in China, see Nōshōmu-shō, Nōmukyoku (Honda Iwajirō), *Shinkoku sanshigyō chōsa fukumeisho* (1899); Tōa Dōbunkai, *Shina keizai zensho*, vol. 12 (1908); D.K. Lieu, *The Silk Industry of China* (1941); Shih Min-hsiung, *The Silk Industry in Ch'ing China* (1976); L. Li, *China's Silk Trade* (1981).
17. CR, Shanghai for 1865, p. 137.

18. Calculated from *Annual Statement of the Trade of the United Kingdom*, corresponding years. For the silk industry in Britain, see F. Warner, *The Silk Industry of the United Kingdom* (1921); A.L. Dunham, *The Anglo-French Treaty of Commerce of 1860 and the Progress of the Industrial Revolution in France* (1930), pp. 252 ff.; R.C. Rawlley, *Economics of the Silk Industry* (1919), p. 271 ff.

19. Durant & Co.'s Circular, 1 January 1874, in JMA, PCMR 42; H.W. Eaton & Sons' Circular, London, 1 January 1873, Table A, in JMA, PCMR 41; *Annual Statement of the Trade of the United Kingdom*, 1876–1890.

20. CR, Kanagawa for 1862, p. 210.

21. Durant & Co.'s Circular, 4 January 1861, in JMA, PCMR 41.

22. Ibid., 4 January 1862, in JMA, PCMR 41.

23. Ibid., 4 January 1862 and 1 January 1863, both in JMA, PCMR 41.

24. Ibid., 1 January 1864, in JMA, PCMR 41.

25. Eaton's Circular, London, 3 January 1862, in JMA, PCMR 41.

26. H.W. Eaton & Sons' Circular, London, 1 January 1873; Arlès-Dufour & Co. [Silk Circular], Lyons, 27 October 1862, both in JMA, PCMR 41.

27. H.W. Eaton & Sons' Circular, London, 1 January 1873, Table A, and Durant & Co.'s Circular, 4 January 1861, both in JMA, PCMR 41.

28. Waithman, Jacomb, & Hogg's Circular, 1 January 1864, and Durant & Co.'s Circular, 8 September 1863, both in JMA, PCMR 41.

29. Waithman, Jacomb, & Hogg's Circular, 1 January 1864, in JMA, PCMR 41.

30. Arlès-Dufour & Co. [Silk Circular], Lyons, 31 July 1869, in JMA, PCMR 40; J.H. Clapham, *Economic Development of France and Germany* (4th edn, 1936), p. 253.

31. Jacomb, Hogg & Co.'s Price Current for China Mail, 25 November 1867, in JMA, PCMR 41; CR, Kanagawa for 1873, pp. 56–7.

32. 'Report by Mr. Adams on the Deterioration of Japanese Silk' (1871), pp. 2–3.

33. CR, Kanagawa for 1869, pp. 4–5; for 1870, p. 6; for 1874, p. 30; for 1877, p. 55.

34. CR, Kanagawa for 1874, p. 32.

35. 'Report by Mr. Adams on the Central Silk Districts of Japan' (1870), p. 11, in *BPP* (1870).

36. Jacomb, Hogg & Co.'s Price Current for China Mail, 25 Nov. 1867, in JMA, PCMR 41; *Silk Supply Journal*,1, 8 (October 1870), p. 136; Durant & Co.'s Circular, 2 January 1871, in *Silk Supply Journal*,1, 9 (January 1871), pp. 169, 170; H.W. Eaton & Sons' Cir-

cular, London, 7 April 1869, in JMA, PCMR 40.

37. Kilburn, Kershaw & Co.'s Report, quoted from *Silk Supply Journal*, 1, 13 (January 1872), p. 240.

38. L. Clugnet, *Géographie de la Soie* (1877), p. 143.

39. E. Pariset, *Histoire de la Fabrique Lyonnaise* (1901), pp. 339–41, 345, 348, 357; P. Clerget, *Les Industries de la Soie en France* (1925), p. 11.

40. Italy, Ministero de Agricoltura, Industria e Commercio, *Annuario Statistico Italiano*, 1889–90 (1891), p. 684; ibid., 1895 (1896), p. 410; ibid., 1904 (1904), p. 253. For the development of the silk industry in Italy, see J. Tambor, *Seidenbau und Seidenindustrie in Italien* (1929).

41. Arlès-Dufour & Co. [Silk Circular], 16 January 1869, and Frederick Huth & Co.'s Bi-monthly Silk Circular, London, 1 January 1869, both in JMA, PCMR 40; Pariset, op. cit., pp. 371, 381–2.

42. M.A. Perret, *Monographie de la Condition des Soies de Lyon* (1878), pp. 88–9.

43. CR, Shanghai for 1865, p. 140; for 1878, p. 24; Kanagawa for 1880, p. 41; for 1881, p. 36; for 1883, p. 13.

44. CR, General Report on the Trade of Japan for 1884, p. 106.

45. See IMC, *Reports on Trade at the Treaty Ports in China*, for 1876, Pt I, p. 32.

46. E. Pariset, *Les Industries de la Soie* (1890), p. 213–4; J. Bouvier, *Le Crédit Lyonnais de 1863 à 1882* (1961), Tome 1, pp. 281–2.

47. M. Laferrère, *Lyon: Ville Industrielle* (1960), pp. 173–4; IMC, *Reports on Trade at the Treaty Ports in China*, for 1876, Pt I, p. 8.

48. Tambor, op. cit., S. 122.

49. H.W. Eaton & Sons' Circular, London, 4 January 1873, and 5 January 1874, both in JMA, PCMR 41.

50. CR, Kanagawa for 1875, p. 46.

51. Ibid.

52. See 'Commercial History and Review of 1876', *Economist*, 1750 (10 March 1877), p. 15.

53. *Shōkyō nenpō* (for 1879/80), No. 5, p. 8.

54. J. Schober, *Silk and Silk Industry* (1930), p. 248; V.S. Clark, *History of Manufacture in the United States* (1929), vol. 1, pp. 326, 575.

55. W.C. Wyckoff, 'Report on the Silk Manufacturing Industry of the United States', in USA, Department of the Interior, Census Office, *Report on the Manufactures of the United States at the Tenth Census* (1880) (hereafter *Tenth Census*), pp. 18, 19.

56. For general descriptions of the silk industry before 1860, see F. Allen, *American Silk Industry, Chronologically Arranged, 1793–1876* (1876); *Tenth Census*, pp. 1–19; Clark, op. cit. vol. 1, p. 289;

A.S. Bolles, *Industrial History of the United States from the Earliest Settlements to the Present Time* (1879), pp. 427–43.

57. Clark, op. cit., vol. 2, p. 449.
58. *Tenth Census*, p. 19.
59. F. Allen, 'Silk Manufactures', in USA, Department of Interior, Census Office, *Twelfth Census of the United States* (1900), Manufactures, Pt III, Special Reports on Selected Industries (hereafter *Twelfth Census*), p. 203.
60. USA, Department of Interior, Census Office, *Ninth Census of the United States* (1870), vol. 3, p. 624; *Tenth Census*, p. 25; B. Rose, 'Silk Manufactures', in *Eleventh Census of the United States* (1890), Pt III (hereafter *Eleventh Census*), p. 226; *Twelfth Census*, p. 230.
61. Mason, op. cit., pp. 42–3, 45–6.
62. See USA, Department of Commerce, Bureau of the Census, *Commerce and Navigation of the United States*, for 1864–1900. For the history of the tariff on silk manufactures in the United States during this period, see Mason, op. cit., pp. 56–102; F.W. Taussig, *The Tariff History of the United States* (8th edn, 1931), pp. 248, 268–9, 297, 337–40. On the details of the Dingley Act, see Silk Association of America, *Annual Report* (for 1898), pp. 62–8.
63. USA, Department of Commerce, Bureau of the Census, *Historical Statistics of the United States: Colonial Times to 1970*, Pt I (1975), p. 8.
64. *Tenth Census*, p. 17; *Twelfth Census*, pp. 222, 223; *Eleventh Census*, p. 222.
65. *Twelfth Census*, p. 223.
66. Ibid., p. 208; L.R. Wells, *Industrial History of the United States* (revised edn, 1926), pp. 377–8.
67. *Tenth Census*, p. 19; Mason, op. cit., p. 16.
68. Bolles, op. cit., pp. 438, 442.
69. Mason, op. cit., pp. 17–18, 21–5. See also Silk Association of America, *Annual Report* (for 1875), pp. 164–7.
70. *Commerce and Navigation of the United States*, for 1869, pp. 90–1. The Trans-Continental Railway shortened the transportation time between San Francisco and New York from 22 days by sea to 6 days by rail.
71. *Commerce and Navigation of the United States*, for 1871, 1876–86.
72. Mason, op. cit., pp. 18, 19; Tomioka Seishijō-shi Hensan Iinkai (ed.), *Tomioka seishijō-shi* (1977), vol. 1, [189], pp. 408–12.
73. *Shōkyō nenpō* (for 1879/80) stated that 'Demand from silk manufactures in the United States was brisk, and, since there has been a tendency to purchase even coarse and low-classified silk at a high price, which might otherwise have been sold only at a

low price in the European market, exports to the United States have increased considerably.' (p. 30.)

74. CR, Kanagawa for 1877, p. 57; *Shōkyō nenpō* (for 1880/81), No. 5, p. 284. See also Eguchi Zenji and Hidaka Yasoshichi (eds), *Shinano sanshigyō-shi* (1937), vol. 3, pp. 469, 1435. For deniers see above, note 7.

75. In weaving, better-quality threads tended to be used for the warp, but the weft tended to use thread in greater quantities (*Yushutsu jūyōhin yōran*, Sanshi (1896), p. 76; *Dainihon sanshi kaihō*, No. 29, p. 31). According to an estimate by Takahashi Nobusada, the average worldwide percentage of warp and weft used in silk-manufacturing districts was 40 per cent and 60 per cent respectively (Ishii Kanji, *Nihon sanshigyō-shi bunseki* (1972), p. 53). However, it was usual practice for manufacturers occasionally to use silk designated for the warp as weft, or vice versa, if this was convenient and suited the kind of fabric being made (*Yushutsu jūyōhin yōran*, Sanshi (1896), p. 76).

76. *Shōkyō nenpō* (for 1878/79), No. 5, pp. 14–15; *Shōkyō nenpō* (for 1883/84), No. 3, pp. 85–6; *Tōkyō keizai zasshi*, 5 March 1881, p. 223; CR, Kanagawa for 1878, p. 41.

77. Clark, op. cit., vol. 2, p. 450. It was also partly because, as a result of the *Rengō kiito niazukarisho jiken* in 1881, 'many manufacturers there [United States], who had up to that time used Japan silks, discarded them in favour' of Italian raws' ('Review of the Silk Season' by Vivianti Brothers, Yokohama, 10 April 1882 (Extract from the *Japan Herald*), in T.B. van Buren to J.C.B. Davis, No. 617, 28 March 1882, in *Despatches from United States Consuls in Kanagawa, 1861–1897*, vol. 12). See below, p. 132.

78. DCRTF, No. 38, Kanagawa for 1885, p. 7.

79. CR, Kanagawa for 1884, p. 54; Yokohama Prices Current and Market Report, Nos 516 (20 March 1889), 532 (19 December 1889) and 573 (1 July 1891), in JMA, PCMR 82; Griffin & Co.'s Silk Trade Review, No. 89, Yokohama, 31 December 1883, in JMA, PCMR 82; J.M. & Co, Silk Report, Yokohama, 1 August 1887, and 18 October 1887, in JMA, A7/200.

80. *Yushutsu jūyōhin yōran*, Sanshi (1896), pp. 27–8, 76.

81. *Commerce and Navigation of the United States*, for 1890/91, p. 130; 1895/96, vol. 1, pp. 179–81; for 1899/1900, vol. 1, p. 336. For *habutae*, see Diplomatic and Consular Reports (Miscellaneous Series, No. 672), 'Reports on the Raw Silk Industry of Japan and on Habutae (Japanese Manufactured Silk)', in *BPP* (1909), pp. 33–55.

82. *Shōkyō nenpō* (for 1880/81), No. 5, p. 256; Eguchi and Hidaka (eds), op. cit., vol. 3, pp. 625–7.

83. *Yushutsu jūyōhin yōran*, Sanshi (1896), pp. 37, 40; Imanishi, op.

cit., pp. 73–4; Hara Gōmei Kaisha, op. cit., pp. 14–16; *Dainihon sanshi kaihō*, No. 28 (October 1894), p. 42.

84. DCRTF, No. 1118, Foreign Trade of Japan for 1891, pp. 11–12.
85. *Yushutsu jūyōhin yōran*, Sanshi (1896), pp. 41, 80.
86. *Dainihon sanshikai hōkoku*, No. 1 (April 1892), pp. 1–2; *Yushutsu jūyōhin yōran*, Sanshi (1896), pp. 39–88; R.V. Briesen, *Beikoku ni okeru Nihonshi ni kansuru hiken* (1896).
87. Briesen, op. cit., pp. 3–5; *Yushutsu jūyōhin yōran*, Sanshi (1896), p. 80; *Yushutsu jūyōhin yōran*, Sanshi (1901), p. 25; Hara Gōmei Kaisha, op. cit., pp. 14–15.
88. CR, Kanagawa for 1868, p. 7, and Hyōgo and Ōsaka for 1868, p. 25.
89. CR, Kanagawa for 1874, p. 32.
90. 'Kiito Yokohama yushutsu shirabe', 3–2, [117], in *Yokohamashi-shi*, Shiryō-hen, vol. 1 (1960), p. 282; Yamaguchi Kazuo, *Meiji zenki keizai no bunseki* (expanded edn, 1963), p. 15.
91. 'Report by Mr. Adams on the Central Silk Districts of Japan' (1870), pp. 13–14.
92. Yokohama Shiyakusho, *Yokohamashi shikō: Sangyō-hen* (1932), pp. 108–9; Gunmaken Naimubu (ed.), *Gunmaken sanshigyō enkaku chōsasho*, Kiito-no-bu (1903), I, pp. 40–43.
   In the Italian type of silk reeling two reelers operated together with one person who was boiling cocoons, while in the French type the same reeler operated both the reeling and the boiling of cocoons.
93. For the Tomioka Filature, see Tomioka Seishijō-shi Hensan Iinkai (ed.), op. cit. For filatures during the early Meiji period, see Smith, *Political Change and Industrial Development in Japan* (1955), pp. 56–8. Note, however, that he shares in the general tendency to overestimate the role of the Tomioka Silk Filature as a pilot firm in the development of the silk industry. On this, see Furushima, *Sangyō-shi*, pp. 236–8.
94. Kajinishi Mitsuhaya (ed.), *Gendai Nihon sangyō hattatsu-shi: Seni* (1964), Pt I, p. 97.
95. Tomioka Seishijō-shi Hensan Iinkai (ed.), op. cit., vol. 1, pp. 52–3.
96. Notification calling for Information respecting Silk Culture by the Home Department (March 1870), in 'Further Paper respecting Silk Culture in Japan', pp. 3–4, in *BPP* (1870); Sano Ei, *Dainihon sanshi*, Seishi (1898), pp. 213 ff. See also *Yokohamashi-shi*, vol. 3, Pt. I, pp. 86–123.
97. Calculated from Nōshōmushō, *Nōsan-hyō* and *Nōshōmu tōkei-hyō*.

98. For the development of the silk industry in the Fukushima area, see Fujita Gorō, *Nihon kindai sangyō no seisei* (1948), ch. 3; Ōishi Kaichirō, *Nihon chihō zaigyōsei-shi josetsu* (1961), pp. 174–206; Yamaguchi (ed.), *Nihon sangyō kinyū-shi kenkyū*, ch. 4; Ebato Akira, *Sanshigyō chiiki no keizai-chirigakuteki kenkyū* (1969), ch. 6.

99. For the development of the silk industry in the Gunma area, see Gunmaken, op. cit.; Yamaguchi (ed.), ibid., ch. 5; Ebato, ibid., chs 4, 5; Ishii Kanji, 'Zaguri seishigyō no hatten katei', *Shakai keizai shigaku*, 28, 6 (1963).

100. See Yamaguchi (ed.), ibid., p. 571.

101. For the development of the silk industry in Nagano, see Hirano-mura Yakuba, *Hirano sonshi* (1932), vol. 2; Eguchi and Hidaka (eds), op. cit.; Yagi Haruo, *Nihon kindai seishigyō no seiritsu* (1960); Yamaguchi (ed.), ibid., ch. 2; Ebato, op. cit., chs 1, 2; Kitajima Masamoto (ed.), *Seishigyō no tenkai to kōzō* (1970).

102. Eguchi and Hidaka (eds), op. cit., vol. 2, pp. 1105–20.

103. Ibid., vol. 3, pp. 1124–5; Yamaguchi, *Meiji zenki keizai no bunseki*, p. 134; *Yokohamashi-shi*, vol. 3, Pt I, pp. 529, 531.

104. See Yamaguchi (ed), *Nihon sangyō kinyū-shi kenkyū*, pp. 10–12, 25–34, 37–74; *Yokohamashi-shi*, vol. 4, Pt I (1965), pp. 397–450; Ishii, *Nihon sanshigyō-shi bunseki*, pp. 163–215; Ishii Kanji, 'Nihon Ginkō no sangyō kinyū', *Shakai keizai shigaku*, 38, 2 (1972).

105. *Shōkyō nenpō* (for 1878/79), No. 5, p. 17.

106. Eguchi and Hidaka (eds), op. cit., vol. 3, p. 1018.

107. Nōshōmushō, *Nōshōmu tōkei-hyō*, corresponding years.

108. Eguchi and Hidaka (eds), op. cit., vol. 3, pp. 909 ff.

109. Hiranomura Yakuba, op. cit., vol. 2, p. 482.

110. Note, however, that the average rice price in Nagano Prefecture shows a downward trend in the late 1880s and then an upward trend in the early 1890s (*Nōshōmu tōkei-hyō*, for 1885–95). This suggests that up to the late 1880s, at least, their substantial wages increased even though nominal wages changed very little.

111. Eguchi and Hidaka (eds), op. cit., vol. 3, pp. 1341–3; *Yokohamashi-shi*, vol. 4, Pt I, pp. 171, 203; Nōshōmushō, *Nōshōmu tōkei-hyō*, corresponding years.

    For discussion of the low wages of female reelers and their working conditions, see Nōshōmushō, Shokkōkyoku, *Shokkō jijō (Kiito)* (1903), pp. 127–59; Sumiya Mikio, *Nihon chinrōdō shiron* (1955), pp. 163–74; Ishii, *Nihon sanshigyō-shi bunseki*, ch. 3.

112. See *Shokkō jijō (Kiito);* Eguchi and Hidaka (eds), op. cit., vol. 3, pp. 1132–1232.

113. *Yokohamashi-shi*, vol. 4, Pt I, pp. 54–76.
114. Nihon Tōkei Kenkyūjo (ed.), *Nihon keizai tōkei-shū* (1958), p. 106.
115. Ishii, *Nihon sanshigyō-shi bunseki*, pp. 49–50, 57, 444–50. Ishii Kanji suggests that this new type emerged as early as 1880, but I do not think it had very much significance as far as American consumers of Japanese silk were concerned.
116. *Yokohamashi-shi*, vol. 4, Pt I, pp. 82–3.
117. Ibid., vol. 3, Pt I, pp. 477–8; vol. 4, Pt I, p. 203.
118. Mizunuma Tomoichi, 'Meiji kōki ni okeru kiito yushutsu no dōkō', *Shakai keizai shigaku*, 28, 5 (1963), pp. 14, 18–19. For details of silk exports by Japanese merchants, see *Yokohamashi-shi*, vol. 3, Pt I, pp. 581–601; vol. 4, Pt I, pp. 120–49, 158–70.
119. *Yushutsu jūyōhin yōran*, Sanshi (1896), pp. 28–34; ibid. (1901), pp. 85–99.
120. Yamaguchi (ed.), *Nihon sangyō kinyū-shi kenkyū*, pp. 10, 19.
121. 'Report by Mr. Adams on the Central Silk Districts of Japan' (1870), pp. 13–14; 'Commercial Morality of the Japanese', *Board of Trade Journal* (November 1890). See also Yokohama Shōgyō Kaigisho, *Yokohama kaikō gojūnen-shi* (1909), vol. 2, pp. 538–9.
122. 'Rengō kiito niazukarisho kokuchisho' (1881), in Yokohama Shōgyō Kaigisho, op. cit., vol. 2, pp. 536–8; Yokohama Shiyakusho, *Yokohamashi shikō: Sangyō-hen*, pp. 441–2.
123. Yokohama Shōgyō Kaigisho, op. cit., vol. 2, pp. 535–6. For similar price manipulation in silkworm egg transactions, see 'Sanshu shōhō', in *Meiji bunka zenshū*, vol. 9 (1929), pp. 83–4.
124. See *Yokohamashi-shi*, vol. 4, Pt II, pp. 455–534; CR, Kanagawa for 1881, Pt II, pp. 38–9; T.B. van Buren to W. Blains, No. 572, 10 October 1881 (Recent Trouble in the Silk Trade), in USA, *Despatches from United States Consuls in Kanagawa, 1861–1897*, vol. 12. There are a number of studies of this affair, for instance *Yokohamashi-shi*, vol. 3, Pt I, pp. 753–98; ibid., vol. 3, Pt II, pp. 106–24; Unno Fukuju, *Meiji no bōeki* (1967), chs 3–6.
125. See Yokohama Shōgyō Kaigisho, op. cit., vol. 2, pp. 541–6; Fujimoto Jitsuya, *Kaikō to kiito bōeki* (1939), vol. 3, ch. 13; *Yokohamashi-shi*, vol. 3, Pt I, pp. 641–52, 690–1, 694–717.
126. *Yushutsu jūyōhin yōran*, Sanshi (1896), pp. 28–32; ibid. (1901), pp. 85–8.
127. 'Export of Silk from Yokohama, Japan, for the Season 1866–67', undated, in JMA, PCMR 46; 'Answers to Queries addressed to H.B.M. Consul at Kanagawa by the Board of Trade in a letter dated 17th November 1869', in F. Lowder to H.S. Parkes, Kanagawa, 7 May 1870 (FO 262/200).

128. 'Seishi shijunkai kiji' (1885), pp. 96–7; DCRTF, Nos 1084, 1255, 1421, 1600, 1971, Yokohama for 1891–3, 1895, 1896.
129. Japanese scholars have stressed the enormous profits gained by Western merchants, owing to the difference in price between Yokohama and the international market at London and Lyons (see, in particular, Takahashi Keizai Kenkyūjo, *Nihon sanshigyō hattatsu-shi* (1941), vol. 1, pp. 64–5). However, this view stems from a miscalculation of the exchange rates. For details, see Sugiyama, 'Bakumatsu Meiji-shoki ni okeru kiito yushutsu no sūryōteki saikentō', *Shakai keizai shigaku*, 45, 3 (1979).
130. For Arlès-Dufour & Co., see Bouvier, op. cit., Tome I, pp. 283–6.
131. Marriner and Hyde, *The Senior, John Samuel Swire*, p. 191.
132. Allen and Donnithorne, *Western Enterprise in Far Eastern Economic Development*, p. 245.
133. See also ibid., p. 61; *Yokohamashi-shi*, vol. 4, Pt I, pp. 149–58.

5: The Development of Tea Exports

1. IMC, *Reports on Trade at the Treaty Ports in China*, for 1876, Pt I, p. 36.
2. P. Griffiths, *The History of the Indian Tea Industry* (1967), p. 125. For British tea consumption, see P. Mathias, 'The British Tea Trade in the Nineteenth Century', in D. Oddy and D.S. Miller (eds), *The Making of the Modern British Diet* (1976).
3. Nōshōmushō, Nōmukyoku, *Chagyō gairan* (1914), p. 59.
4. See W.H. Ukers, *All About Tea* (1935), vol. 1, pp. 219–21, 223, 234, 292.
5. CR, Nagasaki for 1865, p. 6, and Kanagawa for 1865, p. 245.
6. *Yokohamashi-shi* vol. 3, Pt I, p. 487. Prices of tea exported from Yokohama were higher than those from Kōbe, which meant that the quality of this tea was superior to that from Kōbe (ibid., p. 488).
7. Nōshōmushō, Nōmukyoku, *Yushutsu jūyōhin yōran*, Nōsan-no-bu, Cha (December 1896), p. 52.
8. CR, Kanagawa for 1862, p. 211, and for 1866, p. 255; Arthur Capel & Co.'s Tea Circular, London, 8 January 1867, in JMA, PCMR 35.
9. CR, Kanagawa for 1867, p. 309.
10. Paske-Smith, *Western Barbarians in Japan and Formosa*, p. 214.
11. Exports to Canada decreased rapidly after 1903, due to competition from Indian and Ceylon tea (see *Yokohamashi-shi*, vol. 4, Pt I, p. 250). Japanese tea ceased to be quoted on the London

market in 1881 (*Shōkyō nenpō*, for 1883, No. 5, p. 41; *Economist*, 1985, 10 September 1881, p. 1146).

12. CR, Hyōgo and Ōsaka for 1884, p. 14.
13. Ukers, op. cit., vol. 2, p. 18. For the tea industry in Fukien and Formosa, see also R.P. Gardella, 'The Boom Years of the Fukien Tea Trade, 1842-1888', in E.R. May and J.K. Fairbank (eds), *America's China Trade in Historical Perspective* (1986).
14. IMC, *Reports on Trade at the Treaty Ports*, Pt I, p. 55; *Reports on the Trade at the Ports in China*, for 1865, Pt II, p. 129; *Returns of Trade at the Treaty Ports, and the Trade Reports*, for 1884, Pt I, p. 4.
15. CR, Shanghai for 1868, p. 24; IMC, *Returns of Trade and Trade Reports*, for 1891, Pt I, p. 3, and for 1893, Pt II, Shanghai, p. 219.
16. *The Tea Cyclopaedia* (1881), pp. 266, 332; Nōshōmushō, Nōmukyoku, *Chagyō ni kansuru chōsa* (1912), pp. 473-4.
17. J.E. Craig, Jr, 'Ceylon', in W.A. Lewis (ed.), *Tropical Development, 1880-1913*, p. 229.
18. D.M. Forrest, *A Hundred Years of Ceylon Tea, 1867-1967* (1967), pp. 148, 290.
19. CR, Kanagawa for 1865, p. 241.
20. 'Reports on the Production of Tea in Japan', p. 10-11, in *BPP* (1873).
21. G.K. Sarkar, *The World Tea Economy* (1972), pp. 21, 58. E.W. Gilboy has suggested that coffee demand was generally inelastic between 1875 and 1918 ('Time Series and the Derivation of Demand and Supply Curves: A Study of Coffee and Tea, 1850-1930', *Quarterly Journal of Economics*, 48 (1934), p. 685).
22. *Chagyō ni kansuru chōsa*, pp. 3, 249.
23. Nōshōmushō, *Yushutsu jūyōhin yōran*, Cha (1901), pp. 27-8.
24. CR, Kanagawa for 1865, p. 244; IMC, *Reports on the Trade at the Ports in China*, for 1865, p. 129; 'Reports on the Production of Tea in Japan', p. 10.
25. CR, Report by Mr. Malet on the General Features of Chinese Trade for the Year 1872, p. 227; IMC, *Reports on Trade at the Treaty Ports in China*, for 1876, Pt I, p. 33. The unprofitable situation in the tea trade continued for the following three decades.
26. Nōshōmushō, Nōmukyoku, *Yushutsu jūyōhin yōran*, Cha (February 1896), p. 27, and ibid. (December 1896), pp. 53-60; Ukers, op. cit., vol. 2, p. 59; Nihon Chagyō Kumiai Chūō Kaigisho, *Nihon cha bōeki gaikan* (1935), pp. 83-4.

Japanese tea 'was becoming popular, especially in Western States, where the water is so much impregnated with lime' (*The Tea Cyclopaedia*, p. 286). It was said that Americans first boiled green tea, using their coffee-making equipment, and then drank it with sugar and/or milk (*Nihon cha bōeki gaikan*, p. 84).

27. CR, Kanagawa for 1872, p. 40; CR, Hyōgo and Ōsaka for 1873, p. 20.
28. CR, Summary of Commercial Reports for the Year 1876, p. 6; CR, Kanagawa for 1877, p. 59.
29. Hsiao Liang-lin, *China's Foreign Trade Statistics* (1974), p. 117; *Nihon bōeki tōkei* (expanded and revised edn, 1980), p. 153.
30. IMC, *Reports on Trade at the Treaty Ports in China*, for 1869, p. 13; for 1876, Pt I, p. 32.
31. IMC, *Returns of Trade at the Treaty Ports*, Pt I, corresponding years.
32. IMC, *Returns on Trade at the Treaty Ports*, for 1881, Pt II, Foochow, p. 7; IMC, *Decennial Report*, 1892–1901, vol. 1, p. 479; IMC, *Reports on Trade at the Treaty Ports in China*, for 1876, Pt I, p. 36; IMC, *Returns of Trade at the Treaty Ports, and Trade Reports*, for 1883, Pt I, p. 165; IMC, *Returns of Trade and Trade Reports*, for 1896, Pt I, xii.
33. IMC, *Reports on Trade at the Treaty Ports in China*, for 1876, Pt I, pp. 59, 118; DCRTF, No. 1951, Shanghai for 1896, p. 14; IMC, *Decennial Report*, 1892–1901, p. 482.
34. 'Reports on the Production of Tea in Japan', p. 12; Extract from the *Japan Mail*, 31 May 1873, in CR, Review of the Import Trade of Japan, and of the Tea and Silk Season of 1872–73, p. 93; CR, Kanagawa for 1880, p. 42.
35. CR, Kanagawa for 1868, p. 4; CR, Kanagawa for 1869, p. 7.
36. CR, Hyōgo and Ōsaka for 1876, p. 14.
37. CR, Kanagawa for 1876, p. 42.
38. CR, Summary of Commercial Reports for the Year 1876, p. 6.
39. CR, Hyōgo and Ōsaka for 1876, p. 14.
40. CR, Kanagawa for 1881, p. 42.
41. CR, Kanagawa for 1882, p. 14.
42. IMC, *Returns of Trade at the Treaty Ports, and Trade Reports*, for 1883, Pt I, p. 3.
43. *Commerce and Navigation of the United States*, 1882–3, Pt I, p. 44, and 1883–4, Pt I, p. 57.
44. *Shōkyō nenpō* (for 1883), Pt II, No. 4, p. 56.
45. DCRTF, No. 1083, Hyōgo and Ōsaka for 1891, p. 8.
46. DCRTF, No. 1811, Report for First Six Months of the Year 1896 on the Foreign Trade of Japan, p. 7; *Chagyō ni kansuru chōsa*, p. 249; *Chagyō gairan*, pp. 57–9; Ukers, op. cit., vol. 2, p. 278; Griffiths, op. cit., pp. 588–9.
47. CR, Hyōgo and Ōsaka for 1877, p. 29.
48. Nōshōmushō, *Yushutsu jūyōhin yōran*, Cha (February 1896), p. 28.

49. *Chagyō gairan*, pp. 76–80.
50. Ibid., pp. 81–4. Of course, this leaves open the question of whether 1 lb of tea produces as much drinkable liquid as 1 lb of coffee, but it is doubtful whether consumers made such calculations.
51. *Chagyō ni kansuru chōsa*, pp. 354–5.
52. Chagyō Kumiai Chūō Kaigisho, *Nihon chagyō-shi* (1914), p. 36; *Nihon cha bōeki gaikan*, p. 53.
53. Yamaguchi Kazuo, 'Cha bōeki no hattatsu to seichagyō', in Ohara Keishi (ed.), *Nichibei bunka kōshō-shi*, vol. 2 (1954), p. 139; *Nihon cha bōeki gaikan*, pp. 56, 66, 74; *Yokohamashi-shi*, vol. 2, pp. 645–76; Nōshōmushō, Nōmukyoku, 'Seicha shūdankai nisshi' (1884), p. 371; CR, Kanagawa for 1868, p. 5.
54. *Nihon cha bōeki gaikan*, p. 59; Yamaguchi, *Bakumatsu bōeki-shi*, pp. 200–1, and 'Cha bōeki no hattatsu to seichagyō', p. 149. For details of tea production, see H. Gribble, 'The Preparation of Japan Tea', *Transactions of the Asiatic Society of Japan*, 12 (1885).
55. 'Reports on the Production of Tea in Japan', pp. 18–19.
56. CR, Nagasaki for 1859, p. 6, and Kanagawa during the Half Year ended 31st December 1860, p. 280.
57. 'Reports on the Production of Tea in Japan', p. 11.
58. CR, Nagasaki for 1868, p. 32; for 1869, p. 49. The commercial treaties of 1858 fixed the general export duty for tea at 5 per cent of the declared price, but this was later revised to 3.5 *ichibus* per 100 kin. However, while 'tea, fired and packed on the spot is charged full 3½ bus per picul on all grades', the duty for 'bancha' from Nagasaki was only 0.75 *ichibus* (CR, Nagasaki for 1869, p. 49).
59. CR, Nagasaki for 1870, p. 52.
60. CR 1873, Nagasaki for 1873, p. 82; DCRTF, No. 403, Nagasaki for 1887, p. 2.
61. 'Reports on the Production of Tea in Japan', p. 10.
62. 'Seicha shūdankai nisshi', pp. 368, 370.
63. 'Reports on the Production of Tea in Japan', p. 9; 'Seicha shūdankai nisshi', p. 371. Alternative dates for the first tea refiring establishment in Kōbe are given by other sources. According to *Nihon chagyō-shi* (p. 37) it was 1872, but according to *Nihon cha bōeki gaikan* (p. 72) it was mid-1869.
64. 'Reports on the Production of Tea in Japan', p. 13. Figures may be underestimates, because 'the Chamber of Commerce have (*sic*) not, until recently, taken any notice of some minor shipments.'
65. *Nihon cha bōeki gaikan*, pp. 131, 132, 152; DCRTF, No. 404, Hyōgo and Ōsaka for 1887, p. 4.

66. CR, Review of the Import Trade of Japan, and of the Tea and Silk Season of 1872–73, p. 94.
67. Yamaguchi, *Meiji zenki keizai no bunseki*, pp. 18, 19. See also Furushima Toshio, *Shihonsei seisan no hatten to jinushisei* (1963), pp. 74–8.
68. Tōyō Keizai Shinpōsha, *Meiji Taishō kokusei sōran* (1927), p. 517, Table 534.
69. *Nihon chagyō-shi*, pp. 38, 39; *Nihon cha bōeki gaikan*, pp. 90, 91; Sanpei Takako, *Nōka kanai sho-kōgyō no hensen katei* (1934), pp. 121, 140–4; Yamaguchi, 'Cha bōeki no hattatsu to seichagyō', p. 167.
70. *Nihon cha bōeki gaikan*, p. 116; *Yokohamashi-shi*, vol. 3, Pt I, p. 490; vol. 4, Pt I, p. 284.
71. Yamaguchi, *Bakumatsu bōeki-shi*, p. 198; *Nihon cha bōeki gaikan*, pp. 109–10, 149–62; Shizuoka Shiyakusho, *Shizuokashi-shi*, vol. 3 (1973), p. 549.
72. *Nihon chagyō-shi*, p. 38; CR, Kanagawa for 1877, p. 59.
73. *Nihon chagyō-shi*, pp. 39, 40; *Nihon cha bōeki gaikan*, p. 111.
74. CR, Kanagawa for 1881, p. 42; CR, Hyōgo and Ōsaka for 1882, p. 14.
75. 'Seicha shūdankai nisshi', pp. 26–7, 50, 356, 362.
76. *Nihon cha bōeki gaikan*, pp. 89, 92; CR, Kanagawa for 1876, p. 42.
77. CR, Kanagawa for 1877, p. 59.
78. *Yokohamashi-shi*, vol. 3, Pt I, pp. 722, 723, 725–8, 731–9.
79. *Nihon cha bōeki gaikan*, pp. 114–15; *Nihon chagyō-shi*, pp. 42–3.
80. 'Seicha shūdankai nisshi', pp. 4–5, 122.
81. *Nihon chagyō-shi*, pp. 43–5, 69–72.
82. Ibid., p. 83; DCRTF, No. 1260, Hyōgo and Ōsaka for 1892, p. 18.
83. *Nihon chagyō-shi*, p. 89.
84. Ibid., pp. 94, 97; *Nihon cha bōeki gaikan*, p. 135. For a detailed account of the Japan Tea Co., see *Yokohamashi-shi*, vol. 4, Pt I, pp. 260–5.
85. *Nihon chagyō-shi*, p. 107; *Nihon cha bōeki gaikan*, pp. 136–7.
86. *Nihon cha bōeki gaikan*, p. 137; *Nihon chagyō-shi*, p. 118.
87. *Nihon chagyō-shi*, pp. 125–6.
88. Japan, Department of Agriculture and Commerce, *Japan in the Beginning of the 20th Century* (1904), p. 155.
89. *Chagyō ni kansuru chōsa*, pp. 2, 250; *Yushutsu jūyōhin yōran*, Cha (December 1896), p. 28.
90. DCRTF, No. 1779, Yokohama for 1895, p. 7; No. 2189, Hyōgo and Ōsaka for 1897, p. 13. For Shizuoka Prefecture, see *Yushutsu jūyōhin yōran*, Cha (1901), pp. 308-12.

91. *Yushutsu jūyōhin yōran,* Cha (February 1896), pp. 102, 116.
92. *Nihon cha bōeki gaikan,* pp. 53, 129.
93. Ibid., pp. 130–4; Ukers, op. cit., vol. 2, pp. 223–8. Butterfield & Swire left the tea business in 1892. See also *Yokohamashi-shi,* vol. 3, Pt I, pp. 603–14.
94. Kaikō Sanjūnen Kinenkai, *Kōbe kaikō sanjūnen-shi* (1898), vol. 2, pp. 650–2.
95. 'Reports on the Production of Tea in Japan', p. 11.
96. *Yushutsu jūyōhin yōran,* Cha (February 1896), pp. 28–51.
97. *Nihon cha bōeki gaikan,* p. 156; *Yokohamashi-shi,* vol. 3, Pt I, p. 723.
98. *Yushutsu jūyōhin yōran,* Cha (February 1896), p. 30.
99. Ukers, op. cit., vol. 2, p. 214.
100. CR, Shanghai for 1874, p. 140.
101. CR, Kanagawa for 1882, p. 14. See also *Shōkyō nenpō* (for 1882), No. 2, p. 27. According to the Yokohama Prices Current and Market Report (No. 333, 23 November 1880), the freight rates to San Francisco, and to New York via San Francisco, levied by the Pacific Mail and by Occidental and Oriental steamers, were 2 cents and 3 cents per lb gross respectively (*Despatches from United States Consuls in Kanagawa, 1861–1897,* vol. 11).
102. CR, Kanagawa for 1878, p. 44; DCRTF, No. 219, Kanagawa for 1886, p. 6.
103. CR, Kanagawa for 1881, p. 43; for 1882, p. 16; for 1883, p. 148.
104. DCRTF, No. 38, Kanagawa for 1885, p. 10; No. 208, Hyōgo and Ōsaka for 1886, p. 3; No. 219, Kanagawa for 1886, p. 6; Innis, *A History of the Canadian Pacific Railway,* p. 193; Musk, *Canadian Pacific, 1883–1968,* pp. 1, 2, 28.
105. DCRTF, No. 1084, Yokohama for 1891, p. 12.
106. *Nihon cha bōeki gaikan,* pp. 131, 152.
107. DCRTF, No. 1084, Yokohama for 1891, pp. 11–12; DCRTF, No. 1600, Yokohama for 1894, p. 12.

6: The Development of Coal Exports

1. See above, p. 34.
2. G.A. Lensen, *The Russian Push toward Japan* (1959), pp. 278–9, 301, 417, 426; Graham, *The China Station,* pp. 288–91.
3. W.J.C. R. H. v. Kattendyke, *Nagasaki kaigun denshūjo no hibi* (1964), pp. 68–9.
4. Tōkyō Daigaku Shiryō Hensanjo, *Dainihon komonjo* (Bakumatsu gaikoku kankei monjo) 34 (1969), pp. 34–7, 159–60.
5. CR, Nagasaki for 1869, p. 56; for 1870, p. 55; for 1871, pp. 26–7; for 1872, pp. 64–5.

6. Lensen, op. cit., pp. 448–9; Ishii Takashi, *Meiji ishin no kokusaiteki kankyō*, vol. 1, p. 90; Yasuoka Akio, 'Bakumatsu Meiji-shoki no Nichiro ryōdo mondai to Eikoku', in Kokusai Seiji Gakkai (ed.), *Nichiei kankei no shiteki tenkai (Kokusai seiji*, 58, 1978).

7. Harry Parkes to Lord Stanley, Yeddo, 11 September 1867, in *BPP* (1867–8), LXIX [3990].

8. A.W. Kirkaldy, *British Shipping* (1914), p. 459.

9. *First Report of Carnarvon Commission* (3 September 1881), A. Holt's statements 248–50, p. 10, and 356, p. 13 (CAB 7/2).

10. Hyde, *Blue Funnel*, p. 31.

11. C.E. Fayle, *A Short History of the World's Shipping Industry* (1933), pp. 231, 246, 247.

12. *First Report of Carnarvon Commission*, A. Holt's statements 246, 387, Captain Steel's statements 911, 957, 999, and Adm. Sir A.C. Key's statement 2241 (CAB 7/2); *Final Report of Carnarvon Commission* (22 July 1882), T.H. Ismay's statements, p. 600 (CAB 7/4).

13. W.S. Lindsay, *History of the Merchant Shipping and Ancient Commerce*, vol. 4 (1876), pp. 408, 409.

14. Cable, *A Hundred Year History of the P. & O., 1837–1937*, pp. 135–6, 166. See also G. Blake, *The Ben Line* (1956), p. 42.

15. Kirkaldy, op. cit., p. 464; Hyde, *Far Eastern Trade*, p. 106. For the trade on the Yangtze and China Coast, see Kwang-Ching Liu, *Anglo–American Steamship Rivalry in China* (1962).

16. IMC, *Reports on Trade at the Ports in China*, for 1865, p. 126 (Appendix).

17. 'Abstract of Mercantile Opinions of the Trade of Shanghae during 1866', in CR, Shanghai for 1866, p. 100.

18. The import duty levied on imported foreign coals was fixed by treaty at 5 candarine (0.05 taels) per picul. Its influence on the cost of coal was therefore negligible.

19. IMC, *Reports on Trade at the Ports in China*, for 1865, p. 126 (Appendix). See also CR, Shanghai for 1870, p. 5.

20. CR, Nagasaki for 1871, p. 26.

21. 'Abstract of Mercantile Opinions on the Trade of Shanghae during 1867', in CR, Shanghai for 1867, p. 110. See also CR, Shanghai for 1872, p. 141.

22. *NCH*, CI, 15 March 1877, 12 October 1888.

23. D.A. Thomas, 'The Growth and Direction of Our Foreign Trade in Coal during the Last Half Century', *Journal of Royal Statistical Society*, 66 (1903), p. 489; H.S. Jevons, *The British Coal Trade* (1915), pp. 684–91; K.H. Burley, 'The Organization of the Overseas Trade in New South Wales Coal, 1860 to 1914', *Economic Record*, 37, 79 (1951), p. 405.

24. CR, Shanghai for 1872, p. 141; Thomas, op. cit., p. 486.
25. E.A.V. Angier, *Fifty Years' Freights, 1869–1919* (1920), pp. 6, 8, 9. Calculated from the sterling–tael exchange rates in Hsiao, *China's Foreign Trade Statistics*, p. 190.
26. *NCH*, CI, 14 September 1872, 21 September 1872, 17 October 1872, 24 October 1872. Mitsubishi and the Pacific Mail began to carry coal at 1 dollar per ton in 1874 (CR, Shanghai for 1874, p. 140).
27. Freight informations in *NCH*, CI. See also CR, Nagasaki for 1882, p. 39. For the China freight market, see Hyde, *Far Eastern Trade*, pp. 24–5.
28. *NCH*, 24 June 1876, p. 613.
29. CR, Shanghai for 1875, p. 23; CR, Shanghai for 1876, p. 12.
30. CR, Shanghai for 1870, p. 6. See also CR, Nagasaki for 1870, p. 54.
31. CR, Shanghai for 1865, p. 85.
32. CR, Nagasaki for 1874, p. 17.
33. CR, Shanghai for 1874, p. 131.
34. CR, Shanghai for 1875, p. 23. See also ibid. for 1878, p. 18.
35. 'The Mines of Japan', *Japan Mail*, 27 January 1876, in *Despatches from United States Consuls in Kanagawa, 1861–1897*, vol. 9.
36. *NCH*, 15 March 1870, p. 192. See also Waseda Daigaku Shakai Kagaku Kenkyūjo (ed.), *Ōkuma monjo*, vol. 4 (1961), p. 272.
37. CR, Nagasaki for 1875, p. 73.
38. CR, Nagasaki for 1876, p. 55. See 'Tea Ships', *Hongkong Daily Press*, 9 July 1880.
39. Henry Gribble & Co.'s Circular, Nagasaki, 4 December 1873, in JMA, PCMR 76.
40. CR, Nagasaki for 1867, p. 288; 'Report by Mr. Plunkett on the Mines of Japan', in *BPP* (1875), p. 463; 'Report by Mr. Plunkett on Coal Mines at Karatsu', in *BPP* (1875), p. 505.
41. CR, Nagasaki for 1870, p. 54; John Thorne & Co.'s Coal Circular, Shanghai, 4 January 1871, 21 September 1871, 9 October 1872, 23 October 1872, and 20 November 1872, in JMA, PCMR 74, 75.
42. John Thorne & Co.'s Coal Circular, Shanghai, 24 December 1866, 3 March 1868, 20 April 1872, 6 September 1872, 26 February 1873, 30 May 1873, 27 June 1873, 25 July 1873, 5 November 1873, 3 December 1873, in JMA, PCMR 46, 75, 76; *NCH*, CI, 7 September 1872.
43. *NCH*, CI, 22 August 1874, 4 October 1877, 6 December 1881.
44. For instance, *NCH*, CI, 20 December 1881, 12 April 1882, 16 June 1882, 28 February 1883, 25 April 1884, 16 May 1884, and 2 March 1888.
45. *NCH*, CI, 29 May 1891.
46. *NCH*, CI, corresponding years.

47. For the importance of fluctuations in freight rates, see *NCH*, CI, 22 April 1887, 10 September 1887, and 16 October 1891.
48. *NCH*, CI, 28 March 1890, 19 September 1890, 11 December 1891, 22 July 1892, 19 August 1892, 1 September 1893.
49. *NCH*, CI, 15 September 1893. See sections on the structure of the coal market in Hong Kong and Singapore.
50. *NCH*, CI, 19 January 1894.
51. *NCH*, CI, 6 July 1894. During the war the situation was apparently that 'Foreign consumers can still obtain Coals for their use, but only under guarantee that the same is not for sale to natives' (*NCH*, CI, 14 September 1894).
52. *NCH*, CI, 26 October 1894, 23 November 1894; Ōkurashō, *Gaikoku bōeki gairan* (for 1894), p. 293.
53. *NCH*, CI, 21 June 1895, 16 August 1895, 25 September 1896, 14 January 1898.
54. Nihon Kōgakukai, *Meiji kōgyō-shi: Kōgyō-hen* (1930), pp. 734–5. Formosan coal was treated separately from Chinese coal in the official statistics. For Formosan coal, see USA, *Foreign Relations of the United States* (for 1869), China, Formosa, pp. 97–100; 'Note on the Formosa Coal-Fields', *NCH*, 14 January 1875; 'The Coal Mines at Formosa' (Extract from the *London and China Express*), *NCH*, 6 July 1878; 'Report on Kelung Colliery, for the Year 1879', in IMC, *Reports on Trade at the Treaty Ports*, for 1879, Pt II, pp. 281–4.
55. *NCH*, CI, 24 September 1897, 24 December 1898. For the Kaiping coal mines and the development of the Chinese coal industry in general, see E.C. Carlson, *The Kaiping Mines* (1957), chs 1–3; Chang Kuo-hui, 'Chung-kuo chin-tai mei-k'uang ch'i-ych chung ti kuan shang-hsi yü tzu-pen-chu-i fa-sheng wen-t'i', *Li-shih yen-chiu* (1964), No. 3. See also 'Coal-mining in the North', *NCH*, 31 January 1882, pp. 117–8.
56. *Final Report of Carnarvon Commission*, p. 15 (CAB 7/4); B. Boxer, *Ocean Shipping in the Evolution of Hong Kong* (1961), pp. 9, 14.
57. In the *Hongkong Blue Book* it is stated under the subject of 'Imports & Exports' that 'There being no Custom House, it is impossible to give the information required.'
58. These figures are available from No. 597 (28 October 1875) of the *Overland China Mail*. For Japanese consular reports, see Tsunoyama Sakae, 'Japanese Consular Reports', *Business History*, 23, 3 (1981).
59. Bottomley & Hughes' Market Report, No. 34 (5 January 1875); W. Kerfoot Hughes' Market Report, Nos 82–4 (14, 21, 28 December 1875), both in JMA, PCMR 64.
60. Bottomley & Hughes' Market Report, Hong Kong, No. 43, 9 March 1875, in JMA, PCMR 64.
61. Nōshōmushō, Nōmukyoku, *Yushutsu jūyōhin yōran*, Kōzan-no-

bu. Sekitan (1896). pp. 6–7, 29.
62. John A. Sandilands' Market Report. Hong Kong. No. 29 (15 April 1873); Bottomley & Hughes' Market Report. Hong Kong. No. 34 (5 January 1875), both in JMA, PCMR 64.
63. Bottomley & Hughes' Market Report. Hong Kong. No. 60 (8 July 1875), in JMA, PCMR 64.
64. *Overland China Mail*. CS. 29 March 1879.
65. Angier. op. cit., pp. 14, 18, 21. Calculated from figures in CR. Summary of Commercial Reports for the Year 1876, pp. 40–1.
66. Bottomley & Hughes' Market Report. No. 34 (5 January 1875), in JMA, PCMR 64.
67. *NCH*. CI. 27 November 1873; Bottomley & Hughes' Market Report, No. 34.
68. *Overland China Mail*. CS. 6 September 1880; *China Overland Trade Report*, 6 September 1880.
69. *Overland China Mail*. CS. 31 May 1880; *China Overland Trade Report*, 31 May 1880.
70. See *Overland China Mail*. CS. 25 December 1883, 14 April 1885, and 13 April 1886.
71. 'The Hongay Coal Supply'. *Overland China Mail*. 27 January 1898, p. 31. See also 'The Tongking Coal Mines'. *NCH*. 15 June 1889. pp. 729–30.
72. *Gaikoku bōeki gairan* (for 1892). p. 249; *Yushutsu jūyōhin yōran*. Sekitan (1896), pp. 37, 57.
73. See Chiang Hai Ding, *A History of Straits Settlements Foreign Trade, 1870–1915* (1978); K. Sugihara, 'Patterns of Asia's Integration into the World Economy, 1880–1913', in Fischer, McInnis and Schneider (eds), *The Emergence of a World Economy*.
74. *Final Report of Carnarvon Commission*, Appendix No. 4, p. 271 (CAB 7/4).
75. DCRTF, No. 589, Nagasaki for 1888, p. 6; Ueda Jushirō, 'Ueda Yasusaburō nenpu'. in *Mitsui bunko ronsō*, 7 (1973). pp. 318–19.
76. Straits Settlements, *Annual Reports*, for 1890, p. 128.
77. DCRTF, No. 1443, Nagasaki for 1893, p. 4; Sumiya Mikio, *Nihon sekitan sangyō bunseki* (1968), pp. 92–3.
78. Nōshōmushō, *Yushutsu jūyōhin yōran*, Sekitan (1897). pp. 40, 47.
79. Straits Settlements, *Annual Reports*, for 1893, pp. 187, 199; *Gaikoku bōeki gairan* (for 1894), p. 299.
80. Straits Settlements, *Annual Reports*, for 1894, p. 259. See also *Yushutsu jūyōhin yōran*, Sekitan (1897). p. 43.
81. DCRTF, No. 1459, Hyōgo and Ōsaka for 1893, p. 26; Straits Settlements, *Annual Reports*, for 1897, p. 344, and for 1898, p. 247;

Gaikoku bōeki gairan (for 1893), p. 218, and ibid. (for 1897), p. 279.

82. Thomas, op. cit., p. 494.
83. A.B. Ghosh, 'India's Foreign Trade in Coal before Independence', *Indian Economic and Social History Review*, 6, 4 (1969), p. 437.
84. Straits Settlements, *Annual Reports*, for 1900–5. After a sharp rise in working costs in the first decade of the twentieth century, due to increases in the price of coal and other expenses, the Blue Funnel line was forced to change from Japanese to cheaper coal from Australia and India (Hyde, *Blue Funnel*, p. 130).
85. CR, 'Report by Mr. Plunkett on the Mines of Japan', p. 460. See also Sumiya, *Nihon sekitan sangyō bunseki*, pp. 98, 99.
86. Gaimushō, *Dainihon gaikō monjo*, vol. 2 (for 1869), Pt III, p. 252.
87. CR, Nagasaki for 1860, 1875 and 1890.
88. CR, Nagasaki for 1866, p. 238.
89. CR, Nagasaki for 1872, p. 64.
90. *Gaikoku bōeki gairan* (for 1895), p. 474.
91. K.R. Mackenzie to J.M. & Co. (Hong Kong), Nagasaki, 23 February 1860 (JMA, B10/ 4/46). See also Fox, *Britain and Japan*, p. 330.
92. CR, Nagasaki for 1867, p. 238; IMC, *Reports on Trade at Ports in China*, for 1865, p. 126 (Appendix).
93. CR, Nagasaki for 1870, p. 59; for 1872, p. 64; for 1875, p. 67; for 1876, p. 55; for 1877, p. 70.
94. CR, Nagasaki for 1869, p. 56; 'Report by Mr. Plunkett on the Mines of Japan', p. 461. There are many sources of information on the Takashima coal mine. For details, see Sugiyama, 'Thomas B. Glover: A British Merchant in Japan', pp. 127ff.
95. 'Report by Mr. Plunkett on the Mines of Japan', p. 461.
96. Ōkurashō, 'Kōbushō enkaku hōkoku', p. 117.
97. Extract from the *Nagasaki Rising Sun*, in *NCH*, 6 July 1878, p. 19.
98. Endō Masao, 'Meiji-shoki ni okeru rōdōsha no jōtai', in Meiji Shiryō Kenkyū Renrakukai (ed.), *Meiji zenki no rōdō mondai* (1960), p. 74. See also CR, Nagasaki for 1877, p. 70.
99. Murakushi Nisaburō, *Nihon tankō chinrōdō shiron* (1976), pp. 32, 61, 63; Watanabe Tōru, 'Meiji zenki no rōdō shijō keisei o megutte', in Meiji Shiryō Kenkyū Renrakukai (ed.), *Meiji zenki no rōdō mondai*, p. 115.
    The *naya-seido* was abolished in 1897, against the background of the establishment of a formal labour market for coal miners (Murakushi, pp. 107 ff., 111–12, 135, 139, 143). The influence of

this system on the development of the coal industry is a matter of some controversy. For discussion, see Sumiya, *Nihon chinrōdō shiron*, pp. 253–61, and 'Naya-seido no seiritsu to hōkai', *Shisō*, 434 (1960); Murakushi, ibid., Pt I; Tanaka Naoki, *Kindai Nihon tankō rōdō-shi kenkyū* (1984), pp. 191 ff.

100. A.C. Jones to Assistant Secretary of State, No. 31, 26 February 1881, in *Despatches from United States Consuls in Nagasaki, 1860–1906*, vol. 3.
101. CR, Nagasaki for 1876, p. 56.
102. Kasuga Yutaka, 'Kanei Miike tankō to Mitsui Bussan', *Mitsui bunko ronsō*, 10 (1976), pp. 206–7; Tanaka Yasuo, 'Mitsui Bussan Kaisha Shanghai shiten "naijō" ', *Mitsui bunko ronsō*, 7 (1973), p. 203.
103. Kasuga, ibid., pp. 211, 231, 233, 236.
104. 'Kōbushō enkaku hōkoku', p. 109; CR, Nagasaki for 1879, p. 49.
105. Shibagaki Kazuo, *Nihon kinyū shihon bunseki* (1965), pp. 54–5; Matsumoto Hiroshi, *Mitsui zaibatsu no kenkyū* (1979), pp. 427–9.
106. Kasuga, op. cit., pp. 189, 255.
107. Hashimoto Tetsuya, 'Miike kōzan to shūjin rōdō', *Shakai keizai shigaku*, 32, 4 (1966), pp. 47, 53, and '1900, 1910-nendai no Miike tankō', *Mitsui bunko ronsō*, 5 (1971), p. 15; Kasuga, op. cit., pp. 196, 198, 211–12, 270, 273.
108. CR, Nagasaki for 1882, p. 39.
109. Murakushi, op. cit., p. 74.
110. Ibid., p. 81; Tanaka, *Kindai Nihon tankō rōdō-shi kenkyū*, pp. 191–239. Contemporary reports on the working conditions at Takashima were later compiled in Meiji Bunka Kenkyūkai (ed.), *Meiji bunka zenshū*, vol. 21 (1929), and *Meiji bunka zenshū* (new edn), vol. 15 (1957). See also 'Takashima tankō jimuchō nisshi batsuyō', in Rōdō Undō Shiryō Iinkai (ed.), *Nihon rōdō undō shiryō*, vol. 1 (1962); *Rising Sun and Nagasaki Express*, 4 July 1888, in Hidemura *et al.* (eds), *Meiji zenki Hizen sekitan kōgyō shiryō-shū* (1977).
111. Kasuga, op. cit., p. 233; Tanaka ibid., ch. 3.
112. Mitsui Senpaku Kabushiki Kaisha, *Sōgyō hachijūnen-shi*, pp. 520–1, 536–7, quoted by Saitō Yoshihisa, 'Mitsui Bussan Kaisha ni okeru kaiungyō', in Yasuoka Shigeaki (ed.), *Zaibatsu-shi kenkyū* (1979), pp. 123, 126.
113. Tanaka, 'Mitsui Bussan Kaisha Shanghai shiten "naijō" ', p. 204.
114. Kasuga, op. cit., p. 261, 266, 276–8, 288–9, 296.
115. Endō, op. cit., p. 91.
116. Kasuga, op. cit., pp. 290, 298-301, 304–5.

117. Ibid., p. 307.
118. Masuda Takashi to Ueda Yasusaburō, No. 16, 11 January 1886; Ueda to Masuda, No. 82, 13 September 1888, in Tanaka, 'Mitsui Bussan Kaisha Shanghai-shiten "naijō"', p. 222–3, 279. See also *Gaikoku bōeki gairan* (for 1890), pp. 120–1.
119. 'Ueda Yasusaburō nenpu', pp. 318–19; Sumiya Mikio, *Nihon sekitan sangyō bunseki* (1968), p. 265.
120. Sumiya, ibid., pp. 221–2, 227, 243, 245–6, 252.
121. DCRTF, No. 1098, Nagasaki for 1891, pp. 5–6. See also DCRTF, No. 1638, Hyōgo and Ōsaka for 1894, p. 55.
122. DCRTF, No. 1253, Nagasaki for 1892, p. 6; No. 1584, Nagasaki for 1894, p. 5; No. 1638, Hyōgo and Ōsaka for 1894, p. 50.
123. Kasuga Yutaka, 'Mitsui zaibatsu ni okeru sekitangyō no hatten kōzō', *Mitsui bunko ronsō*, 11 (1977), pp. 166–84.
124. Takanoe Mototarō, *Chikuhō tankō-shi* (1898), p. 80; DCRTF, No. 2355, Nagasaki for 1898, p. 11.
125. DCRTF, No. 1937, Foreign Trade of Japan for 1896, p. 13.
126. Sumiya, *Nihon sekitan sangyō bunseki*, pp. 349–51, 364, 369.
127. *Gaikoku bōeki gairan* (for 1897), p. 280; Kasuga, 'Mitsui zaibatsu ni okeru sekitangyō no hatten kōzō', p. 236–37.
128. Ōkurashō, *Dainihon gaikoku bōeki nenpyō*, for 1896, pp. 18–19, 270.
129. Kaikō Sanjūnen Kinenkai, *Kōbe kaikō sanjūnen-shi*, vol. 2, p. 375.
130. *Yushutsu jūyōhin yōran*, Sekitan (1896), pp. 30–35.
131. DCRTF, No. 403, Nagasaki for 1887, p. 4.
132. *Yushutsu jūyōhin yōran*, Sekitan (1896), p. 42.
133. For a discussion of these factors, see B.T. Hirsch and W.J. Hausman, 'Labour Productivity in the British and South Wales Coal Industry, 1874–1914', *Economica*, 50 (1983).
134. Schlote, *British Overseas Trade*, p. 87; N.K. Buxton, *The Economic Development of the British Coal Industry* (1978), pp. 91–8.
135. A.J. Taylor, 'The Coal Industry', in R. Church (ed.), *The Dynamics of Victorian Business* (1980), pp. 53–4.
136. B.R. Mitchell, *Economic Development of the British Coal Industry, 1800–1914* (1984), p. 289.
137. R.H. Walters, *The Economic and Business History of the South Wales Steam Coal Industry, 1840–1914* (1977), pp. 5, 6, 316, 319. For the South Wales coal industry, see also Jevons, *The British Coal Trade*, ch. 5; J.H. Morris and L.J. Williams, *The South Wales Coal Industry, 1841–1875* (1958).
138. Walters, op. cit., p. 306, figure 6 facing p. 310, pp. 312–3, 358;. M.J. Daunton, *Coal Metropolis: Cardiff, 1870–1914* (1977), p. 56.
139. Thomas, op. cit., p. 508; Walters, op. cit., pp. 323, 363, 364.
140. K.H. Burley, 'The Overseas Trade in New South Wales Coal and

the British Shipping Industry, 1860–1914', *Economic Record*, 36, 75 (1960), pp. 394, 403.
141. DCRTF, No. 2004, Nagasaki for 1896, p. 6.
142. *Nihon bōeki seiran*, pp. 105, 269.

Bibliography

(Unless otherwise stated, the place of publication for Western-language books is London, and for Japanese-language books Tokyo.)

1. Contemporary Manuscripts and Official Publications

(i) in Western Languages

China
  Imperial Maritime Customs, Shanghai
    Returns of Trade at the Treaty Ports, 1864, 1865, 1867–1881.
    Reports on Trade at the (Treaty) Ports in China, 1864–1881.
    Returns of Trade at the Treaty Ports, and Trade Reports, 1882–1886.
    Returns of Trade and Trade Reports, 1887–1899.
    Decennial Report on the Trade, Navigation, Industries, etc., of the Ports open to Foreign Commerce in China, 1882–1891, 1892–1901.
    Silk (Special Series, No. 3), 1881.
France
  Direction Générale des Douanes, *Tableau Décennal du Commerce de la France*, 1857–1866, 1867–1876, 1877–1886, 1887–1896, Paris.
Italy
  Ministero de Agricoltura, Industria e Commercio, *Annuario Statistico Italiano*, 1889–90, 1895, 1900, 1904, 1905–1907, Roma.
Japan
  Imperial Department of State for Agriculture and Commerce, *General View of Commerce and Industry in the Empire of Japan*, Paris, 1900.
  Department of Agriculture and Commerce, *Japan in the Beginning of the 20th Century*, Tokyo, 1904.
United Kingdom
  Admiralty, *Navy List*.

British Parliamentary Papers
  *Annual Statement of the Trade and Navigation of the United Kingdom
  with Foreign Countries and British Possessions.*
Commercial Reports
  (Embassy and Consular Reports relating to China and Japan
  up to 1899 are compiled in Irish University Area Studies Series,
  British Parliamentary Papers, CHINA, vols. 6–21, and *British
  Parliamentary Papers, JAPAN* (Shannon, 1971), vols. 1–10).
'Copy of Report of the Committee on Expense of Military Defences
  in the Colonies' (1860, XLI [282]).
'A Return of the Quantity of Coal purchased by the Government
  for the Use of Her Majesty's Navy in the Years 1857, 1858, and
  1859, distinguishing Welsh from Hartley Coal' (1860, XLII
  [348]).
'An Account for Five Years ending the 31st day of December 1859
  of the Quantity of Steam Coal, Annually Purchased for the Use
  of Her Majesty's Navy, and Supplied to the Several Depôts
  Abroad' (1860, XLII [363]).
'Correspondence respecting Affairs in Japan' (1864, LXVI
  [3242], [3303]).
'Report made by the late Mr. Arbuthnot to the Lords of the
  Treasury on the Subject of Japanese Currency' (1866, L
  [513]).
'Correspondence respecting the Revision of the Japanese Com-
  mercial Tariff' (1867, LXXIV [3758]).
'Report by Mr. Adams on the Central Silk Districts of Japan'
  (1870, LXV [C.27]).
'Further Report from Mr. Adams on Silk Culture in Japan' (1870,
  LXV [C.72]).
'Further Paper respecting Silk Culture in Japan' (1870, LXV
  [C.194]).
'Third Report by Mr. Adams on Silk Culture in Japan' (1871,
  LXVII [C.243]).
'Report by Mr. Adams on the Deterioration of Japanese Silk'
  (1871, LXVII [C.388]).
'Reports on the Production of Tea in Japan' (1873, LXVI
  [C.740]).
'Report of the Commissioners appointed to inquire into the
  several matters relating to Coal in the United Kingdom', 3 vols
  (1871, XVIII [C.435]).
'Report by Mr. Plunkett on the Mines of Japan' and 'Report by
  Mr. Plunkett on Coal Mines at Karatsu' (1875, LXXIV [C.
  1355]).
'Report on the Import Trade of Great Britain with Japan' (F.O.

Miscellaneous Series. No. 7) (1887, LXXXII [C.4924]).
'Reports on the Native Cotton Manufactures of Japan' (F.O. Miscellaneous Series, No. 49) (1887, LXXXII [C.4924-19]).
'Foreign Trade Competition: Opinions of H.M. Diplomatic and Consular Officers on British Trade Methods' (1899, XCVI [C.9078]).
'Japan: Notes on the Foreign Trade and Shipping of Japan, 1872-1900' (F.O. Miscellaneous Series, No. 564) (1902, CIII [Cd.787]).
'Reports on the Raw Silk Industry of Japan and on Habutae (Japanese Manufactured Silk)' (F.O. Miscellaneous Series, No. 672) (1909, XCII [Cd.4447]).
Board of Trade, *Board of Trade Journal*, 1887-1914.
Jardine Matheson Archive (University Library, Cambridge)
I. Sections on Accounts, etc.
A1/79-95: General Ledgers, Shanghai Branch, 1850-1886.
A1/96-98: General Ledgers, Yokohama Branch, Pre-1874-1883.
A7/292-301: Summary Accounts, Imports and Exports, 1867/68-1884/85.
A7/390: Adventure to and from Japan, 1859/60-1864/65.
II. Correspondence Section
B4/1-5: Private Letters (unbound), Japan, 1857-1887.
B7/37: Correspondence (unbound), Shanghai, 1859-1872.
B10/1-9: Correspondence (unbound), Japan, 1859-1892.
C49/1, 2: Letter Books, Shanghai to Japan, 1859-1869.
III. Prices Current and Market Reports
1, 2: New York, 1843-1878.
3: San Francisco, 1870-1873, 1877-1878.
34-39: Europe (Great Britain), Tea Circulars, 1861-1880.
40-43: Europe, Silk Circulars, 1860-1884.
46, 74-76: China and Japan, Circulars, 1869, 1871-1873.
62-68: Hongkong and other ports, 1862-1900.
71: Hongkong Fortnightly Prices Current and Market Reports, 1879-1892.
72: Jardine, Matheson & Co., Hongkong and Shanghai, 1865-1873.
73, 77-79: Shanghai and other ports, 1849-1892.
80-82: Japan, 1871-1891.
Manchester Chamber of Commerce, Manchester
Archives of the Manchester Chamber of Commerce (Archives Department, Central Library, Manchester)
M8/2/7-10: Proceedings of the Manchester Chamber of Commerce
Monthly Record, 1890-1940.

Papers in the Public Record Office, London
 ADM 1/5824, 5825: In-Letters.
 ADM 125: China Station Records.
  56 General Subjects and Coal, 1900–1903.
  84 Stores, Coal, Ship's Complements and Docks, 1880–83.
 CAB 7/2–4: The Royal Commissioners appointed to inquire into
  the Defence of British Possessions and Commerce Abroad
  (Carnarvon Commission), First Report (3 September 1881),
  Second Report (23 March 1882), and Final Report (22 July
  1882).
 FO 46: Japan, General Correspondence.
 FO 262: Japan, Embassy and Consular Archives.
 PRO 30/6/122–126, 131: Carnarvon Papers.
Papers of John Swire and Sons Ltd. (Library of the School of
Oriental and African Studies, London) JSSI 1,2: Out- and In-
Letters of John Swire and Sons.
Hong Kong
 Blue Book (of Statistics), 1860–1900.
Straits Settlements
 Annual Reports, 1886–1910.
 Blue Books of Statistics, 1880–1910.
United States of America
 Consulate, Kanagawa, *Despatches from United States Consuls in
  Kanagawa, 1861–1897* (The National Archives, Washington, 1948,
  No. 135, 22 reels).
 Consulate, Nagasaki, *Despatches from United States Consuls in
  Nagasaki, 1860–1906* (The National Archives, Washington, 1948,
  No. 131, 7 reels).
 Department of Commerce, Bureau of the Census,
  Commerce and Navigation of the United States, 1864– , Washington.
  Statistical Abstract of the United States, 1878– , Washington.
  Thirteenth Census of the United States taken in the Year 1910, vol. X,
   Manufactures, Washington, 1909.
 Department of Commerce and Labor, Bureau of Statistics, 'Seri-
  culture in Italy, China, and Japan' (No. 296), in *Monthly Consular
  Reports*, Washington, May 1905.
 Department of the Interior, Census Office,
  The Statistics of the Wealth and Industry of the United States (Ninth
   Census, vol. 3), Washington, 1872.
  Report on the Manufactures of the United States at the Tenth Census
   (1880), Washington, 1883.
  *Report on the Manufacturing Industries in the United States at the
   Eleventh Census* (1890), Part III (Selected Industries), Washington,
   1895.
  Twelfth Census of the United States (1900), Manufactures, Part III,
   Special Reports on Selected Industries (Census Reports, vol. 9),
   Washington, 1902.

Foreign Relations of the United States, 1861–1900, Washington.

(ii) in Japanese

Gaimushō [Ministry of Foreign Affairs] (ed.),
  (Dai) Nihon gaikō monjo [Japanese Diplomatic Documents], vol. 1 (1868) –.
Jōyaku isan [A Collection of Japanese Treaties], 1884.
Tsūshō isan [Japanese Commercial Reports], 1894–1913.
Kenshi Orimono Tōshikki Kyōshinkai, 'Sanshi shūdankai kiji' (August 1885); 'Seishi shijunkai kiji' (August 1885) [Conference reports on sericulture and silk reeling].
Naikaku Tōkeikyoku [Cabinet Bureau of Statistics], *Nihon teikoku tōkei nenkan* [Statistical Yearbook of the Japanese Empire], 1882–.
Naimushō [Ministry of Home Affairs],
  Fuken bussan-hyō [Surveys of Prefectural Products], for 1873 and 1874.
  Zenkoku nōsan-hyō [Nationwide Surveys of Agricultural Products], for 1876–78.
Nōshōmushō [Ministry of Agriculture and Commerce],
  Chagyō gairan [An Outline of the Tea Industry], 1914.
  Chagyō ni kansuru chōsa [A Survey of the Tea Industry], 1912.
  Ifutsu no sanshigyō [The Silk Industry in Italy and France], 1916.
  Kōgyō iken [Views on Encouraging Industries], 1884.
  Kōzan hattatsu-shi [A History of the Development of the Japanese Mining Industry], 1900.
  'Meiji jūsannen mentō kyōshinkai hōkoku' [Report on the 1880 Competitive Exhibition for Cotton and Sugar], No. 2, June 1880.
  Nōsan-hyō [Nationwide Surveys of Agricultural Products], for 1879–82.
  Nōshōkō kōhō [Report on Agriculture, Commerce and Industry], No. 1 (1885)–No.46 (1888).
  Nōshōmu tōkei-hyō [Statistics of Agriculture and Commerce], 1886–.
  Ōbei sanshigyō shisatsu fukumei taiyō [A General Report of the Silk Reeling Industry in Europe and the United States], by Honda Iwajirō, 1897.
  Seicha shūdankai nisshi [Conference Reports on Tea], 1884.
  Shinkoku sanshigyō chōsa fukumeisho [A Report of the Survey into the Silk Reeling Industry in Ch'ing China], by Honda Iwajirō, 1899.
  Shokkō jijō [Factory Working Conditions], 1903.
  Yushutsu jūyōhin yōran, Nōsan-no-bu, Sanshi [An Outline of Major Export Articles: Silk], 1896, 1901, 1906, 1909.
  Yushutsu jūyōhin yōran, Nōsan-no-bu, Cha [An Outline of Major

Export Articles: Tea], February 1896, December 1896, and 1901.

Yushutsu jūyōhin yōran, Kōzan-no-bu, Sekitan [An Outline of Major Export Articles: Coal], 1896, 1897.

Zenkoku seishi kōjō chōsa-hyō [Nationwide Surveys of Silk Reeling Factories], 1895, 1898, 1902, 1906.

Ōkurashō [Ministry of Finance],
Dainihon gaikoku bōeki nenpyō [Annual Returns of Foreign Trade for the Japanese Empire], 1882– .

Gaikoku bōeki gairan [An Outline of Japanese Foreign Trade], 1890–.

Kahei seido chōsakai hōkoku' [Reports of the Committee for Investigating the Currency System] (1895).

'Kōbushō enkaku hōkoku' [The History of the Ministry of Industry], 1888.

Shōkyō nenpō [The Annual Commercial and Market Report], 1878–1883.

2. Journals and Newspapers

(i) in English

China Overland Trade Report, Hong Kong, 1878–88.

Economist, London, 1859–1900.

Hongkong Daily Press, Hong Kong, 1880–1900.

Journal of the Silk Supply Association (*Silk Supply Journal*, after no.2), The Silk Supply Association, nos 1–13 (15 January 1870–15 January 1872).

London Gazette, 30 October 1863; 12 September 1879.

Nagasaki Express, Nagasaki, 1870.

North China Herald and Supreme Court & Consular Gazette, Shanghai, 1870–1900.

Overland China Mail, Hong Kong, 1870–1900.

(ii) in Japanese

Dainihon saishikai hōkoku (later *Dainihon sanshi kaihō*) [Report of the Imperial Japanese Silk Association], Dainihon Sanshikai, nos 1–57, 1892–7.

Tōkyō keizai zasshi [Tokyo Economic Journal], 1879–1900.

3. Books and Monographs

(i) in Western Languages

Ahvenainen, J. *The Far Eastern Telegraphs*, Helsinki, 1981.

Aldcroft, D.H. (ed.) *The Development of British Industry and Foreign Competition, 1875–1914*, 1968.

——and H.W. Richardson *The British Economy, 1870–1939*, 1969.

Allen, F. *American Silk Industry, Chronologically Arranged, 1793–1876*, New York, 1876.

——*The Silk Industry of the World at the Opening of the Twentieth Century*, New York, 1904.

——'Silk Manufactures', in USA, Census Office, *Twelfth Census of the United States* (1900), Manufactures, Pt III, Special Reports on Selected Industries.

Allen, G.C. *A Short Economic History of Modern Japan*, 3rd revised edn, 1972.

——and A.G. Donnithorne *Western Enterprise in Far Eastern Economic Development*, 1954.

Amin, S. *Accumulation on a World Scale*, New York, 1974.

Andrew, A.P. 'The End of the Mexican Dollar', *Quarterly Journal of Economics*, vol. 18 (May 1904).

Angier, E.A.V. *Fifty Years' Freights, 1869–1919*, 1920.

Ashworth, W. *An Economic History of England, 1870–1939*, 1960.

——*A Short History of the International Economy since 1850*, 3rd edn, 1975.

——'The Late Victorian Economy', *Economica*, new series, vol. 33, no. 129 (February 1966).

——'Economic Aspects of Late Victorian Naval Administration', *Economic History Review (EHR)*, 2nd series, vol. 22, no. 3 (December 1969).

Baba, M. and M. Tatemoto 'Foreign Trade and Economic Growth in Japan: 1858–1937', in L. Klein and K. Ohkawa (eds), *Economic Growth: The Japanese Experience since the Meiji Era*, Homewood, 1968.

Baran, P. *The Political Economy of Growth*, New York, 1957.

Bartlett, C.J. *Great Britain and Sea Power, 1815–1853*, Oxford, 1963.

——'The Mid-Victorian Reappraisal of Naval Policy', in K. Bourne and D.C. Watt (eds), *Studies in International History*, 1967.

Baster, A.S.J. *The Imperial Banks*, 1929.

——'The Origins of the British Exchange Banks in China', *Economic History, A Supplement to the Economic Journal*, vol. 3, no. 9 (January 1934).

Beasley, W.G. *Great Britain and the Opening of Japan, 1834–1858*, 1951.

——*Select Documents on Japanese Foreign Policy, 1853–1868*, 1955.

——*The Modern History of Japan*, 2nd edn, 1973.

——*The Meiji Restoration*, 1973.

Blackburn Chamber of Commerce, *Report of the Mission to China, 1896–97*, Blackburn, 1898.

Blake, G. *The Ben Line*, 1956.

Bolles, A.S. *Industrial History of the United States from the Earliest Settlements to the Present Time*, Norwich, Conn., 1879.

Bouvier, J. *Le Crédit Lyonnais de 1863 à 1882*, Paris, 2 tomes, 1961.

Boxer, B. *Ocean Shipping in the Evolution of Hong Kong*, Chicago, 1961.

Brockett, L.P. *The Silk Industry in America*, New York, 1876.

Burley, K.H. 'The Overseas Trade in New South Wales Coal and the British Shipping Industry, 1860–1914', *Economic Record*, vol. 36, no. 75 (August 1960).

——'The Organization of the Overseas Trade in New South Wales Coal, 1860 to 1914', *Economic Record*, vol. 37, no. 79 (September 1961).

Buxton, N.K. *The Economic Development of the British Coal Industry*, 1978.

Cable, B. *A Hundred Year History of the P. & O., 1837–1937*, 1937.

Cain, P.J. *Economic Foundations of British Overseas Expansion, 1815–1914*, 1980.

——and A.G. Hopkins 'The Political Economy of British Expansion Overseas, 1750–1914', *EHR*, 2nd series, vol. 33, no. 4 (November 1980).

——and A.G. Hopkins 'Gentlemanly Capitalism and British Expansion Overseas II: New Imperialism, 1850–1945', *EHR*, 2nd series, vol. 40, no. 1 (February 1987).

Carlson, E.C. *The Kaiping Mines (1877–1912)*, Cambridge, Mass., 1957.

Cayez, P. *Crises et Croissance de l'Industrie Lyonnaise, 1850–1900*, Paris, 1980.

Charlesworth, N. *British Rule and the Indian Economy, 1800–1914*, 1982.

Chiang, H.D. *A History of Straits Settlements Foreign Trade, 1870–1915*, Singapore, 1978.

Chittick, J. *Silk Manufacturing and Its Problems*, New York, 1913.

Clapham, J.H. *Economic Development of France and Germany*, 4th edn, Cambridge, 1936.

Clark, V.S. *History of Manufactures in the United States*, 3 vols, New York, 1929.

Clerget, P. *Les Industries de la Soie en France*, Paris, 1925.

Clowes, W.L. *The Royal Navy: A History*, vol. 7, 1903 (reprint, New York, 1966).

Clugnet, L. Géographie de la Soie, Lyon, 1877.

Cohen, P.A. *Discovering History in China: American Historical Writing on the Recent Chinese Past*, New York, 1984.

Collis, M.S. *Wayfoong: The Hongkong and Shanghai Banking Corporation*, 1965.

Craig, J.E., Jr 'Ceylon', in Lewis (ed.), *Tropical Development, 1880–1913*, 1970.

Daniels, G. 'The British Role in the Meiji Restoration', *Modern Asian Studies*, vol. 2, no. 4 (October 1968).

Daunton, M.J. *Coal Metropolis: Cardiff, 1870–1914*, Leicester, 1977.

Deakin, B.M. (with T. Seward) *Shipping Conferences*, Cambridge, 1973.

Dean, B. *China and Great Britain*, Cambridge, Mass., 1974.

——'British Informal Empire: The Case of China', *Journal of Commonwealth & Comparative Politics*, vol. 14, no. 1 (March 1976).

Deane, P. and W.A. Cole *British Economic Growth, 1688–1959*, 2nd edn, Cambridge, 1969.

Dore, R.P. (ed.) *Aspects of Social Change in Modern Japan*, Princeton, 1967.

Dunham, A.L. *The Anglo-French Treaty of Commerce of 1860 and the Progress of the Industrial Revolution in France*, Ann Arbor, 1930.

Eldridge, C.C. *Victorian Imperialism*, 1978.

——(ed.) *British Imperialism in the Nineteenth Century*, 1984.

Ellison, T. *The Cotton Trade of Great Britain*, 1886.

Emery, R.F. 'The Relation of Exports and Economic Growth', *Kyklos*, vol. 20, Fasc. 2 (1967).

Fairbank, J.K. *Trade and Diplomacy on the China Coast*, Cambridge, Mass., 1953.

——'The Creation of the Treaty System', in J.K. Fairbank (ed.), *The Cambridge History of China*, vol. 10, Cambridge, 1978.

——E.O. Reischauer and A.M. Craig *East Asia: Tradition and Transformation*, Boston, 1973.

Farnie, D.A. *The English Cotton Industry and the World Market, 1815–1896*, Oxford, 1979.

Fayle, C.E. *A Short History of the World's Shipping Industry*, 1933.

Feinstein, C.H. 'Home and Foreign Investment: Some Aspects of Capital Formation, Finance and Income in the United Kingdom, 1870–1913' (unpublished Ph.D. thesis, University of Cambridge, 1959).

Feuerwerker, A. 'Economic Trends in the Late Ch'ing Empire, 1870–1911', in J.K. Fairbank and K.C. Liu (eds), *The Cambridge History of China*, vol. 11, 1980.

Fieldhouse, D.K. *Economics and Empire, 1830–1914*, 1973.

——' "Imperialism": An Historiographical Revision', *EHR*, 2nd series, vol. 14, no. 2 (December 1961).

Fischer, W., R.M. McInnis and J. Schneider (eds) *The Emergence of a World Economy, 1500–1914*, vol. II, Stuttgart, 1986.

Fletcher, M.E. 'The Suez Canal and World Shipping, 1869–1914', *Journal of Economic History*, vol. 18, no. 4 (December 1958).

Forrest, D.M. *A Hundred Years of Ceylon Tea, 1867–1967*, 1967.

Fox, G. *British Admirals and Chinese Pirates, 1832–1869*, 1940.

——*Britain and Japan, 1858–1883*, Oxford, 1969.

Frank, A.G. *Capitalism and Underdevelopment in Latin America*, New York, 1967.

——*Latin America: Underdevelopment and Revolution*, New York, 1969.

Gallagher, J. and R. Robinson 'The Imperialism of Free Trade', *EHR*, 2nd series, vol. 6, no. 1 (August 1953).

Gardella, R.P. 'The Boom Years of the Fukien Tea Trade, 1842–1888', in May and Fairbank (eds), *America's China Trade in Historical Perspective*, Cambridge, Mass., 1986.

Gerschenkron, A. *Economic Backwardness in Historical Perspective*, Cambridge, Mass., 1962.

Ghosh, A.B. 'India's Foreign Trade in Coal before Independence', *Indian Economic and Social History Review*, vol. 6, no. 4 (December 1969).

Gilboy, E.W. 'Time Series and the Derivation of Demand and Supply Curves: A Study of Coffee and Tea, 1850–1930', *Quarterly Journal of Economics*, vol. 48 (August 1934).

Graham, G.S. *The Politics of Naval Supremacy*, Cambridge, 1965.

——*The China Station: War and Diplomacy, 1830–1860*, Oxford, 1978.

Greenberg, M. *British Trade and the Opening of China, 1800–42*, Cambridge, 1951.

Gribble, H. 'The Preparation of Japan Tea', *Transactions of the Asiatic Society of Japan*, vol. 12, 1885.

Griffiths, P. *The History of the Indian Tea Industry*, 1967.

Gull, E.M. *British Economic Interests in the Far East*, 1943.

Hanson, J.R., Jr *Trade in Transition: Exports from the Third World, 1840–1900*, New York, 1980.

Hanley, S.B. and K. Yamamura *Economic and Demographic Changes in Preindustrial Japan, 1600–1868*, Princeton, 1977.

Hao, Yen-p'ing *The Comprador in Nineteenth Century China*, Cambridge, Mass., 1970.

Harley, C.K. 'The Shift from Sailing Ships to Steamships, 1850–1890', in D.N. McCloskey (ed.), *Essays on a Mature Economy*, 1971.

Hemmi, K. 'Primary Product Exports and Economic Development: The Case of Silk', in K. Ohkawa, B.F. Johnson, and H. Kaneda (eds) *Agriculture and Economic Growth: Japan's Experience*, Tokyo, 1969.

Hirsch, B.T. and W.J. Hausman 'Labour Productivity in the British and South Wales Coal Industry, 1874–1914', *Economica*, no. 50 (May 1983).

Hirschmann, A.O. *The Strategy of Economic Development*, New Haven, 1958.

——'The Commodity Structure of World Trade', *Quarterly Journal of Economics*, vol. 57, no. 4 (August 1943).

Hirschmeier, J. and T. Yui *The Development of Japanese Business, 1600–1973*, 2nd edn, 1981.

Hirst, F.W. *Gladstone as Financier and Economist*, 1931.

Hobsbawm, E.J. *Industry and Empire*, 1968.

Hongkong Daily Press *The Chronicle and Directory for China, Japan, and the Philippines*, for 1864, 1865, 1866, 1868, 1870, 1871, 1880, 1893, Hong Kong.

Hoston, G. *Marxism and the Crisis of Development in Prewar Japan*, Princeton, 1986.

Hsiao Liang-lin *China's Foreign Trade Statistics, 1864–1949*, Cambridge, Mass., 1974.

Huber, J.R. 'Effect on Prices of Japan's Entry into World Commerce after 1858', *Journal of Political Economy*, vol. 79, no. 3 (May/June 1971).

Hyde, F.E. *Blue Funnel*, Liverpool, 1956.

——*Far Eastern Trade, 1860–1914*, 1973.

Imlah, A.H. *Economic Elements in the Pax Britannica*, Cambridge, Mass., 1958.

Imperial Japanese Navy, Hydrographic Department *The Distance Tables*, Tokyo, 1937.

Imperial Japanese Silk Conditioning House (Honda Iwajirō) *The Silk Industry in Japan*, Yokohama, 1909.

Innis, H.A. *A History of the Canadian Pacific Railway*, Toronto, 1923.

Jansen, M.B. (ed.) *Changing Japanese Attitudes toward Modernization*, Princeton, 1965.

Jevons, H.S. *The British Coal Trade*, 1915.

Johnson, R.E. *Far China Station: The U.S. Navy in Asian Waters, 1800–1898*, Annapolis, 1978.

Jones, F.C. *Extraterritoriality in Japan and the Diplomatic Relations Resulting in its Abolition, 1853–1899*, New Haven, 1931.

Kalix, Z., et al. (eds) *Australian Mineral Industry: Production and Trade, 1842–1964*, Canberra, 1966.

Kemp, T. *Historical Patterns of Industrialization*, 1978.

——*Industrialization in the Non-Western World*, 1983.

Kennedy, P.M. *The Rise and Fall of British Naval Mastery*, 1976.

——'Continuity and Discontinuity in British Imperialism, 1815–1914', in Eldridge (ed.), *British Imperialism in the Nineteenth Century*, 1984.

Kenwood, A.G. and A.L. Lougheed *The Growth of the International Economy, 1820–1960*, 1971.

Kirkaldy, A.W. *British Shipping*, 1914.

Kuznets, S. *Modern Economic Growth*, New Haven, 1966.

——'Quantitative Aspects of the Economic Growth of Nations: X.

Level and Structure of Foreign Trade: Long-Term Trends', *Economic Development and Cultural Change*, vol. 15, no. 2, Pt II (January 1967).

Laferrère, M. *Lyon: Ville Industrielle*, Paris, 1960.

Latham, A.J.H. *The International Economy and the Underdeveloped World, 1865–1914*, 1978.

League of Nations (F. Hilgerdt) *Industrialization and Foreign Trade*, Geneva, 1945.

LeFevour, E. *Western Enterprise in Late Ch'ing China*, Cambridge, Mass., 1968.

Lensen, G.A. *The Russian Push toward Japan*, Princeton, 1959.

Lewis, W.A. *Tropical Development, 1880–1913*, 1970.

——*Growth and Fluctuations, 1870–1913*, 1978.

——'World Production, Prices and Trade, 1870–1960', *Manchester School*, vol. 20, no. 2 (May 1952).

Li, L.M. *China's Silk Trade: Traditional Industry in the Modern World, 1842–1937*, Cambridge, Mass., 1981.

Lieu, D.K. *The Silk Industry of China*, Shanghai, 1941.

Lindsay, W.S. *History of the Merchant Shipping and Ancient Commerce*, vol. 4, 1876.

Liu, Kwang-Ching *Anglo-American Steamship Rivalry in China, 1862–1874*, Cambridge, Mass., 1962.

Lipman, W. *Public Opinion*, New York, 1922.

Lockwood, S.C. *Augustine Heard and Company, 1858–1862*, Cambridge, Mass., 1971.

Lockwood, W.W. *The Economic Development of Japan*, expanded edn, Princeton, 1968.

——(ed.) *The State and Economic Enterprise in Japan*, Princeton, 1965.

——'Japan's Response to the West: The Contrast with China', *World Politics*, vol. 9, no. 1 (October 1956).

Louis, W.R. (ed.) *Imperialism: The Robinson and Gallagher Controversy*, New York, 1976.

Lowe, P. *Britain in the Far East*, 1981.

Mackenzie, C. *Realms of Silver*, 1954.

McMaster, J. *Jardines in Japan, 1859–1867*, Gronigen, 1966.

——'The Takashima Mine: British Capital and Japanese Industrialization', *Business History Review*, vol. 37, no. 3 (Autumn 1963).

Marder, A.J. *British Naval Policy, 1880–1905*, 1940.

Margrave, R.D. 'The Emigration of Silk Workers from England to the United States of America in the 19th Century, with Special Reference to Coventry, Macclesfield, Paterson, N.J., and South Manchester, Connecticut' (unpublished Ph.D thesis, University of London, 1981).

Marriner, S. *Rathbones of Liverpool, 1845–73*, Liverpool, 1961.

——and F.E. Hyde *The Senior, John Samuel Swire, 1825–98*, Liverpool, 1967.

Mason, F.R. *The American Silk Industry and the Tariff*, Cambridge, Mass., 1910 (American Economic Association Quarterly, 3rd series, vol. 11, no. 4).

Mathias, P. *The First Industrial Nation*, 2nd edn, 1983.

——'The British Tea Trade in the Nineteenth Century', in D.J. Oddy and D.S. Miller (eds), *The Making of the Modern British Diet*, 1976.

Mauldon, F.R.E. *The Economics of Australian Coal*, Melbourne, 1929.

May, E.R. and J.K. Fairbank (eds) *America's China Trade in Historical Perspective*, Cambridge, Mass., 1986.

Medzini, M. *French Policy in Japan during the Closing Years of the Tokugawa Regime*, Cambridge, Mass., 1971.

Minami, R. *The Economic Development of Japan*, 1986.

Mitchell, B.R., *Economic Development of the British Coal Industry, 1800–1914*, Cambridge, 1984.

——and P. Deane *Abstract of British Historical Statistics* Cambridge, 1962.

Morris, J.H. and L.J. Williams *The South Wales Coal Industry, 1841–1875*, Cardiff, 1958.

Moulder, F.V. *Japan, China, and the Modern World Economy*, Cambridge, 1977.

Murphey, R. *The Outsiders: The Western Experience in India and China*, Ann Arbor, 1977.

Musk, G. *Canadian Pacific, 1883–1968*, revised edn, 1968.

Myrdal, G. *Asian Drama: An Inquiry into the Poverty of Nations*, 3 vols, New York, 1968.

Nakamura, T. *Economic Growth in Pre-war Japan*, Yale, 1983.

Nicholas, S.J. 'The Overseas Marketing Performance of British Industry, 1870–1914', *EHR*, 2nd series, vol. 37, no. 4 (November 1984).

Norman, E.H. *Japan's Emergence as a Modern State*, New York, 1940.

North, D.C. *The Economic Growth of the United States, 1790–1860*, Englewood Cliffs, NJ, 1961.

Nurkse, R. *Problems of Capital Formation in Underdeveloped Countries*, Oxford, 1953.

O'Brien, P. 'European Economic Development: The Contribution of the Periphery', *EHR*, 2nd series, vol. 35, no. 1 (February 1982).

Oddy, D.J. and D.S. Miller (eds) *The Making of the Modern British Diet*, 1976.

Ohara, K. *Japanese Trade and Industry in the Meiji-Taisho Era,* Tokyo, 1957.

Ohkawa, K. and H. Rosovsky *Japanese Economic Growth: Trend Acceleration in the Twentieth Century,* Stanford, 1973.

——and M. Shinohara (eds) *Patterns of Japanese Economic Development,* New Haven, 1979.

Owen, R. and B. Sutcliffe (eds) *Studies in the Theory of Imperialism,* Harlow, Essex, 1972.

Palma, G. 'Dependency and Development: A Critical Overview', in D. Seers (ed.) *Dependency Theory,* 1981.

Pariset, E. *Les Industries de la Soie,* Lyon, 1890.

——*Histoire de la Fabrique Lyonnaise,* Lyon, 1901.

Parry, C. (ed.) *The Consolidated Treaty Series,* vols 119, 120, New York, 1969.

Paske-Smith, M. *Western Barbarians in Japan and Formosa in Tokugawa Days, 1603–1868,* Kōbe, 1930.

Pelcovits, N.A. *Old China Hands and the Foreign Office,* New York, 1948.

Perret, M.A. *Monographie de la Condition des Soies de Lyon,* Lyon, 1878.

Platt, D.C.M. *Finance, Trade, and Politics in British Foreign Policy, 1815–1914,* Oxford, 1968.

——'The Imperialism of Free Trade: Some Reservations', *EHR,* 2nd series, vol. 21, no. 2 (August 1968).

——'Further Objections to an "Imperialism of Free Trade", 1830–60', *EHR,* vol. 26, no. 1 (February 1973).

Porter, B. *Britain, Europe and the World, 1850–1982,* 1983.

Rabino, J. 'The Statistical Story of the Suez Canal', *Journal of the Royal Statistical Society,* vol. 50, Pt III (September 1887).

Ranft, B. 'The Protection of British Seaborne Trade and the Development of Systematic Planning for War, 1860–1906', in B. Ranft (ed.) *Technical Change and British Naval Policy, 1860–1939,* 1977.

Rawlley, R.C. *Economics of the Silk Industry,* 1919.

Rawski, T.G. 'Chinese Dominance of Treaty Port Commerce and Its Implications, 1860–1875', *Explorations in Economic History,* vol. 7, no. 4 (Summer 1970).

Redford, A. *Manchester Merchants and Foreign Trade,* vol. 2 (1850–1939), Manchester, 1956.

Remer, C.F. *The Foreign Trade of China,* Shanghai, 1926.

Robinson, E.A.G. 'The Changing Structure of the British Economy', *Economic Journal,* vol. 64, no. 255 (September 1954).

Robinson, R. and J. Gallagher with A. Denny *Africa and the Victorians: The Official Mind of Imperialism,* 2nd edn, 1981.

——and J. Gallagher 'The Partition of Africa', in F.H. Hinsley (ed.)

The New Cambridge Modern History, vol. XI, Cambridge, 1962.

—— 'Non-European Foundations of European Imperialism', in R. Owen and B. Sutcliffe (eds) *Studies in the Theory of Imperialism*, 1972.

Rose, B. 'Silk Manufactures', in *Eleventh Census of the United States* (1890), Pt III.

Rostow, W.W. *The Stages of Economic Growth*, 2nd edn, Cambridge, 1971.

—— *The World Economy: History and Prospect*, 1978.

Sandberg, L.G. 'Movements in the Quality of British Cotton Textile Exports, 1815–1913', *Journal of Economic History*, vol. 28, no. 1 (March 1968).

dos Santos, T. 'The Crisis of Development Theory and the Problems of Dependence in Latin America', in H. Bernstein (ed.) *Underdevelopment and Development*, Harmondsworth, 1973.

Sarkar, G.K. *The World Tea Economy*, Calcutta, 1972.

Saul, S.B. *Studies in British Overseas Trade, 1870–1914*, Liverpool, 1960.

—— *The Myth of the Great Depression, 1873–1896*, 2nd edn, Basingstoke, 1985.

Schlote, W. *British Overseas Trade from 1700 to the 1930s*, Oxford, 1952.

Schober, J. *Silk and the Silk Industry*, 1930.

Semmel, B. *The Rise of Free Trade Imperialism*, Cambridge, 1970.

Shaw, A.G.L. (ed.) *Great Britain and the Colonies, 1815–1865*, 1970.

Shih, Min-hsiung *The Silk Industry in Ch'ing China*, Ann Arbor, 1976.

Shively, D.H. (ed.) *Tradition and Modernization in Japanese Culture*, Princeton, 1971.

Silk Association of America *Annual Report*, 1872–, New York.

Simon, M. 'The Pattern of New British Portfolio Foreign Investment, 1865–1914', in A.R. Hall (ed.) *The Export of Capital from Britain, 1870–1914*, 1968.

Skinner, G.W. 'Marketing and Social Structure in Rural China', *Journal of Asian Studies*, vol. 24, nos 1, 2 (November 1964, February 1965).

Smith, T.C. *Political Change and Industrial Development in Japan*, Stanford, 1955.

Sugihara, K. 'Patterns of Asia's Integration into the World Economy, 1880–1913', in Fischer *et al.* (eds) *The Emergence of a World Economy, 1500–1914*, vol. II, 1986.

Sugiyama, S. 'Thomas B. Glover: A British Merchant in Japan, 1861–1870', *Business History*, vol. 26, no. 2 (July 1984).

—— 'The Impact of the Opening of the Ports on Domestic Japanese

Industry: The Case of Silk and Cotton', *Economic Studies Quarterly*, vol. 38, no. 4 (December 1987).

Sumiya, M. and K. Taira (eds) *An Outline of Japanese Economic History, 1603–1940*, Tokyo, 1979.

Tambor, J. *Seidenbau und Seidenindustrie in Italien*, Berlin, 1929.

Taussig, F.W. *The Tariff History of the United States*, 8th edn, New York, 1931.

——*Some Aspects of the Tariff Question*, Cambridge, Mass., 1931.

Taylor, A.J. 'The Coal Industry', in Aldcroft (ed.) *The Development of British Industry and Foreign Competition, 1875–1914*, 1968.

——'The Coal Industry', in R. Church (ed.) *The Dynamics of Victorian Business*, 1980.

The Tea Cyclopaedia, Calcutta, 1881.

Temin, P. *Causal Factors in American Economic Growth in the Nineteenth Century*, 1975.

Thomas, D.A. 'The Growth and Direction of Our Foreign Trade in Coal during the Last Half Century', *Journal of Royal Statistical Society*, vol. 66 (September 1903).

Tiedemann, A.E. 'Japan's Economic Foreign Policies, 1868–1893', in J.W. Morley (ed.) *Japan's Foreign Policy, 1868–1941*, New York, 1974.

Toby, R. *State and Diplomacy in Early Modern Japan*, Princeton, 1984.

Tomlinson, B.R. 'Writing History Sideways: Lessons for Indian Economic Historians from Meiji Japan', *Modern Asian Studies*, vol. 19, no. 3 (July 1985).

Tsunoyama, S. 'Japanese Consular Reports', *Business History*, vol. 23, no. 3, (November 1981).

Tyson, R.E. 'The Cotton Industry', in Aldcroft (ed.) *The Development of British Industry and Foreign Compeitition, 1875–1914*, 1968.

Walters, R.H. *The Economic and Business History of the South Wales Steam Coal Industry, 1840–1914*, New York, 1977.

Ward, R.E. (ed.) *Political Development in Modern Japan*, Princeton, 1968.

Warner, F. *The Silk Industry of the United Kingdom*, 1921.

Watkins, M.H. 'A Staple Theory of Economic Growth', *Canadian Journal of Economics and Political Science*, vol. 24, no. 2 (May 1963).

Wells, L.R. *Industrial History of the United States*, revised edn, New York, 1926.

Woodruff, W. 'The Emergence of an International Economy, 1700–1914', in *The Fontana Economic History of Europe*, vol. 4, Pt. II, 1973.

Wyckoff, W.C. *The Silk Goods of America*, New York, 1879.

——'Report on the Silk Manufacturing Industry of the United States', in *Tenth Census* (of the United States).

Ukers, W.H. *All About Tea*, 2 vols, New York, 1935.

USA, Department of Commerce, Bureau of the Census, *Historical Statistics of the United States: Colonial Times to 1970*, 2 vols, Washington, 1975.

Yasuba, Y. 'Freight Rates and Productivity in Ocean Transportation for Japan, 1868–1943', *Explorations in Economic History*, vol. 15, no. 1 (January 1978).

(ii) in Japanese and Chinese

Andō Yoshio (ed.) *Kindai Nihon keizaishi yōran* [A Handbook of Modern Japanese Economic History], 2nd edn, 1979.

Ariizumi Sadao 'Kikai seishi bokkō-ki ni okeru ichi seishi burujoajii no shōgai' [The Life of a Silk Producer during the Boom in Filatures], Kyōto Daigaku Dokushikai (ed.), *Kokushi ronshū*, no. 2, Kyōto, 1959.

Briesen, R.V. *Beikoku ni okeru Nihonshi ni kansuru hiken* [A Personal View on the Japanese Silk in the United States Market], Yokohama, 1896.

Chagyō Kumiai Chūō Kaigisho *Nihon chagyō-shi* [A History of the Japanese Tea Industry], 2 vols, 1914 and 1936.

——*Nihon cha bōeki gaikan* [A General Survey of the Japanese Tea Trade], 1935.

Chang Kuo-hui, 'Chung-kuo chin-tai mei-k'uang ch'i-yeh chung ti kuan shang-hsi yü tzu-pen-chu-i fa-sheng we-t'i' [The Relations between Officials and Merchants in Modern Chinese Coal-mining Enterprises and the Problem of the Birth of Capitalism], *Li-shih yen-chiu*, no. 3 (1964).

Chōgin-shi Kenkyūkai (ed.) *Henkaku-ki no shōnin shihon* [Merchant Capital in a Period of Transition], 1984.

Ebato Akira *Sanshigyō chiiki no keizai-chirigakuteki kenkyū* [Studies in the Silk-producing Districts of Japan from the Viewpoint of Economic Geography], 1969.

Egashira Tsuneharu 'Takashima tankō ni okeru Nichiei kyōdō kigyō' [Joint Anglo-Japanese Enterprise at the Takashima Coal Mine], in Nihon Keizaishi Kenkyūjo (ed.) *Bakumatsu keizaishi kenkyū*, 1935.

Eguchi Zenji and Hidaka Yasoshichi (eds) *Shinano sanshigyō-shi* [A History of the Shinano Silk Industry], 3 vols, Nagano, 1937.

Endō Masao 'Meiji-shoki ni okeru rōdōsha no jōtai' [The Situation of Workers in the Early Meiji Period], in Meiji Shiryō Kenkyū Renrakukai (ed.) *Meiji zenki no rōdō mondai*, 1960.

Fujimoto Jitsuya *Kaikō to kiito bōeki* [The Opening of Japan and the Silk Trade], 3 vols, 1939.

Fujino Shōzaburō *Nihon no keiki junkan* [Japan's Trade Cycles], 1965.

Fujita Gorō *Nihon kindai sangyō no seisei* [The Formation of Modern Japanese Industry], 1948.

Furushima Toshio, *Shihonsei seisan no hatten to jinushisei* [The Development of Capitalist Production and the Landlord System], 1963.

——*Sangyō-shi* [A History of Industry], III, 1966.

——and Andō Yoshio (eds) *Ryūtsū-shi* [A History of Distribution], II, 1975.

Gonjō Yasuo, 'Furansu shihonshugi to kaikō' [French Capitalism and the Opening of Japan], in Ishii and Sekiguchi (eds) *Sekai shijō to bakumatsu kaikō*, 1982.

Gunmaken Naimubu (ed.) *Gunmaken sanshigyō enkaku chōsasho* [A Survey of the Development of the Gunma Silk Industry], Kiito-nobu, I, II, 1903.

Hara Gōmei Kaisha *Ōbei sangyō ippan* [An Outline of the Silk Reeling Industry in Europe and the United States], Yokohama, 1900.

Harada Toshimaru and Miyamoto Matao (eds) *Rekishi no naka no bukka* [The Role of Commodity Prices in History], 1985.

Hashimoto Jūbei *Kiito bōeki no hensen* [A History of the Silk Trade], 1902.

Hashimoto Tetsuya 'Miike kōzan to shūjin rōdō' [The Miike Coal Mines and Convict Labour], *Shakai keizai shigaku*, vol. 32, no. 4 (December 1966).

——'1900, 1910-nendai no Miike tankō' [The Miike Coal Mine in the Early Twentieth Century], *Mitsui bunko ronsō*, no. 5 (November 1971).

Hayakawa Naose *Kiito to sono bōeki* [Raw Silk and the Raw Silk Trade], revised edn, 1928.

Hayami Akira *Nihon ni okeru keizai shakai no tenkai* [The Development of an Economic Society in Japan], 1973.

Hayashi Reiko 'Kokunai shijō seiritsu-ki ni okeru shūsanchi tonya' [The Role of Distributive Wholesalers during the Formation of the Domestic Market], in Sakasai Takahito *et al.* (eds) *Nihon shihonshugi*, 1978.

Hidemura Senzō *et al.* (eds) *Meiji zenki Hizen sekitan kōgyō shiryō-shū* [Historical Documents concerning the Coal Industry in the Hizen District during the First Half of the Meiji Period], 1977.

Higuchi Hiroshi *Nihon tōgyō-shi* [A History of the Japanese Sugar Industry], 1956.

Hiranomura Yakuba (ed.) *Hirano sonshi* [The Topography of Hiranomura], 2 vols, Hiranomura, Nagano, 1932.

Hora Tomio *Bakumatsu ishin-ki no gaiatsu to teikō* [Western Impact during the Late Tokugawa and Early Meiji Periods and the Resistance to it], 1977.

Imanishi Naojirō *Ōbei sanshigyō shisatsu fukumeisho* [A Report on the Sericulture and Silk Reeling Industries in Europe and the United States], Yokohama, 1902.

Ishii Kanji *Nihon sanshigyō-shi bunseki* [An Historical Analysis of the Japanese Silk Industry], 1972.

——*Kindai Nihon to Igirisu shihon* [British Capital and Modern Japan], 1984.

——'Zaguri seishigyō no hatten katei' [The Development of Sedentary Silk Reeling], *Shakai keizai shigaku*, vol. 28, no. 6 (August 1963).

——'Nihon Ginkō no sangyō kinyū' [The Bank of Japan and its Industrial Financing], *Shakai keizai shigaku*, vol. 38, no. 2 (July 1972).

——'Igirisu shokuminchi ginkō-gun no saihen' [The Reorganization of British Colonial Banks in East Asia in the 1870s and 1880s], *Keizaigaku ronshū*, vol. 45, nos 1, 2 (April and October, 1979).

——'Ginkō sōsetsu zengo no Mitsui-gumi' [Mitsui before and after the Establishment of the Mitsui Bank], *Mitsui bunko ronsō*, no. 17 (December 1983).

——and Sekiguchi Hisashi (eds) *Sekai shijō to bakumatsu kaikō* [The Opening of Japan and the World Market], 1982.

Ishii Mayako, 'Jūkyū-seiki no Chūgoku ni okeru Igirisu shihon no katsudō' [The Activities of British Capital in Nineteenth-Century China], *Shakai keizai shigaku*, vol. 45, no. 4 (December 1979).

Ishii Takashi *Bakumatsu bōeki-shi no kenkyū* [Studies in Late Tokugawa Trade History], 1944.

——*Nihon kaikoku-shi* [A History of the Opening of Japan], 1972.

——*Meiji ishin no kokusaiteki kankyō* [The International Environment at the Time of the Meiji Restoration], expanded and revised edn, 3 vols, 1973.

Iwata Jin 'Nihon shihonshugi seiritsu katei ni okeru haikyū soshiki no henkaku: Satōgyō o chūshin ni shite' [Changes in Sugar Distribution in the Formative Period of Japanese Capitalism], *Mita gakkai zasshi*, vol. 32, no. 7 (July 1938).

Kaikō Sanjūnen Kinenkai *Kōbe kaikō sanjūnen-shi* [A History of the Thirty Years following the Opening of the Port of Kōbe], 2 vols, Kōbe, 1898.

Kajinishi Mitsuhaya (ed.) *Gendai Nihon sangyō hattatsu-shi: Seni* [A History of the Development of Modern Japanese Industry: The Textile Industry], Pt I, 1964.

——'Shihonshugi no ikusei' [The Development of Japanese Capitalism], in *Iwanami kōza: Nihon rekishi*, vol. 16, 1962.

Kasuga Yutaka 'Kanei Miike tankō to Mitsui Bussan' [Mitsui Bussan and the Miike Coal Mines], *Mitsui bunko ronsō*, no. 10 (November 1976).

——'Mitsui zaibatsu ni okeru sekitangyō no hatten kōzō' [The Structure of Development of the Mitsui Coal Industry], *Mitsui bunko
ronsō*, no. 11 (November 1977).

Katsu Kaishū *Kaigun rekishi* [A History of the Japanese Navy], vol. 8
of *Kaishū zenshū* [Complete Works of Katsu Kaishū], 1928.

Kattendyke, W.J.C.R.H.v. *Nagasaki kaigun denshūjo no hibi* [The Early
Days of the Naval Training School at Nagasaki], translation,
1964.

Kawakatsu Heita 'Jūkyū-seiki matsuyō ni okeru Eikoku mengyō to
higashi-Ajia shijō' [International Competition in Cotton Textiles in
East Asia in the Late Nineteenth Century], *Shakai keizai shigaku*,
vol. 47, no. 2 (August 1981).

Kitajima Masamoto (ed.) *Edo shōgyō to Ise-dana* [Edo Commerce and
Ise Merchants], 1962.

——*Seishigyō no tenkai to kōzō* [The Development and Structure of the
Suwa Silk Reeling Industry during the Late Tokugawa and Early
Meiji Periods], 1970.

Matsui Kiyoshi (ed.) *Nihon bōeki-shi* [A History of Modern Japanese
Trade], 3 vols, 1959–63.

Matsumoto Hiroshi *Mitsui zaibatsu no kenkyū* [Studies in the Mitsui
Zaibatsu], 1979.

Meiji Bunka Kenkyūkai (ed.) *Meiji bunka zenshū* [Selected Materials
of Meiji Culture], vol. 9, Keizai-hen [Economic Affairs], 1929; vol.
21, Shakai-hen [Social Affairs], 1929; new edn, vol. 15, Shakai-hen
[Social Affairs], 1957.

Meiji Bunken Shiryō Kankōkai (ed.), *Meiji zenki sangyō hattatsu-shi
shiryō* [Materials on the Development of Industry in the Early Meiji
Period], 1959–76.

Meiji Shiryō Kenkyū Renrakukai (ed.) *Kindai sangyō no seisei* [The
Formation of Modern Japanese Industry], 1958.

Minami Ryōshin *Nihon no keizai hatten* [The Economic Development
of Japan], 1981.

Miyamoto Mataji *Zoku Nihon kinsei tonyasei no kenkyū* [Further
Studies in the Wholesale System of Tokugawa Japan], Kyōto,
1954.

Miyata Michiaki 'Shin-matsu ni okeru gaikoku bōekihin ryūtsū kikō
no ichi-kōsatsu' [A Study in the Distribution of Imported Goods in
Late Ch'ing China], *Sundai shigaku*, no. 52 (March 1981).

Mizunuma Tomoichi, 'Meiji zenki Takashima tankō ni okeru gaishi
to sono haijo katei no tokushitsu' [Foreign Capital in the
Takashima Coal Mine during the Early Meiji Period and the
Nature of the Process by which it was expelled], *Rekishigaku
kenkyū*, no. 273 (February 1963).

——'Meiji kōki ni okeru kiito yushutsu no dōkō' [Silk Exports during
the Late Meiji Period], *Shakai keizai shigaku*, vol. 28, no. 5

(March 1963).

Murakushi Nisaburō *Nihon tankō chinrōdō shiron* [Studies in the History of Wages and Labour in Japanese Coal Mines], 1976.

Nakamura Satoru *Meiji ishin no kiso kōzō* [The Basic Structure of the Meiji Restoration], 1968.

——'Kaikō' [Japan's Opening of the Ports to Foreign Trade], in Rekishigaku Kenkyūkai and Nihonshi Kenkyūkai (eds) *Kōza Nihonshi*, vol. 5, 1970.

Nakamura Takafusa *Senzenki Nihon keizai seichō no bunseki* [An Analysis of Economic Growth in Prewar Japan], 1971.

Nihon bōeki seiran, see Tōyō Keizai Shinpōsha.

Nihon bōeki tōkei [Japan's Trade Statistics] (expanded and revised edn), Shiryō-hen, vol. 2 of Yokohamashi (ed.) *Yokohamashi-shi*, 1980.

Nihon cha bōeki gaikan, see Chagyō Kumiai Chūō Kaigisho.

Nihon Cha Yushutsu Hyakunen-shi Hensan Iinkai *Nihon cha yushutsu hyakunen-shi* [Hundred Years of Japanese Tea Exports], 1959.

Nihon chagyō-shi, see Chagyō Kumiai Chūō Kaigisho.

Nihon Ginkō, Tōkeikyoku *Meiji-ikō honpō shuyō keizai tōkei* [A Collection of Major Economic Statistics for the Meiji Period onwards], 1966.

Nihon Kōgakukai *Meiji kōgyō-shi: Kōgyō-hen* [A History of Industry in the Meiji Period: Mining], 1930.

Nihon Tōkei Kenkyūjo (ed.) *Nihon keizai tōkei-shū* [Collected Statistics of the Japanese Economy], 1958.

Nōrinshō *Nōrinshō ruinen tōkei-hyō, 1868–1953* [Statistics on Agriculture], 1955.

Ohara Keishi (ed.) *Nichibei bunka kōshō-shi: Tsūshō sangyō-hen* [A History of Japanese–American Cultural Exchanges: Commerce and Industry], 1954.

Ohkawa Kazushi *et al.* (eds) *Chōki keizai tōkei* [Estimates of Japanese Long-Term Economic Statistics since 1868], 14 vols, 1966– .

——(eds), *Kokumin shotoku* [National Income] (LTES, vol. 1), 1974.

——and Minami Ryōshin (eds) *Kindai Nihon no keizai hatten* [The Economic Development of Modern Japan], 1975.

Ōishi Kaichirō *Nihon chihō zaigyōsei-shi josetsu* [An Introductory History of Local Finance and Administration in Modern Japan], 1961.

——(ed.) *Nihon sangyō kakumei no kenkyū* [Studies in the Japanese Industrial Revolution], 2 vols, 1975.

Oka Yoshitake *Kindai Nihon seiji-shi* [A Political History of Modern Japan], I, 1967.

Ōkurashō, Zeikanbu, *Nihon kanzei zeikan-shi shiryō* [Materials on the History of Japanese Customs and Tariff Rates], 3 vols, 1958.

Ōsaka Shiyakusho (ed.) *Meiji Taishō Ōsakashi-shi* [The History of the City of Ōsaka in the Meiji and Taishō Periods], vols 3, 4, Ōsaka, 1933.

Ōuchi Hyōe and Tsuchiya Takao (eds) *Meiji zenki zaisei keizai shiryō shūsei* [Collected Materials on the Financial and Economic History of the Early Meiji Period], 20 vols, 1931–6.

Rōdō Undō Shiryō Iinkai (ed.) *Nihon rōdō undō shiryō* [Materials on the Japanese Labour Movement], vol. 1, 1962.

Saitō Yoshihisa 'Mitsui Bussan Kaisha ni okeru kaiungyō' [The Shipping Business of Mitsui Bussan Kaisha], in Yasuoka Shigeaki (ed.) *Zaibatsu-shi kenkyū*, 1979.

Sangyō Shinkō Dōmeikai *Zen sekai kiito taisei* [General Trends in the World Silk Industry], 1892.

Sano Ei *Dainihon sanshi* [The History of the Silk Industry in Japan], 1898.

Sanpei Takako, *Nōka kanai sho-kōgyō no hensen katei* [The Process of Change in Domestic Rural Industries], 1934.

Shakai Keizaishi Gakkai (ed.) *Atarashii Edo jidaishi-zō o motomete* [In Search of New Approaches to the History of Tokugawa Japan], 1977.

Shiba Yoshinobu, 'Meiji-ki Nihon raijū kakyō ni tsuite' [Overseas Chinese in Japan during the Meiji Period], *Shakai keizai shigaku*, vol. 47, no. 4 (December 1981).

Shibagaki Kazuo, *Nihon kinyū shihon bunseki* [An Analysis of Japanese Financial Capital], 1965.

Shibahara Takuji *Nihon kindaika no sekaishiteki ichi* [The Place of Japan's Modernization in World History], 1981.

Shibata Michio and Shibata Asako 'Bakumatsu ni okeru Furansu no tainichi seisaku' [French Policy towards Japan in the Late Tokugawa Period], *Shigaku zasshi*, vol. 76, no. 8 (August 1967).

Shinbo Hiroshi *Kinsei no bukka to keizai hatten* [Prices and Economic Development in Tokugawa Japan], 1978.

——'Bakumatsu Meiji-ki no kakaku kōzō' [Cost Structures during the Late Tokugawa and Meiji Periods], *Shakai keizai shigaku*, vol. 33, no. 1 (April 1967).

Shizuoka Shiyakusho *Shizuokashi-shi* [The History of the City of Shizuoka], vol. 3, Shizuoka, 1973.

Shōda Kenichirō *Nihon shihonshugi to kindaika* [Japanese Capitalism and the Modernization of Japan], 1971.

Sugiyama Shinya 'Bakumatsu Meiji-shoki ni okeru kiito yushutsu no sūryōteki saikentō' [A Quantitative Review of Japan's Raw Silk Exports in the Late Tokugawa and Early Meiji Periods], *Shakai keizai shigaku*, vol. 45, no. 3 (October 1979).

——'Nihon sekitangyō no hatten to Ajia sekitan shijō' [The Asian

Coal Market and the Development of the Japanese Coal Industry].
Kikan gendai keizai, no. 47 (April 1982).
——'Nihon seishigyō no hatten to kaigai shijō' [Overseas Markets
and the Development of the Japanese Silk Industry], *Mita gakkai
zasshi*, vol. 76, no. 2 (June 1983).
——'Higashi-Ajia ni okeru "gaiatsu" no kōzō' [Rethinking the
Western Impact on East Asia], *Rekishigaku kenkyū*, no. 560
(October 1986).
Sumiya Mikio *Nihon chinrōdō shiron* [A Study of the History of Wage
Labour in Japan], 1955.
——*Nihon sekitan sangyō bunseki* [An Analysis of the Japanese Coal
Industry], 1968.
——'Naya-seido no seiritsu to hōkai' [The Formation and Collapse of
the *Naya-seido*], *Shisō*, no. 434 (August 1960).
Takahashi Keizai Kenkyūjo *Nihon sanshigyō hattatsu-shi* [A History of
the Development of the Japanese Silk Industry], 2 vols, 1941.
Takamura Naosuke *Nihon bōsekigyō-shi josetsu* [An Introductory
History of the Japanese Cotton Industry], 2 vols, 1971.
Takanoe Mototarō *Chikuhō tankō-shi* [Coal Mining in the Chikuhō
Region], 1898.
——*Nihon tankō-shi* [Coal Mining in Japan], 1908.
Tanaka Naoki *Kindai Nihon tankō rōdō-shi kenkyū* [Studies in the
History of Coal Mine Labour in Modern Japan], 1984.
Tanaka Osamu 'Kōbushō shokan jigyō no haraisage to Miike tankō
no haraisage' [The Sale of the Miike Coal Mines and of the Enter-
prises owned by the Ministry of Industry], in Ōtsuka Hisao *et al.*
(eds) *Shihonshugi no keisei to hatten*, 1968.
Tanaka Yasuo 'Mitsui Bussan Kaisha Shanghai-shiten "naijō" '
[Confidential Letters of the Shanghai Branch of Mitsui Bussan
Kaisha], *Mitsui bunko ronsō*, no. 7 (November 1973).
Tashiro Kazui *Kinsei Nitchō tsūkō bōeki-shi no kenkyū* [Studies in
Japanese–Korean Trade during the Tokugawa Period], 1981.
Tōa Dōbunkai *Shina keizai zensho* [A Complete Survey of the Chinese
Economy], vol. 2 (1907), vol. 12 (1908).
Tōa Kenkyūjo *Shina sanshigyō kenkyū* [Studies in the Chinese Silk
Industry], 1943.
Tōkyō Daigaku Shiryō Hensanjo *Dainihon komonjo: Bakumatsu
gaikoku kankei monjo* [Old Japanese Documents: Documents on
Late Tokugawa Foreign Relations], 34, 1969.
Tomioka Seishijō-shi Hensan Iinkai (ed.) *Tomioka seishijō-shi* [The
Tomioka Silk Filature], 2 vols, Tomioka, 1977.
Tōyō Keizai Shinpōsha (ed.) *Meiji Taishō kokusei sōran* [A General
Survey of Japan during the Meiji and Taishō Periods], 1927.
——*Nihon bōeki seiran* [A Statistical Survey of Japan's Foreign Trade],

1935, reprint 1975.

Tsunoyama Sakae *Cha no sekaishi* [The World History of Tea], 1980.

Tsūshō Sangyōshō (ed.) *Shōkō seisaku-shi* [The Official History of Japanese Commercial and Industrial Policy], vols 5, 6 (Foreign Trade), 1965.

Uchida Naosaku *Nihon kakyō shakai no kenkyū* [Studies in Japan's Chinese Community], 1949.

Ueda Jushirō 'Ueda Yasusaburō nenpu' [A Chronological Record of the Life of Ueda Yasusaburō], *Mitsui bunko ronsō*, no. 7 (November 1973).

Umemura Mataji 'Bakumatsu no keizai hatten' [Economic Development in the Late Tokugawa Period], in *Kindai Nihon kenkyū*, no. 3, 1981.

Unno Fukuju *Meiji no bōeki* [Foreign Trade in the Meiji Period], 1967.

——'Meiji shonen no bōeki mondai' [Trade Problems in the Early Meiji Period], in *Iwanami kōza: Nihon rekishi*, vol. 15, 1962.

Waseda Daigaku Shakai Kagaku Kenkyūjo (ed.) *Ōkuma monjo* [Documents relating to Ōkuma Shigenobu], 5 vols, 1958–62.

Watanabe Tōru 'Meiji zenki no rōdō shijō keisei o megutte' [On the Formation of the Labour Market in the Early Meiji Period], in Meiji Shiryō Kenkyū Renrakukai (ed.) *Meiji zenki no rōdō mondai*, 1960.

Yagi Haruo *Nihon kindai seishigyō no seiritsu* [The Formation of the Modern Japanese Silk Reeling Industry], 1960.

Yamaguchi Kazuo *Bakumatsu bōeki-shi* [A History of Trade during the Late Tokugawa Period], 1943.

——*Meiji zenki keizai no bunseki* [An Analysis of the Economy of the Early Meiji Period], expanded edn, 1963.

——(ed.) *Nihon sangyō kinyū-shi kenkyū: Seishi kinyū-hen* [Studies in the History of Japanese Industrial Financing: The Silk Reeling Industry], 1966.

——(ed.) *Nihon sangyō kinyū-shi kenkyū: Bōseki kinyū-hen* [Studies in the History of Japanese Industrial Financing: The Cotton Spinning Industry], 1970.

——'Cha bōeki no hattatsu to seichagyō' [The Japanese Tea Industry and the Development of the Tea Trade], in Ohara (ed.), *Nichibei bunka kōshō-shi*, vol. 2, 1954.

Yamamoto Shigeru *Jōyaku kaisei-shi* [A History of the Revision of the Unequal Treaties], 1943.

Yamamoto Yūzō, 'Bakumatsu Meiji-ki no Yokohama yōgin sōba' [Mexican Dollar Exchange Rates at Yokohama in the Late Tokugawa and Early Meiji Periods], in Shinbo Hiroshi and Yasuba Yasukichi (eds), *Kindai ikō-ki no Nihon keizai*, 1979.

Yamashita Naoto 'Nihon teikokushugi seiritsu-ki no higashi-Ajia sekitan shijō to Mitsui Bussan' [Mitsui Bussan and the East Asian Coal Market during the Formation of Japanese Imperialism], in Shakai Keizaishi Gakkai (ed.), *Enerugii to keizai hatten*, Fukuoka, 1979.

Yamazawa Ippei 'Kiito yushutsu to Nihon no keizai hatten' [The Role of Raw Silk Exports in Japan's Economic Development], *Keizaigaku kenkyū*, no. 19 (January 1975).

——and Yamamoto Yūzō *Bōeki to kokusai shūshi* [Foreign Trade and the Balance of Payments] (LTES, vol. 14), 1979.

Yasuoka Akio 'Bakumatsu Meiji-shoki no Nichiro ryōdo mondai to Eikoku' [British Attitudes towards the Sakhalin Question and Japanese–Russian Relations, 1854–1875], in Nihon Kokusai Seiji Gakkai (ed.), *Nichiei kankei no shiteki tenkai*, no. 58 (March 1978).

Yokohamashi (ed.) *Yokohamashi-shi* [The History of the City of Yokohama], vols 2–5; Shiryō-hen [Volumes on Documents], vols 1, 2, 4, Yokohama, 1959–71.

Yokohama Shiyakusho *Yokohamashi shikō: Sangyō-hen* [A Draft History of the City of Yokohama: Industry], Yokohama, 1932.

Yokohama Shōgyō Kaigisho *Yokohama kaikō gojūnen-shi* [A History of the Fifty Years since the Opening of Yokohama], 2 vols, Yokohama, 1909.

Index